Collective Political Violence

Collective Political Violence
*An Introduction to the Theories
and Cases of Violent Conflicts*

Earl Conteh-Morgan

ROUTLEDGE
NEW YORK AND LONDON

Published in 2004 by
Routledge
29 West 35th Street
New York, NY 10001
www.routledge-ny.com

Published in Great Britain by
Routledge
11 New Fetter Lane
London EC4P 4EE
www.routledge.co.uk

Routledge is an imprint of the Taylor and Francis Group.

Printed in the United States of America on acid-free paper.

10   9   8   7   6   5   4   3   2   1

Library of Congress Cataloging-in-Publication Data

Conteh-Morgan, Earl, 1950–
    Collective political violence : an introduction to the theories and
cases of violent conflicts / Earl Conteh-Morgan.
        p.   cm.
    Includes bibliographical references.
    ISBN 0-415-94743-X (hardcover : alk. paper)—ISBN 0-415-94744-8
(pbk. : alk. paper)
        1. Political violence.   I. Title.
JC328.6.C67   2003
303.6–dc21   2003008988

Contents

Preface

The increasing scope and intensity of violent political conflicts is creating a strong demand for courses on conflict, war, or peace, as well as a growing demand for suitable textbooks. The decision to write *Collective Political Violence* grows out of this serious lack of textbooks that comprise an interdisciplinary coverage and competing explanations of civil and interstate wars, genocides, ethnic and identity conflicts, revolutions, and terrorism, among others. Accordingly, this text is written for undergraduates and first year graduate students with the objective of helping them develop a comprehensive understanding of the various factors that can contribute to violence in our contemporary international system. The result is a text based on competing explanations of theories from social-structural, psychocultural, environmental, economic, political, Marxian, and critical approaches, among others, buttressed by case studies to help the student apply theory and concept to concrete situations. The book therefore provides a significant and broad base of factual knowledge to enhance understanding of theoretical perspectives.

Since the last decade of the twentieth century we have witnessed the carnage and suffering caused by old, new, and emerging conflicts in the changing world order. Internal wars in particular are claiming a growing number of lives, accelerating in their own economic destructiveness, and thwarting efforts to foster human rights, democracy, and socioeconomic progress. Where there are no internal wars, we find other elements of instability—demonstrations, violent protests, coups d'état, and the like—that occur on a regular basis. Besides, the new millenium is still characterized by an intensified and expanded reawakening of the most successful political ideology in human history: nationalism. In the roughly two hundred years since its first formulation in the writings of European philosophers, nationalism has caused the political maps of both developed and developing worlds to be completely redrawn, divided, and become a constant point of contention between groups and nation-states. The post–Cold War era is manifesting an even greater number of conflict-related subnationalism and nationalism often reflected in ethnopolitical violence. Thus, the process, problems, and frequent failures of national integration have further become issues of central importance in the contemporary international system. Accordingly

Collective Political Violence is intended to help students acquire an inter-disciplinary understanding of the major conflict-related issues in today's world.

The book is structured around a levels of analysis framework. Chapters 1 and 2 focus on issues of method, trends and concerns in violent political conflicts respectively. Chapters 3, 4, 5, and 6 serve as an introduction to the more theoretical orientations of the various social sciences and their specific contributions of explanations of political violence. In particular, chapter 3 emphasizes social-structural (societal-level analysis), while chapters 4 and 5 underscore individual-level analysis of social conflict. In combination they constitute an introduction to the macro "societal" or "collective" theorizing and set the stage, as well as prepare the student to think about more recent and/or specific applications and refinements to the problems of ethnic conflict (chapter 10), genocides (chapter 11), revolutions (chapters 7 and 8), and Marx's theory of revolutionary change (chapter 9). Thus, chapters 7 to 13 constitute the microtheorizing about ethnic conflict, genocide, revolution, terrorism, and the nexus between environmental degradation and social conflict. Chapter 14 concludes with questions for the student to ponder related to whether military intervention in another country can really be humanitarian. Who is to guarantee obedience to the rules of international humanitarian law? Or what is the relationship between politics, law, power, and authority? These questions are preceded by a concise discussion of changes in peacekeeping in the twenty-first century, and the emerging role of private security firms within weak states.

I owe a great deal of intellectual debt to many in the writing of this book. My first acknowledgment must therefore go to the theorists or authors of the major theories, approaches, or concepts discussed in this text. References to their works can be found in the notes and references section at the end of each chapter. No one could possibly include in a single text all approaches or explanations of violent conflicts that abound in the many academic disciplines. I would also like to thank Eric Nelson of Routledge for identifying two excellent anonymous reviewers who pointed out the strengths and weaknesses of the first draft of *Collective Political Violence*. Eric has been a constant source of motivation and support in the completion of this text.

In particular, I owe a great debt to Carole Rennick of the Information Processing Center (IPC) at the University of South Florida for her patience and understanding during the preparation of the manuscript. She repeatedly added, modified, and rearranged the chapters in response to reviewers' suggestions. I am grateful to Athanasia Fitos for providing invaluable research assistance. She read most of the chapters, identified typos and omissions, and suggested the addition of relevant figures. Zlatko Knezevic and Ekaterina

Fitos are to be highly commended for lending their technical skills as geographers to this endeavor. The map at the beginning of chapter 2 is their contribution.

Finally, as always I would like to register my debt to Patricia, whose quiet, supportive attitude constantly strengthened my resolve, and to Janjay and Tinzie whose still precious childlike behavior constituted a source of invaluable motivation for seeking explanations of collective political violence.

CHAPTER 1

Collective Political Violence
Scope, Assumptions, and Approaches

The focus of this book is to identify the underlying causes of violent conflicts that range from mass protests, riots, civil wars, genocide, interstate wars, to revolutions. Why do we emphasize explanations of these phenomena in this book? The most general and obvious reason is that violent conflict is endemic to nation-states and is becoming inevitable in many societies, particularly with the end of the Cold War. Class cleavages or problems of inequality continue to polarize segments of populations, and the negative effects of abject poverty, economic deprivation, unemployment, or ethnic discrimination continue to widen in scope and deepen in intensity. This results in violent eruptions either between incumbent regimes and specific groups, or between ethnocommunal groups. The scope of this book is therefore quite broad because explanations of the causes of these varied forms of violence are many and different. While the various forms of conflict are significantly different, their causes are also analytically distinct.

With the end of the Cold War, the world is experiencing an increase in intrastate bloodletting that has horrified many observers of world politics. The possibility that zones of conflict will continue to widen and threaten peaceful ones make it increasingly essential that we understand the underlying causes of violent conflicts as a first step toward dealing with them more effectively. In other words, amplification and greater understanding of the sources of societal conflicts is a first and necessary step toward conflict resolution or peacemaking. Over many years, conflict within and among nations has baffled philosophers, scholars, and practitioners alike. Their

1

consequences—death, maimings, institutionalized fear and hatred, population displacement, and destruction of property—mean that they should be avoided at all costs. Although violent conflicts are an integral part of the march of human history, the dramatic changes within nations and in the international system (for example, the divergence among nations along religio-political value systems and socioeconomic distance) seem to be increasing the scope (extent), intensity (gravity), and duration of violent conflicts in the world. The principal imperative of any government is therefore to avoid violent conflicts within and outside its borders. All other goals cannot be meaningfully and effectively pursued where violent conflict abounds. If education, tourism, trade and finance, and other pursuits among human beings are to flourish, and elevate standards of living, then we must understand the causes of violent conflict; and thereby hope that we would be better able to prevent their eruption, and even identify their necessary ingredients before they occur.

On what assumptions is this book based? Seven central assumptions guide our analysis of violent conflicts within and among states. First, the control and distribution of resources underlie group structure and social arrangements within nation-states, and it is these social structural arrangements that constitute the foundation and outcome of power and inequality. Second, because of the realities of power and inequality, competition for and conflict over the control of resources become perennial issues reflected in all relationships and dynamics of social change among groups within the nation state. Resource control shapes behavior and social processes for all actors within the state ranging from the individual to specific groups often manifested in cleavages such as race, gender, class, or religion. Third, while capitalism has become the undisputed economic system in the world following the end of the Cold War, at the same time it produces gross inequalities and social problems such as ethnic discrimination, inflation, or environmental degradation that in turn aggravate tensions among groups in society. Fourth, the primordial sentiments of presumed common ancestry, racial characteristics, or a common ethnolinguistic background, among others, often intensify and prolong the rivalry among groups thereby further aggravating levels of discrimination and raising the stakes in conflict situations. Fifth, this book is also guided by the assumption that there is an inherent duality in the international system: fragmentation/disintegration and integration/stabilizing forces.[1] International society is characterized by conflict within and among nations. Subgroups, the state, and other actors are basically in continuous competition and conflict, as well as in cooperation with each other. Accordingly, a sixth assumption of this book is to emphasize both conflict and cooperation. While conflict is endemic to society and even inevitable to others because of their social structure and group composition, at the same time, the presence of regional organizations like the North Atlantic Treaty Organization (NATO), powerful states like the United States, and the United Nations (UN) encourage groups to resolve and manage their conflicts. Thus peacekeeping operations have increased significantly with the end of the Cold War. However, although peacekeeping perspectives are incorporated in the analysis, the emphasis is on explanations of collective violence. Finally, on a similar level of analysis, this book is based on the assumption that change and continuity, or stability and change are properties of all nation-states, including the international system. They also impact most groups within nation states thereby producing violent conflicts in some. Efforts at ensuring peace and stability have increasingly become the responsibility of the great powers and the UN because meaningful interactions, transactions, production processes, and distribution require an environment free of conflict and disorder. But because the very process of societal organization generates dissatisfaction, violent conflict becomes inevitable in some societies.

There is no single text that has attempted to fully synthesize most of the varied theories of violent conflicts. This book is therefore an attempt at a concise analysis of the individual, group, societal, state, and international sources of collective political violence.

Explaining Collective Political Violence

The meaning of *explanation* and *cause* as they are used in this book require some elaboration because the overall thrust of this conflict analysis project is to present contending explanations of varied aspects of violent conflict.

Many types of explanation are employed in the social sciences, along with many competing notions of what it means "to explain" phenomena, events, or a class of events. The *nomological* mode of explanation will serve our purposes. Nomological (*nomos* is Greek for "law") explanations are generalized statements to explain a particular event or class of events like riots, civil wars, or even revolutions. Such generalizations or covering laws explain events by linking cause to effect. "Severe economic deprivation leads to internal rebellion" is an example of a generalized, lawlike statement connecting cause to effect. Internal rebellion is, no doubt, the effect, and severe economic deprivation is the cause, because our nomological statement implies that severe economic deprivation is an antecedent of internal rebellion. Stated differently, *cause* implies a sequence in time between event X and event Y. Thus severe economic deprivation occurs prior to internal rebellion.

Most hypotheses in the social sciences are expressed as lawlike statements connecting independent variables (causes) to dependent variables (effects) in terms of a tendency or probability.[2] It is then the task of the researcher to confirm the expectation implied in the hypothesis through substantiating data or empirical testing.

In the analysis of violent conflict, social scientists generally employ either normative theory or empirical theory. Normative theory focuses on pre-scriptive concerns (ought, must, should). The emphasis is on how things *should* or *ought* to be. Examples include ethical questions of what is right or wrong in the conduct of war, or what activities and behaviors are morally acceptable or unacceptable. What should be the conditions for a just war? What practices or techniques are considered unethical or immoral in war? Such normative concerns are not the major focus of this book, although they will be discussed when and where relevant.

Based on our discussion above of explanation and nomological cause and effect, our primary focus will be on the second kind of theory: empirical or causal theories. Their emphasis is not on how things ought to be but why are they the way they are. The objective of empirical theory is the explanation of behaviors—in this case, violent conflict behaviors such as riots, civil wars, genocides, or revolutions.

Theories

Theories in the social sciences are essentially explanations concerning the causes of human behavior. Theories of collective political violence, for ex-ample, consist of explanations about what causes phenomena such as rebel-lions, civil wars, violent demonstrations, and so on, and what determines this cause and effect relationship. In conflict analysis many theories or ex-planations are put forward by scholars from different disciplines about why collective violence occurs. Theories of conflict consist of explanations about what causes the various types of collective violence that plague the world. Generally, theories are constructed through reasoning: that is the use of premises (one or more statements) of an argument to infer another state-ment called the "conclusion." This means that theories are developed in three different ways: through induction, deduction, or a combination of the two. In inductive reasoning the analyst conducts reasoning from the partic-ular (observation of the facts or data) to the general (conclusions). In other words, it is a bottom-up approach in which the premises provide evidence only for the conclusion. As a researcher learns more about, for example, specific revolutions, and as hypotheses are tested, theories are constructed and reformulated. In deduction the top-down approach is used to reason from the general to the particular, and the premises lead necessarily to the conclusion. An example would be deducing the theory of revolution from a more comprehensive, general theory about societies.

In the social sciences, most explanations fall under the inductive method of analysis rather than the deductive method. Similarly, in the natural sciences many explanations are also inductive. Inductive explanations have an *explanandum* and an *explanans*.[3] The explanandum is the problem, phenomenon, thing, or event to be explained and it is the conclusion of an inductive argument. The explanandum may be an individual event or phenomenon such as the Iraqi invasion of Kuwait, or a more general class of events, such as interethnic conflicts in developing countries. The explanans explains the explanandum. The explanandum is deduced from the explanans. In other words, the explanans are the premises, and the explanandum is the conclusion of an inductive argument. The explanans comprises two types of statements: (1) a set of universal (lawlike) generalizations (the covering laws), and (2) a set of initial statements or conditions (the particular facts of the problem, event, or situation).

However, in inductive explanations, the generalizations are statistical rather than universal in the explanans. This means that the explanandum cannot be deduced from the explanans with certainty. The explanans imply probability in relation to the explanandum. It provides support or evidence for the explanandum but does not guarantee certainty for the explanandum. In other words, in inductive argument, the explanans could be true and the explanandum could still be false. An inductive argument takes the following form:

Problem or event:	Why do people in Los Angeles riot?
Explanans:	If people are economically deprived there is 80 percent probability they will engage in riots.
	The people of Los Angeles are economically deprived.
Explanandum:	The people of Los Angeles engage in riots.

In this example, the generalization is statistical or based on probability. The probability here is 80 percent that the people of Los Angeles will riot.

Deductive explanations contain the most powerful type of arguments because they explain individual as well as general events, and their conclusions must be true if their premises are true. Similar to inductive explanations, they consist of the explanandum and the explanans. The deductive argument follows this form.

Problem or event:	Why did the Rwandan genocide occur?
Explanans:	If a totalitarian regime faces bitter opposition from a minority group, it will resort to genocide to silence that opposition.
	The Hutu regime of Rwanda was a totalitarian regime.
	The Hutu regime of Rwanda faced serious opposition from the Tutsi minority.
Explanandum:	The Rwandan Hutu regime resorted to genocide against the Tutsi minority.

In this example, the event (genocide against the Tutsi minority) is explained by deducing it from a universal generalization or covering law, as well as a set of initial conditions that provide support for the antecedent condition of the covering law.

Provided both the explanans and explanandum are true, the deductive explanation is a powerful form of argument that is capable of explaining with certainty both individual and general events. However, deductive explanations so far have limited applicability to the social sciences. The reason for their limited use is that the explanans require a universal generalization, and the social sciences have few, if any, undisputed universal generalizations. The example listed above may not be the best, because there may be instances of minority opposition to a totalitarian regime that do not result in genocide. The best illustrations of the deductive method are usually from the natural sciences.

Within each theory are concepts (terms, or common names) that identify social phenomena, events, or ideas. Riot, aggression, violence, frustration, and so on, are all concepts. They refer to general phenomena rather than unique, specific phenomena.

Our analysis so far underscores the fact that social scientists use the scientific approach, which employs a logical, systematic method of analysis designed to describe, explain, and predict observable phenomena or sets of events.[4] The ultimate objectives of analysis using the scientific method are to describe, explain, and predict. In the area of conflict analysis, for example, political scientists would attempt to describe, explain, or predict such varied conflict-related phenomena as wars, genocides, or revolutions.

Analyzing social phenomena also underscores the interdependence of description (establishing facts) as a basic level of analysis, and explanation (answering the question, Why?), a higher level of analysis that requires thinking in causal terms about classes of events rather than about discrete events highlighted in description. In conflict analysis, for example, the class of events (phenomena) we seek to describe is the varied forms of violent conflict (the dependent variable), which we will then seek to explain using the source categories (the independent variables) or predictor variables found in the varied theories.

In description, the attempt is to ascertain the facts and figures by answering the questions what, when, who, where, or how. The conflict analyst may ask: When do riots occur? Where do they tend to occur? How extensive are most riots? Are lower-income people more likely to participate in protests than higher income people? Because it ascertains the facts, description generally precedes explanation and prediction. Explanation attempts to answer "why" types of questions in order to make more sense out of what description has established. Why are leaders of revolutionary movements often very educated? Why are rapidly modernizing, more affluent societies more likely to experience revolution than slowly modernizing, less affluent societies? Explaining questions such as these engage the mind of the conflict analyst. Prediction grapples with questions about what will occur in the future. The attempt is to predict the conditions under which, for example, a civil war is likely to occur in country X in the future. Prescription, finally, attempts to deal with the normative aspects of observable phenomena. The focus is often on "ought," "must," or "should" types of analysis. For example, what should Liberian officials do to prevent the eruption of another civil war in the country?

Levels of Theory

Theories can be divided on the basis of the scope or breadth of their application to social phenomena (events, problems, or real world situations). In the area of political theories, for example, David Easton made a distinction between three levels of theory: empirical generalizations, middle-ranged theories, and general theories, in ascending order of complexity and sophistication.[5] Empirical generalizations relate two or more concepts in a general statement such as: advanced democracies never go to war with each other.

A middle-ranged theory is a set of interrelated generalizations that explain only a certain aspect of a discipline. An example would be a theory of arms race between two hostile nations in international relations. Other examples of middle-ranged theories are: the relationship between defense spending and interstate wars; economic deprivation and the incidence of riots; or social (ethnic) heterogeneity and domestic instability. Middle-ranged theories do not attempt to explain the entire spectrum of politics or international relations. They are, in other words, partial theories because they do not attempt to account for all the changes, events, or problems within a political system. Some theorists refer to middle-ranged theories as "islands" of theory because they are still quite distant from each other in terms of relatedness.[6] The assumption among many theorists is that the accumulation of middle-ranged theories will someday lead to the construction of theories of increasing complexity and sophistication.

A general theory or a grand theory is one that provides a framework for a complete explanation of political reality. The scope of a general theory extends beyond a particular event, problem, or real world situation. A general theory, in other words, encompasses all aspects of the subject. It should also incorporate and explain both empirical generalizations and middle-ranged theories into its structures. However, most social scientists attempt only to explain a specific aspect of the political process because a grand theory linking or comprising both empirical generalizations and middle-ranged theories along with explanations has yet to be developed.

General theory or grand theory		
middle-ranged or partial theory	middle-ranged or partial theory	middle-ranged or partial theory
Empirical generalization		

Fig. 1.1: Levels of Theory.

Requirements of a Good Theory

This book is one of competing theories of collective violence. It is therefore essential for the student to be aware of what constitutes good theory. In general, a theory, framework, model, or explanation must go beyond mere description and must obey the following requirements:

1. It must be comprehensive or applicable to various situations, and must include relevant variables.
2. It must be cohesive, with all its segments strongly linked to each other with identical variables in its separate paths. In other words, a good theory must be logically consistent.
3. It must be empirical or applicable to concrete situations. This requirement underscores the plausibility, or the intuitive sense of the theory.
4. As a result of the third requirement, a theory must have the greatest validity or empirical evidence to support it or enhance its explanatory power. Some theories, because of the assumptions built into them, tend to have little empirical support in real world situations.
5. It must be parsimonious, or be able to explain the problem or event with as little complexity as possible. However, the world itself and many social phenomena tend to be complex and multifaceted. A simplified theory may result in the loss of relevance and explanatory power.
6. It must be open to verification. In other words, a good theory must be testable and falsifiable.
7. Finally, it must be clear and causal in the relationship between and among variables, and in terms of considering and linking units or factors at multiple levels of analysis. Stated differently, it must attempt to interconnect with other theories and thereby underscore multicausality as opposed to unicausality.

The various theories and approaches that are discussed in this book inevitably fall into a level of analysis (individual, group, societal or state, and international) framework. An individual level of analysis, for example, assumes that a theory of collective political violence (for example, a rebellion) is best explained by focusing on the nature of humans or to be specific nature of the leader of the rebellion who organizes others against the state. In the case of World War II, for instance, it was the psychological makeup of Adolf Hitler that led to German aggression in Europe.

At the group level of analysis, the basic focus is the small group rather than the individual as the cause of political violence. The influential group within a revolutionary movement is responsible for the decision to revolt against the status quo. Or it could be the small group of powerful officials within the national government that is responsible for the state's decision to go to war. Interethnic conflicts would also fall into this level since ethnic groups within a state could be incited to violence by their ethnic elite.

The basic contention for the state level of analysis is that there are certain characteristics inherent in the state that predispose it to war or aggression, compared to other states that lack such characteristics. Similarly, the international system level of analysis assumes that interstate wars are caused by the structure of the international system itself. Issues of status and power configuration, balance of power, empirical hegemony, issues of global economic dislocation or boom, are all factors important in the cause of collective violence. However, instead of overemphasizing one level of causation to the exclusion of others, it makes more sense to view collective political violence (riots, rebellions, civil wars, genocides, revolutions, and interstate wars) as the result of multiple causation, or the combined effects of individual, social-structural, and global systemic factors.

Broad Theoretical Approaches

It is important to reflect, for a moment, on the seminal revolutions of the past four centuries, or on the numerous active civil wars being waged, in any one year, in our international system. To what could these conflicts be attributed? Now reflect for a moment on the socioeconomic problems that underlie these violence-ridden countries and episodes: poverty, unemployment, ethnopolitical discrimination, exploitation, scarcity, inequality, and so on. Why are these problems very much a part of states and contemporary society to the point where they generate violent conflicts, despite the existence of national, regional, or local governments and international institutions that are expected to ensure peace and stability? Conflict analysis provides us with explanatory frameworks, models, or theoretical approaches to help us better understand or sharpen our understanding. In this section, we will briefly analyze theoretical approaches to understanding collective political violence.

What have been referred to as the "Great Revolutions" (the French, American, Russian, Chinese, and so on), the postcolonial conflicts of newly independent nations, and the post–Cold War conflicts that erupted after 1989, increasingly impel theorists to raise numerous questions about collective violence that they are unable to answer. In particular, the different theories or explanations put forward have differed about collective violence, and they are far from arriving at any universally accepted conclusions about why collective violence occurs. The lack of agreement, obviously, stems from the various approaches used in explanations of particular conflict situations. While attempts to answer the who, what, when, how, or where questions (descriptive analysis) may be less difficult, their answers to the question, Why? (explanation) often generates significant differences. The varied theories on collective violence fall largely under three dichotomies: Marxian versus Non-Marxian, contingent versus inherent, and micro versus macro.

Marxian versus Non-Marxian Approaches

The Marxian tradition in the analysis of conflict is also referred to as the conflict perspective and it constitutes a radical view because its advocates are generally those who encourage radical social change. It is labeled Marxian because it was developed, in particular, by the famous German philosopher Karl Marx, who was also a journalist and a political radical, and is often referred to as the "godfather of conflict."[7] Marx, for instance, argued that revolutions, in particular, are inevitable because of the very nature of the structure of society. In societies, the existing social system reflects the vested interests of those who own and control the resources. In other words, society's institutions, its political system and economy, are designed to allow those who have power to exploit those who do not. The consequence is that the rest of society becomes alienated or psychologically separated from those in power in two ways: materially through monopolistic control over the economic system; and socially, through stratification in the form of the class system.[8] For Marx, revolutions in particular, are "normal" because they resolve the basic contradictions that are built into the social arrangements. To achieve equity and social unity, the economic and social separation between the powerful haves and the powerless have-nots must be eliminated. Strong adherents to this view believe that the individual can be reunited with society only through the elimination of private property and the class system. Critics of the existing social structure focus on the very high levels of inequality that generate a vicious circle of poverty, ignorance, deprivation, hunger, disease, crime, and ultimately violent eruptions. Instead of society being viewed as functional for the majority, rather the intense inequality and lack of access to key resources is defined as problematic. For the Marxian perspective, the major concern is realizing equality for all, rather than maintenance of the existing contradictory social order. The Marxist explanation of revolution is elaborated more fully in chapter 10.

Non-Marxian Theories

Many theories of collective violence are an attempt to discredit Marxism. Functionalism, theory of mass society, and rational choice explanations that underscore incentives as a condition for participation in collective violence, among others, fall into this category. The functionalist perspective tends to be conservative and thus to emphasize why societies persist even though conflict is endemic to society. The emphasis is on the traditional arrangements that allow society to persist and are manifested in economic equilibrium, peaceful adaptation to change, and normative and political conformity to the maintenance of political stability. One of functionalism's foremost modern theorists is Talcott Parsons. He viewed society as governed by self-correcting processes that produce equilibrium or a steady state. Social systems are maintained and regulated through a process of value integration in which commonly held values are central to ensuring the perpetuation of society. Parsons, in particular, argued that every major social institution functioned to contribute to the viability of society as a whole. Every social system (from families to entire societies) is comprised of four functionally distinct dimensions. These are the adaptive (political), goal attainment (economic), integrative (legal), and latent pattern-maintenance (religious) aspects of social life. Thus, societies persist and revolutions are not inevitable because of the adaptive capacity of societies through institutional differentiation and functional subsystems whose ultimate goal is the realization of the "moral community."[9] In the Marxian and non-Marxian conceptions of conflict, society is viewed in terms of power/stratification and a natural organism respectively. In the case of the former, social order or hierarchy is based on power, whereas in functionalism, it is based on nature. Accordingly, national integration, peace, and stability are achieved by access to economic resources and systemic authority respectively.

Functionalism, mass society theory, and other explanations of collective violence that constitute a response to the Marxian tradition will be analyzed in more detail in later chapters of this book.

Micro and Macro Approaches

Most theories in the area of conflict analysis fall into two categories: micro and macro theories, or reductionist and holistic approaches to the study of violent conflicts. The micro approach attempts to explain the underlying causes of conflict in the nature of human beings, whereas the macro approach focuses on society's or state's structure and institutions. This micro/macro dichotomy corresponds to specific disciplines in academia. For example, biologists, psychologists, social psychologists, sociobiologists, psychobiographers, decision-making theorists, and rational choice theorists underscore the behavior of individuals, and from there generalize to collective behavior of groups. On the other hand, the focus on groups, collectivities, institutions, social classes, ethnocommunal or religious entities, political movements, cultural systems, nation-states, or the structure of the international system to explain collective violence has been the domain of political scientists, sociologists, anthropologists, organization and communication experts, international relations theorists, and geographers, among others.

However, in some theories of conflict, the micro/macro distinction is not so clear-cut because some theorists might blend both dimensions to produce a psychosocial or psychocultural explanation of collective violence.[10] For such theorists, a better explanation of collective violence is achieved when psychological (nature of human beings) explanations are combined with societal (nature of structures and institutions) explanations. The underlying assumption of such theories is that the inherent tendency of humans to resort to collective violence has to be aroused by contingent conditions in society such as political or economic deprivation before an individual or group can engage in collective violence. While the focus of analysis seems to be on the individual, the underlying assumption is that if enough individuals experience blocked opportunities (deprivation) they become a group of frustrated individuals who are likely to engage in collective violence, especially when a catalyst is present. Similarly, in rational choice explanations of collective violence, while decision makers or economists may focus on members within organizations who attempt to further their interests through collective effort, the ultimate decision to participate in such efforts is an individual choice. Thus, rational choice theorists would conclude that the decision whether or not to participate in collective violence is a rational choice based on cost-benefit analysis by the individual confronted with either negative or positive incentives.[11] But very often this decision-making dilemma of the individual takes place within a revolutionary or political movement, or an organization.

Such efforts to blend micro (individual) and macro (societal) factors to explain collective violence has helped to dilute the methodological chasm that historically divided micro and macro views on collective violence. For example, a sharp cleavage used to exist between psychologists and sociologists around the early 1900s, expressed in Émile Durkheim's statement that "every time that a social phenomenon is directly explained as a psychic phenomenon, one may be sure that the explanation is false."[12] Along the same

Table 1.1: Contending Approaches

APPROACH	ACADEMIC DISCIPLINE	PRIMARY FOCUS
Micro	Psychology, social psychology, biology, rational choice/game theory	Nature of human beings, behavior of individuals
Macro	Sociology, anthropology, political science, systems theory	Group interactions, cultural and social structure, institutions, social classes, interstate relations
Micro/Macro	Social psychology, psychohistorical, and psychocultural analysis	Fusion of individual and behavior, social-structural factors

lines is the enduring antipathy between Freudian analysis and Marxist dialectic. The sharp division between the two general fields is, again, explainable in the fact that psychologists analyze human problems through an emphasis on the anxieties, tensions, fears, and other internal psychic dynamics of the individual, which are eventually projected into the external environment. Conversely, sociologists are known to study human problems via social structures and institutions, and to interconnect the effects of dysfunctions within those structures and institutions to the psychological well-being of individuals. However, the methodological and substantive chasm between micro and macro approaches to the study of collective violence has been narrowed by the prevalence of psychosocial and/or psychocultural analyses.

The Contingency-Inherency Dichotomy

Another broad classification of theories of collective violence is the contingency/inherency dichotomy of Harry Eckstein.[13] In other words, the most basic starting point for choices in theorizing about or studying collective violence lies between regarding it as either "contingent" (conditional) or "inherent" (routine) in political life. Where collective violence is viewed as contingent, its occurrence is said to depend on conditions that occur accidentally, or on the presence of unusual (aberrant) conditions, or conditions that involve a great deal of chance. Thus a theorist can identify factors that increase the probability of, say, a civil war within a country. The analyst wants to know what caused a civil war to erupt in a society where "normally" none was expected to occur. The occurrence of the civil war is thus an abnormality, an aberration, or unusual. What caused the war? Why did it occur? These are the questions explored within this contingency approach to explanations of collective violence.

Conversely, something is inherent if either it will always happen (for example, economic recession) or if the potentiality for it to happen always exists and actuality can only be obstructed. It is contingencies (chance occurrences that hinder or facilitate) that determine the inevitable, and when, as well as whether or not it occurs. Just as contingencies can be controlled and are not random, so is inherence not outright inevitability. For example, it is a fact that a jumbo jet can malfunction and crash, but when or how it will malfunction and crash is not fully predictable, nor is it inevitable. Similarly, a well-functioning social system could dysfunction, but when and how is not easily predictable. In other words, in the real world, contingency and inherency are almost always interrelated and difficult to separate. In studies of collective violence, for example, what may seem clearly contingent to one analyst may seem just as clearly inherent to another.

However, because of the more obvious antithetical nature of the two approaches, the distinction between contingency and inherency is often stated in opposed terminologies: abnormality versus normality, irregularity versus regularity, extrinsic versus intrinsic, or accidental versus purposive, among others. In the end, it is essential to note that the objective of the contrasts is to arrive at a better explanation, and not necessarily the absolute truth, because in real situations of collective violence contingent and inherent conditions are to a large extent intertwined.

To sum up this section on the contingency/inherency approaches, we need to broadly relate them to actual theories of collective violence that fall within their domain. First, contingency explanations inspire many psychocultural theories (for example, relative deprivation) because the assumptions underlying these theories is that collective violence is the consequence of the frustration of a group's rights by extraordinary causes. Thus, if the group should resort to violence, it is not that it is disposed to violence, but because the proclivity toward normal pacific competition (petitions, electoral competition, pressure group politics, and the like) has been blocked. Thus the violence that ensues is more of an emotional outburst than a rational, cost-benefit, or coolly calculated behavior. The contingency approach therefore assumes that human nature and by implication groups would rather resort to peaceful resolutions of disputes before they escalate into violent conflicts.[14] The key issue for theorists is thus to explain the frequency of collective violence.

On the contrary, in the inherency approach, the resort to collective violence is seen as one way for individuals or groups to maximize political influence and increase leverage over decisions. It is viewed as extreme but "normal." Since there are other channels of acquiring power that are pacific, the use of collective violence is thus a rational choice or a tactical route that involves cost-benefit calculation. Violence is not automatically chosen, it is chosen only after peaceful methods of power seeking are blocked, and only if the prospects for success are guaranteed if violence is employed. Prior use of violence, or violence as a part of the culture, does not affect the decision to resort to violence. Similarly, affective (emotional) factors are assumed to play a minor role.

Conflict theorists whose explanations fall into the contingency approach emphasize relative deprivation as a cause of systemic breakdown and/or individual pathologies. The argument is that the disposition to individual or collection violence is "inherent," but it lies dormant until aroused by contingent (extrinsic) forces that generate enough frustration and anger to escalate into violence. Relative deprivation theories would thus encompass violence resulting from the exclusion of competent individuals from societal institutions, the inability of rigid or poorly developed political structures to absorb groups or individuals mobilized by rapid socioeconomic modernization, systemic overload or disequilibrium, and peasant rebellions caused by the encroachment of market economies that upset traditional peasant life and at the same time produce cultural and economic frustrations due to intrusive and inappropriate new arrangements that replace traditional arrangements. In other words, the contingency approach includes both micro and macro theories, or a combination of the two. Gurr's explanation of collective violence is essentially microtheoretical (individual-level focus) whereas Huntington's modernization theory underscores the macrocosmic (societal) level of analysis.[15] Both approaches aim to explain collective political violence.

The inherency approach emphasizes collective violence as an aspect of the rational pursuit of self-interest and underscores the inevitability of conflict, or conflict as part of the march of history. Conflict as an extreme but "normal" process is reflected in theories that fall within the inherency approach: resource mobilization theory, strategic interaction models, political process theory, theory of group dynamics, and political contention theory. Charles Tilly, perhaps the foremost theorist of the inherency approach, uses the concept of "collective action" in his work *From Mobilization to Revolution* to stress the fact that violent action is purposeful and therefore not aberrant, but rather a tactical choice by groups in their political struggles against those in power who monopolize influence, access, and resources.[16] Accordingly, a group of individuals who share a common interest will organize, mobilize their resources, and if the opportunity is available, will engage in collective action, all as part of a normal political process.

In sum, the contingency approach is part of the large family of culturalist theories—theories based on learned orientations to action. Conversely, inherency theories are related to rationalist theories—theories based on the notion that actions are chosen by calculations of cost-efficiency.

Diagnostic Approach, Individual, and Social Pathologies

Generally, works on political violence are broad ranging and include philo-sophical approaches, historical descriptions, attempts at theory building, and various types of analyses related to ethnoviolence, genocide, or rebel-lions, among others. According to David Apter, causes related to institutional weakness and blockages, normative insufficiencies, injustices, or inequities are "diagnostic" in their approach.[17] This is the approach that suggests that political violence is a result of the unjustly treated deciding to redress the injustice outside the legal framework of society. It is a rational response to injustice, except that the means used is extralegal and/or violent.

The initiation of many of these violent conflicts is attributed to indi-viduals. Thus there is the prevalent view of political violence as individual pathology. This is the view that those inclined to use violence have some personality disorder: they are the malcontents, meddlesome, troublemak-ers, or lacking in self-control. They take on the task of redressing perceived or real injustices either in others or in society as a whole. They are inclined to disregard the rules and regulations that ensure societal stability and good citizenship.

Finally, if political violence can be viewed as individual pathology, then it can also be approached as social pathology. The pathological condition may be a consequence of asymmetrical relationships related to power and access, inequality based on class distinctions, or structural inequities embedded in a specific political economy such as capitalism or socialism. Macro analyses such as social-structural theories or Marxism view political violence as a manifestation of systemic breakdown. Changes in macro systems such as the transition from monarchy to democracy or capitalism to socialism are viewed by some as a result of the inevitable march of history to its ultimate end.

The approaches discussed above are attempts to engage in a scientific study of the underlying causes of violent social change within states and in our contemporary international system. Conflict analysis as a modern field of study first emerged in the 1920s and 1930s with the "Natural History" school of revolution.[18] Further developments in the field took place in the postcolonial era in response to the instability (coups, civil wars, riots, rev-olutions, and so on) that characterized the new nations of the developing regions of Asia, Africa, and Latin America. In particular, psychocultural and social-structural explanations were developed to help make sense out of the volatility that characterized these new states.

The period of European colonial hegemony had held the varied ethno-communal societies together as colonial territories prior to their entrance into the comity of nations as sovereign nation-states. But with independence, the situation became highly volatile in many of these new states—coups and countercoups, border disputes, and other forms of violent power struggles resulted. Shaking the foundation of the political infrastructure inherited from the colonial powers was a flood of new political parties, a "revolution of rising expectations" on the part of both the new elite and the population in general, new concerns by specific ethnocommunal groups who were no longer protected by the hegemony of the colonial regime, and inexperienced regimes and a new power elite directly confronted, for the first time, with the sensitive issues of ensuring ethnic balance and power sharing. Violent conflicts and disruption in many developing countries were thus not the exception, but the rule.

Similar to the decline of the traditional feudal order in France, Germany, and England, the post–World War II international system became more diverse, complex, and complicated with many new problems accompanying the new bipolar configuration of power that pitted two ideologically opposed superpowers, the United States and the Soviet Union, against each other and created many new problems for the new nations related to power, inequality, urbanization, and development. Similarly, a flood of competing political and economic ideologies sprung up among the new nations. Marxism, African Socialism, Maoism, and Marxism-Leninism all competed with capitalism and Western democracy.

Problems that had not been evident under European hegemony were now social problems. For example, perceptions of inequality became more intense as ethnocommunal groups perceived that the control of material resources by the dominant group meant that resources were distributed unequally. Consequently, the inadequacy of institutions created by colonial rule, coupled with actual and perceived injustice, created tensions that often escalated into violent conflicts.

Critical Theory: Constructivism and Feminism
Social Constructivism

While the many social science perspectives discussed in this text underscore positivist (system of observable scientific facts) thinking, it is also useful to briefly mention critical approaches such as constructivism and feminism as equally powerful tools in the analysis of collective political violence. In contrast to the neorealist, neoliberal, or Marxist approaches that underscore material power as the principal source of authority, influence, and struggle for dominance, social constructivists would emphasize both material and discursive (communicative) power as avenues for a better understanding of wars, revolutions, genocides, and so on. In particular, constructivists argue that violent political behavior could be explained and even understood by focusing on the role of norms and ideas as determinants of such behavior.

Accordingly, constructivists often make reference to Max Weber, who stressed that, "We are *cultural beings,* endowed with the capacity and the will to take a deliberate attitude towards the world and to lend it *significance.*"[19] Along the same line of argument, Émile Durkheim, the French sociologist, emphasized the concept of social facts, or the primacy of ideas and beliefs ("la conscience collective").[20]

To a large extent, the assumptions of social constructivism are different from those of positivism. While positivists specify a priori assumptions about the true nature of actors' interests and incentives, social constructivists believe that actors create social reality. John Ruggie identified three assumptions of social constructivism that eventually translate into causal beliefs.[21] The first assumption is that to a large extent, it is group affiliations that "construct" peoples' identities, ideas, and goals. A causal belief—such as the belief that nuclear weapons in the hands of rival nations will produce or threaten stability—is often the result of nations as actors defining their interests in the process of defining situations.

A second assumption of social constructivism is that shared ideas are shaped by historical circumstances. In other words, norms that specify or define reality can change significantly over time thereby introducing completely new interests and shared ideas both within and among nations. For example, constructivist empirical studies have documented the changing nature of ideas about human rights, international support for the termination of apartheid, the changing nature of humanitarian intervention, or the decrease in the sacrosanct nature of state sovereignty, among others. More obvious cases include the fact that colonialism and slavery were perfectly permissible internationally one or two centuries ago, and now both are unacceptable.

A third assumption of social constructivism is that issues of conflict and cooperation are determined by socially constructed understandings among groups, nations, or the international system. For instance, in the international system, it is not the proliferation of nuclear weapons that really concerns the United States, but who possesses them. Thus, nuclear warheads in the hands of Israel are of no concern to the United States, but they cause great concern when in the hands of Iraq or North Korea.

With regard to the stability of the international system, constructivists would argue that international society is comprised of values, rules, and institutions that are commonly shared by states and thereby guarantee global systemic stability such as a balance of power.[22] Often these norms that eventually become shared norms and beliefs emanate from the core to periphery in the international system (for example, the rapid spread of efforts to democratize society in many developing nations, or the increased spread of light arms to developing countries). As ideas or beliefs become more shared they develop into "intersubjective beliefs," or what John Searle refers to as "collective intentionality." Collective intentionality, according to Searle can "will" the rules of behavior, interactions, or the game to change.[23] Examples would be the end of slavery or colonialism, or the ongoing changes in state sovereignty, humanitarian interventions, or the creation of global human rights through collective intentionality.

Many conflicts and disputes in the world, their intensity, and the level of participation in them by groups or states could be explained in terms of how the identities, ideas, and goals of the actors are affected. The socially constructed understandings and perceptions or interpretations of such actors shape the way in which conflict and/or cooperation unfold. For instance, it could be argued that rebels, whether in Angola, Colombia, or Sri Lanka, their understandings of who they are, as well as what they consider legitimate and want to achieve, had their origins in their social environment—an environment perhaps characterized by injustice, inequality, and oppression. In other words, the social relationships (exploitation, corruption, and the like) in which actors (states, groups, individuals) find themselves determine how they interpret events and others' actions, define interests, and how they pursue goals—whether peacefully or through the use of violence.

There is no doubt that changes in norms, values, and beliefs in the recent post–Cold War past have ended some violent systems in the world, such as apartheid in South Africa, oppressive communist control in Eastern and Central Europe, and the blatant dictatorial behavior of leaders in many developing states of the world. The positive outcome of all these normative developments is the spread of a more comprehensive peacekeeping and peace-building agenda, as well as the spread of a culture of human rights and democracy. The questions that social constructivists will continue to grapple with include: When do old norms change? What causes them to change? Is it when they are too costly to sustain that they change? How do actors accept the new norms? Do actors persuade or coerce others to accept new norms?

Constructivism as an approach is a useful theoretical lens in understanding the true nature of things such as class, gender, and racial issues, among others. Within these units emancipation occurs when the accurate picture (view) of things is understood. When agents (individuals, groups, or nations) and events are contextualized in a normative and material structure it becomes easier to understand and even evaluate the resulting political action (cooperation or conflict). For example, rebellious behavior may be better understood in the context of a corrupt, insensitive, oppressive, and patrimonial behavior of inept power elite in a situation of resource scarcity and economic deprivation. The goal is to examine human behavior (cooperative or conflictual) in an effort to understand it. A violent event can only take on meaning if it is considered in relation to other meaningful events. That meaning can be found in structures. In this sense constructivism emphasizes *understanding* and not necessarily *explanation*. Understanding implies a profound and complex appreciation of the phenomenon. According to Valerie Marcel: "Explanation entails revealing a causal chain of events that allows one to find an underlying and universally valid truth. Understanding on the other hand consists in making sense of the event for oneself."[24] For instance, in order to understand group rebellion, one must get a sense of the rebels' worldview, their motivation within a normative-material social structure. The use of abstract models of actor rationality are not useful for a proper understanding of political behavior because decision makers' choices are largely shaped and determined by values that other groups in society share and take seriously.

Feminist Perspectives

Many of the theoretical perspectives discussed in this text satisfy the traditional statist conflict, security, and peacekeeping agenda, which emphasize balance of power struggles, or interest-based explanations of collective political violence. Traditional international relations, for example, has traditionally analyzed issues of conflict and peace either from a structural perspective or at the state-centric level with its emphasis on rational decision makers attempting to maximize their options vis-à-vis other state actors. The feminist perspective regarding conflict, violence, or war is one of those analytical categories that shed new light on our understanding of collective political violence. It underscores changing collective identities, the role of culture, or normative factors broadly defined to show how identities, interests, and power impact women in particular within and across societies.[25] In other words, the methods feminism uses to understand war and peace are quite different from those used by traditional international relations theories. The latter focus on interstate relations, balance of power struggles, and national interests as though groups within nations do not matter. Feminists explicitly focus on the marginalization of women in international politics, in matters of war, and the insecurity of entire segments of society because of the injustices of hierarchical social relations perpetrated by a male-dominated world.

Feminists from radical, socialist, liberal, or other perspectives characterize gender relations as relations of inequality and subordination. Radical and socialist feminism in particular use the term *patriarchy* to describe the obvious male dominance and female subordination in societies around the world.[26] For liberal feminists, the problem of female subordination is a result of the socialization of men and women into different roles. The consequence for women has been discrimination, prejudice, and marginalization.

In particular, many feminists utilize a critical theoretical approach as a way to better understand how societal hierarchies that subordinate women are socially constructed and maintained. The study of gender accordingly focuses on issues of power and hierarchy between elite men and marginalized groups. Radical feminists, for instance, argue that women have been relegated to a household (private) position to take care of men and children. This overwhelming male dominance is a result of the biological inequality and differences between the male and female, and particularly women's reproductive roles.

In terms of disciplines and methodologies, while traditional theorists (neorealists, neoliberals, Marxists, and so on) use a top-down approach to try to understand conflict, security, and peace, feminists use a bottom-up approach, emphasizing social relations, and examining ways to emancipate women and other marginalized groups. Feminists direct our attention to the devaluation of women's work and the increasing feminization of poverty all over the world.[27] In other words, while women do not experience the same type of oppression across race, class, and society, they are nonetheless disproportionaltely relegated to the bottom of the socioeconomic ladder in all countries. While the subordinate position of women in the world has not produced a world war, or directly caused a civil war or revolution in any society, feminists like Susan Okin nonetheless believe that women should not be marginalized by their sex.[28] They should instead be guaranteed security, equality with men, and freedom of choice.

The condition of women, according to feminists, is reinforced by traditional mainstream assertions that the state is a neutral arbiter. Power relations are, in other words, male dominated. They exclude women from elite decision-making positions in states, positions that constitute the "public" domain of society. Women are confined to the "private" sphere of life with its focus on the household and rearing children. In critical-theoretical terms therefore, gender structures are socially constructed and maintained through power relations, and are variable across time. The aim of feminism is to emancipate women, especially since knowledge in the dominant disciplines, such as international relations, constitutes a structure of domination because it has largely been produced by men and for their benefit. For instance, the myth is generally perpetuated that wars are fought to guarantee the security of women, children, and other "vulnerable" segments of society. In reality, according to feminists, these groups suffer the highest level of casualties in war. Thus, while traditional theorists examine the causes and consequences of wars, feminists are concerned about what happens during wars, in particular their impact on women and other segments of society.

Feminists have also underscored an atrocity often suffered by women during war: rape. Wartime rape is an integral part of wars. During the immediate post–Cold War conflicts in the Balkans, rape was used as a systematic military strategy. In ethnic wars, rape is used as a weapon of demoralization against entire societies. During the Rwandan genocide, for example, more than 250,000 women were raped.[29] These women were stigmatized, made outcasts in their communities, and their children were labeled "devil's children." The 1937 "Rape of Nanking" describes approximately 20,000 cases of rape that occurred within the then capital city of China when the Japanese army seized it. According to the International Military Tribunal for the Far East held in Tokyo in 1946:

> Death was a frequent penalty for the slightest resistance on the part of a victim or the members of her family who sought to protect her. Even girls of tender years and old women were raped in large numbers throughout the city, and many cases of abnormal or sadistic behavior in connection with the rapes occurred. Many women were killed after the act and their babies mutilated. . . .[30]

The civil wars that are raging in many parts of the world, whether in Africa, Asia, or elsewhere, have rape as a common denominator. Rape, in other words, has been generally used as a weapon of violence to intimidate, violate, injure, and at times kill many women. During the Vietnam War American soldiers commonly employed rape as a weapon. In one episode, members of an army platoon subjected two female Vietnamese detainees "to multiple rapes, sodomy, and other mistreatments." According to an eyewitness report, both were subsequently murdered; one of them was shot once in the neck and twice in the head.[31] In war-ravaged societies, as the men disappear, are killed, or go into hiding, they leave the women behind as the sole caregivers for the old and young.

According to feminism the effects of war on women reveal the unequal gender relations that are integral to military activities. The argument that war protects vulnerable groups becomes a myth, and war itself is a cultural construction because it is not inevitable, as realists assert. Some feminists suggest that it is in fact women who are more attuned to peace, since it is men who generally articulate militaristic rhetoric. In other words, the link between masculinity and war has been emphasized by many feminist writers. While women play the role of cooks, nurses, sex slaves, or "wives" of rebels, it is the males who are given the attributes of brave, battle-hardened, and the like. Women are associated with peace movements such as the Women's Strike for Peace in the United States in the early 1960s to protest escalation of the Cold War. In more recent marches for peace around the world, women were substantially represented.

While war does not have the same impact on women as it does on men, the outcome of some revolutions tend to alter gender relations. The many revolutions and wars of independence in the developing world during the 1960s and 1970s specifically stated their intent to achieve gender equality. According to Stephanie Urdang:

> particularly important is the insistence that their fight stretches beyond victory on the battlefield to the more fundamental question of establishing a new and just society in each of their countries, one that brings the end to all forms of exploitation. Within this context liberation movements have all—in varying degrees—emphasized the liberation of women.[32]

At times women have been instrumental in starting revolutions. For instance, the women textile workers' strike on International Women's Day triggered the Russian Revolution, but women did not play a significant role in subsequent events. The Bolsheviks considered them the most backward segment of the working class. The marginalization of women was equally pervasive in the Chinese Revolution and the Cuban Revolution, as well as the Vietcong struggle against the United States. In these struggles women played largely supportive roles as messengers, scouts, and nurses rather than as combatants. They played crucial roles in areas that were already liberated. To a large extent, women were put into gender typical roles as teachers, nurses, and support for male fighters. Thus, the marginalization of women eventually meant that the goal of eliminating gender inequality was never achieved. Socialist revolutions in Mozambique, Nicaragua, and Cuba did not totally emancipate women.[33] Even socialist revolutions have often relegated feminist issues to a secondary role, and emphasized instead economic development and social stability.

As with other approaches or perspectives in the social sciences, feminists are not united about what constitutes female oppression, or how to go about destroying those structures of domination that have generally been produced by and for elite men. Just as the condition of women vary from region to region and across time, so do liberal, socialist, and radical feminists differ in their interpretation of the gender problem.

In sum, many approaches are used in efforts to explain collective political violence: micro-explanations that focus on individual frustration; social-structural explanations that focus on inequality in society and the role of institutions, social classes, cultural systems, critical theories, and the like; as well as a mixture of individual psychological factors and the nature of the political system. The next chapter identifies some of the most recent trends and provides a general introduction to concerns that have risen to prominence since the end of World War II and the Cold War.

Notes

1. See for example, J. A. Camilleri, *The End of Sovereignty? The Politics of a Shrinking and Fragmenting World* (Aldershot: Edward Elgar, 1992).
2. For details, see Robert B. Smith, *An Introduction to Social Research.* Vol. 1 of Handbook of Social Science Methods (Cambridge, MA: Ballinger, 1983).
3. See Dickinson McGaw and George Watson, *Political and Social Inquiry* (New York: Wiley, 1976).
4. See Kenneth R. Hoover, *The Elements of Social Scientific Thinking* (New York: St. Martin's, 1984).
5. Easton discusses this three-tiered classification in terms of "singular generalizations," "narrow-gauge theory," and "broad gauge" or "systematic theory." For details, see David Easton, *The Political System: An Inquiry into the State of Political Science* (New York: Alfred A. Knopf, 1959).
6. For details, see, among others, Glen H. Snyder and Paul Diesing, *Conflict Among Nations: Bargaining, Decision-Making, and System Structure in International Crisis* (Princeton: Princeton University Press, 1977).
7. For more details on Marx and his life see George Soule, *Ideas of the Great Economists* (New York: The New American Library, 1952); and Mostafa Rejai, *Comparative Political Ideologies* (New York: St. Martin's Press, 1984).
8. See, among many other works, Gerd Hardach et al., *A Short History of Socialist Economic Thought* (New York: St. Martin's Press, 1978).
9. See Talcott Parsons, "Some Reflections on the Place of Force in Social Process," in *Internal War,* ed. Harry Eckstein (Glencoe, IL: The Free Press, 1964), 34.
10. Among many others, see A. S. Cohan, *Theories of Revolution: An Introduction* (New York: Wiley, 1975); T. R. Gurr, *Why Men Rebel* (Princeton: Princeton University Press, 1970); and Edward N. Muller, *Aggressive Political Participation* (Princeton: Princeton University Press, 1979).
11. For details, see among others, Mancur Olson, *The Logic of Collective Action: Public Goods and the Theory of Groups* (Cambridge: Harvard University Press, 1971).
12. See Abraham Kardiner and Edward Preble, *They Studied Man* (New York: American Library Mentor Books, 1963), 102.
13. Harry Eckstein, "Theoretical Approaches to Explaining Collective Political Violence," in *Handbook of Political Conflict,* ed. T. R. Gurr (New York: Free Press, 1980).
14. For details, see Harry Eckstein, "Theoretical Approaches to Explaining Collective Political Violence," in *Handbook of Political Conflict,* ed. T. R. Gurr.
15. See, for example, T. R. Gurr, *Why Men Rebel* (Princeton: Princeton University Press, 1970); and Samuel P. Huntington, *Political Order in Changing Societies* (New Haven: Yale University Press, 1968).
16. Charles Tilly, *From Mobilization to Revolution* (Reading, MA: Addison-Wesley, 1978).
17. David Apter, ed., *The Legitimization of Violence* (Washington Square: New York University Press, 1997), introduction.
18. For details, see, Jack A. Goldstone, ed., *Revolutions: Theoretical, Comparative and Historical Studies* (Fort Worth: Harcourt Brace College Publishers, 1994).
19. Max Weber, *The Methodology of the Social Sciences,* trans. E. Shils and H. A. Finch (Glencoe IL: Free Press, 1949), 81.
20. Émile Durkheim, *The Rules of Sociological Method,* trans. E. G. Catlin (New York: Free Press, 1938).
21. John Ruggie, *Constructing the World Polity: Essays on International Institutionalization* (New York: Routledge, 1998).
22. See, for example, Nicholas G. Onuf, *World of Our Making: Rules and Rule in Social Theory and International Relations* (Columbia: University of South Carolina Press, 1989).
23. John R. Searle, *The Construction of Social Reality* (New York: Free Press, 1995).
24. Valerie Marcel, "The Contructivist Debate: Bringing Hermeneutics (Properly) In," paper presented at the 2001 ISA Conference, February 21, 2001, 9.
25. For details, see, J. Ann Tickner, *Gendering World Politics* (New York: Columbia University Press, 2001).

26. See, for example, Georgina Waylen *Gender in Third World Politics* (Boulder: Lynne Rienner Publishers, 1996).
27. See, for example, Nancy J. Hirshmann and Christine DiStefano, eds., *Revisioning the Political: Feminist Reconstructions of Traditional Concepts in Western Political Theory* (Boulder: Westview Press, 1996).
28. Susan Okin, "Is Multiculturalism Bad for Women?" in *Susan Moller Okin with Respondents,* ed. Joshua Cohen, Matthew Howard, and Martha C. Nussbaum (Princeton: Princeton University Press, 1999).
29. See, for details, Elizabeth Royte, "The Outcasts." *New York Times Magazine,* January 19, 1997.
30. William Brennan, "Female Objects of Semantic Dehumanization and Violence," http://www.fnsa.org/v1n3/brennan/.html, January 20, 2003.
31. William Brennan, "Female Objects of Semantic Dehumanization and Violence," p. 2.
32. Stephanie Urdang, "Women in national liberation movements," in *African Women South of the Sahara,* eds., M. Hay and S. Stichter (London: Longman, 1984).
33. For details, see, Georgina Waylen, *Gender in Third World Politics* (Boulder: Lynne Rienner Publishers, 1996).

Key Terms

contingency approach
deductive reasoning
description
empirical theories
explanation
inductive reasoning

inherency approach
nomological explanations
normative theory
prediction
prescription

Discussion Questions

1. What is the difference between deductive and inductive reasoning?
2. Compare and contrast Marxism and non-Marxism approaches to explaining collective political violence.
3. What are the differences between description, explanation, and prescription as levels of analysis?
4. Outline and discuss the three levels of theory.
5. What disciplines are closely associated with micro approaches to understanding violence?
6. Outline the differences between contingency and inherency approaches to explaining violent conflicts.

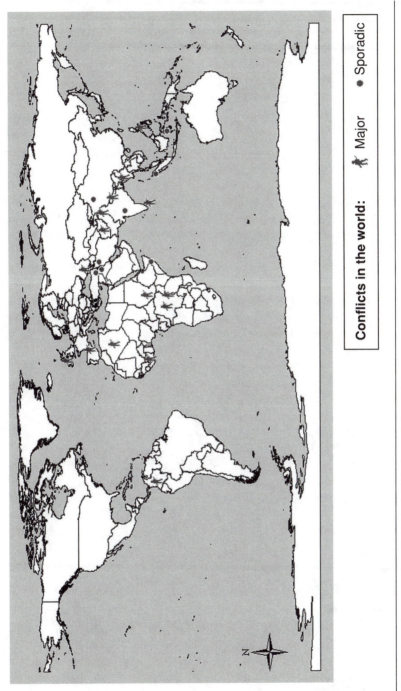

Conflicts in the world: 🏃 Major • Sporadic

Fig. 1.2: Hot Spots Around the World, March 2003. *Source:* Z. K. and E. F.

CHAPTER 2

Trends in Collective Political Violence

Cold War, Nation Building, and Post–Cold War Conflicts

Disputes that escalate into violent conflicts are essentially issues that divide different social entities along incompatible goals. Violence erupts as a consequence of the mutual hostilities that result from the incompatibilities dividing the rival actors. Intergroup conflict, for example, may arise because of competition to obtain resources that are present in limited supply. The severity of the conflict may be analyzed in several generally variable ways: in terms of whether the incompatibilities between contenders is mild, moderate, or intense, or by the scope (extent), intensity (destructiveness), and duration of mutual hostilities, which are in turn an indication of the quantity and quality of the means mobilized in the struggle over incompatible goals.

This chapter summarizes the evolving trend of organized political violence since the end of World War II to the post–Cold War era. The nature and underlying causes of these wars are categorized into: (1) Cold War conflicts that were motivated by superpower empire-building efforts; (2) nation-building conflicts caused by differences over what the proper boundaries of the new state should be, or over the most appropriate goals and policies of a political community; and (3) post–Cold War conflicts characterized largely by a widening scope and intensity of intergroup violence caused by the end of superpower imperial hegemony and a transformation in the bipolar structure of power and influence of the Cold War. The conflicts in Somalia, the former Yugoslavia, or in the Caucasus region erupted following the end of the Cold War.

Decolonization Process

Following the end of World War II, the first type of violent conflicts to occur were the anticolonial wars characterized by riots and violent struggles of long duration in the form of guerrilla wars, repressive actions, and counterinsurgency operations. In sub-Saharan Africa, for example, Angola, Namibia, and Mozambique experienced anticolonial wars. But generally, a large part of the decolonization process was nonviolent. A combination of factors led to the fall of colonial empires: nationalist agitations by indigenous elite groups prompted widespread demands for constitutional reforms that eventually culminated in political independence; in the metropoles (Britain, France, Belgium, and so on) the support for the continuation of colonial relations came under attack for both economic and ideological (the shift in world systemic values away from colonial possessions) reasons; World War II and it devastating impact on European powers made the colonial powers less capable of holding on to their possessions, and at the same time increased the confidence of indigenous elites in their demands for self-rule.[1] To a large extent, the economic exhaustion brought on by World War II spawned a lack of political will by the colonial powers to hold on to colonial possessions. The colonial empires that had taken centuries to establish rapidly broke down, and power was handed over to indigenous elites who inherited the territorial boundaries created by European colonial rule.

Between 1942 and 1982, the major colonial powers—Britain, France, the Netherlands, Belgium, and Portugal—engaged in a massive decolonization process and granted independence to more than eighty countries. Extensive and severe organized violence occurred in only a handful of countries during this period of decolonization. In all about 14 of the 82 newly independent states experienced at least occasional acts of organized violence by at least two warring parties. The intense and extensive cases of violence were notably the French colonial wars in Indochina (1946–54) and Algeria (1954–62). In Indochina about 95,000 French soldiers died in a conflict that lasted more than eight years, and in Algeria 18,000 died in roughly seven years of fighting.[2] These numbers do not include the countless more war deaths of the national liberation fronts of both countries (Indochina and Algeria), nor are civilian deaths included.

Other instances of organized political violence in decolonization struggles include: the British in Malaysia (1948–59), Kenya (1953–56), Cyprus (1955–59), South Yemen (1963–67), and South Rhodesia (now Zimbabwe) (1967–79); the Dutch in Indonesia (1945–49); the French in Tunisia (1952–54),

Morocco (1952–56), and Cameroon (1955–63); and the Portuguese in Angola (1961–74), Guinea-Bissau (1963–74), and Mozambique (1964–74).[3]

In these areas of decolonization conflicts, the Portuguese were the most reluctant to give up their possessions, while Belgians transferred power to indigenous elites rapidly. Britain's decolonization was more peaceful than that of France. The conflicts were essentially wars of independence from European colonial rule or some form of foreign domination such as that between the apartheid regime of South Africa and the South West Africa (Namibia) People's Organization (SWAPO) insurgent group.

Types of Conflict
Superpower Empire-Building or Cold War Conflicts

Many of the Cold War induced conflicts were "proxy" wars—that is wars where a client group of one superpower fought against another client group associated with the other superpower. It was the way the superpowers (the United States and the Soviet Union) expressed their mutual hostility, and manifested their attempt to get control of an ideologically contested territory, such as Angola in the 1970s and 1980s. The conflicts tended to be of low intensity, based largely on guerrilla warfare. They were also characterized by a massive flow of refugees and violence as well as exploitation directed at civilians by warring factions. The strong adherence to the principle of noninterference in domestic affairs kept the United Nations, the great powers, and even regional organizations from direct peacekeeping military intervention.

Cold War conflicts were motivated by causes that were overtly ideological as the superpowers competed fiercely to build empires and maintain them. The partition of Europe and the Korean War set the trend for these conflicts, which were in turn widened in scope and intensified by the collapse of European colonial hegemony over their overseas territories between the late 1950s and the mid-1960s. The period at the end of the Vietnam War (1975–80) was a period of rapid change that produced conflicts in various parts of the world. The East-West Cold War rivalry, which for a long time had been confined to the Indochina peninsula, was not being actively played out in other parts of the developing world. After a long and bloody war of independence by the people of both territories in southern Africa, Mozambique and Angola erupted into violence following the abrupt nature of Portuguese decolonization in 1974. Mozambique, the former territory, after nearly a century under Portuguese rule, won its independence in 1975 following ten years of anticolonial warfare. With independence the conflict was eventually transformed into a Cold War civil conflict as the socialist Mozambiquan government engaged in a devastating civil war against apartheid South Africa and the U.S.-backed Mozambique National Resistance (Renamo): Renamo was a vicious guerrilla movement responsible for severe and widespread atrocities against civilians and for the murder of more than 100,000 people, mostly civilians.[4] Similarly, Angola fought its war of independence in the 1960s until it gained independence in 1975, only to be gripped by a Cold War conflict that pitted the government—made up of the Popular Movement for the Liberations of Angola (MPLA) supported by the Soviet Union and Cuba—against the National Union for the Total Independence of Angola (UNITA)—made up of pro-Western rebels sponsored by the United States and South Africa.

Another region of Cold War tensions was the Horn of Africa where Ethiopia, initially aligned with the United States, became a client of the Soviet Union in 1977. The United States immediately aligned with Somalia. What occurred was a switch in patron-client relationships. In the Sahara, tensions erupted between Morocco, Algeria, and Mauritania over the decolonization of Spanish (Western) Sahara in 1974. Both Morocco and Mauritania wanted to annex the territory. In Latin America, conflicts increased after the fall of Somoza and the rule of the Sandinistas in Nicaragua in 1979. The guerrilla movements in El Salvador were revived. In Asia, meanwhile, the Soviets invaded Afghanistan in 1979, and the United States sponsored the Mujahadeen with arms, money, and logistical support. In Sri Lanka violent conflict erupted for the first time in 1977 between Tamils, backed by India, and the Sri Lankan state.[5] Within the same time frame (1975–80) the civil war in Lebanon, which started in 1974, was raging, the Shah of Iran was overthrown in 1979, and Iran was thrown into political turmoil. Increased guerrilla activity continued in the Philippines and sporadic fighting was taking place between Chad and Libya. Thus, within five years, the international system experienced a surprisingly rapid change of scenery.

During the Cold War period, many conflicts took the form of brief unilateral military interventionist actions by either one or the other superpower against a regime or in favor of the client government or faction in a civil war. In other words, the objective of such intervention was to prevent a government switching from one ideological persuasion to another, or to encourage such a switch. Interventions by the Soviets in Hungary (1956) and Czechoslovakia (1968); and by the United States in the Dominican Republic (1965), Grenada (1983), and Panama (1989) were to a large extent motivated by ideological/Cold War considerations.[6] Similarly, indirect U.S. military interventions such as the Bay of Pigs fiasco against Cuba in 1961, and the Contra struggles against the Sandinista regime in the early 1980s were also impelled by Cold War considerations.

Nation-Building Conflicts

While some civil conflicts were underlined by Cold War motivations, many others were just part of the nation-building efforts after independence and manifested in power struggles between elite groups. Various national elites competed violently to acquire and consolidate the levers of power within a state. At times the domestic struggles were further complicated and intensified by ideological polarization, by interference from neighboring states in internal conflicts, and by attempts at territorial secessions because of cultural or economic differences. It could be argued that most violent conflicts since World War II have been due to nation-building efforts. Accordingly, most casualties in conflicts within nations have been lost in nation-building struggles. Examples of very severe cases are China from 1945 to 1950 (about one million deaths), Nigeria from 1967 to 1970 (also about one million deaths), and Colombia from 1949 to 1962 (about 300,000 deaths).[7] These are some of the more notable examples with minimal Cold War motivations.

Nation-building conflicts are usually produced by two types of disputes: (1) disagreement over what the proper boundaries of the state or political community should be; and (2) disagreement over redefining the goals and policies of the state or political community. The first type of conflict often involves attempts by one ethnic group or geographical unit to secede or break away from a country whose boundaries are artificial because they were determined by European colonial powers without careful attention to ethnic and geographic realities.[8] Many past conflicts (for example, the Nigerian civil war and some ongoing wars such as the Sri Lankan civil war) are examples of violent disputes over the effort to define the proper boundaries of the state. The second type of conflict arises not because of disagreements over the boundaries of the state, but because of ideological differences over the purposes and policies of the state. These types of conflicts were common during the Cold War. For instance, the Angolan civil war was initially based on ideological differences between the Marxist incumbent regime and the Western-supported UNITA Movement of Jonas Savimbi. Similarly, many of the violent conflicts in Central and South America that involved state terrorism and the disappearance of thousands of individuals were underlined by struggles to redefine the ideological goals and policies of the state.

It is estimated that between 1945 and 1994 violent conflicts claimed 18 million lives. East Asia, Central and South Asia, and sub-Saharan Africa account for more than 15 million of the fatalities. In particular, more than 10 million people died in East Asia, including two million in the Vietnam conflict, three million in Korea, and one million in the Pol Pot massacres in Cambodia. The deaths from other regions include close to 3 million in central and south Asia, 2.6 million in sub-Saharan Africa, 447,000 in Latin America, and 972,000 in the Middle East.[9]

In essence, conflicts in the developing world, whether during the Cold War or after, originated as internal conflicts. They were simply nation-building conflicts intensified by U.S.–Soviet rivalry. The significance of external factors was perhaps overemphasized during the Cold War. The Afghan civil war was seen as a case of Soviet expansionism versus an Afghan nation that refused to be dominated; and the Angolan civil conflict was prolonged by U.S., Soviet, and Cuban involvement. Thus, the withdrawal of Soviet and U.S. influences from these conflicts in the early 1990s was not sufficient to bring peace to many of these nations, an indication that local causes were just as important in the conflict escalation. In these conflict-ridden societies in Africa, Latin America, and Asia, the effect of internal factors (for example, ethnic, regional, and religious rivalries) had become deep-seated causes of conflict. A decade or more of fighting had also transformed these societies into militarized, self-perpetuating war economies.

Post–Cold War Conflicts

From Angola to the Balkans, from Nagorno-Karabakh to Somalia, the number of internal conflicts has increased following the end of the Cold War. There are certain underlying characteristics of all these violent post–Cold War outbreaks. First, the patron-client relationships with the superpowers ended abruptly, thereby curtailing the support and external backing these states used to receive. Somalia, Afghanistan, Angola, and other states that experienced violent conflicts found themselves alone and without their superpower patron.[10] A drastic reduction of foreign aid ensued because ideological threat (on the part of the United States) could no longer be used as a justification for resource transfers to erstwhile client states. Because these states are economically and institutionally weak, they are either collapsing or experiencing a more fierce competition for scarce resources.

Second, the eruption of violent internal conflicts in many countries could be attributed to the rapid disintegration of authoritarian and totalitarian regimes that used to hold historically hostile communities together. The coercive power of despotism and authoritarianism held together artificial states in a condition of coerced unity. It was Alexis de Tocqueville who stated that it is when constraints are loosened and conditions are finally improving that explosive tensions are more likely to develop.[11] Revolutions or serious uprisings against a coercive state are rare. Revolts or violent conflicts are more likely to occur in societies that are markedly improving or are in the process of effecting reforms. The former Yugoslavia is a good example of how the weakening of federal institutions unleashed claims by the member nations that were tantamount to mutual incompatibilities. Somalia is an example of what happens when the coercive state suddenly comes to an end—the consequent mutual incompatibilities are expressed in collective political violence.

Moreover, the weakening of authoritarianism spawned by the end of superpower hegemony coincided with domestic developments in client states

Table 2.1: Types of Conflict

TYPE OF CONFLICT	SELECT EXAMPLES
Decolonization	Mozambique (1964–74)
	Malaysia (1948–59)
	Tunisia (1954–54)
Cold War	Angola (1976–91)
	Vietnam (1959–75)
	Loas (1960s–70s)
Nation-building	Nigeria (Biafra War, 1967–70)
	Sri Lanka (1970s–present)
	Ethiopia (1978–91)
Post–Cold War	Somalia (1991–present)
	Serbia (1997–99)
	Albania (1997)

2

like the crisis of neopatrimonialism. Neopatrimonialism developed in many former colonial states to fill the postcolonial vacuum where the new elites found themselves with no legitimacy or moral basis to demand compliance of citizens. In such a system, the rulers treat matters of state as their personal affair, personal rule is based on personal loyalty, the armed force is personally loyal to the regime. Strongmen, who are personally loyal to the head of state, command a web of patron-client networks to reward loyal supporters, all important positions in society are filled by loyal followers of the strongmen, and rulers resort to coercion for survival and to maintain the system because they lack legitimacy.[12] Neopatrimonialism ends up ex- #2 cluding many from economic and political opportunities, thereby creating disillusionment and opposition to the regime. Moreover, because neopatrimonialism does not encourage efficient use of state resources, it contributes to the dislocation of national economies. Thus, the combined effect of external factors and the negative effects of neopatrimonialism intensified the clamor for political reforms, which produced violent conflicts in some countries.

The efforts at transition from authoritarianism to democratization gave rise to centrifugal, and for the most part, ethnic tensions, with groups resorting to violence because of insecurity that produces fierce competition for power and resources. The consequence could be further polarization of the state into even smaller ethnic groups, clans, tribes, or other feuding communities. In this post–Cold War era, societies have become more fragmented as the withdrawal of the superpowers produced the military breakup of conflicts. Armed movements split into rival factions headed by local warlords.

The consequence is increased anarchy reflected in the proliferation of rebel groups whose survival is based on the power of the gun.

Case Studies

The Vietnam Conflict

The Vietnam War is an example of a conflict that had anticolonial, Cold War, and nation-building ingredients. Except for the brief Japanese occupation of Indochina (Vietnam, Laos, and Cambodia) during World War II, France had since the 1870s been the dominant colonial power in the region. After World War II, Ho Chi Minh, who had led the Vietnamese effort to expel the Japanese, expected the Western powers to support the longstanding demands for Vietnamese independence. When France refused to grant independence to its territories in Indochina, the Vietnamese, under the leadership of Ho Chi Minh, fought an anticolonial war (the French Indochina War) that ended with the defeat of France in 1954.[13] Cold War overtones were manifested in the fact that during the war, the insurgent Vietnamese, known as the Vietminh, received external support from the U.S.S.R. and China, and were therefore viewed by the West as instruments of international communism. On the other hand, the French had received substantial assistance from the United States before their defeat at Dien Bien Phu.

The Geneva conference convened in 1954 called for the establishment of three states: Laos, Cambodia, and Vietnam (French Indochina). A further arrangement of the Geneva conference called for the division of Vietnam into the socialist Republic of Vietnam (North Vietnam) and the Republic of Vietnam (South Vietnam) until political unification could be accomplished by a general election within two years. The United States refused to sign the Geneva Accords, and instead began to treat South Vietnam as a sovereign, independent, anticommunist state. The U.S. refusal to sign the accords in support of free and fair elections was due to the overwhelming knowledge that the Vietnamese would support a united Vietnam under Ho Chi Minh.[14] The United States viewed the entire issue as a contest between communism and Westernism, and urged Ngo Dinh Diem to proclaim an independent Republic of Vietnam in the south.

While the Vietminh may have perceived U.S. actions as a replacement of French colonialism, the United States, on the other hand, saw the issue in zero-sum terms: the loss of Vietnam could have a domino effect and speed up the global communist conspiracy masterminded by Moscow and Peking. The Cold War dimension of the conflict began in 1957 when the Communist rebels, known as the Vietcong, began terrorist attacks in South Vietnam. The United States in turn responded by providing support in the form of military advisers. By 1963, approximately 17,000 Americans were serving in South Vietnam.

The Vietcong and the Vietnamese National Liberation Front, formed in 1960, continued to intensify their attacks and increase their gains. As the scope and intensity of their attacks increased, U.S. involvement correspondingly increased in terms of military assistance and deployment of troops. Similarly, South Vietnamese troops conducted counterinsurgency operations against rebel camps in North Vietnam, Laos, and Cambodia. The scope of U.S. involvement increased during the Johnson administration (1963–68) through direct participation in the fighting, massive bombings of North Vietnam, and the deployment of more than 500,000 American troops.[15]

While the scope of U.S. involvement widened during the Johnson administration, the destructiveness of violent conflict between the United States and North Vietnam actually began in August 1964, after the Gulf of Tonkin incident. The incident involved an attack on August 2 by a North Vietnamese torpedo boat against a U.S. destroyer. The United States in retaliation initiated bombing raids of North Vietnamese military facilities in the gulf, and repeated bombing missions against North Vietnamese bases in Laos and Cambodia in the following years. The extent of external participation in the Vietnam conflict also widened when in mid-1965, Australia, New Zealand, and South Korea contributed forces to the conflict. Thailand and the Philippines also participated on the side of the United States in subsequent years. Moreover, the destructiveness of the conflict would deepen with the widespread use of napalm, and the establishment of "free-fire zones," within which even civilians were considered "legitimate targets," and the mining of the North Vietnamese harbors of Hanoi and Haiphong. By 1975, after U.S. troops had been withdrawn from the conflict, the United States had lost close to 60,000 men, and had used more than 7 million tons of bombs on Indochina. Vietnamese casualties probably amounted to some 2 million deaths. South Korea lost bout 4,000 troops, while Thailand and Australia each lost about 5,000.[16] By far most of the casualties were civilian. The war in French Indochina started as a war underlined by predominantly anticolonial causes, transformed into an East-West conflict involving direct U.S. participation against indirect Soviet and Chinese involvement. In the final analysis, it was also a conflict over: (1) defining the proper boundaries of the Vietnamese state; and (2) deciding the policy (ideological) posture the state should adopt in its effort to modernize.

Finally, a peace agreement calling for U.S. withdrawal was signed in Paris in 1973. The catalyst for U.S. withdrawal was no doubt the instability the conflict caused in the United States: it polarized U.S. public opinion and spawned riots and violent demonstrations in American cities and universities. Supporters of U.S. involvement viewed the issue as one about containing communism, whereas opponents of the war saw it as a blatant disrespect for the human rights and territorial integrity of Vietnam. In 1975, the South Vietnamese government was taken over by a combination of North

Vietnamese and Vietcong forces, and a United Communist Vietnam was established. The United States and Vietnam did not establish diplomatic relations until 1997; and Vietnam following the end of the Cold War is on its way to instituting political and economic liberalization.

The Angolan Civil War

Angola is another example of a country that experienced decolonization, Cold War, and nation-building conflicts. As a Portuguese colony along with Guinea-Bissau, Cape Verde, Mozambique, and São Tomé and Príncipe since the seventeenth century, a bloody anticolonial guerrilla war erupted in the 1960s. The beginning of armed revolt was an indication that the Portuguese colonial administration invested little effort to prepare its colonies for self-rule. In February 1961, the Union of Angolan People (UPA) initiated terrorist attacks against European settlers, and in March it merged with the Marxist-oriented Movimento Popular de Liberação de Angola (MPLA) to intensify and widen the guerrilla warfare.[17] A protracted anticolonial war raged on until 1974 when the right-wing Portuguese dictatorship of Marcello Caetano was overthrown in Lisbon because of mounting Portuguese casualties, war costs, and inability to crush the insurgency. The new military government in Lisbon implemented a unilateral cease-fire and granted independence to all its territories on July 27, 1974. Angola formally gained independence on November 11, 1975. The independence (anticolonial) struggle for the colonies was very intense with more than one hundred thousand people killed, including a large number of civilians and Portuguese troops.

Immediately following independence, Angola fragmented and plunged into civil war over control of power. Thus, an initial struggle for independence was transformed by external forces into a war that had little to do with Angola's own interests. The United States, collaborating with Zaire and South Africa, supported one faction, the alliance of the National Front for the Liberation of Angola (FNLA) and the Union for the Total Independence of Angola (UNITA); while the Soviet Union and Cuba supported the other, the Marxist-oriented MPLA. The MPLA won an indecisive victory in February 1976 against its U.S.-supported rivals.[18] For key interventionist powers—the U.S. and U.S.S.R.—intervention became a means to promote their global ideological objectives. In the global struggle for power between the United States and U.S.S.R., intervention of one form or another was almost inevitable, because nonintervention would automatically help the other side.

The Angolan civil war intersected with the U.S.-Soviet rivalry; however, it was primarily an internal conflict, not merely an appendage of their global competition or the external interventions of other nations. The internal divisions within Angola had existed in embryonic form since the collective mobilization against the Portuguese during the colonial era. At various stages in the past, each of the movements—FNLA, MPLA, UNITA—had accused the other of collaborating with the Portuguese to promote its own military and political interests. The Portuguese responded to the Angolan collective struggle with military means and by pitting one movement against another, just as they earlier had set one ethnic group against another to colonize the country. There was evidence of ethnic rivalry from the outbreak of the civil war in 1975. MPLA support came first and foremost from the *assimilado* intellectuals of Luanda and the Kibundu peoples of northwestern Angola. FNLA support was rooted in the Bakongo of northern Angola, while UNITA was founded mainly among students and politically conscious peasants from the Ovimbundu people of central and southern Angola.[19]

In order to invite external support to continue the civil war, UNITA claimed that the MPLA was not only dominated by the Soviets and Cubans, but was run by *mestiços*, whites and Mbundus, while other ethnic groups were excluded. Persistent ethnic, political, and ideological divisions largely underlined the external direct and indirect interventionist efforts by the United States, U.S.S.R., Cuba, South Africa, and Zaire.

By 1988, the new détente (relaxation of tensions) between the United States and U.S.S.R. gradually transformed the war between the MPLA and UNITA. With the Bicesse Accords of May 1991, the first postindependence war between the two entities came to a gradual end, although sporadic fighting between the two groups continued. Both sides also agreed to a cease-fire, national elections in 1992, and demobilization of both armies and their integration into a 50,000-man national force.[20] However, because of the limited number of UN peace monitors, insufficient funds, and a lack of commitment to demobilization by UNITA forces, violence soon erupted. The UN monitors could do nothing to stop violations of the Bicesse Accords. All they could do was take note of violations and report to their superiors. Within days of the end of the elections on September 30, 1992, anger degenerated into violence. The immediate reason for the violence was that the MPLA-controlled radio and TV announced the government party's victory even before the polls had closed.

The next two years were characterized by bloody confrontations as the MPLA and UNITA struggled for control of the central highland cities of Huambo and Cuito.[21] The struggle killed thousands of civilians. The MPLA government slowly overturned many of the UNITA victories. By the end of 1993, a new round of talks began in Lusaka, Zambia, as the war settled to a familiar stalemate. The Lusaka Accords of November 1994 were more flexible in terms of implementation because they contained no strict deadlines for demobilization and elections. Between 1995 and 1998 the UN set up demobilization camps throughout the country. In the meantime, there were sporadic armed confrontations between UNITA and the MPLA, as well as several incidents in which UN peacekeepers and monitors were attacked, or their plan shot down by UNITA forces. By the end of 1999, the MPLA was in control of most of the country. For the next two years, the Angolan War continued in the form of sporadic fighting because of UNITA's lack of commitment to any of the peace accords it had signed. However, a dramatic development took place in February 2002, when the longtime leader of UNITA, Jonas Savimbi, was killed in an ambush by government commandos. The following month the two sides signed a cease-fire. The cease-fire ceremony attended by representatives from the UN, the United States, Russia, and Portugal approved a plan for the demobilization of 50,000 UNITA troops.

The Sri Lankan Civil War

In conflicts that arise between ethnic majorities and minorities, the latter often accuse the former of violating their political rights and/or civil liberties. In the Sri Lankan conflict, for example, the Tamil insurgent groups emphasize their lack of human rights and the refusal of the Sri Lankan state (dominated by the majority Sinhalese) to grant them national self-determination. The Sri Lankan problem, like so many postcolonial problems in developing regions of the world, is one of disagreements over what constitutes equity and fairness, defining the proper boundaries of the political community, and differences over what the goals of the polity should be.

Before the arrival of Europeans (Portuguese, Dutch, and the British), who exercised hegemony over the island, there Sri Lanka was home to two distinct kingdoms that thrived in close proximity to each other, the Tamil kingdom in the north and the Sinhala kingdom in the south. In order to ensure effective administration, the British during colonial rule (1815–1948) amalgamated the two distinct groups and the island and governed it as the colony of Ceylon.[22] With the acquisition of independence in 1948, control of the island eventually fell to a Sinhala-dominated government, which renamed the island Sri Lanka.

The divisive effects of ethnic differences have played an important role in politics since independence. But these effects were intensified after 1972 when the first republican constitution entrenched the position of the Sinhalese majority while discarding minority interests, especially those of the Sri Lankan Tamils. The Tamil people, for example, claim that the Sinhala-dominated state instituted, after independence, a series of laws that amounted to discrimination against Tamils by making Sinhala, instead of English, the only official language of the country; restricting Tamil admissions to higher education; allocating minimal investment resources to Tamils; and restricting recruitment of Tamils into the security forces, among others.

In the 1970s a small number of Tamils launched violent attacks against political elites of the Sri Lankan state. Tamil politicians advocated a separate Tamil state in 1977. The Tamil United Liberation Front (TULF) resolved to campaign for political independence based on the Tamil nation's right to self-determination.[23] Their decision was based on the rationale that the Tamil people of Sri Lanka constitute a distinct nation endowed with their own history, traditions, culture, language, and traditional homeland. In 1983, civil war erupted after anti-Tamil riots in the majority Sinhalese areas. The armed struggle of the Tamil people for a separate state is manifested in the Tamil Tigers or the Liberation Tigers of Tamil Eelam (LTTE).

The severity of the civil war has been confined in the northeast where Sri Lankan Tamil groups claimed a Tamil homeland (Eelam). For a while, the separatists received some external support from India, until 1987 when the Sri Lankan and Indian governments worked out a resolution to the conflict. The agreement included some concessions to Tamil demands and devolution of power to the provinces. An Indian peacekeeping force was also stationed in the northeast region. However, the LTTE, the most powerful Sri Lankan Tamil group, believed that the agreement was not far-reaching enough. Between 1988 and March 1990 sporadic fighting took place between the Indians and the LTTE. By 1991, a short period after the Indians withdrew, the war between the government and the LTTE erupted again.

Other Tamil groups, in particular the Indian Tamils (descendants of immigrants who worked on the plantations during British colonialism) and the Moors (Muslims), are also part of the minority population. However, the Indian Tamils have largely succeeded in maintaining a neutral stance in the conflict, whereas the Moors have been active participants because they oppose the LTTE's claim to represent all Tamil-speaking minorities. Apart from ethnicity, class and generational tensions also underlie the Sri Lankan civil war. The LTTE insurgents target not only Sinhalese hegemony but other Sri-Lankan Tamil political groups as well, including the Tamil minority dominated by the English-speaking elite.[24] In 1987 a Sinhalese group, the Janatha Vimukthi Peramuna (JVP), launched a violent campaign against the government. The JVP not only resented the Indian presence on the island, but also believed that the peace pact contained too many concessions to Tamil demands. Its supporters comprised young Sinhalese in rural and semiurban areas who felt excluded from the political process. The JVP threat to the government subsided when the security forces killed most of its leaders in late 1989. However, the socioeconomic forces that generated support for the JVP are still in place, and future extralegal challenges to the state from Sinhalese groups are likely. This is because the government's response to the LTTE and JVP has been characterized by gross violations of human rights that have reduced confidence in the prospects for a genuine Sri Lankan democracy.

Table 2.2: A Select Number of Violent Conflicts

LOCATION	DATE	TYPE OF CONFLICT	ACTORS
Niger	Sept. 1999	Internal ethnic rebellion	Niger government and rebels
Saudi/Yemen	1998	Interstate/border war	Saudi Arabia vs. Yemen
Kosovo	1998–99	Internal ethnic rebellion and foreign intervention	Yugoslav/Serbian government vs. Kosovo Liberation Army (KLA) rebels and NATO
Nepal	1996–present	Internal rebellion	Nepal government vs. rebels
Burundi	1994–present	Civil war/ethnic conflict	Burundi government vs. Hutu rebels
Mexico	1994–present	Civil war/ethnic conflict	Mexican government vs. Zapatista rebels
Algeria	1992–present	Civil war	Algerian government vs. Islamic rebels
Egypt	1992–present	Urban guerrilla war	Egyptian government vs. Islamic rebels
Sierra Leone	1991–present	Civil war	Sierra Leone government vs. rebels
Somalia	1991–present	Civil war/clan warfare	Various Somali clans and militia groups
Israel-Palestine	2000–present	Ethnic clashes	Israel vs. Palestinians in the West Bank and Gaza
Turkey	1984–present	Internal ethnic rebellion	Turkish government vs. Kurdish rebels
India	Mid-1980s–present	Internal ethnic rebellion (Bodo rebellion)	Indian government vs. Tribal guerrillas
Spain/France	1958–present	Ethnic separatist rebellion	Spanish and French governments vs. Basque Fatherland and Liberty guerrilla group (ETA)

Before the Indians withdrew from their peacekeeping role, they helped to bolster their allies, the moderate, pro-Indian, pro-provisional council Eelam People's Revolutionary Liberation Front, by helping them establish their own armed group, the Tamil National Army (TNA), so that they could protect Tamils and even destroy the LTTE. But the TNA proved to be no match for the experience and fierceness of the LTTE. In 1990 there was a brief lull in the fighting. The LTTE soon launched simultaneous attacks on government positions (especially police stations) and engaged in terrorist acts and assassinations.[25] These attacks resulted in the killing of the Sri Lankan minister of defense and the May 1991 killing of Rajiv Gandhi, then head of the main opposition party, who had supposedly urged the Indian government to oust the pro-LTTE government in Tamil Nadu.

Between 1991 and 1995 renewed violence marked the relationship between the government and the LTTE. The fighting was mostly confined around the Jaffna peninsula, although the LTTE launched a number of bombing attacks on Colombo and other areas of the south. The government had the upper hand in the struggle to control the Jaffna Peninsula, and by mid-1996 the Sri Lankan army was in total control of the peninsula. The LTTE has permanently resorted to a war of attrition and criminal attacks against civilians. It is capable of continued rebellion because of the massive support it receives from Tamils in the diaspora. The government meanwhile continues to work on plans for devolution of power to the provinces and power sharing in the central government with moderate Tamil groups. The causes of these violent conflicts range from the struggle over land, efforts to overthrow an incumbent government, border disputes, a reaction against government neglect, struggle over resources, and attempts at secession, among others. In early 2002, a jointly agreed cease-fire between the government and the LTTE entered into force. The truce has now held for one year.

The End of the Twentieth Century and Irregular Violent Conflicts

Irregular violent conflicts characterize many of the armed struggles that erupted when the Cold War rivalry between the United States and the Soviet Union ended. Somalia, Sierra Leone, Rwanda, and the former Yugoslavia, among others, constitute a new but important class of violent clashes because of their chaotic and brutal nature. In irregular violent struggles combatants often perpetrate violence and cruelty against not only each other but against the civilian population as well. Combatants are characterized by a lack of formal military training, and often those with formal military training (that is members of the national army) tend to defect to the guerrilla forces.[26] Child soldiers form a substantial segment of the combatants in irregular warfare.

The Liberian civil war and the conflict in Sierra Leone, for instance, are, based on their character, good examples of irregular violent struggles. Motivations of the combatants, most of whom have experienced years of political, economic, and other deprivations, were often based on factors other than politics. For them, instant economic gratification was seen in their ability to pillage and loot the countryside. The personal gratification that had so long eluded them was obtained through their ability to carry guns and terrorize, maim, rape, and kill the civilian population without remorse. At times in these conflicts, the distinction between professional soldier and rebel fighter becomes blurred. In the Sierra Leone conflict, for example, close to 50 percent of some 14,000 soldiers became soldier-rebels (sobels) who operated on both sides of the conflict, motivated by their own economic self-interest or personal gratification.[27]

The actors in irregular conflicts are often diverse: national armies linked to the government that may effectively control only the capital, one or more warlords controlling a resource-rich territory, and a number of civil defense forces, composed largely of ethnic-based hunter guilds with little or no training in counterinsurgency techniques. In particular, the insurgents are often disaffected and marginalized members of society excluded from the political and economic benefits available to those who are part of the patronage system—the network of patron-clients that distributes opportunities and resources to members. The primary reason for insurgency therefore seems to be economic in nature. For example, in the Sierra Leone conflict, the Revolutionary United Front (RUF) rebel force has never articulated a detailed and specific political agenda. Its strategy was one of terrorizing the civilian population, acts of looting, pillaging, and killing, among others.

Finally, in irregular violent conflicts the methods used by all sides are usually similar. The protagonists operate as roving bands in areas with exportable natural resources such as diamonds, or where agricultural crops are grown, and where the opportunities to attack aid convoys or civilian minibuses, are the greatest. In the process loot is taken from defenseless civilians; forced recruitment and the commandeering of slave labor is also carried out. Only rarely do rebel forces attack each other head on. For the most part, they prey on civilians. In some of the irregular conflicts, there is often an element of frequent shifts in alliances among the protagonists based on military, political, and economic expediencies. Some government soldiers in Sierra Leone have often switched to the rebel side when it was expedient to do so.

The irregular violent conflicts of the end of the twentieth century are largely a result of violence waged by economically, politically, and socially deprived members of society who believed they had no future in their respective countries. Often a privileged class excludes a significant segment of the population from government largesse and the networks of the patronage system. These conflicts are therefore not always based on ethnic hatreds or differences, although the existence of marginalization could be exploited by an ethnic elite for its own end. Moreover, one major cause of irregular warfare is state collapse or failure because of the state's inability to provide social, economic, and other governmental services to the general population.[28] In Sierra Leone, for instance, weak corrupt governments, institutional collapse, and the failure of the traditional patronage system—which caused self-interested rulers to redirect control of critical resources under private commercial interests, rather than traditional patronage clients—sparked widespread revolt in many forms. While irregular warfare may be underlined by multifaceted historical, cultural, economic, military, political, and social factors, in the final analysis, they are resource wars.

Finally, there are several key aspects of irregular warfare that set it apart from other forms of armed struggle. Rebellions, insurgencies, guerrilla warfare, and civil war are all examples of fighting grouped at the lower end of the spectrum of conflict. These can be either regular or irregular in nature. The differences in the two lie, first, in the underlying causes of the conflict; second, in the manner in which the conflict is conducted; and third, by the very nature of the combatants themselves. Where irregular warfare occurs, members of the armed forces exhibit a degree of lawlessness, indiscipline, and professional incompetence that makes them indistinguishable from the irregular forces they fight against. Embodied in the conduct of irregular warfare is the presence of an extraordinary level of disorganized violence directed by the combatants toward each other and particularly toward the civilian population. This violence is frequently waged on a random, terroristic, and indiscriminate basis. Its objective is primarily to prevent the civilian population from joining the opposition, rather than winning their suport for a defined political or social platform. A second objective is to seize property for personal use as part of a process in which looting to obtain the spoils of war is a way of payment for services rendered to one's militia. Violent behavior by government forces is usually a result of the absence of military professionalism, which can be characterized by professional ethos, discipline, regard for human rights, and corporate loyalty by the armed forces to the state as an institution.

In sum, violent conflicts that have affected countries such as Algeria, Burundi, Cambodia, Ethiopia, Liberia, Mexico, Sri Lanka, or the former Yugoslavia, can be categorized as either anticolonial, Cold War, nation-building, or post–Cold War struggles. In many cases, these conflicts became transformed from decolonization to either Cold War, nation-building, or post–Cold War struggles.

Notes

1. In the case of African colonial territories, see, for example, P. Gifford and W. M. Roger Louis, eds., *Decolonization and African Independence: The Transfers of Power, 1960–1980* (New Haven: Yale University Press, 1988).
2. For further details, see Herman van der Wusten, "The Geography of Conflict since 1945" in *The Geography of War and Peace*, eds. David Pepper and Alan Jenkins (Oxford: Basil Blackwell, 1985).
3. See, among others, I. Kende, "Wars of Ten Years (1967–1976)," *Journal of Peace Research* 15: 227–42; and Dan Smith, *The State of War and Peace Atlas* (London: Penguin, 1997).
4. For details, see Francois Jean, ed., *Populations in Danger* (London: John Libbey & Co. Ltd., 1992).
5. See H. D. Tillema, *International Armed Conflict Since 1945: A Bibliographic Handbook of Wars and Military Interventions* (Boulder, CO: Westview, 1991).
6. For details, see H. K. Tillema, *Appeal to Force: American Military Intervention in the Era of Containment* (New York: Crowell, 1973).
7. More details can be found in M. Small and J. D. Singer, *Resort to Arms: International and Civil Wars, 1816–1980* (Beverly Hills: Sage, 1982).
8. In the case of Africa, see Ali Mazrui, "The Anatomy of Violence in Contemporary Black Africa," in *Africa: From Mystery to Maze*, ed. Helen Kitchen (Lexington, MA: D.C. Heath & Co., 1976).
9. See International Institute for Strategic Studies, *The Military Balance, 1997/98.*
10. In the case of African states, for example, see *Current History* 98: 628 (May 1999).
11. For details, see Alexis de Tocqueville, *The Old Regime and the Revolution* (Chicago: University of Chicago Press, 1998).
12. For details, see Christopher Clapham, ed., *Private Patronage and Public Power* (London: Frances Pinter, 1982).
13. See P. Davidson, *Vietnam at War: The History, 1946–1975* (Novato, CA: Presidio, 1988).
14. For further details, see Stanly Karnow, *Vietnam: A History* (New York: Viking, 1983).
15. See, for example, David P. Barash, *Introduction to Peace Studies* (Belmont, CA: Wadsworth Publishing Co., 1991).
16. See M. Small and J. D. Singer, *Resort to Arms: International and Civil Wars 1816–1980* (Beverly Hills: Sage Publications, 1982).
17. For a more detailed account, see J. Marcum, "Angola: Twenty-five Years of War," *Current History* 185: 511 (1986).
18. See R. Lemarchand, ed., *American Foreign Policy in Southern Africa: The Stakes and the Stance* (Washington, D.C.: University Press of America, 1981).
19. For details, see K. Sommerville, *Angola: Politics, Economics and Society* (London: Frances Pinter, 1986).
20. On Angola, see James Ciment, ed., *Encyclopedia of Conflicts Since World War II*, Vol. I (Armouk: M. E. Sharpe, 1999).
21. For details, see Anthony Pereira, "The Neglected Tragedy: The Return to War in Angola," *The Journal of African Studies* (Winter 1994).
22. See Jonathan Spencer, ed., *Sri Lanka: History and the Roots of Conflict* (New York: Routledge, 1990).
23. For details, see A. J. Wilson, *The Break-up of Sri Lanka: The Sinhalese-Tamil Conflict* (Honolulu: University of Hawaii Press, 1988).
24. See William McGowan, *Only Man Is Vile: The Tragedy of Sri Lanka* (New York: Farrar Strauss Giroux, 1992).
25. For further details, see David Little, *Sri Lanka: The Invention of Enmity* (Washington, D.C.: United States Institute of Peace, 1994).
26. For more details on irregular warfare, see Jeffrey B. White, "Irregular Warfare: A Different Kind of Threat," *American Intelligence Journal* (1996).
27. See *Analytical Study of Irregular Warfare in Sierra Leone and Liberia.* SAIC-98/6039 (Englewood, Colorado: Foreign Systems Research Center).
28. For details on Sierra Leone, see Earl Conteh-Morgan and Mac Dixon-Fyle, *Sierra Leone at the End of the Twentieth Century—History, Politics, and Society* (New York: Peter Lang, 1999), Chapter 5.

Key Terms

anarchy	guerrilla warfare	nation-building
artificial states	insurgencies	neopatrimonial system
Cold War	irregular wars	proxy wars
decolonization	marginalized groups	state failure
détente		

Discussion Questions

1. What is the difference between decolonization, Cold War, and nation-building conflicts? Pg 29
2. What are the characteristics of a political system based on neopatrimonialism? Pg 35
3. Discuss what is meant by proxy wars. What examples can you identify? Pg 31
4. "Irregular warfare" has become a feature of internal conflicts in the twenty-first century. Discuss the characteristics and causes of such conflicts. pg 45

CHAPTER 3

Social-Structural Theories and Violent Change

The popularity of Marxism, and the anxieties it caused in Europe and North America following the Russian Revolution and the Great Depression of the 1930s intensified the search for alternative theoretical models to Marxism. Much of non-Marxist social science is therefore devoted to a refutation of premises by Marxist sociology that revolutionary change in society is inevitable because society is characterized by inherent (inbuilt) contradictions—that is the division of society into classes that reflect the mode of production, or political economy. First, non-Marxian theorists argue that not all structural change comes in the form of an alteration of the classes and class relations in society. Second, they further argue that while social change is common, or conflict is endemic to society, it is by no means inevitable that social change must always be in the form of revolution. This chapter reviews some of the older and more notable non-Marxist social-structural explanations of violent change.

Functionalism

The functionalist analysis of social change represents one of those non-Marxian theories of social change. Integral to functionalism are the interrelated concepts of structure and function. Functionalism underscores the idea of society as an organism whose entire system has to be in good working order for systemic equilibrium to be maintained. For example, an organism and a society are similar in that each represents an integrated whole, maintains a certain degree of structural continuity, undergoes intrasystemic transformations at the level of some of its parts, and involves internal processes that perform specific functions. Accordingly, functionalism by its use of the analogy of the organismic model underscores the attributes of interdependence, equilibrium, and differentiation in every society.[1] Interdependence refers to the interconnections or interactions among social actors and social relations that comprise a social structure. Equilibrium refers to the regulatory mechanisms of socialization, adaptation, goal attainment, and social control that continuously attempt to preserve social-structural equilibrium or stability. Differentiation refers to the institutionalization of social roles and organizations and their related processes, outcomes, and functions.

Thus, functionalism attempts to show how social systems persist or perpetuate themselves by maintaining their structural balance and how social systems handle change by adjusting their essential variables and overall structure. In other words, the social system maintains its equilibrium by retaining the necesssary forms of social organization and patterns of action, while abandoning dysfunctional patterns. In order to underscore the idea of systems maintenance or survival, functionalists attempt to identify "functional prerequisites," or "needs," or "essential variables" of society.[2]

Apart from being homeostatic (that is, self-regulating), a system is generally considered open, or designed to receive inputs from its environment. The system in turn influences environmental conditions to maintain the stability of the system. In particular, the functional prerequisites must be satisfied if a system is to survive or remain in adequate working order. Four of these prerequisites are emphasized by functionalists such as Talcott Parsons, or theorists of revolutions such as Chalmers Johnson. The first, socialization or pattern maintenance, corresponds to the religious sectors of social life and involve, in particular, the inculcation in children of societal values and norms. Adaptation to the environment as another prerequisite underscores the political sectors of society related to the differentiation and allocation of roles, as well as the distribution of scarce resources. A third prerequisite, goal attainment, focuses on the economic sectors of social life, and is concerned with the formation and development of policies for achieving systemic goals. The fourth and final prerequisite, integration and social control, is preoccupied with the legal sectors of social life, justice, law and order, or ways in which problems of deviancy are prevented or solved.

In other words, a system is a set of interrelated variables (functional prerequisites) that generally change over time (or exhibit dynamism) because in open systems, in particular, other nonsystemic or environmental factors affect the value of the systemic variables. The homoeostatic system is one particular kind of open and dynamic system. The functional prerequisites (essential variables, or needs) in an open system must be maintained within

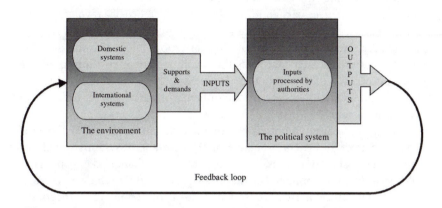

Fig. 3.1: The Political System. The environment encompasses all the actors that place supports or demands on a political system. These actors articulate their interests through supports and demands, which are input into the political system. Inputs are in turn processed by authorities, and output as decisions and policies. The decisions and policies are fed back into the environment and the environment responds accordingly by placing new inputs through supports and demands, and the cycle continues. *Source:* Adapted from David Easton's Systems Theory.

certain predetermined critical limits (or values) for the system to be in adequate working order. When the environment undergoes change, the values of the systemic variables also change to compensate for environmental changes. It is possible that with radical and sudden environmental change the system may break down because it is no longer in adequate working order.

Political scientists, for example, represent a social system as comprised of an environment from which inputs into the political system emanate. The political system then responds (reacts) to the inputs through outputs (laws, rules, regulations) for the society. It is often an input-output process represented by a single feedback loop. In other words, environmental conditions through the feedback loop send information to the system, which determines whether the system needs to change so as to maintain stability with respect to the functional prerequisites.

When the system is incapable of adequately responding to radical environmental conditions, it becomes first disequilibrated, followed by a loss of authority, and then, given a catalyst or precipitating factor, a revolution or some form of collective violence occurs.[3] Stated differently, a disequilibrated system is a necessary condition for revolutions, and could be manifested in a situation where the society's predominant values are out of sync with justice, equity, or distributional fairness. Such discrepancy between theory and practice regarding ethical social values eventually results in a loss of authority as the second necessary condition for the occurrence of a revolution. The system loses legitimacy or acceptability and is thus challenged. A catalyst, or accelerator, could take the form of state bankruptcy, defeat in war, or catastrophic natural disaster that leads the revolutionary opposition to believe that it is capable of defeating the power elite. This is often the motivation for direct military attacks against incumbents, or the reason for the onset of guerrilla warfare.

Faced with a disequilibrated system, the elite would either: (1) allow the system to undergo structural change, or (2) maintain the system through coercion, repression, or oppressive means. Structural change takes two forms: conservative change initiated by the elite, or revolutionary change. A system maintained by force is often transformed into a police state. Thus, the social-structural characteristics of a given society affect an individual's decision to join a revolutionary movement.

Society as a social system is self-regulating toward equilibrium or some preferred normative structure to which the members of society strongly adhere. Since the system is homeostatic or self-regulating, the self-regulating mechanisms automatically adjust toward equilibrium or neutralize negative influences emanating from the external environment. For example, sanctions that are part of socialization and social control automatically counteract tendencies toward systemic disequilibrium. Stated differently, the concept of equilibrium underscores the constant need to preserve a given normative order to stabilize some structure of the sytem. Whenever changes occur in the system's environment or within the system that alter the system-environment relationship, the self-regulating mechanism will operate to maintain the system's preferred state. Thus, because of inherent systemic problems related to scarcity of resources relative to society's rising expectations or weaknesses in the socialization process or the negative effects of competing societies, change is endemic to all systems in order to ensure equilibrium.

In sum, in functionalism, a society is viewed in these ways:

1. A system is characterized by interdependent parts.
2. A system persists because it is assumed to be homeostatic (self-regulating) and therefore fundamentally in a state of equilibrium.
3. Integration of the system is a function of the positive contribution of the different social forces within the system.
4. Systemic or social integration is achieved through the mechanisms of institutionalization, socialization, and social control, all of which contribute to value consensus—the adherence of most members of a given system to the goals and principles of the social system.

5. Conflicts, dysfunctions, or strains are endemic to a social system, but they tend toward self-resolution or become nonproblems through institutionalization.

6. Social change, instead of being violently revolutionary, is generally viewed as a gradual and adjustive process through differentiation and adaptation to extrasystemic pressures.[4]

Functionalism as an explanation of why societies persist and avoid collective violence is open to serious criticisms. For example, it is not specified how successful socialization, or goal attainment, should be, or even how much social control is necessary. Such issues are largely unanswered by the analysis. There are not specifics on when a given system is, or is not, in equilibrium. Virtually all the components of the system are unspecified labels that fail to spell out levels, degrees, scope, or intensity of disequilibrium that will trigger rebellion within a system.

Theories of Collective Behavior

Neil Smelser's Theory of Collective Behavior

Smelser's theory of collective behavior is an attempt to articulate a theory of group reaction to a system that is not in adequate working order, or a systemic disequilibrium. Collective behavior, according to Smelser, is action produced by a generalized belief in the existence of extraordinary forces (threats, conspiracies, crises, etc.) that are at work in the wider environment.[5] These generalized beliefs that produce group behavior also involve an assessment of the serious consequences that will result if the collective attempt to reconstitute social action is either successful or unsuccessful. His theory of structural strain and group action characterizes collective behavior as: (1) uninstitutionalized—or originating in response to an unstructured situation; (2) a consequence of the failure or inadequacy of conventional modes of dealing with a situation, which is thus an attempt to reconstitute all or part of the social order; and (3) guided by a generalized belief manifested in the existence of negative or threatening forces. In other words, Smelser's definition of collective behavior comprises: (1) uninstitutionalized mobilization whose aim is (2) to reconstitute a component of social action on the basis of (3) a generalized belief.

For Smelser, examples of major types of collective behavior are: the panic, the craze, the hostile outburst, the norm-oriented movement, and the value-oriented movement. Any of these collective behaviors are produced by general determinants and a unique combination of determinants. The former explains why collective behavior occurs at all, whereas the latter explains why one form of collective behavior occurs rather than another. The determinants in sequence and in combination eventually lead up to collective behavior. Through this value-added process, because each stage must satisfy a certain pattern or combination before the next stage can contribute its particular effect (value) to the end result (or collective behavior). Each stage is therefore a necessary condition for the appropriate and effective addition or impact in the next stage.

Determinants of Collective Behavior

Smelser next applies this value-added logic to the outbursts of collective behavior, which is a result of an elaborate sequence of determinants. These determinants not only follow an elaborate sequence, they also combine in a definite pattern, with the possibility that one determinant may appear in many varieties or assume unique combinations. Alternative behavioral possibilities become remote as the varied forms of determinants combine. Smelser's determinants of collective behavior are: (1) structural conduciveness, (2) structural strain, (3) growth and spread of a generalized belief, (4) precipitating factors, (5) mobilization of participants for action, and (6) operation of social controls.

The above determinants follow a temporal sequence. Any or all of them may lie dormant for any length of time until activated in a definite pattern to contribute to the process of collective behavior. Collective behavior can only occur if they are activated in a definite pattern. The most general determinant is structural conduciveness and is a necessary condition for the activation of the other five. Structural conduciveness refers to social conditions that increase the propensity for groups to engage in collective behavior. For example, a well-populated but neglected ethnic minority section of a city (such as a ghetto or shanty town) constitutes a structural feature that is more conducive to ethnic or race riots than areas with middle-class residential patterns. Structural strain refers to a conflict between opposing societal practices, for example, conflict between justice or equal opportunity and blatant discrimination practices in employment and other societal opportunities. The major types of strain such contradiction produces are ambiguity (for example, normative vagueness), socioeconomic or political deprivations, conflicts, and discrepancies, which lead to typical episodes of collective behavior. When the strain falls within the scope established by the condition of conduciveness, together the two combine to minimize the range of possible alternative final outcomes.

Before the affected group can engage in collective action it must accept as meaningful the combined situations of structural conduciveness and strain. This takes the form of accepting a general belief that communicates the meaning to potential collective behavior participants by: (1) identifying the origin or source of the strain; (2) attributing certain characteristics to this source; (3) recommending that certain action be taken to deal with the strain; for example, the belief that, (a) the city elites are the source of the strain, or (b) they are part of a conspiracy to keep our ethnic group permanently in a marginalized position; and therefore (4) we ought to use violence to get their attention and thereby regain some equality vis-à-vis other groups that are more accepted.

Precipitating factors provide the context toward which collective behavior can be channeled, especially when they strongly correspond with the other determinants. They provide an immediate, catalyzing effect on the entire collective behavior process. Through the mobilization of participants for action, panic, hostility, agitation for reform, or revolution erupt. It serves as the only remaining necessary condition to bring the affected group into action. The final determinant (operation of social controls) serves to counteract collective behavior. As counterdeterminants they are meant to prevent the escalation of collective behavior, and are of two kinds: (1) those social controls that minimize conduciveness and strain, thereby preventing collective behavior, and (2) those that are mobilized after a collective episode has begun. They determine the scope, intensity, duration, or direction of the conflict episode.

The value-added logic of these determinants assume a progression of scope, intensity, or substance.[6] That is, the six determinants of collective behavior are parts of one process. They are multiple determinants of some single outcome. There is also a continuity of locus implied, for the determinants must be communicated to persons of similar enough experience so that these conditions will be interpreted in a like manner.

The Components of Social Action

For Smelser, both violent collective behavior and conventional (nonviolent) collective behavior can be analyzed within the same framework—that is both fall within the context of societal values and involve an assessment of the situation in which they occur. Smelser's components of social action involve roles (for example, husbands, physicians, teachers, citizens) and organizations (for example, political parties, firms, families) as units of analysis. Thus, his conception of "social system" encompasses not only interaction at the societal level but even informal interpersonal relations involving two persons. His four basic components of social action include values, norms, mobilization or motivation into organized action, and situational facilities. Values refer to the broad guiding principles for social behavior, such as the value of democracy. Norms are specific regulatory principles through which values are to be realized, for example, rules for elections. Norms are also wide ranging and include formal and informal rules as well as tacit or unconscious understandings. Mobilization for organized action includes organized participants in pursuit of valued ends, division of roles among participants, as well as what the system of rewards will be. Situational facilities are facilitators or hindrances to the attainment of group goals. They include knowledge of environmental factors, concrete goals, means used to assess the situation, and the like.

Panic as a form of Collective Behavior

For Smelser, panic as an example of collective behavior is only possible as a result of the existence of: (1) structural conduciveness, (2) structural strain (the perceived presence of some imminent danger of uncertain and uncontrollable proportions), (3) anxiety—resulting from knowledge of the imminent or threatening danger, (4) hysterical belief (fear), which is a result of fear of a specific threatening agent such as financial collapse, (5) mobilization against or away from the identified imminent and threatening danger, and (6) social controls—for panic control.[7] While the first five conditions are facilitators of panic, social controls would comprise values such as faith, norms, reassurance, drills, and the like to minimize or even reverse panic.

Panic is thus a reaction to an unstructured situation characterized by lack of information or knowledge about environmental conditions, or an unstructured situation not directly structured by agents, norms, or values. For panic to occur, structural conduciveness is the first condition that must exist. In relation to panic, it refers to: (1) the degree to which danger can arise, (2) the communication of danger, and (3) restricted opportunity to escape. For example, financial panic as a collective behavior is dependent on the extent to which danger (danger from financial panic) is communicated and the feasibility of escape from such danger. Factors that are equally important are: (1) the degree to which the dangers of economic fluctuation exist, or whether the institutional controls (for example, unemployment insurance, savings deposit insurance, etc.) are effective; (2) whether news about financial crises can be rapidly communicated; and (3) whether people in the event of a financial panic have only restricted means of disposing of their assets.

In sum, for Smelser, all types of collective behavior are interrelated because they all have the six general determinants combined in a definitive value-added pattern. They also involve the reconstitution of a component of social action: all five types (panic, craze, hostile outburst, norm-oriented movement, and value-oriented movement) of collective behavior follow each other in a hierarchy of increasing intensity, complexity, and inclusiveness.

Smelser's *Theory of Collective Behavior* has often been applied to Germany, under the Weimar Republic, which it is argued was characterized by structural conditions conducive to the rise of value-based mass movements coupled with severe strains on the society's culture, values, norms, and so on. Hitler provided the leadership and articulated a value-based belief within which the central focus of strain could be located. Thus, although the theory tends to be abstract and based on universal variables, its focus is nonetheless on concrete factors that determine change. Smelser focuses largely on single, short-term episodes of change rather than on long-term developments. Strain or conflict are viewed as consequences of modernization and a manifestation of both small-scale changes within a society and those on a wider scale.

Mass Society Theory

The theory of mass society as another alternative to Marxist explanation of revolution is a strictly structured analysis of the production of militant social movements. It belongs to the view that violent social movements sprang disproportionately from the ranks of the socially dislocated. Such individuals, it was held, were very susceptible to manipulation by distant and cynical elites.

In William Kornhauser's *Politics of Mass Society* (1959), he argued that people who lack intermediate ties to established social institutions are easily susceptible to mobilization by movements that seek radical and extreme goals, and also operate outside the established channels of institutional politics.[8] The lack of attachments to work, community, or other proximate associations leaves people open to support for mass political behavior. The ideal society for Kornhauser is a society where, to a large extent, all political activities are expressed in the context of established institutions, and in gradual incremental stages. In contrast, collective violence is caused by mass politics, and stems from people being weakly attached to institutionalized political and socioeconomic life and seeking political ends directly. The probability of civil violence results when such unattached individuals seek political ends directly. In particular, for Kornhauser: "Violence in words and deeds is the hallmark of the mass movement uncommitted to institutional means. Mass behavior then, involves direct, activist modes of response to remote symbols."[9] In other words, political instability ensues when self-interest overrides general commitments to abstract principles.

The development of mass society theory was inspired by the emergence of the Nazis and their accession to power in Germany in 1933. Revolutionary mass movements like Nazism arise when traditional structural arrangements break down. In Germany at the tend of World War I, the situation altered tremendously, creating a serious discrepancy between widely held societal values and the environment. Among other environmental changes, the German people were presented with a new republic in place of a monarchy, defeat in war instead of expected victory, and the reality of a completely new political situation.

In explaining the advent of the revolutionary mass movement, mass society theory underscores three major terms: (1) *atomization* of the individual, (2) the emergence of *new ideologies*, and (3) the rise of *totalitarianism*. First, a severe atomization of the individual occurs as group attachments are lost. In the case of the German people a number of developments led this process of loss of group attachments: a severe treaty (the Treaty of Versailles) due to loss of the War, ineffective attempts to stabilize a dislocated economy, inability to contain the effects of the depression and its effects on the people, and the loss of their once stable lifestyle.[10] In response to atomization, new ideologies emerge to replace the loss of security or sense of community. In Germany in the 1930s, communism, social democracy, and the Nazi party struggled for power. Thus, the environment became highly unstable as a result of riots, strikes, and street fights among competing factions along with citizen participation. People were ready to embrace new ideologies in their search for a community to replace the lost community. Eventually one party gains victory, resulting in totalitarianism, or total domination of the society by an elite group. In Germany, the Nazis became the leaders of a new dominant order characterized by a dictator, Hitler, and a reign of terror. Initially, the individual supports the totalitarian movement because it provides security, but with continued state terror people are appalled at the monstrosity they helped create. The Nazis capitalized on the frustration and discontent of the German people. Germany in the 1920s and 1930s was confronted with acute political instability and economic malaise, including unemployment and depression. The humiliation of their defeat in the war haunted them, and the resentment of the people intensified.

As a form of collective behavior, mass behavior exhibits four characteristics. First, the focus of attention tends to be removed from everyday life and personal experiences. In the case of the German people their focus of attention was on the harsh effects of the Treaty of Versailles, which had contributed to the destruction of their stable lifestyle. Second, reaction to remote effects is often direct and manifested in strikes, riots, and street fights. In Germany, violence was a frequent form of interaction among Nazis, socialists, and communists. Third, mass behavior is characterized by highly unstable support for the competing ideologies. In Germany, support for political parties shifted regularly. Finally, mass behavior takes on the character of a mass movement when it becomes organized around a program and acquires a sustained effort and definite goal. In Germany, for example, the Nazis set out to address Germany's political and economic problems and to restore to the German people their sense of national pride and integrity.

In Germany, the objective of the Nazis was to unite the German people by incorporating the working classes into a harmonious nationalist and democratic state. Thus, the groups for whom Nazism as a mass movement had the greatest appeal were the unattached intellectuals, the marginal, and insulated working classes. Their classlessness and unattached characteristics made them ready candidates for membership in the movement. The concept of marginality is integral to mass society theory. For example, Hitler was marginal to German society because he had certain background attributes that made him different from the mainstream (bulk) of German population. He was: (1) Austrian rather than German by birth, (2) Catholic and leader in a predominantly Protestant society, and (3) of petit bourgeois (lower middle class) background in a society and time when leaders were drawn largely from the upper and upper-middle classes. According to mass society theory, an individual's marginality becomes significant when he tries to move into the majority group. Hitler aspired to mainstream, and always thought of himself as German. In Germany, Hitler needed to be a part of the state (chancellor), part of the political process, before he could become absolute ruler over Germany. The German population, in quest of lost security in the 1930s, rallied around their new charismatic leader, hoping he would provide a new stable environment.

Mass society theory falls under the general category of irrational social movements. It is a structuralist view of the emergence of militant social movements. Irrational social movements generally give birth to crowd action that is sustained and even becomes extensive in scope over time. It is characterized by the manipulation through intense mass propaganda of people who have lost their communal or group attachments. Hitler and Stalin are now generally considered personalities that effectively manipulated socially dislocated persons, such that their activities culminated in the development of violent social movements. In other words, a socially rootless population becomes very susceptible to manipulation, and is likely to become the target of marginal and self-serving elites.

Finally, theories of collective behavior like mass society theory have never gained the same prominence and respectability as other theories of collective violence. By the mid-1960s, collective behavior analysis was eclipsed by more appealing and analytically rigorous works by theorists such as J. C. Davis, Huntington, Gurr, Rudé, or Tilly, among others. Collective behavior theory came under attack because critics doubted whether mass, riotous, or rebellious behavior is "abnormal" or "disorganized." Underlying crowd action, in other words, could be a purposeful, goal-directed response to societal interests and a desire to sustain or recapture "traditional" social life. Other critics viewed the occurrence of collective behavior as a result of "new norms" rather than the absence of traditional structural arrangements or culture. The new theoretical views became predicated on the argument that the factors that produce collective violence developed well before the actual episodes of violent eruptions. In particular, for the new political and psychological theories, collective violence was a result of persistent social conditions that produced discontent and erupted in social conflict.

Contrasting Functionalism and Conflict Theories

In general, in the structural-functional approach, social change is viewed as dysfunctional unless it occurs slowly and promotes a harmonious equilibrium. Accordingly, functionalists advocate maintenance of the status quo. They do not blame the political system or social structure for individual and group disadvantages, but instead they argue, for example, that people are poor because they are lazy and immoral. They also believe that with a combination of hard work and luck, anyone can become rich. To a large extent, functionalists contend that: (1) inborn differences among people are responsible for social inequality; (2) success and failure in the workplace can be accounted for by the individual's level of intelligence, achievement motivation, and other psychological traits; (3) success is a sign of divine grace; and (4) in the final analysis, the individual should be responsible for his or her failure.[11]

In contrast to the functionalist perspective, theories that emphasize the inevitability of conflict explain instances of social disorganization by tracing them to the social structure of a society. Institutions as part of the social structure and society may be disrupted and weakened during periods of rapid social change. For example, as societies change from traditional to modern, so does the structure of the family change from an extended family structure consisting of parents, children, grandparents, and other relatives, to a nuclear family structure consisting only of parents and their children. With this transformation in the structure also come new problems such as the welfare of the elderly, single parents, and above all inadequate socialization of the children since both parents may be busy trying to earn a living. Social disorganization may therefore consist of a situation where in society: (1) elements of socialization (norms, mores, etc.) and social control may become progressively weakened, (2) the relationship between the social system and its physical environment may be poor, and (3) some segments of the population are arbitrarily prevented from achieving their economic, political, and other goals.[12]

The structural-functional perspective, on the other hand, argues that the poor are in fact poor because they adhere to a distinctive subculture characterized by a certain set of norms that reinforce a cycle of poverty from one generation to the next. This subculture is not confined to one racial group, region, or nation. Moreover, this cycle of poverty and its distinctive subculture tends to occur in capitalist economies with their emphasis on profit-making at the expense of the low-income population. The consequence is a persistently high rate of unemployment, low wages, and a lack of a social safety net for the disadvantaged. The functionalist perspective attributes poverty to personal incompetence and inferiority. However, the negative conditions produced by capitalist economies tend to generate chronic deprivation and despair, especially among those who are forced to live in urban slums. By and large chronic deprivation is socially undesirable and potentially dangerous in terms of system stability.

Implicit in functionalism is the idea that societies ensure stability through socialization or the process whereby the meanings, ideas, and actions appropriate for a particular society are internalized. This is simply the process of learning the culture. In the case of the child, the family, the schools, and the media play an important part in producing a citizen that is essentially molded into the pattern of that society. In comparison to the family, the formal system of education (schools) is even more conservative in its effect of transmitting the attitudes, values, and training necessary for the maintenance of law, order, and stability in society. In traditional societies (villages and less industrialized regions), it is the secret society, age groups, initiation ceremonies, and the mores of society that transmit this conservative effect, which helps to produce and maintain the stabilizing structures and functions of society.

In addition to the family and the educational system, in developed countries in particular, the media plays a very powerful socialization function because it reinforces the existing values and practices of society. According to sociologist Herbert Gans, major television networks (CBS and NBC) and major periodicals (*Newsweek* and *Time Magazine*) portray eight clusters of enduring values: ethnocentrism, altruistic democracy, responsible capitalism, small town pastoralism, individualism, moderatism, social order, and national leadership.[13] These values are status quo enhancing or conservative and stabilizing in their effect. Particularly because of the combined socialization effects of family, educational system, and media, members of society generally manifest similarities in many fundamental respects.

In terms of integration and social control (the legal aspects) of functionalism, the idea is that the state is a body of institutions based on law that exist to maintain order and stability. In American society, for example, liberal democratic theory embodies the functioning of the order model. The body of rules that constitute law enacted by representatives are considered to be in the interest of the people. They are also viewed as essentially neutral and applied without bias toward any individual or group. The result is interest group pluralism based on compromise and consensus among the various interest groups within American society.

In contrast to the legal order of functionalism is the critical view of American society based on the following assumptions: (1) the state exists to serve the economic elite, that is the owners of large corporations and financial institutions; (2) the law and legal system are simply a reflection of the interests and needs of the ruling class; and (3) since the law reflects the interests of the power elite, challenges to the status quo or domestic order are successfully defeated.[14] In other words, the law is partial to the needs and interests of the ruling class.

Radical or conflict theories of society contend that order and stability in society is maintained because some segments of society coerce other segments into proper and acceptable behavior aimed at maintaining the status quo, or political-economic and social system. In American society, for example, instances of the state's efforts to maintain the status quo are numerous, and include: the FBI's concern with internal security, which dates back to 1936, when President Franklin Roosevelt directed J. Edgar Hoover to investigate domestic communist and fascist organizations in the United States; between 1969 and 1973 the Internal Revenue Service (IRS) monitored the activities of 99 political organizations and 11,539 individuals; between 1967 and 1973 the National Security Agency (NSA) monitored the overseas telephone calls and cables of approximately 1,650 Americans and U.S. organizations, as well as almost 6,000 foreign nationals and groups; beginning in 1957 the FBI monitored the activities of civil rights leader Martin Luther King Jr., and also effectively contained the threat posed by the Black Panther Party during the 1960s; and currently, the FBI frequently infiltrates and monitors the activities of right-wing extremist groups such as the Aryan Nation and other neo-Nazi movements.[15] Such activities and many more fall under the need to maintain the status quo, and are done in the name of "national security."

The Sociocultural Environment of Peaceful Societies

The stabilizing and socializing effects of a common culture are especially evident in the study of peaceful societies by anthropologists. Where socialization is effective, and especially in smaller and more homogeneous societies, the members of society tend to be alike in fundamental ways. However, in large and more diverse societies, the sources of dissimilarities are many and are located in social class, religion, ethnicity, and geographic location, among others. According to anthropologists, violence in many preindustrial societies, in rain forests, deserts, or similar settings, is determined more by social structure than by either the inevitability of violence as Marxist

Table 3.1: Major Themes in Functionalist and Conflict Perspectives

FUNCTIONALISM	CONFLICT PERSPECTIVES
Society is characterized by self-regulating mechanisms that ensure peace and stability	Society is dynamic and characterized by a constant struggle for power among groups
Violent conflicts and other forms of disorganization result from rapid social change	Violent conflicts are caused by inequities related to structural dislocations
Collective violence is illegitimate by definition	Collective violence can be legitimate because the structures of power and dominance produce imbalances in the political economy that lead to instability
People rebel because they have not been socialized to accept and obey the customs of society	Rebellion occurs because the powerful in society enact laws and perpetuate structures of inequality at the expense of the disadvantaged
Stratification and inequality are not only inevitable but necessary	The stratification (especially the distributive) system is unjust, and is the source of a great deal of instability
The solution against the occurrence of violence is to maintain a stable balance among the functional needs of society	The elimination of inequities and inequitable social structures will solve the problem of instability

scholars would argue, or by instincts as sociobiologists and biologists would argue.

Their conclusion is derived from the study of the social structure and culture of peaceful societies such as the Mbuti (Pygmies) of the Congo forest, the San of the Kalahari desert in Southern Africa, the Semai of Malaya, the Zuni Indians of the American Southwest, and the Arapesh of New Guinea, among others. In many of these societies, the culture and social structure emphasize egalitarianism (the absence of elitism or class differences) and contempt for physical combat or the use of violence to settle disputes. Instead, values such as communal ownership, sharing, trickery, and deception rather than the use of violence are used and admired. Members who deviate from the accepted norms of society are socially ostracized rather than subjected to physical punishment or violence.

In particular, the Mbuti Pygmies of the Congo rain forest are said to be at peace not only with themselves but with their environment as well. They are egalitarian in terms of social structure because there are not formal leaders in a Mbuti band. Division of labor is along age and gender lines, but even here the roles are not formalized or rigid, but rather flexible. Their subsistence existence is based on cooperation, especially in hunting. Sharing is integral to the culture; as a result, after the hunt all band members share the meat. It is unthinkable to them not to share. Politics among the Mbuti is based on consensus. When there is a dispute, the community discusses it until they arrive at a solution acceptable to all. The emphasis is on peace and thus there is little or no reference to rights and wrongs. Members of the community often sing to the unborn child, and after the child is born, it is not only the parents that feel responsible for it, but members of the community feel a collective responsibility for the child as well. Their cooperative and egalitarian values are so strong that even games of competition (e.g., tug-of-war) are made into a comedy. For example, as the males begin to win in a tug-of-war involving males versus females, one of the males goes into role acting by adjusting his clothing, talking like a woman, and joining them.[16] According to Jean-Pierre Hallet, the Pygmies of the Ituri forest in the Congo have eighteen commandments including laws about interpersonal relationships such as prohibition against cruelty toward children, murder, disrespect toward parents and elders, adultery, theft, and slander, as well as ecological laws that prohibit wanton slaughter of animals, cutting tall trees, wasting foods, and setting traps for animals, among others.[17]

In conclusion, while structural functionalists view socialization as necessary to produce stability, order, and law-abiding citizens in a society, conflict perspectives (especially Marxism) view socialization as a process that many groups in society are led to accept uncritically, and often the disadvantaged may accept a system that does not benefit them in any way. Since the disadvantaged may consider it just, they are in fact in a state of false consciousness, according to Karl Marx. Since the sources of dissimilarities that may eventually produce collective political violence are found in social class, religion, ethnicity, and the like, radical conflict theorists seriously challenge the functionalist view that societies are harmonious and stable. According to the conflict perspective, it is because social structures are not well balanced and functional that even a modern society tends to experience severe tensions and conflicts. The reality is that the lack of proper balance between interrelated and interdependent parts of society result in the continuous struggle by different groups in society to obtain scarce and valued resources or rewards.

The order model of structural functionalism emphasizes shared values, which produce a society in harmony and in a state of equilibrium. However, theorists who emphasize the inevitability of conflict operate on the basic assumption that human societies are continuously in a state of flux because individuals and groups are constantly in competitive relationships with one another. The result is a competitive self-interested behavior that produces confrontation, fluidity, and discontinuity rather than integration, stability, and equilibrium. This condition is found in societies because social interactions take the form of competition and confrontation between and among social groups such as trade unions, political parties, and ethnoracial or ethnoreligious categories. Thus, conflict in society can take nonviolent forms as well, which may be contained in entirely institutionalized forms— elections, use of the media, strikes or bargaining, recourse to the courts, and so on—or it may occur in more informal settings, such as crimes against persons or property, war, and violence.

Finally, conflict in society ranging from antisocial behavior to full-blown revolutionary activity may result from the unequal access to societal opportunities and other pursuits sanctioned by the culture. Often, the deprived groups are, on the one hand, asked to orient their conduct toward the prospect of accumulating wealth, and on the other hand, they are largely denied the opportunities to do so within the context of the structures and institutions of society. This lack of harmony between certain aspects of the culture (goals and norms) and the social structure (opportunities, or access to means) leads to structural inconsistency. The consequences of such structural inconsistency are violence either in the form of antisocial conduct and/or revolutionary activities.

Notes

1. For details on the varied dimensions of functionalism, see Herman Strasser and Susan C. Randall, *An Introduction to Theories of Social Change* (London: Routledge and Kegan Paul, 1981).
2. See, for example, Talcott Parsons, *The System of Modern Societies* (Englewood Cliffs, NJ: Prentice-Hall, 1971); and R. Collins, *Conflict Sociology: Toward an Explanatory Science* (New York: Academic Press, 1975).
3. For details, see Chalmers Johnson, *Revolutionary Change* (Boston: Little, Brown & Co., 1966).
4. See A. R. Radcliffe-Brown, *A Natural Science of Society* (Glencoe, IL: Free Press, 1957).
5. Neil J. Smelser, *Theory of Collective Behavior* (New York: Free Press, 1962).
6. See, for example, Neil J. Smelser, *Essays in Social Explanation* (Englewood Cliffs, NJ: Prentice-Hall, 1968).
7. In *Social Change in the Industrial Revolution* (London: Routledge, Kegan & Paul, 1959), Smelser uses the example of the British cotton industry to show how the process of modernization generates strains through social differentiation. It is a study of the social conditions and disintegrative mechanisms that led to the industrial revolution of eighteenth-century England. In particular, Smelser's theory has been applied to the Nazi revolution by Susan C. Randall, and Herman Strasser in "Change of the Social System, Social Groups, and Social Relationships," in Herman Strasser and Susan C. Randall, *An Introduction to Theories of Social Change* (London: Routledge, Kegan & Paul, 1981), 220–74.
8. William Kornhauser, *The Politics of Mass Society* (Glencoe, IL: Free Press, 1959).
9. William Kornhauser, *The Politics of Mass Society*, p. 46.
10. Many aspects of turbulence in the political economy of Germany in the 1920s and 1930s are detailed in Albert Speer, *Inside the Third Reich* (New York: Macmillan, 1970).
11. For further details, see Thomas J. Bernard, *The Consensus-Conflict Debate* (New York: Columbia University Press, 1983); and Mark Abrahamson, *Functionalism* (Englewood Cliffs, NJ: Prentice-Hall, 1978).

12. For details, see Graham C. Kinloch, *Society as Power: An Introduction to Sociology* (Englewood Cliffs, NJ: Prentice-Hall, 1989); and Michael Parenti, *Power and the Powerless* (New York: St. Martin's Press, 1978).

13. Herbert J. Gans, *Deciding What's News* (New York: Pantheon, 1979).

14. See, for example, C. Wright Mills, *The Power Elite* (New York: Oxford University Press, 1956).

15. For details, see D. Stanley Eitzen and Maxine Baca Zinn, *In Conflict and Order: Understanding Society* (Boston: Allyn and Bacon, 1991); and Ward Churchill and Jim Vander Wall, *Agents of Repression: The FBI's Secret Wars Against the Black Panther Party and the American Indian Movement* (Boston: South End Press, 1988).

16. For more details, see C. M. Turnbull, *The Mbuti Pygmies: Change and Adaptation* (New York: CBS College Publishing, 1983); and Luigi Luca Cavalli-Sforza, ed., *African Pygmies* (Orlando: Academic Press, 1986).

17. Jean-Pierre Hallett and Alex Pelle, *Pygmy Kitabu* (New York: Random House, 1973).

Key Terms

altruism	interest group pluralism	social disorganization
atomization	marginality	social system
ethnocentrism	necessary condition	socialization
false consciousness	peaceful societies	structural strain
functionalism	power elite theory	subculture
homeostatic system	precipitating factors	totalitarianism

Discussion Questions

1. What is functionalism? Discuss its main elements in relation to societal stability.
2. Briefly discuss Neil Smelser's theory of collective behavior.
3. Analyze the theory of mass society in relation to the emergence of Nazism in Germany.
4. Compare and contrast functionalism and conflict theories.
5. What are "peaceful societies"? Give examples and briefly discuss one.

CHAPTER 4

The Psychocultural Approach to Explaining Collective Political Violence

The psychocultural approach to explaining collective political violence focuses on individuals and factors at the individual level as units of analysis. The individual is at the center of analysis, but implicitly or explicitly their conditions, feelings, or attitudes are combined into a "collective" or "aggregate." The basic argument is that individual feelings and perceptions are a primary cause of instability. Relative deprivation is considered the primary determinant of instability. The various theorists in these psychological determinants of collective behavior emphasize the state of mind of the masses as a primary cause of revolution and other violent collective change.

These relative deprivation theories are varied, with each emphasizing one factor or the other as a major determinant of collective behavior.[1] The most common variation is found in the standard of comparison put forward as governing individual action. Standards of comparison range from the perceived state of some social unit or group to people's view of a specific reference group perceived as either rivals, similar to their group, or based on some other criterion. The standard for comparison lies strictly within the individual's state of mind or psychic world. Relative deprivation also has a temporal dimension, as an individual's level of relative deprivation changes with time and in relation to some level of expectation. The level of expectation may not be fixed with regard to any reference or outside group.

The Concept of Aggression

Perhaps the earliest modern investigation of the relationship between deprivation and collective violence was the original frustration-aggression studies of Dollard and other Yale scholars.[2] However, their frustration-aggression theory does not explicitly involve relative deprivation because their notion of frustration did not include a dimension of comparison. Subsequent theorists introduced other dimensions related to attitudes, intergroup comparisons, expectations, or individual conceptions of equity and justice. For Dollard and his colleagues, frustration is simply "an interference with the occurrence of an instigated goal-response at its proper time in the behavior sequence."[3] One significant study of the frustration-aggression hypothesis is that which established a strong relationship between lynchings in the American South and specific indicators of economic performance such as per-acre value of cotton.[4] The authors linked such findings to frustration, which produces aggression. In other words, times of recession or poor economic performance would act as a general frustration by "blocking individual goal-directed behavior." The frustration is then displaced onto the others in the form of lynchings of blacks. Expressions of frustration do not take some other form of violent action because landlords, merchants, or politicians who are the actual source of the frustration are in power positions, and thus action taken against them would be foolhardy. Displacing the aggression onto blacks would not be punished. Besides, many of those lynched constituted the "outcast" of an unprotected minority; they were either already arrested, or were hiding from the law.

The concept of aggression has been subject to a variety of meanings because researchers who utilize it have a permanent disagreement about how to define it. Definitions have ranged from aggression as actions that inflict pain on others to behavior that is not socially approved. For most people an action is aggressive in nature if the perpetrator had a socially unjustified motive. This latter conception of aggression introduces a moral evaluation that presents serious difficulties in state-society relations.[5] Who, for example, is to decide what actions or behaviors are socially justified? After all, social standards vary from group to group and from time to time. Many revolutionary groups and their supporters, for instance, would argue that terroristic acts such as bombing a public building with innocent people inside is justified as far as fighting for their cause is concerned. In many developing countries whipping a disobedient child may not be considered violent child abuse, whereas in an advanced industrial society like the United States, it is considered a crime. However, while what constitutes violence is subjective or exists only in the eyes of the beholder, many contemporary theorists who utilize the concept of aggression are largely in agreement with

Dollard and his colleagues that aggression is "behavior whose goal-response is the inflicting of injury on some object or person." In other words, the purpose of aggression is to inflict either psychological or physical injury on the target.

The goal of aggression is self-preservation or self-enhancement by the individual or groups who perceive themselves to be threatened, challenged, or devalued. They may attack the legitimate source of the perception or scapegoat some other target in an effort to reassert their status or standing in the community, or change others' perceptions of them as weak, incompetent, or cowardly. Accordingly, social psychologists identify two broad types of aggression: instrumental and hostile.[6] In the former, the violence is instrumental and aimed at acquiring other noninjury related goals such as material goods, prestige or social approval, an improved self-concept, or even the elimination of a source of discomfort. This type of aggression is often referred to as defensive or self-enhancement violence. Hostile aggression, the second type of aggression, primarily aims at injury of the target. This aggression is a result of people being angered or emotionally aroused, and thus is frequently thought of as affective or emotional aggression. Instrumental and hostile aggression are also referred to respectively as incentive-motivated and annoyance-motivated aggression.[7]

The political turbulence of the 1960s in the United States and in the new nations of the developing world led many scholars utilizing psychosocial approaches to conflict analysis to formulate their own explanations of collective political violence that essentially underscored the frustration-aggression linkage or the concept of relative deprivation.

Relative Deprivation

In the early 1960s, research specifically underscoring the temporal and intergroup dimensions of relative deprivation began with J. C. Davies's "Toward a Theory of Revolution," which identifies the principal determinant of revolution to be the reaction to a short-term economic downturn following a prolonged period of economic and social development.[8] In other words, Davies argued that both successful and abortive revolutions are the result of widespread dissatisfaction produced by a long period of "rising expectations and rising gratification" followed by a short period of sharp reversal, quickly generating a wide and intolerable gap between expectations and gratification. In social-psychological terms, collective violence is a consequence of shattered hopes and aspirations, as well as the individual's fear of losing what had already been gained. Davies applied his argument to several revolutionary events: Door's Rebellion in early-nineteenth-century Rhode Island, the

Russian Revolution of 1917, the Egyptian Revolution of 1952, the American Civil War, the Nazi revolution of 1933, and the rebellions of American blacks in the 1960s. In all studies he theorized economic improvement and rising expectations, followed by a sharp and sudden downturn.

By the mid-to-late 1960s and early 1970s, Ivo and Rosalind Feierabend and their collaborators identified the main source of collective violence to be the psychic gap between expectations and realities.[9] They argued that social conditions produced individual frustration when "want formation" far exceeded "want satisfaction." In other words, the Feierabends focused on "systematic frustration" generated by the modernization process or specific aspects of social change. Indicators of want satisfaction are aggregate measures such as number of physicians and caloric intake per capita; and want formation is manifested in measures such as rates of literacy and urbanization. The modernization process thus involves striking a balance between individual needs and societal capacities to satisfy them. When needs and capacities are out of balance, the outcome is likely to be high levels of social instability.

For Ted Gurr, relative deprivation arises when an individual is deprived of what is justifiably due to him or her—their just deserts. He labels this denial of just deserts as a "discrepancy between value expectations and value capabilities."[10] In other words, the denial, for example, of political or societal opportunities to ethnic or other groups in society constitutes a major source of collective violence. The emphasis is, again, on an intolerable discrepancy between what people want and what they get (a want-get gap) as the crucial determinant of collective political violence. For Gurr, in particular, relative deprivation incorporates both psychological and societal variables as conditions leading to violence. The magnitude of political violence is at the same time dependent first on whether the deprivation is mild, moderate, or intense; and second on what its scope, intensity, and duration is.

The various patterns of relative deprivation—decremental, aspirational, and progressive—for Gurr determine the magnitude of frustration and anger throughout a populace and serve to generate violence in society.[11] In decremental deprivation individuals are angered because of the loss of what they previously had or thought they could have. Such a situation arises when value expectations (wants, aspirations, just deserts) stagnate while value capabilities (means, goods already acquired, conditions of life) are perceived to decline. According to Gurr, people experience relative deprivation in relation to their past condition. Factors that may lead to decremental deprivation are: declining production of material goods in society, deteriorating security or value systems in a society, disproportionate tax burdens directed at one class in relation to others, declining employment opportunities for a particular group in society, such as unskilled labor, and the psychic displacement or instability experienced by people who migrate from rural to urban settings. Decremental deprivation is considered to be probably most prevalent in "traditional" societies where the traditional equilibrium is disturbed. Thus, colonial subjects suffered power deprivations because colonialisim disrupted interpersonal relationships and undermined the authority of traditional rulers. During World War I, the Russian people sacrificed a great deal to the war effort, thereby experiencing the deprivation that provided the basic ingredient for the Russian Revolution. For many theorists—Aristotle, Marx, and Engels among others—decremental deprivation is the major source of political violence.

In aspirational relative deprivation value capabilities remain relatively constant while expectations increase. Individuals are angered because they feel they lack the capacity to acquire new expectations. They generally do not experience a significant loss of what they already have. They may simply be expecting or demanding more material goods, a better political order and system of justice, or new values (for example, political participation or equality with other groups) already enjoyed by other groups. Gurr gives as some of his examples the demands of African Americans in the 1960s, which were more intense than their demands in the 1940s. Another example is the revolution of rising expectations experienced by traditional people when exposed to modern life, or the demonstration effect developed countries provide for developing countries. In such a situation expectation levels significantly increase because an individual, group, or society sets its value expectations by reference to the more advanced value position of some other individual, group, or society.

Progressive relative deprivation refers to a "substantial and simultaneous increase in expectations and decrease in capabilities." Also known as the "J-Curve" hypothesis, it says "revolutions are most likely to occur when a prolonged period of objective economic and social development is followed by a short period of sharp reversal."[12] According to Gurr, progressive deprivation is a special case of aspirational relative deprivation because the long improvement in people's condition produces expectations of continued improvement. It is when value capabilities stabilize or decline after such prolonged improvement that progressive relative deprivation occurs. Conditions leading to progressive deprivation are: economic depression in a booming economy and a society experiencing modernization within a context of rigid economic and political structures. Individuals who experience this deprivation fear that what they have already gained over a long period of time will be lost overnight. According to Gurr, in the United States, the income of blacks relative to whites of comparable education increased rapidly between 1940 and 1950 but then began to slip. By 1960 the relative gains of the past decades were lost. This, coupled with societal reluctance to extend political rights, along with economic decline, resulted in violence. Many conflicts in colonial times could also be attributed to progressive deprivation because colonial officials raised the hopes of colonial subjects with expectations of independence but dashed those hopes with policies that interfered with its attainment. To a large extent, progressive deprivation is strongly related to the reluctance or inability of institutions to accommodate new developments, demands, or ideas. The preconditions of structural inflexibilities or rapid economic decline in a growing economy were some of the factors identified by J. C. Davies in case studies of French, Russian, and Nazi revolutions, as well as the American Civil War and the Egyptian Revolution of 1952.[13]

Finally, Gurr argues that the magnitude of political violence is directly related to three mediating factors that either intensify or dampen violence. These are "normative justifications," "utilitarian justifications," and the "balance of coercive forces" between the state and dissidents. In normative justifications, feelings about the justification for or against violence could increase or decrease the effects of the discrepancy between expectations and capabilities (or the want-get frustration). Stated differently, for rebellion to occur or not will depend, on the one hand, on whether the belief (enhanced by notions of a society that glorifies violence) exists that violence should be used, and, on the other hand, that violence not be used (reinforced by doctrines of nonviolence). Normative justifications determine variations in levels of civil conflict from one nation to another because they act as mediating factors that either augment or decrease political violence. They are evident in traditions—or lack thereof—of violent conflict or ideological commitment or beliefs concerning regime legitimacy/illegitimacy. Utilitarian justifications involve, in large part, tactical cost-benefit calculations focusing on whether political violence is useful or not in the struggle to achieve political goals. The balance of coercion helps to determine the duration of any violent conflict between regime and dissidents. If the balance of coercion (military might or capabilities) is relatively even, strife will be greatest. If it is highly unequal, one side is either totally defeated or goes underground. Gurr also underscores the presence or absence of facilitators of rebellion: transportation networks, geographic (topographic) traits of the country, demographic characteristics (for example, ethnic composition) that could enhance support for rebels, and external support either for rebels or the state.

Psychological theories of collective political violence command a great deal of appeal because they imply commonplace arguments like "when people are pushed too far, they revolt," or "people will not just let you trample on them, they will strike back." Their straightforward or direct appeal has conferred on them a long intellectual pedigree. For example, in Aristotle's *The Politics*, some sort of relative deprivation is emphasized.[14] He argues that while both democracy and oligarchy as political systems are predicated on the idea of justice, they nonetheless fail to guarantee absolute justice. Accordingly, when citizens in both systems fail to realize the level of justice or constitutional rights they expect and aspire to, they resort to sedition. Similarly, in Alexis de Tocqueville's *The Old Regime and the French Revolution* we read:

> Patiently endured so long as it seemed beyond redress, a grievance comes to appear intolerable once the possibility of removing it crosses men's minds. For the mere fact that certain abuses have been remedied draws attention to the others and they now appear more galling; people may suffer less, but their sensibility is exacerbated.[15]

In this passage de Tocqueville directly links the causes of the French Revolution to relative deprivation explanations of revolution.

Relative deprivation theories argue that the rise of popular protest is an inevitable outcome of response to unfulfilled expectations and fair treatment. Thus they explain the rising demands of deprived/marginalized social groups in relation to actual longings for justice and equity. However, critics have been quick to emphasize the deceptiveness of relative deprivation theories because of their great appeal and apparent simplicity. For example, it does not necessarily follow that actual or objective deprivation results in collective violence. In other words, one can be very poor but not revolutionary. The focus is on an individual's perception, not to actual conditions. Conversely, an individual can be well-off but very dissatisfied. Gurr, in *Why Men Rebel*, realizes that frustration does not necessarily lead to rebellion. Thus he emphasized that for frustration to be transformed into rebellion, it has to be politicized.

Do individuals or groups necessarily resort to public action or aggression if they find their social condition or environment unacceptable? Alternative responses are equally worthy of consideration. At times, instead of frustration resulting in aggression against the perceived source of frustration, such as governmental authorities, it is instead displaced onto a scapegoat. For example, much violent action is displaced onto members of disadvantaged minority groups, or against members of antagonistic ethnic, racial, or religious groups. Some relative deprivation theories may assume too often that people channel their aggression against the perceived or actual sources of their frustration. Is it in fact possible that individual frustrations in public life result in aggressions in the domestic (family) sphere? Or do individual frustrations result in neglect of family responsibilities by a father (deadbeat dads), or other forms of deviancy at home or in the immediate neighborhood? Examples, of course, abound of instances where people are exploited, go hungry, or are deprived of human rights, and still do not revolt.

Table 4.1: Major Themes: Causes of Violence

1. Intolerable gap between expectations and gratification.
2. A sudden and sharp economic downturn after a prolonged period of economic and social development.
3. Shattered hopes and aspirations.
4. An imbalance between needs and capacities.
5. A wide and intolerable want-get gap.
6. A discrepancy between dues (rights, just deserts, etc.) and means, or conditions of life.

Relative Deprivation and the American Civil War

Progressive relative deprivation, or the J-Curve pattern of rising and then declining satisfaction, describes, to some extent, the political-economic rise and decline of Southerners in relation to Northerners before the American Civil War. In economic terms, the South suffered deprivation because of the Tariff Act passed in 1828 through the efforts of Northern businessmen. The act raised the prices of manufactured products from Europe that were sold mainly in the South. The objective of the law was to encourage the South to buy the North's products because by 1860, the North was producing over 90 percent of the value of all manufactured goods.[16] However, it angered Southerners that they had to pay more for the goods they wanted either from Europe or from the North. The tariff laws had to a large extent been changed by the time of the Civil War, but they nonetheless became a source of grievance for the South against the North. In addition, the relative economic dissatisfaction of the South vis-á-vis the North continued with the more imminent economic crisis of 1857. The South experienced a panic in 1857 because of a serious downturn in the New York commodities exchange market. The effect on the South was that the demand for cotton in—as well as money exchange with—England ceased. The loss amounted to a third of the value of their major crop (cotton), to the tune of $35 million. The South's progressive relative economic deprivation went hand in hand with a political downturn manifested in changing political power in the federal government. The Northern and Midwestern states were becoming increasingly more powerful as the populations increased. The South eventually lost political power, including a diminution of their dominant power in the Senate, where in the past they had vetoed many laws demanded by Northerners. Thus, as the South lost political influence and experienced a threat to its socioeconomic security, it felt a growing need for freedom from the central federal government in Washington, D.C. The decision by some Southern states to break away led to the Civil War (1861–65).

The American Civil War was, in other words, characterized by a substantial level of economic insecurity and deprivation manifested in the rise of sectional interests, especially the economic and political sectionalism of the early 1800s. The political-economic sectionalism was reflected in: (1) an increase in primary loyalty to the state or region, and not to the entire nation; (2) consideration of political-economic and social problems from a sectional, and not a national point of view; (3) legislators using the powers of the central government to further the interests of their section of the country; (4) the South in particular using the doctrine of states' rights to oppose federal action deemed detrimental to its interests; and (5) the growth in feelings of identifying first and foremost with citizenship of a state or of being a representative of a region, instead of as an American. This widening gap between the conflicting feelings of sectionalism and nationalism would eventually result in civil war that pitted North and South.

The political-economic basis of sectionalism was reflected in the differences between the North, South, and West. The interests of the North and West would later be similar, thereby making the situation more threatening to the South. These sectional differences are outlined in Table 4.2.

The differences between the regions became so acute that even elections became increasingly divisive. In 1820 James Monroe had been reelected popularly by support from all sections of the country. But the election of 1824 turned out to be a sectional struggle to gain control of the presidency. The four candidates were John Quincy Adams of the North, William H. Crawford of the South, Henry Clay of the West, and Andrew Jackson of the far West. No candidate received a majority of the votes because the people voted along sectional lines.[17] The election eventually went to the House of Representatives and resulted in Adams being elected president despite the fact that Jackson had led in the electoral vote.

The presidential election of 1860 served as the trigger for the Civil War. Slavery was a burning issue in that election. The Democratic Party split into two parts: the Northern Democrats nominated Stephen A. Douglas on a platform exposing popular sovereignty; Southern Democrats nominated John C. Breckenridge on a platform calling for the enforcement of the Dred Scott Decision on 1857. In that case, Dred Scott, a black slave, had sued for his freedom on the grounds that his master had taken him for a time into free territory. In that decision the Supreme Court ruled that a slave, not being a citizen, could not bring suit in federal court. Chief Justice Roger B. Taney, who wrote the majority decision, even went so far as to state that: (1) slaves were property; (2) Congress could not deprive any person of the right to take property into the territories of the United States; and (3) the Missouri Compromise of 1820 was unconstitutional since it prohibited taking slaves into the Louisiana Territory north of $36°30'$. The South applauded the Dred

Table 4.2: Major Economic Differences Between North, South, and West

NORTH	SOUTH	WEST
1. Supported the protective tariff to protect its manufacturers against external competition.	1. Opposed the protective tariff because it made the price of goods purchased by the South more expensive.	1. Was not unanimous on the question of the protective tariff. While it wanted a prosperous market in the North for its products, it disliked the higher prices on manufactured goods.
2. Favored the Second United States Bank in order to ensure a stable currency and to provide capital for investment purposes.	2. Opposed the Second United States Bank because, as an agricultural and debtor region, the South wanted cheap money.	2. Also opposed the Second United States Bank because, as an agricultural and debtor region, the West wanted cheap money.
3. Favored improved routes to Western markets, yet disliked the additional taxes necessary to build roads and canals. Overall, was divided on the question of internal improvements at federal expense.	3. Opposed internal improvements at federal expense, because the South had satisfactory water routes to its markets in the North and Great Britain, and had little need of routes to the West.	3. Favored internal improvements at federal expense to provide roads and canals for sending Western agricultural surpluses to Northern markets and seaports.
4. Supported immigration to provide labor for Northern factories.	4. Opposed unlimited immigration, because the immigrants settled in the North and West, thereby reducing the influence of the South in the federal government.	4. Supported immigration to provide settlers for Western lands.
5. Opposed territorial expansion, particularly to the Southwest, because the increase in the number of slave states challenged the influence of the North in the federal government.	5. Supported territorial expansion to the Southwest in order to replenish its supply of lands, which became degraded by continuous cotton cultivation.	5. Supported territorial expansion to provide additional sources of cheap, fertile land.

Scott decision, while the North denounced it in very strong terms.[18] On the other hand, the Republican Party nominated Abraham Lincoln on a platform of opposition to the extension of slavery in the territories, with the promise not to interfere with slavery in the states. The split in the Democratic Party gave the election to Lincoln. He received a majority in the electoral college, although he polled only 40 percent of the popular vote.

To the South, the election of Lincoln was an outrage because they viewed him as a black Republican. The consequence was immediate secession by South Carolina from the Union. Overall, the basic causes of the Civil War were economic, political, and social. The economic differences were reflected in the fact that geographical conditions determined that the North became an industrial region and the South an agricultural region. These economic differences in turn produced bitter regional rivalry on such issues as the protective tariff, the United States Bank, and slavery. Slavery was the most explosive of these issues, since it denied human freedom and violated democratic ideals. A second basic cause of the war revolved around the nature of the federal Union. The South claimed that the federal Union was a compact among the states, and that any state had a right to secede from the Union. The North, on the other hand, insisted that the Union was created by the people as "one nation indivisible" and that no state had the right to secede. Lincoln himself had stated that the Civil War was the struggle over control of the central government. Both the North and South realized that control of the central government would pass to the section that gained the Western region's support. Consequently, the South favored and the North opposed the extension of slavery into the Western territories.[19] With the passage of time, Western interests and Northern interests became linked economically, and primarily by a network of railroads and a mutually beneficial exchange of goods and services. The South, on the other hand, perceived that it was becoming increasingly marginalized and threatened economically by this growing integration between North and South. It became increasingly obvious that: (1) most Western lands were unfavorable for cotton culture, (2) the South was losing the battle for Western support, and (3) the South would remain a peripheral section in the Union. Finally, the clash of worldviews and civilizations between the North and South contributed to the war. Southern culture was based on a small aristocracy of influential planter families whose Southern society was more static than dynamic. In the North, on the other hand, society was more democratic and dynamic. The differences between the two regions resulted in a clash of civilizations and made understanding of respective views almost impossible. Extremists on both sides did not help matters, because instead of compromise and cooperation, extremism dominated relations. While the South emphasized sectional loyalty, the North insisted on national loyalty. The result was civil war.

Relative Deprivation and the Civil Rights Struggles in the United States

Relative deprivation as a pattern of rising and/or declining satisfaction has also been used to explain the conditions of African Americans after 1940. In general antigovernment protests and rebellion directed at governments have underlying cause, and are therefore not random occurrences. They are, in large part, the overt manifestations of the struggle for power and influence between groups, or between groups and the government. During the 1960s, for example, no less than six million Americans engaged in political activities ranging from violent demonstrations to riots and terrorism. At the same time, the great majority of them participated in protest activities that were both legal and peaceful. According to T. R. Gurr:

> In the minority of events that were violent, an estimated 350 people died and more than 12,000 were reported injured. Nearly 100,000 people were arrested, most of them for rioting or looting, but many others for protest activity that exceeded the varying limits of official tolerance.[20]

American society in the 1960s was first galvanized by civil rights demonstrations, or freedom struggles, until after 1965 when protests and mobilization centered around the Vietnam War. Overall, the 1960s were characterized by the Free Speech Movement at the University of California, Berkeley, campus in 1963, and the more violent episodes at San Francisco State in 1968 to 1969, Columbia University in spring 1969, and Kent State University in May 1970.

Many would argue that the Supreme Court decision in Brown versus Board of Education of Topeka acted as the catalyst for further civil rights demands. These demands were especially accelerated when in December 1955, Rosa Parks of Montgomery, Alabama, defied the Southern custom that required blacks to give seats toward the front of buses to whites. Roughly five years later, in February 1960, four freshmen at North Carolina Agricultural and Technical College began a wave of student sit-ins designed to end segregation at Southern lunch counters. These protests became widespread all over the South and resulted in the founding of the Student Nonviolent Coordinating Committee (SNCC) in April 1960.[21] Martin Luther King Jr. became the most effective leader in the civil rights movement because of his skillful use of methods of boycott and nonviolent tactics. His combination of idealism, militancy, and passive resistance helped bring about passage of the Civil Rights Act of 1964. What started in Montgomery with Rosa Parks resulted in the creation of a new regional organization, the Southern Christian Leadership Conference (SCLC), dominated by the clergy, and with Martin Luther King Jr. as its president.

Civil rights activism was targeted at especially the states of Georgia, Alabama, and Mississippi, not just by the SNCC and SCLC, but also by the predominantly white Congress of Racial Equality (CORE) and the National

Association for the Advancement of Colored People (NAACP). In particular, the SNCC's activities targeted the rural and predominantly black areas of Southern states, where white resistance to desegregation and equality was intense. All of the civil rights organizations emphasized voter registration, thereby laying the foundation for sustained black political activity in later years. In many instances political activism escalated into radicalism and violence as manifested in the belief in racial separatism that increasingly characterized the SNCC during the second half of the 1960s. In 1966, for instance, the Black Panther Party was formed by Huey Newton and Bobby Seale. The combined efforts of the SCLC and SNCC were responsible for major Alabama protests in 1965. Violent confrontations between protesters and police caused hundreds of civil rights sympathizers to converge in Selma, Alabama. Soon after the Selma to Montgomery march, Congress passed the Voting Rights Act of 1965, which enabled many southern blacks to register to vote.[22] With the Voting Rights Act, white support for civil rights diminished substantially.

By the late 1960s, the occasional open conflicts of the mid-1960s between civil rights organizations became more open and widespread because of strong challenges from new militant organizations such as the Black Panther Party. As a result of the radicalism of the Panthers, a number of major rebellions erupted during the second half of the 1960s. Radical black civil rights activists were heavily influenced by the black nationalism of Elijah Muhammad and Malcolm X, and by radical pan-Africanism, which viewed the struggle of all black people in the world as a struggle for total liberation from white oppression and repression. After the 1960s, civil rights as a source of violent protests, riots, and rebellion gave way to the Vietnam War protests.

Psychocultural Factors and Ongoing Conflicts

In terms of ongoing conflicts, the Northern Ireland conflict has a large element of psychocultural factors. For instance, in Northern Ireland parades have been interpreted as essentially celebrations of in-group solidarity (Protestants versus Catholics) and therefore manifestations of domination and triumph by Protestants in relation to the resistance and resentment expressed by the Catholic minority. Protestant parades celebrate past victories such as the Battle of Boyne in 1689 when William of Orange's Protestant forces defeated the army of Catholic King James II. Events like parades, with their religious nature, hardly helped to bring members of the two communities together to celebrate a shared experience or cooperate on mutual problems. It has been reported instead that more than 3,000 parades are held in Northern Ireland each year, with the vast majority (over 70 percent) exclusively Protestant in a population size of only 1.5 million.[23]

Parades in Northern Ireland aggravate cultural and political differences, resulting in tensions and anger, as well as increased sectarian feelings. In particular, parades heighten provocation and produce strong emotional responses when they traverse neighborhoods of the rival group. For example, Protestant parades through Catholic working-class neighborhoods have often resulted in violence and death. The parades are part of a psychocultural contest that divides the two groups in Northern Ireland. This division, which has produced emotionally charged situations, has resulted in or perpetuated a condition of competing and unresolvable claims underlined by suspicions and fears of each other. The parades, in other words, reinforce cultural solidarity within groups, but at the same time aggravate out-group competition and prolonged conflict.

Furthermore, because ethnic conflicts, in particular, are subject to psychocultural interpretation, the element of perception or misperception is integral to them. Illusion and distortion based on cultural differences mean that the parties to the conflict operate from different frames of reference. The facts, explanations, and prescriptive aspects of the conflict are often plagued by disagreements. At the same time, grievances and in-group memory are hardly separated into past and present because older grievances can conveniently be indexed to newer ones based on political expediency. The fact that issues are invested with emotional significance makes even what would seem the most trivial issue to an outside observer, no longer trivial, as interactions are viewed in terms of group self-esteem and legitimation.[24] Issues invested with emotional fervor result in rigid and uncompromising attitudes, thereby making it difficult to arrive at conflict resolution. In zones of prolonged ethnic conflict collective/group memory tends to link past experiences with present courses of action underlined by strong emotions. In Northern Ireland, Protestants invoke scenes of past massacres of their group as a rationale for their current resistance. Serbs likewise invoke images of marauding Turks during the Serbian defeat in 1389 as a reason to push for the creation of a greater Serbia. Jewish collective memory underscores episodes of the destruction of the temple and the Holocaust. The selective emphasis is, to say the least, mutually exclusive of each other's concerns, fears, and suspicions. In Northern Ireland, while the Protestants underscore the story of William of Orange and of the Battle of Boyne in 1689, the Catholics ignore it and instead emphasize the meaning of the 1916 Easter Uprising, which for Protestants has little or no significance.

Conflicts based on such strong psychocultural elements—divisive historical experience, contemporary identity, and suspicions and fears about an opponent—become prolonged and intractable because over time they produce cultural claims, threats, and/or rights that solidify and assume the character of nonnegotiable issues. This means that as the conflict is prolonged, new issues crop up that tend to divide the competing communities even further. Examples abound in the Arab-Israeli conflict regarding the status of Jerusalem, the building of new Jewish homes in occupied lands, or Israel's opening an archaeological tunnel under the Muslim holy sites in Jerusalem. In the United States, there is the conflict over flying the Confederate flag in some Southern states, in particular, over the South Carolina state capitol. In African states such as Zimbabwe or Kenya, there are ethnically based land claims that have produced strong cultural and political claims to land now occupied by European settlers.

In sum, conflicts underlined by psychocultural factors are: (1) emotionally charged and therefore explosive, volatile, and intractable; (2) rigidly polarizing resulting in uncompromising postures and mutually exclusive objectives; and (3) characterized by a strong linkage of a group's past experiences to its ongoing struggle against the rival group. They are a classic example of in-group/out-group incompatibilities, fears, and suspicions. Similar to the psychocultural approaches discussed above are explanations that either focus on innate (genetic), or environmental factors, or a combination of the two.

Innate versus Environmental Explanations

Explanations of human aggression or collective political violence can also be categorized in terms of explanations that emphasize either instinctivist behavior, environmental causes, or behaviorism. Stated differently, explanations of aggressive outbursts fall into either genetic (innate) causes, environmental influences, or a mixture of the two. In *The Ego and the Id* (1923) Sigmund Freud put forward an instinctivist explanation of human behavior manifested in a duality of human nature: life instinct(s) (Eros) versus death instinct(s) (Thanatos). According to Freud:

> Starting from speculations on the beginning of life and from biological parallels I drew the conclusion that, besides the instinct to preserve living substance, there must exist another, contrary instinct seeking to dissolve those units and to bring them back to their primeval, inorganic state. That is to say, as well as Eros there was an instinct of death.[25]

Freud argues that extreme forms of human aggression such as homicide and suicide are the result of a struggle between a death instinct (Thanatos) found in everyone, and a life instinct (Eros).[26] This conclusion is based on the premise that humans have in them a lust for hatred and destruction. Both instincts are expressions of a more basic drive—"the pleasure principle"—that produces in humans a motivation to eliminate all pain and do away with all desire. When the pleasure principle is expressed through the death instinct, it leads to suicide. But if it is counteracted by Eros, it results in the displacement of the death instinct onto others in the form of aggression that could even result in homicide. For Freud, peace can be ensured by suppressing the natural interplay of these basic instincts. They should instead be expressed in human creativity and love, or constructive activities such as sports. The family, church, state, or even world government, according to Freud, should intervene to control the tendency toward world anarchy.

Similar to Freud's instinctivist theory is Konrad Lorenz's (1966) *On Aggression*, which argues that human propensity for violence is due to biological factors beyond man's ability to control.[27] This is because the human being is characterized by a continuous accumulation of energy that is occasionally released in the form of violent behavior. The continuous buildup and flow of energy is not necessarily the result of reaction to environmental factors. Violent explosive behavior is likely to occur when enough energy has been accumulated regardless of the absence of stimulus. In other words, the pent-up energy does not depend on external stimuli in order to find expression, although it is usual for either man or animal to find a target (stimuli) at which to direct the violence. Lorenz also argues that aggression is instrumental in the survival of the individual and of the species. He also assumes that intraspecific aggression, or aggression among members of the same species, helps to maintain the balance between individuals of the species and the available habitat. This is accomplished largely through violence that favors the fittest over the weakest, and also ensures the maintenance of a social rank order. For Lorenz aggression is not a threat but a means of survival.

Konrad Lorenz and Edward O. Wilson, who holds a view similar to that of Lorenz, have been criticized for generalizing their observations of insects and animals to human beings.[28] For instance, they ignore the role of sociopolitical and economic circumstances of man's own making in aggression. They also do not make any distinction between defensive and offensive aggression. The former depends on external stimuli, such as a threat to vital interests, before it can erupt. It is therefore not spontaneous or independent. Many conflict theorists would find it difficult to accept that man is naturally endowed with an innate force to destroy. Moreover, does innate aggression, if there is any such thing, serve the survival of the individual and the species? Lorenz's prescription for dealing with human aggression is through athletics or competitive sports. However, sports could be the source of rivalry, misplaced nationalism, and violence. The 1980s and 1990s were characterized by a series of hooliganism in soccer games. Before those decades the world witnessed the massacre of the Israeli Olympic team during the 1972 Munich Olympic games. There have been many more instances of athletic or sports violence that made the global headlines.

Those theorists who argue that environmental conditions are largely responsible for human aggression hold the opposite position to instinctivists.

According to them, human behavior is exclusively determined by the influence of the environment: social and cultural factors as opposed to "inborn" ones. The most extreme formulation of aggression as molded by sociocultural factors was argued by the philosophers of the Enlightenment such as Jean-Jacques Rousseau. Humans, according to these philosophers, were born "good" and rational and it was the combination of bad institutions, bad education, and bad example that resulted in aggressive and evil tendencies. Similar to the arguments of environmentalism are those of behaviorists who downplay and even ignore the subject dimension (feelings or impulses) to analyze human passions or actions that motivate human behavior. According to behaviorists, it is reinforcement that entirely determines behavior.[29] As a result, they downplay the notion of a "nature" of man as a useful tool to analyze various human passions. While they would support the view that the social structure can shape man, and that genetic endowment is important, they nonetheless argue that behavior is determined entirely by reinforcement. Reinforcement can occur in two ways: either through the normal cultural process, or through the stimulus-response structure, where the appropriate reinforcements produce desired behavior.

Erich Fromm in 1973 analyzed thirty primitive cultures from the standpoint of aggressiveness versus peacefulness. He then divided them into three categories: (1) system A or Life-Affirmative societies, (2) system B or Nondestructive-Aggressive societies, and (3) system C or Destructive societies.[30] In Life-Affirmative societies there is little or no hostility, violence, or cruelty among people. There is also an absence of crime, severe punishment, or a war-fighting mentality. Children are treated with love and kindness, and not subject to severe corporal punishment. Women equally experience love and are treated as equal to men as opposed to being exploited or humiliated. In such societies there is little envy, greed, or destructive competition. Corporate ownership of property predominates, as well as a general attitude of contentment, cooperation, trust, and confidence in others and especially in nature. In general such societies emphasize ideas, customs, and institutions as instruments for the preservation and sustenance of life in its entirely. Life-Affirmative societies are far more peaceful than the other two. Erich Fromm placed the Zuni Pueblo Indians, the Mountain Arapesh and the Bathouga, the Aranda, the Semangs, the Todas, the polar Eskimos, and the Mbutus in this category of peaceful life-affirming societies.

In the second category of Nondestructive-Aggressive societies are those that are neither completely peaceful, nor premeated by aggressiveness and war. While competition, hierarchy, and individualism are present, they are not destructive of society. In other words, while aggressiveness and war are normal occurrences, they do not predominate. Fromm identified fourteen groups that fall into this category of nondestructive aggression. Among

86 · Collective Political Violence

them are the Greenland Eskimos, the Bachigas, the Manus, the Samoans, the Kazaks, the Incas, and the Hottentots.

The third category, Destructive societies, is dominated by interpersonal violence, cruelty, destructiveness, and the like. Violence and treachery are found both within the tribe as well as directed outside. The entire atmosphere is one of hostility, tension, and fear. Unlike life-affirming societies, in destructive societies competition, individualism, hierarchy, and war making predominate. Examples of these societies are the Dobus, the Kwakiutl, the Haidas, the Aztecs, the Witotos, and the Ganda. According to Fromm, systems A and B are both life-affirming, while system C is cruel, sadistic, or destructive.

In his analysis of these societies, Erich Fromm was attempting to demonstrate that the instinctivist interpretation of human violence is not a strong argument. The fact that violence and cruelty are minimal in so many societies is an indication that "innate" passion is a weak determinant of aggressive behavior. Fromm also argues that because "the least-civilized societies like the hunter-gatherers and early agriculturalists show less destructiveness than the more-developed ones speaks against the idea that destructiveness is part of human 'nature'."[31] In other words, while violence, destruction, and cruelty are not a part of human nature they are nonetheless widespread and at times intense in human interactions.

Erich Fromm argues against the genetic or instinctivist explanation of violence. He maintains that aggression is more the result of social conditions than innate predisposition. In particular, he argues that malignant as opposed to defensive aggression needs to be controlled because it is expressed in the form of sadism and masochism. It is often alienated people who express malign aggression. Such people are usually also ready candidates for recruitment into nationalist organizations.

Anthropological Perspectives

Anthropological studies on violence are numerous. In particular, cultural anthropological studies related to conflict and violence in both state and nonstate societies focus on meaning systems, rituals and symbolism, language and communication, reciprocity and scarcity of resources, gender, and ethnicity and identity.[32] Under the general subject of cultural imperialism conflicts occur over material resources such as land, food, and commercial items. In addition to these are conflicts that revolve around beliefs such as witchcraft, revenge, and other factors. In preindustrial societies in particular, what determines whether war will ensue are cultural constraints and individual and collective behavior. According to C. A. Robarcheck, "warfare or nonviolence, like other behaviors, occur when they are perceived and selected from among a field of possible alternatives as viable means of achieving specific, largely culturally defined, goals."[33] In other words, while economic deprivation or struggle over resources may count as a factor in warfare, often warfare is more related to purely cultural factors. Accordingly, some types of conflict are manifested in the form of tournaments. Their objective is to acquire prestige, or to satisfy some religious imperative. Head-hunting among the Marind-Anim of New Guinea was undertaken for two related reasons: to satisfy a religious imperative and to increase fertility and population through the capture of children.

However, warfare in many nonstate societies is also partly determined by influences and interactions with external state actors or societies. For example, the construction of ethnicities or "tribal" groups produce not only interethnic animosities, but are responsible for many of the violent conflicts that abound in Africa today. The favored policy of European powers toward native peoples was divide and conquer. Colonialism exacerbated the differences between Hutu and Tutsi, or between the Baganda in Uganda and other societies, among many others. If it is not indigenous intersocietal wars that are aggravated, it is often the hostile reaction of societies that are invaded, leading to warfare between the invaders and local people. In the case of the Yonomami, R. B. Ferguson argues that their aggressiveness was largely a result of European impingement on their society in the form of disease, different settlement patterns, and new wants, related to the increasing shortage of game.[34] The consequence was increased levels of tension in social groups. Thus, according to Ferguson, Yonomami culture and violent behavior has also been shaped by the external factors of European colonialism.

Whereas full-scale war is absent in many nonstate societies, there is often the prevalence of revenge behavior and feuding. In many societies, such as among the Melanesian, feud is often a way of avoiding full-scale warfare. Feuding could be interpreted as a form of institutionalized conflict that operates to maintain the social order because large-scale warfare could lead to a very dysfunctional society. The institutionalization of conflict behavior is also often manifested in symbols that carry messages, instigate social action, or define an individual's place within society. Along the same lines as symbolism—the expression or manipulation of symbolic forms and patterns of symbolic action—are communication patterns that deal with intracultural conflict through language. Edward Hall refers to speech communities that are either "high" or "low" context.[35] In the former, discourse is indirect, abstract, metaphorical, and based on broad frameworks, whereas in the latter, discourse is is direct, unambiguous, and precise.

In the area of cross-cultural negotiations, there is often a clash between systems of meaning and understanding predicated on symbolism. Raymond

Cohen, for example, argues that the continued failure in negotiations related to the Israelis and Egyptians for nearly fifty years was a result of their different conceptions of time, the role of violence, and the community.[36] These differences, which are social, cultural, and historical, impeded negotiations. Coupled with these differences were how the different styles of verbal communication complicated efforts to foster peace between the two countries.

Just as feuding in many simple societies is used to prevent large-scale warfare, so also is reciprocity used to reinforce the cohesion of society. In reciprocity corporate sharing is emphasized so that even small surpluses are shared with other members of a community. The give and take of scarce goods cements bonds of indebtedness between community members thereby reinforcing the cohesion of society. Accordingly, anthropologists have attempted to understand conflict through the concept of reciprocity. For example, how do societies negotiate and adapt during periods of resource scarcity? Does past reciprocal behavior enable societies to accommodate periods of resource scarcity? These questions are relevant because environmental degradation, natural disasters, and prolonged scarcity may challenge the reliability of reciprocity as a cohesion-enhancing method. For example, studies by Charles D. Laughlin and Ivan Brady show that during periods of extreme conditions, reciprocity is restricted, leading to more self-interested behavior.[37] Similarly, Colin Turnbull found that among the Ik of northeastern Uganda food sharing is restricted during times of severe and prolonged environmental crisis.[38]

Generally, preindustrial or simple societies are conflictual because of the presence of fraternal interest groups. These are power groups of related males perpetuated through the practice of polygyny—the practice whereby a man can have more than one wife. In other words, these are societies with the male supremacist complex. According to Keith F. Otterbein, societies with fraternal interest groups are characterized by extensive conflict, rape, feuding, internal war, and intraclan executions.[39] There is of course no society that neatly fits this pattern of behavior. The behaviors of rape, feuding, internal war, and capital punishment are interrelated because rape can lead to feud, and a feud can then escalate into an ambush or internal war. Otterbein also discusses societies without fraternal interest groups. These societies have little conflict, no rape, no feuding, no internal war, and community-wide executions. Again, this, like the fraternal interest group society, is an ideal type.

The extreme form of societies without fraternal interest groups may be peaceful societies as briefly discussed in chapter 3. These societies generally contradict the widespread notion that violence is a part of human nature. They are not as numerous as violent societies but they are found in various parts of the world. They include, among many others, the Amish of North

America, the Buìd of the Philippines and the Chewong of Malaysia. The general tendencies of peaceful societies are: small with egalitarian structures, relatively high gender equality, corporate ownership and sharing, and decision making through group consensus. Nonviolence is the foundation of their worldviews, values, attitudes, enculturation practices, and conflict resolution procedures.[40] According to Marc Ross, these peaceful societies have:

> Psychocultural practices which build security and trust; a strong linkage between individual and community interests and high identification with the community so that individuals and groups in conflict trust that its interests are their own; a preference for joint problem solving which leaves ultimate control over decisions in the hands of the disputants; available third parties (sometimes in the form of the entire community) to facilitate conflict management; an emphasis on the restoration of social harmony that is often at least as strong as the concern with the substantive issues in a dispute; the possibility of exit as a viable option; and strategies of conflict avoidance.[41]

The existence of peaceful, nonviolent societies strongly suggests that violence and war are not inevitable features of national and international society.

Notes

1. For a summary and critique of relative deprivation and related psychological theories, see James B. Rule, *Theories of Civil Violence* (Berkeley: University of California Press, 1988), chapter 7.
2. John Dollard et al., *Frustration and Aggression* (New Haven: Yale University Press, 1939).
3. John Dollard et al., *Frustration and Aggression*, p. 7.
4. For details, see Carl Houland and Robert Sears, "Minor Studies in Aggression, VI: Correlation of Lynchings and Economic Indices," *Journal of Psychology* 9 (1940): 301–10.
5. For details, see Leonard Berkowitz, "The Frustration-Aggression Hypothesis: An Examination and Reformulation," *Psychological Bulletin* 106 (1989): 59–73.
6. See, for example, Seymour Feshbach and Adam Fraczek, eds., *Aggression and Behavior Change: Biological and Social Processes* (New York: Praeger, 1979).
7. In particular, see Dalf Zillman, *Hostility and Aggression* (Hillsdale, NJ: L. Erlbaum Associates, 1979).
8. J. C. Davies, "Toward a Theory of Revolution," *American Sociological Review* 27 (1962): 5–19.
9. Ivo Feierabend and Rosalind Feierabend, "Systemic Conditions of Political Aggression: An Application of Frustration-Aggression Theory," in *Anger, Violence and Politics*, ed. Ivo Feierabend et al. (Englewood Cliffs, NJ: Prentice Hall, 1972).
10. See T. R. Gurr, "A Causal Model of Civil Strife: A Comparative Analysis Using New Indices," *American Political Science Review* 62 (1968): 1104–24.
11. For details on relative deprivation, see T. R. Gurr, *Why Men Rebel* (Princeton: Princeton University Press, 1970), chapter 2.
12. T. R. Gurr, *Why Men Rebel*, p. 52.
13. See J. C. Davies, "The J-Curve of Rising and Declining Satisfactions as a Cause of Revolution and Rebellion," in *Violence in America: Historical and Comparative Perspectives*, ed. Hugh Davis Graham and T. R. Gurr (Beverly Hills: Sage, 1979).
14. Aristotle, *The Politics*, ed. Ernest Barker (New York: Oxford University Press, 1958).
15. Alexis de Tocqueville, *The Old Regime and The French Revolution* (Garden City, NY: Doubleday, 1955), 177.
16. For further details, see among many other works, Timothy H. Donovan et al., *The American Civil War* (Wayne, NJ: Avery Pub. Group, 1987).

17. See, for example, Stephen B. Oates, *The Approaching Fury: Voices of the Storm, 1820–1861* (New York: Harper Collins Publishers, 1997).

18. For details, see Don E. Fehrenbacher, *The Dred Scott Case: Its Significance in American Law and Politics* (New York: Oxford University Press, 2001).

19. See, for example, B. Collins, *The Origins of America's Civil War* (London: Edward Arnold Ltd., 1981).

20. T. R. Gurr, "A Comparative Study of Civil Strife," in *The History of Violence in America: Historical and Comparative Perspectives*, ed. Hugh Graham and T. R. Gurr (New York: Praeger, 1969), 514.

21. See, for example, Clayborne Carson, *In Struggle: SNCC and the Black Awakening of the 1960s* (Cambridge, MA: Harvard University Press, 1981).

22. For details, see Taylor Branch, *Parting the Waters: America in the King Years, 1954–1963* (New York: Simon & Schuster, 1988).

23. For details, see N. Jarman, *Material Conflicts: Parades and Visual Displays in Northern Ireland* (New York: Berg, 1997).

24. See, for example, M. H. Ross, "Psychocultural Interpretation Theory and Peacemaking in Ethnic Conflict," *Political Psychology* 16 (1995): 523–44.

25. Sigmund Freud, "Civilization and Its Discontents," in *Standard Edition of the Complete Psychological Works of Sigmund Freud*, ed. J. Strachey (London: Hogarth Press, 1886–1939).

26. For more on this, see Erich Fromm, *The Anatomy of Human Destructiveness* (New York: Holt, Rinehart and Winston, 1973).

27. Konrad Lorenz, *On Aggression*, trans. Marjorie Kerr Wilson (New York: Harcourt Brace Jovanovich, 1974).

28. Edward O. Wilson, *On Human Nature* (Cambridge: Harvard University Press, 1978).

29. For details, see Erich Fromm, *The Anatomy of Human Destructiveness* (New York: Holt, Rinehart and Winston, 1973); and B. F. Skinner, *Science and Human Behavior* (New York: Macmillan, 1953).

30. Erich Fromm, *The Anatomy of Human Destructiveness*.

31. Erich Fromm, *The Anatomy of Human Destructiveness*, p. 177.

32. For details, see Christos N. Kyron, Jason Pribilsky, and Robert A. Rubinstein, "Cultural Anthropology Studies of Conflict," in *Encyclopedia of Violence, Peace, and Conflict*, Vol 1, ed. Lester Kurtz (San Diego: Academic Press, 1999), 89–99.

33. C. A. Robarcheck as quoted in Andrew J. Strathern and Pamela J. Steward, "Anthropology of Violence and Conflict," in *Encyclopedia of Violence, Peace, and Conflict*, Vol 1, ed. Lester Kurtz (San Diego: Academic Press, 1999), 94.

34. R. B. Ferguson, "Explaining War," in *The Anthropology of War*, ed. J. Haas (Cambridge: Cambridge University Press, 1990), 26–55.

35. For details, see Edward Hall, *The Silent Challenge* (Greenwich, CT: Fawcett Publications, 1969).

36. Raymond Cohen, *Culture and Conflict in Egyptian-Israeli Relations: A Dialogue of the Deaf* (Bloomington: Indiana University Press, 1990).

37. C. D. Laughlin and I. A. Brady, eds., *Extinction and Survival in Human Populations* (New York: Columbia University Press, 1978).

38. C. M. Turnbull, *The Mountain People* (New York: Simon and Schuster, 1972).

39. K. Otterbein, *Feuding and Warfare: Selected Works of Keith Otterbein* (New York: Gordon & Breach Science Publishers, 1994).

40. For more details, see Douglas P. Fry, "Peaceful Societies," in *Encyclopedia of Violence, Peace, and Conflict*, Vol 2, ed. Lester Kurtz (San Diego: Academic Press, 1999), 719–34.

41. Marc H. Ross, *The Culture of Conflict: Interpretations and Interests in Comparative Perspectives* (New Haven, CT: Yale University Press, 1993), 59–60.

Key Terms

aspirational relative deprivation	frustration-aggression hypothesis
conflict	in-group/out-group
conflict resolution	instrumental violence
decremental relative deprivation	progressive relative deprivation
frame of reference	relative deprivation
frustration	violence

Discussion Questions

1. What is relative deprivation? How is it related to frustration and aggression?
2. Discuss the American Civil War in terms of the frustration-aggression hypothesis.
3. Select one aspect of relative deprivation and discuss it in terms of the black struggle for civil rights.
4. What are the major criticisms of relative deprivation as a psychological interpretation of violent conflicts?
5. Compare and contrast innate and environmental explanations of violence.

CHAPTER 5

Collective Political Violence as Rational Choice

Rational choice explanations of collective political violence emphasize individual rather than collective interest as the motivation for participation in collective action to obtain a common objective. Such explanations are theoretically distinct from social-structural, functionalist, or other sociological theories of civil violence. Rational choice is an attempt to introduce utilitarian thought in the study of collective political violence and other social movements. According to utilitarianism, a doctrine developed by the English social philosopher Jeremy Bentham (1748–1832), every social institution was to be assessed by its usefulness (hence utilitarianism) in securing "the greatest good to the greatest number."[1] In particular, the good was to be recognized as anything that increased the pleasure or diminished the pain of any individual. Thus, organizations, associations, or clubs, among others, are pervasive in society to increase the good to its members.

Many economists and political scientists, among others, have examined interactions of self-interest decisions in the unfolding of collective actions. The purposeful collective efforts of labor unions, lobbies, social movements, or organizations in general are often analyzed in relation to their role in satisfying the interests of individual participants. The publication of Mancur Olson's *The Logic of Collective Action* in 1965 popularized and expanded the ways in which collective choices may come into conflict with individual ones.[2] According to Olson, the ubiquitous character of associations or organizations in society is directly related to the attempt by groups of individuals with shared or common interests to promote those interests. However, individuals within these associations do not always act to further common or group goals. The objective of many forms of group action is to obtain public goods. Public goods are usually contrasted with private goods. Private goods are characterized by two important attributes: excludability and depletability or exhaustibility.[3] In the first attribute, only those individuals who pay for the good can enjoy its benefits. For example, whoever did not pay for the express train service will not be allowed to use the express train. In the second attribute, the consumption of a private good, such as a loaf of bread, or gallon of gasoline, exhausts, either temporarily or permanently, the supply available for other people.

However, public goods have the attribute of nonexcludability. They are goods or services that, if provided to anyone, automatically cannot be withheld from others. Examples of public goods that are often cited are national defense, police protection, or a public park. A renovated or beautified public park benefits all citizens of a town. In other words, the improved conditions and aesthetics of the park are available to every citizen who decides to use the park. Similarly, whether or not a group of citizens pays taxes, the individuals in that group will automatically benefit from national defense if the country is under attack. A public good, unlike a private good, is not characterized by depletability. The conditions of a renovated and beautified public park are available to all who decide to use its facilities. In terms of definition, a public good is any commodity or service such that if anyone consumes it, it becomes difficult or impossible to exclude others from consuming it, even if they refuse to pay for it, and is such that even when consumed cannot be depleted.

In large groups, or when the potential number of participants to obtain the public good rises above a small number, it becomes irrational for any individual to participate in the collective effort to obtain the good. This is because whether or not one participates in obtaining the public good, one is sure to partake of the benefits of the collective good. In addition, as the number of potential beneficiaries rises, the likelihood that one's participation will make a difference between acquiring or failing to acquire the good is small. In other words, if we view the public good in terms of payment of fees, or participation in order to obtain it, what is known as the "free-rider" problem becomes evident. One individual of a large group or association will expect to enjoy the benefits of the public good regardless of whether he or she pays the required fees or participates in its provision.

There are thus two implications involved in public goods that constitute the free-rider problem. First, nonparticipants or nonpayers cannot be excluded from enjoying a public good, and providers of such goods will find it impossible or difficult to ensure full participation, or collect fees proportionate to the benefit they supply. If, for example, the state makes the payment of income taxes voluntary, how many will willingly pay taxes equal to one-tenth of their annual salary? Yet that amount may be necessary for the state to provide adequate police protection or national defense. In other words, no one will be willing to pay for services he or she can get free. Thus, the provision of public goods or nonexcludable goods like national defense or public health are the responsibility of the state. Private enterprises are therefore not in the business of public goods because they are goods no one will pay for since they can be received free. Second, providing an additional user a public good costs almost nothing because the provision of a public good is not depleted by an additional user. In other words, the zero marginal cost involved in providing public goods and services makes it often impossible to charge a market price for a public good. It is often also undesirable to charge a market price.

The free-rider problem accounts for the large numbers of shared interests that are never seriously pursued or acted upon. Just because individuals share a common interest in obtaining a particular public good does not necessarily mean they will cooperate in collective action to secure that good. The reason is the individual cannot rationally believe that his or her contribution will make a difference in either obtaining or failing to obtain the collective good. Thus, according to Olson, collective action will only occur when selective incentives, or inducements, that can be given to or withheld from participants individually are utilized. Positive incentives (promises or rewards) and negative incentives (threats, coercion, or punishment) are central to the individual's willingness or refusal to participate in procuring the public good.

Rational Choice and Political Violence

Olson's work has little directly to say about collective political violence, but his analysis has a great deal of relevance for individual decision to engage in such activities. Revolutions, riots, civil wars, interethnic conflicts, and rebellions in general are activities that are usually considered to be efforts to secure public goods for members of the affected groups. Yet if one is to apply Olson's logic to them, then one would conclude that participants in revolutionary movements, for example, are more likely to be motivated to participate on a large scale if personal gain can be distinctly separated from the indivisible public good likely to be acquired. In the absence of such individual (personal) gain, the willingness to participate will be low because violent actions such as revolutions or rebellions against the state are generally supposed to be efforts to produce a collective outcome.

Participation in revolutionary activity is infrequent because people are reluctant to incur the cost of participation in a revolution. Average people have generally been socialized into tolerating the status quo.[4] They may also consider revolutionary action futile and risky, or view the existing order of things to be beyond their control. Where negative incentives are absent, the individual is presented with one of two choices: (1) either to actively participate in the revolutionary movement, or (2) to abstain from participation or engage in free-riding with the full knowledge that if success is the outcome, he or she will still consume the public good (the revolution). If everyone opts for free-riding, then the revolution will not succeed.

A rational individual who does not like incurring costs (loss of life, limb, or injury to family members), and in the absence of negative incentives, would be better off not to participate, whether or not other individuals do. Those who ultimately engage in revolutionary action do so on the basis of rational (cost-benefits) analysis. Individuals engage in revolutionary activity because they derive some personal gain—such as a personal conviction that most people in society would fare much better under a revolutionary regime. Leaders of revolutionary movements (such as Lenin, Mao, or Castro, etc.) would obviously not need to be encouraged by rewards or threatened to participate in pursuit of the public good (the revolution). The idea of effecting a revolution is often their brainchild. It is their actions and fervor that give shape and momentum to the movement, and their participation has a substantial impact on the realization of their respective revolutions.

Rational choice theory as an individual interest theory of public action is characterized by "selective incentives" as a requirement to explain participation in the pursuit of public goods. According to Morris Silver, the factors involved in such a self-interest theory of collective political violence are the following: (1) either net gain or loss to the individual from participation rather than free-riding, or remaining neutral; (2) the individual is given a private reward in the form of income, power, and status for his participation if the revolution succeeds; (3) revolutionary victory is likely even if the individual free-rides or remains neutral; (4) should the revolution fail, a private penalty as a cost for participation is imposed on the individual for participation; (5) the individual risks probable injury through participation in revolution; (6) injury could be incurred while participating; (7) psychological or emotional gratification from participation takes the form of duty to country (for example, the American Revolution), class, race, humanity, God, or simply on the taste for conspiracy, violence, and adventure; and (8) involved in the decision whether or not to participate is the value of participant's time and other resources.[5]

Participation in Political Violence as Strategic Calculus

The previous analysis that falls in the realm of game theory assumes that participants in a revolution or any form of collective political violence will seek to maximize their gains or to minimize their losses. Rationality in this sense is defined in terms of utility maximization and disutility minimization. In game-theoretic language, this rule of rational behavior is referred to as the minimax principle.

According to many studies, in great revolutions and other political upheavals a significant proportion of the population participates in the revolutionary activities that lead up to the actual overthrow of the incumbent regime. A controversial and important question in rational choice theory is: Why do individuals from various socioeconomic classes participate?

Many political economists or decision theorists would conclude that the probability that a given individual would be the decisive participant in a significant revolution was remote, so remote in effect that a rational individual would never find it in his or her own interest to participate on instrumental grounds. As a result, a number of explanations for participation in collective political violence are often given. These include citizen duty to country, race, or humanity, minimax regret (the need to avoid substantial regret in case one's participation would have been decisive), private consumption value, the monitoring of participation and sanctions for not participating, and individual participant utility depending on the margin of revolutionary victory as well as victory itself.[6]

The act of revolutionary participation itself has costly effects. Individuals, then, must weigh the cost of participating against its potential benefits. In decision-theoretic terms, a rational individual will participate in revolutionary activities if and only if the potential benefit of participating exceeds the costs.

Another assumption emphasized is that the benefits are determined by two factors: (1) the probability that one's participation is decisive (it makes a difference in the outcome of the revolt), and (2) the increase in utility to the participant when his or her participation is in fact decisive. If the cost of participation is relatively high and the probability of a decisive participation is very low, then a rational individual who may not want to incur costs may choose not to participate even if the individual has strong preferences between the two alternatives.

The individual who considers the high cost of participation may be better off if he does not participate, regardless of whether others do or not. This is especially the case if the individual does not want to incur the cost (arrest, incarceration, or even death) of participation. If the revolution succeeds, he or she would still enjoy the benefits of the revolution since the revolution is like a collective good. The individual would thus be better off as a free-rider.[7]

However, in cases where participation is decisive and would maximize utility because of the expectation of private benefits and the probability of significantly affecting the outcome of the revolution, both leaders and some followers in particular might feel that their participation is very significant to the success of the revolution. They could be motivated by either the expectation of private reward or simply love of country, or both.

In addition, if there are many individuals participating, the probability that an individual is decisive must be incredibly small. Hence the rational individual may be tempted not to participate. However, the individual may derive direct psychological benefit from participation regardless of the outcome. If this direct benefit (psychological satisfaction) is greater than the cost of participating, then participating is not irrational and, in fact, is rational if the individual does not care what the outcome of the revolution is. On the other hand, the individual might believe that his or her participation would profoundly affect the course of the revolution to the extent of offsetting the costs of participation. The individual in this situation is not affected by any paradox of not participating: the assumption being a significant level of participation with many able participants is inconsistent with rational behavior.[8]

A final assumption is to suppose that individuals are not concerned with the probability that their participation is decisive. Participants participate simply to avoid the possibility that if they remain neutral or free-ride the contest between revolutionaries and the incumbent regime ends in a stalemate, or if they realize that their participation would definitely have made a difference in favor of the revolutionaries, they will suffer substantial regret since their participation would have been decisive.[9] In this situation, participation is not motivated by private reward or fear of punishment, but by a fear of the possibility of psychological torment resulting from regret.

Table 5.1: Major Themes

---

1. A successful revolution is like procuring a public good; it is therefore impossible to exclude anyone from consuming it.
2. One is sure to enjoy the benefits of a public good, whether or not they pay for it.
3. People therefore tend to free-ride, or refrain from participating because they know they will enjoy the benefits without paying for it.
4. Incentives are central to the individual's willingness or refusal to participate in procuring the public good.
5. Incentives are of two kinds: negative (coercion, threats of punishment, etc.) and positive (promises of payments and other rewards).
6. Some children who participate in civil wars in developing countries do so out of rational choice: either because they are coerced, promised private benefits, seek revenge for psychological gratification, or they believe it is the only way they can survive.

Conclusion and Critique

For Olson, collective action satisfies "rationality" only when interests could be individually gratified. In other words, action is rational when it gratifies divisible interests of the individual—those interests that the individual can enjoy when no one else enjoys them. Conceivably, one's interests in overthrowing a regime might be divisible if satisfied by occupying a specific high office such as secretary to the revolutionary party. Olson limits his argument to desires such as wealth and pleasure, but excludes abstract causes or interests of broader humanity. Any action that is not likely to produce increased gratification for the individual would not be considered rational pursuit.

Moreover, Olson's argument does not seem to include a willingness on the part of the individual to risk his or her life in pursuit of some collective goal that does not include private reward. Self-interested behavior is assumed to be an integral aspect of collective political violence, absent which widespread participation to acquire collective goals is relatively infrequent.

Olson's theory is an attempt to critique Karl Marx's expectation of class solidarity and action arising out of shared misery on the part of the proletariat and collective action taken by them to end their misery and exploitation by the bourgeoisie. In Olson's logic, individual proletariats are not provided relative incentives and thus may not be willing to participate in revolutionary action. In Olson's own words:

> But even if Marx really had irrational emotional behavior in mind, his theory still suffers, for it is hard to believe that irrational behavior could provide the motive power for all social change throughout human history.[10]

However, when examined in terms of general social action, Olson's theory and critique of Marx are not supported by reality. In any society, people support and vote for issues (positions) they know will be defeated. Similarly, people are willing to die for causes they strongly believe in regardless of overwhelming state and societal opposition to such causes. Most people would not consider exercising one's conscience and supporting a belief, principle, or doctrine, even against great odds to be irrational behavior. Examples include contributing to charities that do not directly or materially benefit the beneficiary, or supporting a losing side based solely on principle. In other words, the affective domain, or emotional commitment by individuals to collective causes, is ignored in Olson's theory.

It is in the behavior of crowds that one can discern the simultaneous interplay of group emotions and rationality. In *La Foule* (the crowd), Gustave LeBon underscores the role of the unconscious and the irrational in political violence.[11] In his book LeBon makes reference to the "law of mental unity of crowds," or the idea that within a collective or crowd individuals take on some characteristics and behavior patterns that are quite distinct from their own. In particular the crowd develops a "collective mind" or even a collective psychosis in which the unconscious predominates, irrationality and emotionality are intensified, instincts dominate, violence pervades, and individuals behave as psychotic beings. The crowd environment can become so contagious that the individual immersed in it ends up losing his or her personal interest to the crowd or collective interest. In addition, crowds are characterized by impulse, irritability, impatience, and intolerance.

Freud is largely in agreement with LeBon because he also emphasizes the aggressiveness, irrationality, emotionality, unpredictability, and anarchistic behavior of crowds. However, Freud attributes these characteristics of group behavior mainly to the role of leadership.[12] Similarly, in George Rudé's *The Crowd in the French Revolution,* the focus is on two questions: (1) Who were the persons that turned out in the streets of Paris? and (2) What was their motivation?[13] With regard to the first question, Rudé found that the French Revolution did not just attract the sans-cullotes (urban poorer classes) but mostly middle class: owners, landlords, merchants, civil servants, shopkeepers, teachers, lawyers, and priests; and lower class: wage earners, journeymen, metal workers, dressmakers, cabinetmakers, shoemakers, builders, engravers, cooks, waiters, tailors, hairdressers, posters, and domestic servants. Thus, in terms of participation, the revolution attracted a large segment of the population.

With regard to the second question, Rudé emphasized the dynamics of political and economic forces. The political forces included the pull of the ideas embodied in the declaration of the rights of man and citizen, and of liberty, equality, and fraternity. In their totality they represented the revolt of the bourgeoisie and working class against the ancien régime. The economic forces were expressed in the people's clamor for basic human needs, especially food. These comprised the principal and most enduring motive of the revolutionaries. Rudé's conclusion is that revolutionary crowds are comprised of men and women motivated by new political ideas and by the imperative of economic necessity.

Similarly, in Dirk Hoerder's *Crowd Action in Revolutionary Massachusetts,* focusing on the period 1765 to 1780, the author also found that the class scope of participation was extensive.[14] Merchants, artisans, laborers, farmers, landlords, owners, lawyers, teachers, priests, and politicians crowded together and revolted. Their grievances were endless and targeted British acts, duties, and taxes. Crowd action encompassed both the urban centers and rural areas. The struggle for liberty, property, and natural rights transcended individual and class differences. Whatever individual rationalities existed were subsumed by one unifying factor—taxation—since all colonials were affected by taxes.

Finally, in most empirical studies of leaders and followers examined by Mostafa Rejai and Kay Phillips, the general conclusion is that participants or followers are normal individuals from both the middle and lower classes who are motivated by political ideals and by the economic necessities of life.[15] Thus, crowd action is rational and understandable. In other words, the crowd can be both emotional and rational at the same time.

The Rational Actor and Game Theory

Rational-choice explanations of collective political violence are predicated on the assumption that, in general, individuals are first and foremost rational beings capable of making rational choices and decisions. In other words, the notion of rationality implies that actors engaged in conflict have a definite and clear idea of the outcome desired and therefore pursue it in the most efficient way possible. While rational-choice theory could be applied to situations of actual conflict as in revolutions or civil wars, it could also be applied to situations of conflict resolution. In both cases, rationality is maximizing behavior or efficiency, or considering all alternatives in order to choose the option that ensures the desired outcome. In the process of making a rational choice, the adversaries are confronted with conflicting options or insufficient or inaccurate information, which tend to increase the degree of uncertainty involved in making decisions or choices.[16] Stated differently, choices made within the context of whether or not to participate in say, insurgency against the government in power, or to negotiate with an adversary in order to arrive at resolution of a conflict, are choices underlined by uncertainty because social systems are unpredictable and the future is almost never certain.

In game theory, the rational actor is faced with a great deal of uncertainty because of the rational choice involved in the various possible acts the actor will choose depending on the structure of the game. Anatol Rapoport, the game theorist, classifies conflicts into three types: "fights," "games," and "debates." Each type has different background criteria, a different pattern of development, and different distribution of outcomes that are predictable.[17] Fights are based on action-reaction processes as in a dogfight, schoolyard fight, or interstate wars, because the actions of each actor serve as starting points for similar counteractions by the other actor. In arms races between two rival nations, for example, one nation tries to outdo the other in terms of expenditure to the point where their defense budgets experience a significant increase each year. In other words, fight-type conflict processes tend to be automatic and emotional, until they escalate into mindless savagery, unless there is a decelerating effect that introduces self-restraint into the process.

In debates, the rivals or adversaries are attempting to change each other's images of reality, motivations, and values. They involve a process of competitive interests and preferences toward a decision that could be accepted by both or all parties as being in their interests. Examples are arms control negotiations or international trade negotiations over tariffs and other preferences. According to Karl Deutsch, one outcome of debates is the principle of mutually acceptable restatement:

> According to this principle, a debate is more likely to lead to the discovery of a mutually acceptable and beneficial solution if each side finds out what the other side is actually saying—that is, if it learns to state for itself the case of its adversaries in a form so clear and appealing as to be acceptable to these adversaries themselves.[18]

Generally, debates involve recognizing and acknowledging the validity of views, as well as the effort made on the part of each rival to convince the other of the truth of its own views.

Games are characterized by strategy and are therefore rational because the actor or player maintains control over his or her own moves, and not necessarily over their outcomes because of the uncertainty and unpredictability involved in events and the wider system in general. Examples of activities characterized by rationality and strategy are games such as poker, bridge, chess, and checkers on the one hand, and in terms of wider systemic activities, war diplomacy, politics, and business competition on the other. Games can take two general forms: zero-sum games and games of partial conflict. Zero-sum games are also referred to as games of total conflict or fixed-sum games, and partial-sum games are nonzero games or variable sum games. In the former, the sum of all payoffs (benefits) to all players equal zero, meaning that anything that one player wins is a loss for the rival player. In the latter case (variable sum games), players not only win something competitively from one another, but are also collectively liable to gain or lose something from an additional player. In other words, in zero-sum games the gains of one player are automatically the losses of another, whereas in non-zero-sum games there is the possibility of mutual beneficial cooperation for all players involved.

Three types of games commonly analyzed in the literature on game theory and international relations are: the games "chicken," the "prisoners' dilemma," and "assurance," which is less widely known than the first two. The game of chicken captures mixed-motive conflict situations and involves mutual threats. In this game two players drive their cars on a remote road and accelerate at high speed straight toward each other. The first player or driver to swerve from the middle of the road in order to avoid a head on collision is referred to as "chicken" and ridiculed and held in contempt by the rest of the gang. The more courageous or reckless driver, who refused to avoid a head-on collision is regarded by them as a hero. In the real world of international politics, major powers in dispute at times threaten each other with deadly force, or even all-out war, and the use of nuclear weapons.

In the game of chicken, each of the two players can choose between two strategies: either cooperate with the other player by swerving to avoid collision, but with the possibility of being disgraced if he should be the first to swerve before the rival player, or defect from their common interest in survival and drive straight at each other to their mutual death, unless one swerves before the other. In other words, each player has control over whether he will cooperate or defect, but the outcome of his decision depends also on the decision taken by his rival.

Table 5.2 represents the game of chicken, where player I chooses between the rows and player II between the columns. C denotes the cooperative option and D the defect option. The pairs of numbers in brackets represent the payoffs or gains to each of the two players, with the first number representing the gain to player I and the second to player II. This means that in Table 5.2, if player I plays the cooperative (C) and player II plays the defect (D) strategy, player I will get a gain or payoff of 1 unit of benefit, while II will get a gain of 4 units. Mutual defection and mutual cooperation gives them the same payoffs or gains. The CC point can be regarded as the best point for both combined. Since the option and knowledge of mutual defection (DD) is a possibility, it is therefore likely to get a situation of effective deterrence.

The prisoners' dilemma is a game that involves threats and promises. In comparison to the game of chicken, it is more realistic. The story goes like this: there was once a governor of a prison who had two prisoners whom he could not execute without a voluntary confession from at least one. He therefore ordered that one prisoner be brought before him. He offered this first prisoner his freedom and a sum of money if he would confess to the crime at least a day before the second prisoner did so, so that the second prisoner could be convicted for the crime and be executed. However, if the second prisoner could confess at least a day before him, then that prisoner would be freed and rewarded, and he (the first prisoner) would be executed. But if both of them confess the same day, they will each be spared of execution and get ten years in prison. If neither of them confesses, then both will be set

Table 5.2: Chicken

		PLAYER II	
		C	D
Player I	C	(3,3)	(1,4)
	D	(4,1)	(0,0)

Table 5.3: Prisoners' Dilemma

		PLAYER II	
		C	D
Player I	C	(3,3)	(1,4)
	D	(4,1)	(2,2)

free without any reward. In the end, the governor told the first prisoner to beware because his fellow prisoner was a crook who might hurry to confess so that he would pocket the reward. After the first prisoner was returned to his cell to think about his answer, the second prisoner was summoned by the governor and told the same. Now each of them will spend the night alone to ponder the dilemma and arrive at a choice.

Table 5.3 represents the prisoners' dilemma, with the top left-hand entry being the mutually beneficial one for both players. There is, however, a strong temptation by either player to defect with the possibility of a (C D) outcome.

While chicken and prisoners' dilemma are widely known, the game of assurance is not. It is not the subject of much analysis, perhaps because the outcomes are obvious since there is no lack of information or uncertainty about what the other player or a rival might do. Each player has full information, knows his payoff and that of his rival. This means that an action or defection by one player will be responded to by a similar defection by the rival player. However, assurance is the structure that would produce the highest level of cooperation. Chicken may be the most conflict prone and the most confused because an adversary does not know what policy or choice the other player might adopt.

Critics often argue that strictly zero-sum games are rare because a dispute that escalates into a war between adversaries could be transformed into a non-zero-sum one where negotiations bring about cooperation and mutual benefits. However, in a situation where a conflict is viewed in strictly zero-sum terms—that is the dismissal of mutually beneficial elements in the conflict—there is very little that conflict resolution can do except to explore

Table 5.4: Assurance

		PLAYER II	
		C	D
Player I	C	(4,4)	(1,3)
	D	(3,1)	(2,2)

ways of getting the adversaries to think of some prospects of compromise. During the Cold War, some key American decision makers perceived the Cold War in zero-sum terms. Hardline American "hawks" perceived most Soviet moves as suspicious, self-interested, and therefore a loss for the United States in the geostrategic competition. Parallel behavior was to be found on the Soviet side. In general, however, variable sum games provide a great deal of insight into real life conflict processes.

Child Participation in Irregular Warfare as a Rational Choice

An integral aspect of the spillover of the Liberian civil war into Sierra Leone in 1991 and the rebel Revolutionary United Front's (RUF) challenge against the All People's Congress (APC) regime is the participation of child soldiers in the scope, intensity, and duration of violent conflict. A large portion of the irregular character of the war (looting, maimings, banditry, etc.) could be understood in terms of the role of child fighters and their voluntary and/or coerced participation in violent acts in particular.[19] The RUF sought to establish a mass base by attempting to recruit large numbers of local youth either through coercion or economic incentives. Thus the participation by child rebels, at times as young as ten years old, could be viewed as a rational choice on their part either because of positive incentives (promises) or negative incentives (threats, coercion).

First, the young were at times seized and transformed into combatants (coercion as a reason for participation), and bullied to support the venture of the RUF. For example, Michael Johnny, an eleven-year-old coerced participant said: "The rebels killed my mother and father and took me along with them to be carrying their looted items on my head."[20] Often to obtain their loyalty, children are tortured or beaten into submission and forced to commit atrocities such as rape or murder as a form of initiation into a life of great cruelty.

Second, the lure or promise of economic incentives ensures child participation in war atrocities. The promise to redistribute stolen and looted goods, or monetary promises from the rebel leadership are used as a motivating factor for the capture of a major town. For example, a 22-year-old ex National Patriotic Front of Liberia (NPFL) fighter stated how easy it was to recruit young fighters for the Sierra Leone war because of the lure of economic gratification, after the end of the Liberian conflict found many of them idle and with no other opportunities. "President Taylor could not integrate us into the Liberian army and I thought coming to Sierra Leone to fight could have helped me out."[21] Other captured youth soldiers said they had been promised diamonds and gold by the deposed Armed Forces Revolutionary Council (AFRC) junta and Liberian officials. Thus, the intense struggle to control the diamond-rich east and southeast of Sierra Leone since 1991, and particularly after the ousting of the AFRC in February of 1998. The RUF leadership targets the diamond-rich regions because they are using them as a resource base to entice and maintain the thousands of young boys who perpetuate most of the violence in the war. In the Sierra Leone conflict, therefore, what began as struggle against an inept regime continues as disputes over control of resources and fruits of victory.

Often the decision to volunteer for economic incentives is not exercised freely, but is driven by socioeconomic factors. Hunger and poverty may drive parents to offer their children for service. On the other hand, children may believe that this is the only way to guarantee regular meals or shelter. Eventually, the child develops a sense of belonging with the rebel force that the impoverished family cannot provide. Thus, child soldiers overwhelmingly are recruited from the poorest and most marginalized sectors of society. Especially susceptible to recruitment are children without families or with disrupted family backgrounds. In Sierra Leone's conflict, the RUF included youth considered socially marginal. Recruitment to the movement was randomly done; for example, anyone who expressed interest in going to Libya for military and ideological training, regardless of competence or ideological fit, was recruited. The majority of those who trained in Libya were either from the loosely structured marginal classes, or those with a troubled social and educational background. Most of the RUF cadre and field commanders were from a category of society that could be described as rough and unruly youth, drug abusers, social deviants, and misfits. These were mostly school dropouts who despise the mainstream values of society and thus viewed the RUF venture as a way to boost their low self-esteem and thereby reverse their status in society.

For the young, war becomes self-perpetuating and eventually a way of life. Thus, another reason for child participation in war is that many of the young fighters know nothing other than the gun. These young ones continue war for no better reason than inertia. They know that no normal life is waiting for them back in their homes, which have been destroyed, or within a political system that has offered them no meaningful life. When this happens, war is not different from banditry. Viewing a life of conflict as a "meaningful" existence may attract volunteers among the impoverished young, the miserable, the starving, and people with no other prospects, no hope, and no reason for hope. In other words, for some, in addition to rebel service providing food, it provides psychological gratification: companionship, excitement, and respect. Apart from the necessity to escape from desperate conditions at home, some children join rebel groups and armed forces because of the prestige of wearing a uniform or for the feeling of doing something important. Related to psychological gratification, others have said they joined to avenge the death of a family member.

The capture and coercive treatment of the very young and their transformation into hardened fighters committing the most atrocious tactics is facilitated by the marginal ("lumpen") elements within the RUF who do not strongly identify with family and societal values. At an early age they exhibited deviant behavior often intensified by habitual drug abuse and the use of violence to resolve even the simplest problems. The rebel RUF leadership, in collaboration with these lumpen elements, use both alcohol and drugs to control the children. In the Liberian civil war, children were urged to take a mixture of cane juice (from sugar cane) and gunpowder, which made them callous to corpses and increased their bravery at the war front. This strategy was no doubt adopted by the RUF in Sierra Leone. The theory apparently is that if a child is intoxicated, he will become hardened and insensitive enough to jump over a fallen friend's body and still keep fighting.

Irregular warfare, especially where it relates to forces comprised of armed individuals or groups who are generally not members of the armed forces, has become heavily dependent on the use of child fighters. This is due to a number of reasons. First, the terrain in many of these conflicts makes it possible for children to operate in it effectively. It also impels rebel leaders to use children as burden bearers (loot carriers) in remote, rugged, or otherwise difficult terrain. Such terrain is usually not suitable to operations by modern forces because it limits their mobility and reduces their technological advantages. In the Sierra Leone conflict, the mobility of the RUF through woods, jungles, and tiny bushpaths impels them to use children in a wide variety of functions. They are often used in support roles as porters, messengers, and cooks.

Moreover, the level of violence in irregular warfare corresponds closely to the military capability of child soldiers. Children are better able to use basic weapons such as the AK-47 or assault rifle, machine guns, mortars, grenades, or land mines. In other words, the light weapon makes the child soldier within the RUF more effective because of ease of operation and the limited time it takes to train them to operate them. The advancement in modern materials and weaponry allow the construction of automatic rifles such as the M-16 or AK-47, which can be carried and operated by even a small child of seven. In addition, the international arms trade has made these assault rifles inexpensive and widely available to even the poorest communities. The consequence is that conflicts like the one in Sierra Leone are transformed into a perennial slaughter.

Child soldiers have increasingly become an integral part of irregular warfare because by its very nature such a conflict is primarily one in which resource mobilization for the war effort is based on options ranging from purchase, banditry, capture, or looting. Thus, the use of child soldiers by the RUF to raid, skirmish, or ambush. In both Liberia and Sierra Leone, warring factions induced children to join them by promising them food, clothing, money, and whatever they could loot from civilians. In the RUF, children who do not take part in actual fighting are used to transport loot and weapons. In general, the logistic requirements of the RUF are less formal, and are simple, irregular, and not heavily mechanized.

Children become an integral part of irregular warfare because such warfare is more heavily influenced by idiosyncratic factors (for example, that of the rebel leader or cadre, or that of children who join it) than by more systemic, widely held values, goals, or tactics. For example, the values, goals, or tactics of the RUF are still baffling, idiosyncratic, and remote to many Sierra Leoneans. Why maim people or burn their homes if the goal is to liberate them from a corrupt system? Thus, one is tempted to conclude that the RUF war is a war directed by a leadership for personal reasons rather than for reasons of liberation and self-determinance.

The lack of an overarching strategic war doctrine by the RUF may be responsible for the random, irrational, and incredible atrocities committed by its child soldiers. The child soldiers probably do not quite understand what they are fighting for because the RUF does not have a well-articulated doctrine. The RUF youth soldiers are used to fighting on their own terms, and based on their whims and caprices. This lack of a formal war doctrine spelling out what they are fighting for is largely responsible for the systematic atrocities perpetrated by the child soldiers.

Finally, in the African context, the use of child soldiers is enhanced because African cultures ingrain in children a respect for elders. Thus, children are easily bullied, manipulated, coerced, or convinced to participate in war because of this deeply held respect for age. In Liberia and Sierra Leone obedience is a strong cultural trait. Children generally do not question orders from elders because they have been raised to follow instructions. This cultural trait increased the use of children in the wars in both countries and intensified the level of violence they perpetrated.

In conclusion, violent actions by RUF child fighters will not occur on a large scale unless child participants are coerced by fear of punishment or death at the hands of their captors. Their atrocities are also widely supposed to be efforts to secure societal goods. Such actions would not occur on a large scale unless the youth participants were motivated by personal gain distinct from the indivisible collective gains (e.g., a new and better-ruled Sierra Leone) likely to be produced. The commission of atrocities is also a way for children to advance within the ranks. Boys are rewarded with ranks or responsibilities for special acts that usually involve some kind of atrocity.

Finally, the networks of social support for children in Sierra Leone has been undermined by the violent conflict that has been raging since 1991. In order to help reintegrate children into society, and prevent fresh eruptions of violence that directly impact children, the power elite need to: (1) help reverse abject poverty and marginalization of entire segments of youth, (2) institute a program of education with the objective of deindoctrination so that child soldiers are sensitized to atrocities and hostile behavior, and (3) reestablish the networks of social welfare between families and communities that have been destroyed by war, as well as by rapid urbanization and the spread of market-based values inimical to the extended family.

Notes

1. See Bhikhu Parekh, ed., *Bentham's Political Thought* (London: Croom Helm, 1973); and Geroge Soule, *Ideas of the Great Economists* (New York: New American Library, 1952).
2. Mancur Olson, *The Logic of Collective Action: Public Goods and the Theory of Groups* (Cambridge, MA: Harvard University Press, 1965).
3. For details, see, among others, William J. Baumol and A. S. Blinder, *Economics: Principles and Policy* (Fort Worth: Dryden Press, 1994).
4. For further details on the rational choice approach, see Barbara Salert, *Revolutions and Revolutionaries* (New York: Elsevier, 1976).
5. Morris Silver, "Political Revolution and Repression: An Economic Approach," *Public Choice* 1 (fall 1971): 89–99.
6. Many of these explanations are common in analysis of voting behavior. For details, see Thomas R. Palfrey and Howard Rosenthal, "A Strategic Calculus of Voting," *Public Choice* 41, no. 1 (1983): 7–54; and W. Ricker and P. Ordeshook, "A Theory of the Calculus of Voting," *American Political Science Review* 62 (1968): 25–42.
7. For details on the payoff structure and other dimensions of the analysis, see Barbara Salert, *Revolutions and Revolutionaries.*
8. This is similar to what is commonly referred to in voting behavior as the voter paradox: the idea that a significant turnout in elections characterized by many eligible voters is not consistent with rational behavior. For details, see Thomas R. Palfrey and Howard Rosenthal, "A Strategic Calculus of Voting," *Public Choice* 41, no. 1 (1983): 7–54.
9. This is similar to the minimax regret idea in voting behavior. For details, see J. Ferejohn and M. Fiorina, "The Paradox of Not Voting: A Decision Theoretic Analysis," *American Political Science Review* 68 (1974): 525–36.
10. Mancur Olson, *The Logic of Collective Action: Public Goods and the Theory of Groups* (Cambridge, MA: Harvard University Press, 1965), 110.
11. Gustave LeBon, *The Crowd: A Study of Popular Mind* (London: Allen & Unwin, 1908).
12. Sigmund Freud, *Group Psychology and the Analysis of the Ego* (New York: Bantam Books, 1960).
13. George Rudé, *The Crowd in the French Revolution* (Oxford: Oxford University Press, 1959).
14. Dirk Hoerder, *Crowd Action in Revolutionary Massachusetts, 1765–1780* (New York: Academic Press, 1977).
15. Mostafa Rejai and Kay Phillips, *Leaders and Leadership: An Appraisal of Theory and Research* (Westport, CT: Praeger, 1997).
16. See, for example, Barbara Salert, *Revolutions and Revolutionaries: Four Theories* (New York: Elsevier, 1976).
17. For details, see Karl W. Deutsch, *The Analysis of International Relations* (Englewood Cliffs, NJ: Prentice-Hall, 1978).
18. Karl W. Deutsch, *The Analysis of International Relations,* p. 131.
19. See *Analytical Study on Irregular Warfare in Sierra Leone and Liberia.* SAIC 98/6039 (Englewood, CO: Foreign Systems Research Center).
20. Reuters Business Briefing/Interpress Service (January 6, 1998).
21. Reuters Business Briefing/Interpress Service (October 5, 1998).

Key Terms

conflict
conflict resolution
free-rider problem
irregular warfare
marginal classes

private goods
public goods
rationality
selective incentives

utilitarianism
variable sum games
violence
zero-sum games

Discussion Questions

1. Discuss the main arguments of rational-choice explanations of violent conflicts.
2. What is the difference between private and public goods? Why is participation in civil wars or revolutions similar to efforts at acquiring a public good?
3. What is rationality? Discuss this concept in relation to the prisoners' dilemma game.
4. There are many resource wars taking place in developing countries. Would you say that the child participants and others engaged in these wars are motivated by rationality?
5. Critique rational-choice theory in terms of scope (extent) of participation by applying it to a specific revolution (French, Russian, Iranian, etc.).

CHAPTER 6

Macro-Structural Theories of War

Introduction

War is integral to human existence and interactions. The reasons for war have been as varied as the differences that intensify divisions among groups, societies, and states. They range from religious differences, economic rivalry, competing ideologies, plunder and adventurism, and subjugation, to idiosyncratic factors connected with delusions of grandeur, wealth, and power, as well as obsessions of world conquest and presumptions of personal affront to individual dignity. Similarly, many wars are determined by ethnonationalist fervor, accidental involvement, the need to restore regional and power balance, interalliance rivalries, inflammatory diplomatic exchanges, or global systemic and historical-structural changes. War, at times, can be viewed as a rational act, especially when viewed through the reasoning of Karl von Clausewitz, who wrote that: "War is politics by other means," and "War is thus an act of force to compel our enemy to do our will."[1] At times, though, war is an irrational act involving unethical behavior.

War can be viewed in the context of levels of analysis: gang warfare, interethnic war as part of a civil war, class warfare as in Marxist analysis, interstate war, and even a global or world war. Our focus here is limited to war in terms of large-scale organized armed hostility or violence between state actors, or with at least one state as a participant. In the modern world of complex interdependence and extensive internationalization, many civil wars have a substantial external dimension because of support from outside parties. Similarly, a war between two state actors has the potential of involving many more states based on shared ideological, economic, or military interests.

In the past, religious wars were more frequent and perhaps more intense than they are today. These wars are motivated by theological differences or spiritual fervor at times underlined by other cleavages such as ethnicity, region, or nation. In the contemporary international system, violence resulting from religious differences is manifested in Northern Ireland, the Sudan, and occasionally in India, Nigeria, or Iraq, among other. Violence ensuing from religion is based on either completely different beliefs between the protagonists or from varied doctrinal differences based on interpretations of the same holy book. The justification for engaging the other side in war is merely the division caused by conflicting beliefs, a division intensified by bigotry, intolerance, and a lack of compassion for the other group.

Economic wars are even more infrequent today than they were in the eighteenth or nineteenth centuries. The age of plunder, which took the form of imperialism (expansion to overseas territories), generated a great deal of violence between Europeans and indigenous people. Among the more notable economically motivated conflicts of the twentieth century were Germany's drive for "lebensraum" (living space), and Japan's intent to form a "co-prosperity sphere."[2] However, in this age of economic globalization, with its widened scope of economic interactions and mutual interests, major wars based on economic motivation seem remote. The cost of modern warfare in terms of arms buildup, mortality rates, industrial destruction, and general environmental degradation are counterproductive to economic prosperity.

The age of plunder was a mixture of economic imperialism and adventurism that lasted until the end of the nineteenth century. The motivation for such adventure was to explore new lands and conquer distant peoples for the power, wealth, and prestige of the crown or the nation. The justification for such conquest took the form of a *mission civilisatrice* (a civilising mission) for the French, or the "white man's burden" for the British. These rationalizations are virtually absurd because in the end they created more national and global problems whose repercussions are still being played out today in the form of wars within states where incompatible cultures were artificially lumped together to form the same state.

Both economic imperialism and adventurism involved control and domination that enhanced the power, wealth, and prestige of the imperialist nation. They ensured the exploiting country cheap labor, an ample supply of raw materials, and enormous profits for a privileged business class. Such hegemony and control created many anticolonial revolts.[3] The age of overt imperialism is over, but many of its effects are being manifested in interethnic wars, genocides, and the many internal wars unfolding in many developing countries today, some of which are motivated by the struggle to control the mining of lucrative minerals such as diamonds or gold.

Furthermore, many of the interstate wars of the twentieth century have been fought to preserve or promote an ideal. Justifications of making the world safe for democracy, to preserve the principle of territorial integrity, or to prevent inhumane treatment of people in distant lands has impelled the United States to engage in major wars. During the Cold War, many Marxists, socialists, Maoists, or communists attempted to promote their own view of an ideal political economy, considered as a solution to all the world's problems. An ideal for many would serve as the only real justification for war and as an effective instrument for stirring up the emotional resources of patriotism or nationalism toward any war effort.

Nationalism and Modern Warfare

The first known modern example of mass mobilization (*Levée en masse*) by humans to fight a war occurred during the French Revolution. First, the revolution of French peasants, urban workers, and part of the merchant class occurred against the old feudal order at the beginning of the Revolution in 1789. Later, in 1793, when the Revolution was threatened by the monarchs of Austria, Prussia, and Hungary, the revolutionary government responded with a mass and compulsory mobilization of the entire French society for war. What in effect amounted to the legitimizing of compulsory state action was stated thus:

> All Frenchmen are permanently requisitioned for service into the armies. Young men will go forth to battle; married men will forge weapons and transport munitions; women will make tents and clothing and serve in hospitals; children will make lint from old linen; and old men will be brought to the public squares to arouse the courage of the soldiers, while preaching the unity of the Republic and hatred against the Kings.[4]

The fervor of nationalism coupled with this broad-based appeal to fight the enemy resulted in the mobilization of more than one million fighting men to serve in the French army from 1793 to 1799. It surpassed any previous army, and under the direction of Napoleon a modern bureaucratic military organization was created. Primary schools were especially created to instruct low-level enlisted men in map reading and written orders. At the same time a merit system was put in place to handle promotion and awards. The old feudal practice of aristocratic right to officer ranks was abolished. The modernization of the army during the revolution resulted in the establishment of very elaborate military division of labor with a highly efficient core of officers with specialization in war strategy, planning, logistics, and development and testing of new weapons.

Many theorists thus point to nationalism as a primary cause of war.[5] Nationalism (devotion to one's country), which originated with the French Revolution, established the first modern army based on mass recruitment made possible by popular feelings of patriotism. In spite of globalization processes that tend to integrate the world's people, the idea of belonging to a nation-state is deeply ingrained in the minds of people, giving them a sense of identity and feeling of pride. The power of the nation-state and its accompanying emotional resource of patriotism is, in other words, still predominant.

In the history of warfare, the role of the power elite has been particularly instrumental in persuading their populace to fight for their respective countries as well as to be prepared to endure the consequences of fighting a war manifested in war casualties and economic hardships of war mobilization. In his classic work *A Study of War*, Quincy Wright emphasized the role of the political elite:

> Since popular support became more necessary with the new technology, the management of opinion became increasingly important. Development of the sentiment of nationalism, identifying the citizen with the state, made it possible to arouse popular enthusiasm for war. . . . National sovereignty, defined by the new international law, became the prevailing value, the dominant sentiment, the political objective and the leading cause of war in the modern period.[6]

Nationalism has since its emergence spawned intense feelings of national superiority of one nation against another. The power elites of eighteenth-century Europe quickly transformed doctrines of national superiority to justify political, economic, and cultural domination of peoples in distant lands through colonial empires. Nationalism became the legitimizing tool for imperialism, power struggles, and the means of diverting attention away from domestic injustice and inequalities by focusing on an external enemy. On the other hand, nationalism has been used as the unifying call of all colonized and oppressed peoples to rise up against alien rule.

In addition to nationalism, another cause of war is the existence of relationships of overt inequality that become intolerable. Stratification and dominance that produce misery and suffering contribute to war. In the worst cases inequality produces feelings of frustration or dehumanizing results that force the dominated to rebel. Many colonial wars were the result of domination in which the colonizers considered themselves intellectually and morally superior, and thereby imposed their will on the colonized. Oppression, authoritarianism, lack of empathy, and inhuman treatment then force the dominated to rebel against the dominant. Examples abound in more recent history of wars against foreign domination: France in Algeria, the Soviet Union in Afghanistan, the Dutch in Indonesia, or the United States in Vietnam, among others.

The varied causes of collective political violence, of which civil war is an example, have already been discussed in previous chapters of this book. The rest of this chapter will focus on the internal-external causes of war as well as historical-structural causes of war involving at least one state as a major participant.

Internal and External Dynamics of War

War has become such a major aspect of interactions among states in the past that war analysts often make reference to a "war system" to describe the ensemble of social institutions, beliefs, and cultural practices that tend to enhance the acceptance of war, weapons systems, and military personnel as an integral part of society and its foreign policy. In advanced industrial societies such as the United States, for example, a cause of, or the possibility of, war during the Cold War in particular was attributed to the military-industrial complex.[7] The complex is described as the conjunction of an immense military establishment and a large arms industry. Specifically, it is composed of: (1) professional soldiers, (2) managers and owners of industries heavily engaged in military supply, (3) senior government officials whose careers and interests are directly linked to military expenditure, and (4) legislators whose districts benefit from defense procurement. At the height of the Cold War, for example, the military-industrial complex expanded to include universities as another major arena for research on weapons systems.

Nation-states are especially prone to engage in war when their national interest is threatened or endangered by the policies and behavior of other nations. Threats to either the independence, territorial integrity, military security, or national sovereignty of a state has impelled many states to declare war against other states. Similarly, the pursuit of a nation's national interest defined as the well-being of its people and interests both within and outside the country has also been a source of interstate wars. For example, in his analysis of U.S. foreign policy, Donald Nuechterlein categorized the nation's national interests into defense of homeland, economic well-being, favorable world order, and promotion of values (ideology).[8] Defense of homeland falls under survival interests because an imminent threat, or massive destruction of the nation is probable. For instance, the United States quickly responded to Japan's attack on Pearl Harbor in 1941. The survival interest from the attack forced the United States to engage in full-scale war against Japan. Another example of a survival interest leading to a near-war situation was the Cuban missile crisis in 1962 caused by the discovery that Soviet medium-range missiles were being installed in Cuba. Their complete installation would have outflanked the U.S. early warning system against missile attack, and thereby seriously undermine the nation's national security. According

to Nuechterlein, national interests can be accorded one of four priorities—
survival, vital, major, or peripheral—depending on the severity of the threat
to the nation-state, as well as on the amount of time that a country has to
decide how it will confront such an external threat.

The internal and external dimensions of the national interest imply that
wars are also characterized by internal and external dimensions. For example, Michael Stohl has emphasized the connection between civil and
international conflicts of a state.[9] The first relationship of the nexus suggests that when a nation-state is involved in external conflict (especially war)
it tends to increase its internal unity, thereby enhancing its internal peace.
This situation is often stated as the in-group/out-group hypothesis. In other
words, when faced with another supposed hostile group, a "we-group" tends
to manifest more cohesion and mutual loyalty and express intense hostility
and belligerence toward the "they-group" or out-group. In the context of
the nation-state, leaders often experience a great deal of popular support
during the initial stages of their nation's involovement in a foreign war. For
example, Americans rallied round the flag and gave President Bush a great
deal of popular support during the Gulf War against Iraq in 1990 to 1991.

The second relationship of the internal-external conflict linkage constitutes the opposite of the first relationship. It suggests that when the nation-
state is involved in external war it tends to experience revolutions or internal
stability. In other words, an increase in internal violence (riots, violent
demonstrations, or revolutions) is associated with external war involvement.
Many examples abound of revolutionary and/or violent internal conflict
situations resulting from external war involvement: the Paris Commune of
1871, the Russian Revolution of 1905, the Chinese Revolutions, the Turkish
Revolution of 1908, and many other revolutions that resulted from World
War I and World War II.[10] More recent examples are the riots and violent
demonstrations that were associated with the U.S. involvement in Vietnam.
Such disturbances or revolutions occur because war produces a situation
conducive to extreme methods of effecting change. The defeated government
especially tends to experience a loss of authority, general societal dissatisfaction, and psychological demoralization. Opposition groups are thus emboldened to challenge the old leadership by pushing for radical social change.

The third relationship in the internal-external conflict linkage is the argument that it is internal conflict or the mere possibility of conflict that tends
to result in external conflict and war. It is argued that groups that are threatened by domestic enemies, in order to ensure their self-preservation, may
resort to a foreign policy of conflict or outright war. By starting a foreign
war or conflict, the leadership aims to deflect the threat away from itself
by uniting a weakly cohesive nation against some real or alleged external
threat. For example, B. Semmel quotes Cecil Rhodes's statement in support

of this relationship: "The Empire, as I have always said, is a bread and butter question. If you want to avoid civil war you must become Imperialists."[11] In support of this relationship, Jean Bodin's (1576) argument is also appropriate: "the best way of preserving a state, and guaranteeing it against sedition, rebellion, and civil war is to keep the subjects in amity with one another, and to this end to find an enemy against whom they can make common cause."[12] Some will argue that the war between Britain and Argentina in 1982 occurred because the military junta annexed the Falkland Islands in order to deflect attention away from the dislocated economy and thereby ensure its surival through the Argentine nationalism that the war unleashed.

Empirical or scientific studies of these relationships generally find no single clear association. Results and conclusions as to the strength of relationships between internal disturbances and external war involvement or vice versa have varied from one study to the next. Nonetheless, the internal-external conflict linkage is an integral aspect of the conflict behavior of states.

Theories of War

Status Disequilibrium and War

The fact that wars have both an internal and external dimension, or that there is an active linkage between internal and external conflict behaviors of nations, is a consequence of a stratified international system of interacting states. The sociological concept of stratification implies dominance, inequality, or hierarchy, in relation to systemic values such as power, wealth, or psychological gratification.[13] In terms of international politics, a nation's position within the stratified international system determines to a large extent what role it will play in world politics. Similarly, in terms of status discrepancy or rank disequilibrium theory, a nation's position within the stratified state structure plays a role in determining its conflict or war behavior.

The international system is characterized by numerous systemic values by which nations are ranked or stratified. For example, nuclear capability, gross national product (GNP), military power, life expectancy, or literacy rate, among many others, are some of the values that nations aspire to and compete for. According to Maurice East, all the political, military, socioeconomic, or psychological criteria can be reduced to three values that in large part correspond to Max Weber's classic categories of class (wealth), power (military force), and status (prestige).[14]

In terms of the stratified international system, some states might rank high or *top dog* (T) in all three values, giving them an overall ranking of TTT. Others might rank low or *underdog* (U) in all three, giving them an overall ranking of UUU. States that rank the same on all three values are said to be in rank equilibrium. On the other hand, those states will be in rank disequilibrium whose rankings are not consistent on all three values. Their ranking would fall under configurations such as: TTU, TUT, UTT, TUU, UTU, and UUT.

Rank disequilibrium is supposed to be associated with the likelihood of a state participating in war. For example, Johan Galtung has suggested that the states more likely to participate in war are those in rank disequilibrium.[15] Similarly, Maurice East has hypothesized that the more rank discrepancy in the international system the more it should experience war. Total underdogs may experience deprivation and thus are dissatisfied with the status quo but are too powerless to effect any change through war. The problem lies with the rank discrepant states that may be top dog in one or two categories but underdog in others. They may have military power but no wealth or prestige. Such states experience differential treatment that produces in them a feeling of dissatisfaction and a strong pressure to compete for the value they lack. Where peaceful means are absent, a state's goal to attain rank equilibrium status may be attempted through force. Just as in the case of relative deprivation at the individual or group levels, rank discrepant states take as their frame of reference total top-dog states, and their leaders may decide to deal with their frustration through aggression. Perhaps rank disequilibrium is most dangerous where prestige is not in equilibrium with the military and/or economic achievements. To be denied the status equal to its achievements definitely creates frustration and anger, which could then be translated into displaced aggression.

Empirical studies focusing on status-discrepant theory have found only modest correlations between the presence of the discrepancy among states and the presence of war in the international system.[16] In other words, wars have occurred that were not largely underlined by the actions of rank discrepant states, or the presence of rank discrepant systems. Nonetheless, the theory has implications for peace studies in general. States that rank high on military power and wealth, for example, should be accorded the diplomatic respect as well as the political and military recognition they deserve, and therefore be given important positions, commensurate responsibility, and the opportunity to participate in decisions that directly affect questions of international peace and stability.

Bipolarity versus Multipolarity

The emphasis on balance of power politics is an inherent aspect of realist theory in international relations, and it underscores the structure of equality and inequality between nations in the international system, where they tend to balance power against each other, especially against those who threaten the status quo. Many major wars have been a consequence of changes in the structure of relations among states. The hypothesized relationship between balance of power and war has a long intellectual pedigree, stretching back as far as Thucydides' history of the Peloponnesian Wars.[17] This relationship is reflected in the theoretical debate among political scientists in particular about the relative merits of bipolar versus multipolar systems. In other words, in terms of peace and stability, which of the two systems is most functional? Functional refers to the capacity to guarantee peace and to maintain itself over time without experiencing major wars. For example, the transformation from bipolar to multipolar or to unipolar could take the form of a cataclysmic widespread war that entirely changes the prevailing configurations of power and states. Such a systemic transformation could result in both fragmentation of states and empires as well as integration of smaller states into empires. Thus, given that both bipolarity and multipolarity are prone to transformation, the major theoretical questions often discussed are: Which power configuration or system is most capable of avoiding wars? Which system is most capable of avoiding widespread wars? What are the inherent differences between bipolarity and multipolarity?[18]

Bipolarity A bipolar international structure is one with two major powers competing for influence with each supported by allies or satellite states. There are many arguments in favor of bipolarity's ability to avoid both wars and major wars. Some of these arguments are listed below:

1. Unnecessary expansionism and conflict are prevented because spheres of influence are respected by both superpowers, thereby producing an effective balance.
2. Both superpowers become very cautious of their behavior toward each other because of the mutual fear that a major war could result in mutual destruction.
3. Careful policy deliberation and systemic behavior become a priority in order to prevent misperception and miscalculation.
4. The superpowers themselves tend to play a leadership role as well as a moderating role vis-à-vis their more aggressive allies or client states.
5. In bipolarity, the existence of only two opposed major camps, or one dyad, makes it unlikely that intercamp warfare might break out across numerous camps or dyads. But in a multipolar system war can break out between more groups of states or between two or more dyads.
6. Balance of power is more predictable and easier to achieve than in a multipolar system. This is because adjustment and balance require less effort since they tend to be automatic, and superpowers rely on their experience in conflict management gained from a succession of crises.

7. Since balance of power is more easily managed, changes may not be so radical that they lead to war.

On the other hand, the arguments against bipolarity emphasize:

1. The zero-sum nature of competition that might be perceived by the losing superpower as a threat to its existence, and thereby precipitate a war.
2. A tightly polarized system lacks third-party mediators that can help defuse or moderate a conflict before it turns violent.
3. Bipolarity is risky because any conflict can easily escalate into a widespread cataclysmic war, especially since interests of great powers are at stake worldwide.
4. Many smaller wars take place in a bipolar system because the superpowers are concerned that their intervention could lead them to directly confront each other.
5. The certainty and predictability that is inherent in bipolarity may lead to more war rather than less because nations are tempted to initiate war when they are more certain of the international environment than when there is ambiguity about it.[19]

Multipolarity Similar to bipolarity, there are many arguments for and against multipolarity. A multipolar system is one in which power and influence are distributed among several relatively equal states. Multipolar systems are reported to be more stable than bipolar systems because:

1. The possibility for positive interactions and joint areas of cooperation increases as the number of important actors in the system increases. The development of overlapping memberships, relationships, and cross-cutting cleavages prevents the development of rigid and uncompromising positions on issues. Thus, the probability that major conflicts will erupt is decreased by the pluralistic system characterized by multiple criss-crossing interactions.
2. In a multipolar system, nations often engage in balance of power politics that tend to discourage dominance by any state or groups of states. The flexibility in alliances also discourages rigidity in alliance systems.
3. A plurality of major actors creates possible opportunities for effective mediation of actual and potential disputes.
4. In a multipolar system, the arms buildup by a potential aggressor is often offset by the combined weapons capability of two or three other nations. As a result, the arms races and the security-insecurity dilemma is not as intense as in a bipolar system with two major powers.

5. In a multipolar system, negative bilateral preoccupations or the sole focus of one nation on the behavior of another decreases. National attention is instead generally dispersed onto the multiple actors that make up the system.
6. In a multipolar system, the existence of cross pressures and overlapping memberships diminish major power polarization and hostility.
7. Because alliances are not rigid, and the system is pluralized, potential aggressors are careful not to start a war that might result in their defeat or in producing a formidable alliance against them. This reasoning is in line with the uncertainty, unpredictability, and ambiguity inherent in multipolar systems.
8. A final and very powerful argument for multipolarity points to the 1815 to 1914 multipolar period as one of relative peace. This period spans the Congress of Vienna in 1815 until the outbreak of World War I in 1914.

On the other hand, there are several arguments against multipolarity, such as:

1. There is a greater likelihood for conflicts to erupt because of an increased number of actors, as well as the greater interaction opportunities.
2. The competition among many great powers increases the diversity of interests and demands, which is more likely to lead to conflict rather than cooperation.
3. The argument that multipolarity enhances peace because a state's attention is not focused on a single rival is considered too restrictive. It is rather more realistic to believe that one group of states can focus attention and vigorously compete against another group of states considered threatening.
4. Misperception, miscalculation, and the probability of war are increased because multipolar systems are inherently characterized by great uncertainty.
5. The plurality of states could result in an unequal distribution of resources, thereby heightening dissatisfaction among actors, which could eventually develop into open hostilities.[20]

In sum, bipolarity is a concept associated especially with the Cold War period when the structure of the international system was viewed as a division around two poles: the United States and its allies and the U.S.S.R. and its satellite states. In bipolarity zero-sum perception characterizes relations between the two poles. On the other hand, multipolarity is a system dominated by a number of centers (at least three poles or centers) not led by any one or two superpowers. Nineteenth-century and early-twentieth-century Europe was a multipolar system with relatively equal nation-state actors characterized by a much wider range of issues.

Power Transition Theory of War

Power transition theorists argue that changes in the distribution of power in the international system is the primary cause of war among great powers. The major proponent of this power transition theory of war, A. F. Organski, challenges the traditional balance of power thesis that equilibrium in the system balances power against power and therefore deters war.[21] Power transition theorists assume that the international system is not anarchic, but to a certain extent is hierarchically organized. Accordingly, they argue that in each historical era a *hegemon* (or single dominant leader) usually guarantees international order in cooperation with a coalition of satisfied powers. However, as potential challengers of the hegemon and the status quo increase in power and wealth through industrialization and modernization, the status quo is disturbed, producing a situation that usually leads to war. The source of war is the loss of leadership by the status quo coalition leader as a result of relative economic decline. As long as the hegemon maintains a preponderance of power plus coalition support, peace is maintained. But when these transitions in equality or inequality cause differences in rates of growth of the members of the system, conflicts are most likely. In particular, major wars are hypothesized to be most probable when the challenger moves to parity with the dominant state. The relative equality is due to simultaneous growth in relation to industrialization, and increased state capabilities that equally increase the capacity of the power elite to mobilize national resources.

In particular, Organski and Jacek Kugler argue that a newcomer to the ranks of the great powers usually challenges the status quo by initiating war because it is dissatisfied with its position in the international system in particular.[22] It therefore desires to rewrite the rules of the system to correspond more to its interests and liking. In this regard, power transition theory draws some of its logic from the theory of status inconsistency or discrepancy.

As to be expected, the hegemonic power feels threatened by the new challenge and might embark on a preemptive strike against the challenger in order to maintain its power and leadership position. The strategic advantage is often on the side of the dominant power because it is usually supported by the stronger alliance that ends up defeating the challenger. However, within fifteen to eighteen years the challenger recovers from the defeat and even outpaces some members of the dominant coalition. More challengers tend to arise in the long run, and individual increases in productivity and overall capabilities are integral to the system.

Organski hypothesizes that the probability of war is greater when the rate of transition is faster. Similarly, Organski and Kugler hypothesize that approximate equality in power distribution between the dominant state and the challenger increases the likelihood of major wars.

The general conclusions of the empirical tests of power transition theory are that the elements of power transition constitute a necessary but not a sufficient condition of war.[23] Power transitions are an important determinant of the outbreak of war. For example, power transition theory adequately explains all of Germany's wars: the Austro-Prussian War (1866); the Franco-Prussian War (1870–71); and the two world wars. All of these wars erupted within five years of equality or near-equality in capabilities between Germany and its major power rival at the time.[24] Such findings tend to lend support to the "parity leads to war" hypothesis. However, there are also several transitions that did not lead to war. These empirical tests use GNP as their measure of power. The theory focuses on a dyadic level of two nation states in a continuing relationship, rather than at the level of an international system.

As a theory, power transition is consistent with commonsense logic: it makes intuitive sense, is fairly parsimonious, and is supported by a small amount of evidence. It also touches on other salient factors at others levels of analysis that also help to explain the initiation of war.

Cyclical Theories of War

Theory of Hegemonic War

In terms of levels of analysis, the power transition theories are dyadic in nature, but cyclical theories and historical-structural theories of war operate at the international level. Theorists of this school emphasize a good understanding of the current structure of the international system through a close analysis of its historical evolution. They argue that the current patterns and cyclical processes, and especially cycles of war, can be explained by examining their origins and developments in previous international systems. There are thus several theories that attempt to understand cycles of war between dominant states and challengers.

One of the cyclical theories of war is the theory of hegemonic war formulated by Robert Gilpin in his *War and Change in World Politics*.[25] Its focus is to explain wars fought between great powers (hegemonic wars) for leadership in the international system. Just like Organski's power transition theory, Gilpin's theory is also a medium-range theory as opposed to a general theory of war.

Gilpin's explanation focuses primarily on wars fought for leadership or dominance in the international system. A hegemonic war is a direct confrontation between the existing hegemon(s) or dominant power(s) and an emerging challenger over the political management and leadership of the international system. According to Gilpin, war is a result of a rising imbalance between governance of the system, on the one hand, and the actual distribution of capabilities, on the other. As the incumbent dominant power steadily loses its previously unchallenged economic and military status, it experiences a discrepancy between power and prestige. This gradual disequilibrium is a result of the instability and unpredictability of growth in rates of national power among nation-states. Power among nation-states is susceptible to cycles of growth and decline related to the *law of uneven growth*. One consequence is the rise and fall of hegemonic powers.

As a neorealist, Gilpin argues that conflict between dominant powers is due more to strategic and national interests than to economic interests.[26] Hegemonic wars are therefore due more to power struggles than economic struggles. Power disequilibrium becomes the significant factor, not economic disparity. This is due to the uneven growth of power, not the uneven development of national economies. However, Gilpin acknowledges that changes in power distribution and growth result from changes in socioeconomic factors such as transportation, communication, technology, prices, capital, population, and military technology, among other factors.

Gilpin notes that the decline of the dominant power is an inevitability and is due to several factors such as the burdens of maintaining dominance or leadership in the system. Such a burden is costly and includes military expenditures, aid to allies, and provision of general economic goods necessary to sustain the global economy. Second, because of uneven rates of growth, there occurs the loss of economic and technological dominance to other states. This is often a result of an increase in consumption on the part of the hegemon, at the expense of innovation, investment, and risk taking. Third, is the availability of military and economic technology in the hands of nonmajor powers. Another factor is the exhaustion of the hegemon's resource base. In addition, as war among the major powers weakens them, there is a tendency for power to shift from the center to the peripheral or nonmajor powers.

According to Gilpin, challengers of the dominant power are motivated to change the status quo when they perceive that the benefits of doing so will surpass the costs. In other words, Gilpin's theory incorporates a rational choice analysis into its explanation. War does not erupt as long as the challenger perceives that it is not profitable to change the system. The incentive to launch a war in order to change the status quo is thus directly related to the change in relative power within the international system. The issues contested are usually the rules of the system, spheres of influence, and distribution of benefits and territories. However, no initiation of war is likely until the cost-benefit ratio of doing so is in favor of the challenger.

Although the dominant power feels threatened by a rising power, it is usually the latter that is most likely to initiate a war as it attempts to expand its new power and influence based on its overall capabilities. The hegemon may also decide to launch a preemptive strike and thereby initiate a war.

In Gilpin's conclusion, neither bipolarity nor multipolarity guarantees peace.[27] The central issue is rather that of power and its distribution and dynamics in the international system. Peace has generally been maintained when the hegemon has been powerful and effective. For example, the long peace between the end of World War II in 1945 to the present has been due to U.S. hegemonic rule. Gilpin argues that a new era of global warfare could result if there is a decline in American preponderance. But he also argues that it is possible that hegemonic decline will not result in global warfare.[28] The two instances of hegemonic governance by Britain (1815–1939) and by the United States (1939 to the present) each have been periods of long peace. However, some observers argue that to a large extent, a primary determinant of the eruption of war is not found in the degree of hegemonic power.

Long Cycle Theory of War

Another well-articulated cyclical theory of major war is George Modelski's and William Thompson's "long cycle" of international politics and war.[29] They assert that the international system comprises major structures: the global system, the world economy, and the world cultural subsystem. System management is sometimes in the hands of a single unit, often a function shared among several states, and sometimes a function that is altogether absent. A world power can dominate the maintenance of order through a reliance on its preponderant military resources. Single world powers that dominated the keeping of world order prior to 1945 relied primarily on naval capabilities, considered the most important contribution to the state's global power projection.[30] The possession of extensive military capabilities enables the world power to provide collective systemic goods such as military security, world organization, and a set of rules for a stable international economic system.

Since 1500, the global system has been shaped by a succession of world powers. The rise and fall of these world leaders has been characterized by cycles, with the beginning of each cycle marked by a global war that decides the configuration of power and which world power will lead in the organization of the system. One consequence of the global war is a heavy concentration, temporarily, of military capabilities in the hands of a single nation-state. The strongest economy is also temporarily located in the territory of the single actor. In time, as the political legitimacy and power capabilities of this state decline, it attracts competitors. Disorder replaces order and power becomes more concentrated. Overall there are four stages that comprise the long cycle: global war, world power, delegitimation, and deconcentration.

Systemic peace and stability are associated with the single world-power state, although these do not last. The long cycle of world leadership lasts for roughly hundred years to three generations. For the initial phase of this period the system is unipolar, indicating that the world-power state manages the system alone. But as its legitimacy and power declines the system steadily drifts into bipolar and multipolar power configurations.

Why is the world system based on a cyclical nature of world leadership? According to Modelski, warfare is at the heart of each cycle, and is the cause of any cycle. Monopoly of global power involves both costs and benefits: while the monopoly confers a great deal of benefits, it also attracts costs in the form of competition, burdens or expenditures related to managing the system.[31] Besides, world powers tend to defend fixed positions and distant frontiers in response to challenges. There is furthermore a strong correspondence between cycles and shifts in the distribution of economic resources among the states of the system.

According to research by long cyclists, the global wars caused by cyclical changes tend to start as relatively small localized wars that then become global when the dominant power or powers decide to participate.[32] The aspiring world power tends to suffer defeat in its challenge against the dominant state. At the end of the war, a new dominant power usually arises from the coalition of allies that supported the previous dominant power against the challenger. The whole process of the global transfer of leadership is usually done smoothly.

Based on common knowledge about World War I and World War II, Germany did not surpass either Britain or the United States in economic or military power prior to the eruption of the war. These two factors limited Germany's global power projection. In particular, Germany was relatively deficient in naval power, making it vulnerable to naval blockades. The United States, as part of the coalition that defeated Germany during World War II, smoothly inherited the status of the world's new leader from Britain, the previous world leader before the outbreak of the war.

According to Thompson, multipolarity is the most unstable system because as the distribution of power in the system becomes more equal, the amount of war increases.[33] But according to power transition and cyclical theories, declining power does not always lead to war. Declining power is more likely to cause war when: (1) the transition is fast-paced and results in rough equality; (2) the shift is of substantial magnitude; (3) there is no history or tradition of cordial relations between the rivals; (4) the status quo does not enhance the interests of the challenger; (5) the challenging forces have a relative military advantage over the defensive forces, and are probably

Table 6.1: A Select List of Twentieth-Century Wars

Anglo-Boer War	1899–1902
Russo-Japanese War	1904–05
Spanish-Moroccan War	1909–11
Italo-Turkish War	1911–12
Balkan Wars	1912–13
World War I	1914–18
Russo-Polish War	1918–20
Greco-Turkish War	1919–22
Poland-Lithuania War	1920
Franco-Syrian War	1920
Sino-Soviet War	1929
Russo-Finnish War	1939–40
World War II	1939–45
Franco-Thai War	1940–41
First Indo-China War	1945–54
Sino-Indian War	1962
Sino-Soviet War	1963–69
Sino-Vietnamese War	1979
Gulf War	1990–91
Peru-Ecuador War	1995–97
Eritrea-Ethiopian War	1998–2000

expected to initiate war first; (6) the benefits of initiating war seem to outweigh the costs; and (7) leaders in the challenger coalition are willing to risk war.[34] Which of the above are necessary, or sufficient, or which combination of them should be present, is not clear.

World System Theory of War

World system theorists, by focusing on international inequality and dependence, attribute the outbreak of war to the nature of capitalism, especially its competitive aspects. In particular, Immanuel Wallerstein and other world system theorists argue that the international political economy is a European-based capitalist world economy that had its beginnings in the modern era, about 1450.[35] But it is a capitalist global economy that no one state or actor is able to monopolize because of its competitive nature as well as the anarchic nature of the international system.[36] The consequence of competition and anarchy is a capitalist world economy with an international division of labor. In addition, this world economy includes three levels: the core, the periphery, and the semiperiphery. Core states are the advanced industrial or have nations. They are at the forefront of technological knowhow and skilled labor. They control wealth that is very disproportionate to their population size. The periphery is made up of less-developed countries characterized mainly by low-wage, labor-intensive raw materials. Largely because of colonial ties, their economies are very dependent on those of the core countries, many of whom were their former colonial masters. The semiperiphery occupies an intermediate position between the core states and the periphery. In other words, they are characterized by some high-tech industrialized production and some low-skilled, low-wage, labor-intensive economic activities. While the semiperiphery may exploit the periphery, it is also an area exploited by the core states. Membership within both the semiperiphery and core is characterized by constant conflict because all states strive for upward socioeconomic mobility.

Just as there is stratification and division of labor among the states of the international system, so also is there division between hegemonic powers and regular core states. According to Wallerstein only three states have achieved real hegemony, and for only brief periods: the United Provinces, from 1620 to 1672; Great Britain, from 1815 to 1873; and the United States, from 1945 to 1967. World wars have been the primary determinant of guaranteeing the hegemonic status of each.[37] The United Provinces achieved their hegemonic status as a result of the Thirty Years' War; Britain achieved hegemonic status as a result of its victory over France in the Napoleonic Wars; and American hegemony was the result of World War I and World War II. Periods of relative hegemonic decline resulted in attempts to impose world empire. Examples are the imperial attempts by Louis XIV, Napoleon, and by Germany in the twentieth century.

In the view of world system theorists, the development and expansion of global capitalism is at the core of the eruption of major wars. This is because capitalism creates conflict among accumulators of capital. War, in Wallerstein's view, is a "struggle to shape the institutional structures of the capitalist world economy so as to construct the kind of world market whose operation would automatically favor particular economic actors."[38] Likewise, Christopher Chase-Dunn argues that, "world wars and the rise and fall of hegemonic powers—can be understood as the violent reorganization of productive relations on a world scale," in order to further internationalize capitalist production.[39] In other words, wars are violent struggles over what form capitalist production should take caused by the challenge of emerging powers against existing hegemonic powers for a greater share of the world economic surplus. The end result of world wars is the emergence of a new hegemonic power whose tenure depends far more on economic factors than on military ones. Often the hegemony of the new power does not last.

Hegemonic status tends to be ephemeral because of uneven capitalist development, which affects productive capabilities in the form of a loss in comparative edge by the hegemonic power in the production of leading industries. For Wallerstein, these changing distributions of power are almost entirely economically driven. While political-military imbalances may be important, they are shaped and produced by economic processes.

According to world systems theorists, the preponderance of power in the hands of the hegemon tends to be short-lived. As a result, there is a constant rise and fall of hegemonic powers and a cyclical nature of war. A four-phase cycle characterizes this rise and fall of hegemonic powers: (1) an ascending hegemonic challenger as a result of severe conflict among rival states to replace the older hegemon, (2) hegemonic victory because the challenger outpaces the declining hegemon, (3) the stage of actual or mature hegemony, and (4) declining hegemony characterized by increased challenges against the hegemony.[40] It is the emerging challenger that initiates world wars, and not the hegemonic core states. However, the challenger always fails because it has difficulty convincing other states to join in an alliance against the hegemonic core states.

While world systems theory is quite appealing as an explanation of major wars, it does not seem to adequately explain the U.S. and German roles during the two World Wars. In other words, Germany's challenge was not directed at the United States, nor was the United States involved in the initial fighting either as a challenger or as the hegemon trying to defend its hegemony.[41]

Kondratieff Waves: Economic Cycles Theory of War

In the 1920s, the Russian economist Nikolai Kondratieff argued that the economies of the major capitalist nations operate on fifty-year cycles or waves related to prices, production, and consumption. These cycles, he argued, are not limited to these major capitalist nations but extend to the international economic system as a whole. His research findings suggested that upswings in economic long waves corresponded to the eruption of major war. The wars, he speculated, may be due to the intense competition for markets and raw materials associated with the increased pace of economic activity, rising prices, and growth in production that accompany upswing phases.[42] While many economists even doubt the existence of K-waves, long cycle theorists nonetheless claim to have found them, and that they correspond to world leadership cycles, with one-hundred-year world leadership cycles equated with pairs of K-waves. Because K-waves are associated with leadership cycles, they are also linked to cycles of global war.[43]

Other scholars have ascertained that most of the wars that erupted between 1780 and 1914 coincided with the upswing of a K-wave, since major wars were preceded by price upswings, and the cessation of major wars also coincided with upswings in K-waves.[44] As a result of the interlocking relationship between the international political system and the global economy,

K-wave theorists also argue that major wars have largely determined the upswing curve.

On the other hand, some other studies have not been able to establish a direct relationship between wars and upswings in K-waves. Instead, the number of wars is about equal in both upswing and downswing periods. However, Joshua Goldstein uncovers within the time frame of 1495 to 1918, a clear link between K-waves and the cycles of war severity, or the number of battle deaths per year. In particular, his findings are that intense wars are more probable in the upswing phase of K-waves. In particular, he found that peaks in warfare occurred near the end of the upswing phases that were part of the nine waves that occurred between 1495 and 1918. According to Goldstein, the causes of major wars lie in the upswing in production that generates a greater demand for resources, which in turn produces greater competition for these resources.[45] The resulting abundance and availability of resources translate into increased supplies of war material for the military, thereby greatly increasing the likelihood of war. War making becomes an attractive option because of the abundance of resources to alleviate the material costs of war. In other words, for Goldstein, it is the combination or conjunction of hegemonic decline and economic expansion that is likely to cause war. Economic expansion without hegemonic stagnation does not present any danger of war.

Relative Power Cycle Theory of War

Another theory of war related to the systemic structure is Charles F. Doran's relative power cycle theory. In his theory he argues that decision making about war is determined by the rise and decline of the relative power of major states.[46] Accordingly, states that comprise the great power central system go through a cyclical path of growth, maturation, and decline where relative power capabilities are concerned. The cycle is shaped and determined by uneven rates of national economic development. These power transitions are useful in attempts to explain the involvement of great powers in extensive wars, as well as the timing of such wars.

The emphasis of Doran's theory is relative power. This means that a state's journey through the cycle depends on its own position within the great power central system reflected in its own internal growth and decline. Thus, a state's position in the cycle of relative power will determine its policies and behaviors within the system of nations. There are four critical points along the cycle that are most likely to contribute to war. First is the lower turning point. This is the stage in which the state becomes a member of the great power system. In other words, the state makes the transition from a declining power to a rising power because its capabilities, relative to others, begin to increase. Second is the first inflection point, which indicates that the rise in the state's relative capabilities is beginning to slow down considerably. This stage is significant because it shows that the initial rapid rise in power will definitely cease. The third stage is the upper turning point where the state's power capabilities relative to other members of the great power system begin to decline. The state makes the transition from a power in ascendance to one in decline. The fourth and final stage is the second inflection point. This is where the state's initial rapid relative decline begins to drop more slowly, an indicator that it may experience a relative rise in the future.[47]

Relative power cycle theory asserts a strong relationship between national behavior, the state's role within the system as reflected in its relative power capabilities. The reasons for war are closely associated with the critical points at which states have arrived within the cyclical path of growth, maturation, and decline. For example, as a state experiences a decrease in power capabilities, its role and interests should decrease accordingly. However, states are prone to hold on to their status, power, and interests with despicable tenacity. Similarly, as a state experiences an increase in power capabilities, its interests and roles correspondingly increase as well. But the other members of the system are often inclined not to facilitate the rising state's transition to great power status. In other words, war may erupt because states are usually unwilling to relinquish power, or allow new members into the great power system. Power shifts at the systemic level produce security threats at the national level among the power elite in the circle of great powers.

The system tends to be in equilibrium when power transition through the power cycle is routine and anticipated. When interests and capabilities are relatively matched, systemic stability is ensured. According to Doran, bipolar and multipolar systems are equally stable and/or unstable. The crucial factor is not the structural difference between the two systems, but the transition between multipolar and bipolar systems that involves a number of great powers in the system going through critical points in the cycle of relative power.[48]

In general, Doran's theory seems to capture more accurately the dynamics of power and war in the international system. This is evidenced in empirical findings related to the major power systems from 1816 to 1965, as well as an investigation of five wars from 1816 to 1975, in particular, the Crimean War, Franco-Prussian War, World Wars I and II, and the Korean War. Average magnitude, severity, and duration of wars were especially found to be much higher for the critical periods.[49] In other words, critical changes in relative power are much better predictors of extensive war among rival nations. It is during one of the critical periods that major powers are more likely to initiate wars that become extensive.

In sum, while micro explanations of war emphasize conflict mostly at the societal, community, or nation-state level, macro level theories focus on: (1) interstate wars, (2) the structure of the international system as a determinant of major wars, (3) the struggle for power between hegemons and aspiring hegemons, (4) status discrepancy among states in relation to power, wealth, and prestige, and (5) long-term causes of major wars because of uneven rates of growth.

Notes

1. Karl von Clausewitz, *On War*, ed. Michael Howard and Peter Paref (Princeton: Princeton University Press, 1976), 75.
2. Lebensraum means "living space." The desire for more living space led to wars by Germany and Japan for control of more territory. For instance, Hitler argued that it was Germany's destiny to control the East and therefore other states must submit to its goal for lebensraum.
3. For a comprehensive analysis of the anticolonial trend, see Fenner Brockway, *The Colonial Revolution* (New York: St. Martin's Press, 1973). In the case of Africa, in particular, see *Decolonization of African Independence: The Transfer of Power, 1960–1980*, ed. Posser Gifford and William Roger Louis (New Haven: Yale University Press, 1988).
4. See William H. McNeil, *The Pursuit of Power: Technology, Armed Force, and Society Since AD 1000* (Chicago: University of Chicago Press, 1982), 192.
5. For more detail, see Francesca M. Cancian and James William Gibson, *Making War—Making Peace: The Social Foundations of Violent Conflict* (Belmont, CA: Wadsworth Publishing Co., 1990), introduction.
6. Quincy Wright, *A Study of War* (Chicago: University of Chicago Press, 1965), 51–2.
7. On the military-industrial complex, see C. Wright Mills, *The Power Elite* (New York: Oxford University Press, 1958); Steven Rosen, ed., *Testing the Theory of Military-Industrial Complex* (Lexington, MA: Heath, 1973); and Michael Parenti, *Democracy for the Few* (New York: St. Martin's, 1988).
8. Donald E. Nuechterlein, *America Overcommitted: United States National Interests in the 1980s* (Lexington: University of Kentucky Press, 1985), chapter 1.
9. Michael Stohl, "The Nexus of Civil and International Conflict," in *Handbook of Political Conflict*, ed. Ted R. Gurr (New York: Free Press, 1980), 297–330.
10. See, for example, Andrew Wheatcroft, *The World Atlas of Revolutions* (New York: Simon and Schuster, 1983).
11. B. Semmel, *Imperialism and Social Reform* (Cambridge: Harvard University Press, 1960), 16.
12. Jean Bodin, *Six Books of the Commonwealth* (Oxford: Oxford University Press, 1955); and A. J. Mayer, *Dynamics of Counter-Revolution in Europe, 1870–1956: An Analytic Framework* (New York: Harper & Row, 1971), 141.
13. On stratification, see Melvin Tumin, *Social Stratification* (Englewood Cliffs, NJ: Prentice-Hall, 1967).
14. Maurice East, "Status Discrepancy and Violence in the International System: An Empirical Analysis," in *The Analysis of International Politics*, ed. James Rosenau, Vincent Davis, and Maurice East (New York: Free Press, 1972).
15. Johan Galtung, "A Structural Theory of Aggression," *Journal of Peace Research* 1(2) (1964).
16. On empirical findings related to status inconsistency, see, among others, Michael D. Wallace, "Power, Status, and International War," *Journal of Peace Research* 8(1) (1971): 23–36; James Lee Ray, "Status Inconsistency and War Involvement in Europe, 1816–1970," *Peace Science Society* (International) Paper 23 (1974): 69–80.
17. For a detailed analysis in relation to the Peloponnesian wars, see James S. Nye, *Understanding International Conflicts* (New York: Longman, 1999).
18. On polarity in general, see A. N. Sabrosky, ed., *Polarity and War: The Changing Structure of International Conflict* (Boulder, CO: Westview, 1985).
19. For a more detailed elaboration of these arguments, see Greg Cashman, *What Causes War? An Introduction to Theories of International Conflict* (Lanham: Lexington Books, 2000), chapter 9; and Kenneth Waltz, "International Structure, National Force, and the Balance of Power," in *International Politics and Foreign Policy*, ed. Richard Rosecrance (New York: Free Press, 1969).

20. For further details, see James E. Dougherty and Robert L. Pfaltzgraff Jr., *Contending Theories of International Relations* (New York: Longman, 1996), chapter 3; and Lloyd Jensen, *Explaining Foreign Policy* (Englewood Cliffs, NJ: Prentice-Hall, 1982).

21. A. F. K. Organski, *World Politics* (New York: Knopf, 1958–68).

22. A. F. K. Organski and Jacek Kugler, *The War Ledger* (Chicago: University of Chicago Press, 1980).

23. A. F. K. Organski and Jacek Kugler, *The War Ledger.*

24. See R. J. Stoll and M. Champion, "Capability Concentration, Alliance Bonding, and Conflict Among the Major Powers," in *Polarity and War,* ed. A. N. Sabrosky (Boulder, CO: Westview, 1985), 67–94.

25. Robert Gilpin, *War and Change in World Politics* (Cambridge: Cambridge University Press, 1981).

26. Robert Gilpin, *War and Change in World Politics,* p. 83.

27. Robert Gilpin, *War and Change in World Politics,* pp. 92–3.

28. For competing views on this, see Charles W. Kegley, ed., *The Long Postwar Peace: Contending Explanations and Projections* (New York: Harper Collins, 1991).

29. George Modelski, "The Long Cycle of Global Politics and the Nation-State," *Comparative Studies in Society and History* 20(2) (April 1978): 214–35; and W. R. Thompson, *On Global War: Historical-Structural Approaches to World Politics* (Columbia: University of South Carolina Press, 1988).

30. See, W. R. Thompson, "Polarity, the Long Cycle, and Global Power Welfare," *Journal of Conflict Resolution* 30(4) (December 1986): 587–615.

31. For details, see Karen Rasler and W. R. Thompson, "Global Wars, Public Debts, and the Long Cycle," *World Politics* 35(4) (July 1983); and Paul Kennedy, *The Rise and Fall of Great Powers* (New York: Random House, 1987).

32. See, for example, W. R. Thompson, "Succession Crises in the Global Political System: A Test of the Transition Model," in *Crises in the World System,* ed. Albert Bergesen (Beverly Hills, CA: Sage, 1983).

33. W. R. Thompson, ed., *Contending Approaches of World System Analysis* (Beverly Hills, CA: Sage, 1983).

34. For further details, see Jack Levy, "Declining Power and the Preventive Motivation for War," *World Politics* 40(1) (October, 1987): 85–8; and Stephen Van Evera, "The Cult of the Offensive and the Origins of World War I," *International Security* 9 (summer 1984): 58–107.

35. Immanuel Wallerstein, *The Modern World-System* (New York: Academic Press, 1974); and *The Capitalist World Economy* (New York: Cambridge University Press, 1979), among others.

36. See, for example, Christopher Chase-Dunn, "Interstate System and Capitalist World Economy: One Logic or Two?" *International Studies Quarterly* 25(1) (March 1981).

37. See Christopher Chase-Dunn, *Global Formation: Structure of the World Economy* (Cambridge, MA: Basil Blackwell, 1989).

38. Immanuel Wallerstein, *Historical Capitalism* (London: Verso, 1983), 64.

39. Christopher Chase-Dunn, "Interstate System and Capitalist World Economy," p. 23.

40. These cycles are discussed in W. R. Thompson, *On Global War: Historical Structural Approaches to World Politics* (Columbia: University of South Carolina Press, 1988), 72.

41. For details, see R. C. North, *War, Peace, Survival: Global Politics and Conceptual Synthesis* (Boulder, CO: Westview, 1990).

42. Nikolai D. Kondratieff, *The Long Wave Cycle* (New York: Richardson & Snyder, 1984), original ed. 1928.

43. See, for example, George Modelski, "The Long Cycle of Global Politics and the Nation-State," *Comparative Studies in Society and History* 20(2) (April 1978): 214–35.

44. See W. R. Thompson and Gary Zuk, "War, Inflation, and the Kondratieff Long Wave," *Journal of Conflict Resolution* 26(4) (December, 1982): 621–44.

45. Joshua S. Goldstein, "Kondratieff Waves as War Cycles," *International Studies Quarterly* 29(4) (December 1985): 411–44; and "Long Waves in War, Production, Prices and Wages," *Journal of Conflict Resolution* 31(4) (December 1987): 573–600.

46. See, among his other works, Charles F. Doran, "War and Power Dynamics: Economic Underpinnings," *International Studies Quarterly* 27 (1983): 419–44; "Systemic Disequilibrium,

Foreign Policy Role, and the Power Cycle: Challenges for Research Design," *Journal of Conflict Resolution* 33(3) (September 1989): 371–401.

47.   Charles F. Doran, "War and Power Dynamics: Economic Underpinnings," p. 420.
48.   Charles F. Doran, "War and Power Dynamics: Economic Underpinnings," pp. 429–30.
49.   See C. F. Doran and W. Parsons, "War and Cycle of Relative Power," *American Political Science Review* 74(1980): 947–65.

Key Terms

balance of power

bipolarity

core

economic wars

hegemonic war

imperialism

in-group/out-group hypothesis

military-industrial complex

multipolarity

nation-state

national interest

nationalism

periphery

power disequilibrium

power transition theory

rank disequilibrium

relative power

semiperiphery

status discrepancy

stratification

war system

zero-sum perception

Discussion Questions

1. Discuss the relationship between nationalism and modern warfare.
2. Analyze the connection between the internal and external dimensions of war.
3. Compare and contrast bipolarity and multipolarity in relation to war.
4. What is the connection between status inconsistency (rank disequilibrium) and war?
5. Discuss and critique any cyclical theory of war.

CHAPTER 7

Revolutionary Leaders and Political Violence

Competing Theoretical Approaches

The history of the human race has been marked by many seminal revolutions such as the French, Russian, Cuban, and Iranian revolutions, among many others, as well as several profound political transformations that have been labeled as revolutionary. In spite of the pervasive nature of revolutionary political activity in both the distant and recent past, studies of revolutionary personnel (leaders, cadres, rank and file) are still scant. Many of the existing analyses on revolutionary elites, or on cadres, and rank and file are based largely on intuition and speculation.

Three principal theoretical approaches characterize the study of revolutionary leadership—that is people actively involved in revolutionary movements and the struggle for power or transformation of their societies.[1] These initiators of revolution (for example, Lenin, Gandhi, Mao, or Castro) planned, executed, and consolidated the revolution and did not just emerge after power seizure and revolutionary consolidation. In particular, the revolutionary elite play the paramount role in organization, mobilization, and ideological indoctrination of paramilitary groups and the masses. One level removed from the leadership are the cadres or middle-level personnel who receive their orders directly from the leadership and are responsible for carrying out specific aspects of organization, mobilization of resources and the masses, indoctrination, coordination, and discipline. They are a kind of transmission belt of information and orders between leaders and the rank and file. In particular, they play a pivotal role in morale building among the

revolutionary masses, clarifying and translating party policy, and performing other activities aimed at movement consolidation and unity.

This chapter summarizes the major theoretical approaches to revolutionary leadership, and examines in the process the factors that motivate
revolutionary leaders as outlined in the theories formulated by the major
theorists in the field of leadership.

In the writings of earlier theorists, the idea of leadership was viewed first
in terms of the "great man," with a focus on his memories, anxieties, passions, traits, whims, or caprices. Such a conception was expressed in classic
works such as Plato's Philosopher King, Niccolo Machiavelli and the Prince,
Thomas Carlyle and the Hero, or Friedrich Nietzsche and the Superman,
among others. A second category of earlier theorists deemphasized the linkage of the great man to his leadership traits, and focused instead on the
imperatives of social forces and the role of situations. Social-structural factors are paramount among such theorists. Examples are Karl Marx and his
focus on class struggles or Adam Smith and the Invisible Hand. A third category of theorists pioneered by William James prefer a fusion of leadership
traits and situational factors. Since the late 1940s, virtually all studies of
leadership underscore the mutual interaction of traits and situations.[2]

Theoretical Approaches to the Study of Revolutionary Leaders

Studies on revolutionary personnel emphasize three theoretical approaches:
the psychoanalytical, the psychohistorical, and the sociological. Psychoanalytical studies rely heavily on the early childhood and psychological experiences of individuals as the source of their revolutionary driving force. By
underscoring the inner dynamics of human personality, they believe they
can correctly identify and locate the impelling force of revolutionary action.
The psychohistorical approach combines the psychological dimension and
the dynamics of society and history to explain revolutionary leadership. The
anxieties, wishes, frustrations, whims, and caprices of early childhood are
viewed in the context of sociohistorical realities. The intersection of psychological motivation with actual life experiences, memories, failures, or guilt
feelings through time help shape the revolutionary impulse. The sociological approach revolves around the concept of charisma—the exceptional or
supernatural qualities of a leader that make him or her attractive, or exercise
a magnetic influence on followers.

The Psychoanalytic Approach

The psychoanalytic approach was pioneered by Sigmund Freud.[3] His analysis of the ego has been applied to leadership in general. Other theorists have
applied this Freudian approach to understanding leadership, specifically to

political and revolutionary personalities. In Freudian analysis, there is a perpetual conflict that takes place between an individual's id (instinctual forces) and his or her superego (social/moral imperatives), which the ego (rationality principle) is incapable of resolving because it is too weak. The development of emotional ties to the leader provides a way of resolving the tension produced by the id/superego conflicts. In other words, left to themselves, the followers cannot measure up to their "ego ideal" (manifested in the superego), and they therefore substitute the leader for the ego ideal.

Freud's pioneering work has been modified, or applied in varied ways by many theorists. One such theorist was Harold Lasswell, whose work focused on the psychological dynamics of the political man.[4] In particular, he argues that the obsession with power on the part of the political personality is a manifestation of psychological compensation for feelings of inadequacy and low self-esteem. Stated differently, the political man, because of inherent feelings of inadequacy and low self-esteem, develops a power-centered personality. His priority becomes the acquisition of power because he can only maintain his personal integrity through the exercise of power. It is this inner psychological drive that is then projected onto public objects and political life and expressed in terms of the public interest.

Lasswell categorized several personality types, including: the agitator, the administrator, and the theorist or ideologue. The agitator combines in his personality trait a commitment to principle, a strong narcissistic behavior, and a dependence on the emotional approval of the people. The administrator tends to displace his private need/motive upon impersonal and concrete objects; his greatest interest is found in "the coordination of effort in continuing activity." The ideologue, according to Lasswell, is plagued by doubt, involved in trivialities, and dogmatic. The ideologue is characterized as follows: "Deep doubts about the self are disposed onto doubts about the world outside, and these doubts are sought to be allayed by ostentatious preoccupation with truth."[5] Lasswell views individuals involved in social movements, including revolutions, in the same manner: they displace private motives upon public objects.

E. Victor Wolfenstein specifically studied the "revolutionary personality" by amplifying Lasswell's displacement hypothesis and applying it to Lenin, Trotsky, and Gandhi.[6] These three leaders, according to Wolfenstein, externalize their hostilities to a wider target: the state. In Freudian analysis the rebellious sons—in the context of the Oedipus complex—directed their aggression against the father. Wolfenstein further employs Erik H. Erikson's model of the eight stages of personality development—oral, anal, genital, latency, adolescence, young manhood, adulthood, maturity—in order to better explain the psychological forces that motivate individuals toward revolutionary action. In Erikson's model, each stage of personality development is characterized by a distinct crisis.[7] A "mature" transition to the next stage requires a successful resolution of each crisis. According to Wolfenstein, the revolutionary impulse originates from the inability of the leader to resolve the crisis of the genital state: the Oedipus complex. The state eventually takes the place of a parent as a target of rebellion for the revolutionary leader. According to Wolfenstein:

> The basic attribute of this personality is that it is based on opposition to governmental authority; this is the result of the individual's continuing need to express his aggressive impulses vis-à-vis his father and the repressive action of governmental officials. The latter permits the individual to externalize his feelings of hatred.[8]

In other words, the revolutionary leader comes to view governmental authority as clearly evil, and thus it should be opposed at all costs and without hesitation. In time the hatred of and opposition to governmental authority develops into a cause that is then enveloped into an ideological framework through which the individual can express justification for hatred and eventual overthrow of governmental authority. According to Wolfenstein, Lenin, Trotsky, and Gandhi, in the end, procured an ideological framework that, among other things, contrasted the role equivalent of a benevolent father (communist society, national independence) to that of a malevolent one (czarism, British imperialism).

Personality and Leadership Development: Gandhi, Lenin, Hitler

The roots of the values held by revolutionary leaders are a result of the guilt feelings that arise out of their early childhood confrontation with parental authority. These values develop and become so entrenched that it is impossible to completely eradicate their influence. According to Freud, the development of the superego is a result of the resolution of Oedipal conflicts occurring in the process of the child internalizing prohibitions in the form of parental scoldings, reproofs, or warnings. Before long, the child develops a conscience that is a manifestation of the superego as well as an attempt by the child to identify with and gain the approval and affection of the parents, and thereby evade parental punishment and displeasure by repressing the behaviors that would produce such penalties. According to Jean Piaget, children are then likely in later years to be rigid and uncompromising about these rules.[9] In most cases the socializing forces of later years modify their view of the rules so that they become less absolutist about them. Freud believed that these early experiences and views about right and wrong (standards and conscience) change very little in adult life because they constitute an iron law of biological and child-parent expectations.

Gandhi, Lenin, and Hitler have been the focus of detailed and varied psychobiographical analysis. While early childhood may not answer all the questions about motive or ambition, it does provide clues to personality and leadership. Mohandas Gandhi was born in 1869 in an upper-class family.[10] His father was prime minister of the principality of Porbandar. They belonged to the Vaisyas caste of farmers and merchants. Within the confines of British colonialism, the father wielded a great deal of political influence. The family was nonetheless known for its integrity and independence. The young Mohandas grew up in an extended family home that included five uncles and their families, as well as his own brothers and sisters. Thus, tolerance, sharing, and a communal life were things that Gandhi learned early in life. He remembered his father as characterized by the values of truthfulness, bravery, and generosity, but also as quick-tempered and strongly inclined to sexual pleasures. According to Erik Erikson, Gandhi as the last child in a polygamous family feared his father and felt unable to measure up to the masculine ideal.[11] Wolfenstein observed that Gandhi "was torn between a desire to submit to his father (and his own superego, the internal manifestation of his father's moral standards) and a desire to replace him in his mother's eyes."[12] To Gandhi, his mother was a model of integrity, saintliness, and an impeccable character. Her religiosity was expressed in consistent fasting and observance of religious rites. He loved as well as feared his father. His relations with both parents—a patriarchal father and a very religious mother—may have intensified the Oedipal conflict in him. But despite what may have seemed like feelings of insecurity in his early life, Gandhi also exhibited, according to Erikson, superiority and a sense of originality.

Vladimir Ilyich Ulyanov (Lenin) was born into a comfortable home and family that was generally described as happy, well adjusted, and normal.[13] Lenin's parents belonged to the middle or upper-middle class. The father was known to be devoted, benevolent, and caring, as evidenced by his involvement with the children's schooling and his mediatory role in the childhood quarrels of his six children. The mother was equally devoted and resourceful. She taught her children to play the piano, sing, and engage in other educational activities at home.

Vladimir was said to have identified with his father, who was often away on official business. According to Wolfenstein, "The high moral rectitude of the father undoubtedly resulted in an unusually demanding superego for the son, so that the young Lenin probably was unable to think or express the feelings of resentment which seem sure to have followed his father's absence and disciplining without experiencing guilt as a consequence."[14] This perpetual interplay of standards and conscience would be a key motivating force for revolutionary activity in later years.

Adolf Hitler was Austrian by birth. Unlike Lenin and Gandhi, he did not experience an easy early childhood. His experience was rather that of a drab, poverty-filled childhood. His home was characterized by fighting and quarreling as Hitler's father increasingly became dependent on alcohol. The father became estranged not only from his wife, but from young Adolf as well. Hitler described his mother in *Mein Kampf* as "giving all her being to the household, and devoted above all to us children in eternal, loving care...."[15] Although Hitler described his father as a dutiful civil servant, he was nonetheless brutal at home, and unwilling to support his family, especially as he became more alcoholic.

According to psychoanalysts, Hitler manifested a sharp dichotomy of attitudes between his father and mother. He loved his mother, but his father he merely respected. Similarly, he equated his love of Germany with the love he had for his mother. He had little love for Austria, which he identified with his father. For Hitler, Germany is the motherland, instead of the more traditional term, *fatherland*.[16] He was also said to have feminized certain German neuter nouns. The distinct contrast between his father and mother led Hitler to become increasingly dependent on the love and affection of his mother. His father was in contrast brutal, uncaring, and at home a petty tyrant who bullied and beat his family. Hitler would later punish Austria (the father) as an act of avenging his mother (Germany). His bitterness over the alleged Austrian aggression against Germany, the "rape" of his motherland by predatory Jews and the aggressive Allies of World War I, among other things, are evidence, according to psychoanalysts, that Hitler had repressed his anguish over traumatic childhood experiences only to project them onto the political arena at the opportune moment, in Germany in the 1920s and 1930s.

These profound psychological forces, and more, may have shaped Hitler's political extremism. His guilt feelings, anxieties, deviant behaviors, and extreme rage at perceived injustice may have shaped Germany's destiny and seriously affected its political and military future.

According to Mostafa Rejai and Kay Phillips, revolutionary elite may in varying levels and combinations share a set of psychological dynamics during their personality development.[17] These dynamics evolve gradually and include: (1) vanity, egotism, narcissism; (2) asceticism, puritanism, virtue; (3) relative deprivation and status inconsistency; (4) marginality, inferiority complex, the compulsion to excel; (5) Oedipal conflict writ large; (6) aestheticism and the romantic streak.

In the early 1980s, Mostafa Rejai and Kay Phillips studied 135 revolutionary leaders from 31 revolutionary movements in 29 countries across 4 centuries. They found that such leaders are generally in their 40s and 50s upon seizing power. They have often been exposed to revolutionary ideology and activity in their teens. They are also either urban-born, or develop a liking for, and continued exposure to, urban cultures. In terms of socioeconomic status, Rejai and Phillips found that 50 percent of revolutionaries are from the middle class, 30 percent are from the lower class, and 20 percent are from the upper class.[18] They are usually mainstream in terms of ethnicity and religion, with some leaning toward atheism as they grow into maturity. Revolutionary leaders are well-educated individuals, with up to 75 percent college or university educated, or with professional experience. The most important situational factors or catalyst that galvanize revolutionary leaders into action are: situations of national crisis or emergency; anticolonial conflicts that result in direct confrontation between subjects and colonizer; the violent historical contests of such countries as Algeria, China, Columbia, Cuba, Mexico, Palestine, South Africa, and Vietnam; and the role of chance.

Many studies on revolutionaries agree on the one characteristic that binds revolutionaries: they were all motivated by a sense of justice/injustice and an accompanying attempt to rectify wrongs. This sense of justice/injustice may be innate, or it may be perceived in social-structural conditions, or it may be personally based and projected on to the wider society.

Other motivations for revolutionary leaders were varieties of nationalism and patriotism expressed as either a desire to get rid of alien rule, oppression, and exploitation, or improve the level of wealth, power, and prestige of their countries.

Revolutionary elite, to a large extent, are noted for physical, social, or psychological traits or characteristics that are distinctly at variance with societal norms, expectations, and practices. Among other things, revolutionaries are individuals characterized by personal psychological traumas experienced during childhood; feelings of insecurity, anxiety, or despair; instances of personal setbacks, humiliation, or failure; experiences with ill health, physical deformity, or frailty; being born out of wedlock; or being a member of a despised minority group. All these and more may have act as motivating forces to regain self-esteem.

The Psychohistorical Approach

In terms of levels of analysis, the psychoanalytic perspective deals largely with the inner psychological conflicts of the individual, whereas the psychohistorical approach combines the sociohistorical and political context and personality dynamics. Pioneered by Erik H. Erikson, it is a merger of psychology and history, and an attempt to link or interrelate the personality conflicts of a "great man" with the historical problems endemic to a particular era.

In Erikson's analysis, eight stages characterize the human life cycle.[19] These stages are distinct, successive, and evolve in a historical setting such that each one contributes in shaping the human personality as it develops through time. The eight stages are: oral, anal, genital, latency, adolescence, young manhood, adulthood, and maturity. According to Erikson, a distinct "crisis" or "turning point" characterizes each stage, and if successfully managed contributes to the development of a fully differentiated and whole personality.

In Wolfenstein's study of Lenin, Trotsky, and Gandhi, he focused on the genital stage of the Oedipal conflict, but in Erikson's study of Martin Luther and Gandhi, the focus is on the turning points of adolescence (Luther) and adulthood (Gandhi). In Luther's case the main emphasis is "identity crisis," the successful resolution of which results in complete personal development. In the case of Gandhi, the focus is on whether one becomes an effective role model in terms of guidance, accomplishments, or actual fatherhood, for the next generation.[20] In other words, for Gandhi the problem is a "generativity crisis." For both Luther and Gandhi, Erikson utilizes a pivotal event as an organizing device for his analysis.

Erikson starts his analysis of Luther with a focus on the event: a fit Luther had in his early twenties in the choir of his monastery. According to eyewitnesses, as he lay on the ground, he raved: "It isn't me!" (German translation) or "I am not!" (Latin translation). Erikson treats this incident as the focal point of Luther's identity crisis, and he tries to fully explain it in terms of Luther's home life and childhood.[21] Luther's parents were known for being strict, and so were his teachers. Inclined to rebelliousness, the young Luther was brooding and aloof, lacked feelings, was susceptible to violent moods, and had a bad temper and a strong capacity to hate. His professors at the University of Erfurt were mostly radical theologians critical of the dogmatic beliefs of the Catholic Church. After he completed his master's degree he underwent a sudden conversion: outrightly defying his father, Luther terminated his academic studies and determined to become a monk. He then joined a very strict monastery where he was ordained in 1507, at the age of twenty-three.

The knowledge and indoctrination Luther gained from his training for priesthood enabled him to formulate his rival theology, which served as a capable and legitimate weapon for his attacks on the Catholic church. In 1517 Luther displayed his ninety-five theses on the church door in Wittenberg. By presenting an alternate Christian paradigm that emphasized the priesthood of all believers, and attacking church dogma and hierarchy, according to Erikson, Luther spoke for and championed the secret wish of millions who had entertained the same feelings but were too intimidated to challenge Roman Catholic hegemony.

In Gandhi's case, Erikson used as a pivotal event the Ahmedabad textile strike in 1918. The strike is viewed by Erikson as a salient event in the development of nonviolence as a transformative technique. It was also noteworthy because it was the first time the 48-year-old Gandhi fasted for a political cause. He affirmed his belief in passive resistance and nonviolence a year later when he launched the mass movement in national civil disobedience. Through the use and practice of techniques of nonviolence, according to Erikson, Gandhi was trying to resolve a crisis of generativity that hung over his adult life. His efforts at nation building were manifested in, and facilitated by, a large following, a vast retinue, an extended family and a nonviolent technique. While at the macro level he was involved in a process of nation building, at the micro and personal level he was involved in self-creation. The way Gandhi dealt with his perennial feelings of severe guilt toward his father (caused by the famous episode of Gandhi making love as his father lay on his deathbed), enduring feelings of depression, personal despair, and humiliation, was to transform the negative Indian identity of inferiority vis-à-vis the British. By accomplishing a transformation at the national level, he did the same on a personal level in terms of his negative self-image. In Gandhi's case, as in Luther's, we are reminded again of the intersection of historical realities and personal conflicts. In the final analysis, the great person adapts the historical context to his or her personal needs.

Gandhi's life was one of persistent guilt over his excessive indulgence in carnal pleasures, his father's carriage accident on his way to his son's wedding, his violation of Hindu prohibitions against meat eating, lying, and smoking, among other things, and his father's passing away while he was in bed with his wife satisfying his carnal needs, rather than nursing his father.[22] Gandhi felt very guilty about the last incident; he felt he had contributed to his father's death because of his lust. These psychological influences also combined with the plight of Indians who went daily to his law office, and his reading of Ruskin, Thoreau, Tolstoy, and others. Thus, a combination of intense personal experiences and social imperatives led Gandhi to gradually shape a political strategy: to dramatize the plight of the Indian people through demonstrations, noncompliance, or passive resistance.

The Sociological Approach

The concept of charisma is the bedrock of the most notable sociological theory of revolutionary leadership. The church historian Rudolf Sohn originally coined this term to refer to divinely inspired leaders, thereby limiting its use to religious contexts.[23] In other words, charisma is a biblical term meaning the "gift of grace." Max Weber, who popularized the concept and with whom it is generally associated, added a secular dimension to it. As presented in his own words:

> There are three pure types of legitimate authority. The validity of their claims to legitimacy may be based on:
>
> 1. Rational grounds—resting on a belief in the "legality" of patterns of normative rules and the right of those elevated to authority under such rules to issue commands (legal authority);
> 2. Traditional grounds—resting on an established belief in the sanctity of immemorial traditions and the legitimacy of the status of those exercising authority under them (traditional authority); or finally
> 3. Charismatic grounds—resting on devotion to the specific and exceptional sanctity, heroism or exemplary character of an individual person, and of the normative patterns or order revealed or ordained by him (charismatic authority).[24]

Other qualities that Weber attributes to a charismatic leader are supernatural or superhuman characteristics that set the individual apart from ordinary men. In fact, there would be no leader-follower relationship, no charisma without the magnetism of supernatural feats—"works," "signs," "proofs," or "miracles." These works provide the basis for the magnetism or "attractiveness" of the leader. Again, Max Weber asserts:

> The charismatic leader gains and maintains authority solely by proving his strength in life. If he wants to be a prophet, he must perform miracles; if he wants to be a warlord, he must perform heroic deeds. Above all, however, his divine mission must "prove" itself in that those who forcefully surrender to him must fare well, he is obviously not the master set by the gods.[25]

Whereas traditional authority rests on the ascriptive, "divine," or cultural attributes of the institution, and rational-legal authority rests on the requirements and necessity of law and order, charismatic authority is grounded in the emotional attachments between leader and followers. The relationship is not necessarily maintained by salaries, promotions, or other official enticements. What binds the followers to the leader and energizes or sustains the leader-follower relationship is a "cause," a sense of "mission" or "calling."

The charismatic leader is viewed as transcending formal institutional settings and endowed with profound innovation and change. Weber emphasizes how charismatic authority repudiates the past and thus constitutes a revolutionary force. Charismatic authority, according to Weber, is most likely to be manifest "in times of psychic, physical, economic, ethical, religious, political distress."[26]

The concept of charisma has been applied to many political upheavals, especially the political developments in the 1950s and 1960s in the developing areas of Africa and Asia. Studies of politics in developing areas have often referred to Nasser of Egypt, Sukarno of Indonesia, Nkrumah of Ghana, or Peron of Argentina among many others, as charismatic leaders. In particular Ann Ruth Wilner applied the concept of charismatic leadership to the situations of crisis under which leaders endowed with magnetism or "attractiveness" emerged in colonial societies.[27]

In other words, situations of perceived or real political, economic, social, or psychological stress culminate into a collective clamor for a leader to emerge as a savior to the nation. Charismatic leadership has also been directly linked to charismatic movement. Robert Tucker equated charismatic leadership with a charismatic social movement. The leader recruits people into the movement whose objective is to bring about profound change in society. Tucker asserts that, "To speak of charismatic leaders, then, is to speak of charismatic movements; the two phenomena are inseparable."[28] Since the leader and movement are interlocked, it means that the charismatic leader emerges at the very beginning of a movement or around that time, thereby underscoring the leader's early career.

James V. Downton views charisma as a "psychological exchange" such that through their interactions, leader and followers succeed in fulfilling certain personality needs.[29] Downton uses the ideas of Freud and Erikson to identify the sources of the follower's commitments that result from the tensions with his or her personality. These tensions result from the inability of the ego to resolve satisfactorily the conflict between the id and the superego. In the case of the follower, for example, ego weakness is the main reason for psychological exchange, or intimate identity with the leader.

In particular, Downton identifies two sources of charismatic appeal for the follower: (1) intrapsychic distance—the follower substitutes the leader as his ego ideal because of the discrepancy between his or her ego and the goals established by the superego; and (2) identity crisis—the result of an underdeveloped ego ideal that does not provide the ego with an adequate identity to help confront the real world. In both cases, identification with the leader alleviates feelings of anxiety, tension, guilt, and insecurity. A relationship with a charismatic leader enhances the follower's sense of identity, autonomy, and self-esteem. In other words, this relationship helps develop the follower's personality by effectively mediating the conflict between the id and the superego.

The psychological exchange between the leader and follower is based on deference and security as personality needs for the leader, on the one hand, and the need for a role model and transcendent authority for the follower, on the other hand. The leader comes to view deferential treatment as a right, which enhances his charismatic quality. In return for the deferential treatment, he performs the functions of provider of security, ideal role model, and transcendent authority performing the duty of the spokesman.

Table 7.1: Summary of Competing Approaches

PSYCHOANALYTICAL	PSYCHOHISTORICAL	SOCIOLOGICAL
Persistent conflict between instincts and social/moral imperatives that the individuals rational nature is unable to resolve.	A merging of psychology and history to show how the personality of the leader is affected by the specific problems of a particular society.	Focus on a leader-follower relationship, and a mutual intimate identity.
The development of emotional ties to the leader is seen as the solution to resolving this perpetual conflict between instincts and moral imperatives.	An emphasis on human life cycles: infancy, adolescence, adulthood, etc. A distinct turning point or event characterizes each stage.	Identifying with the leader alleviates feelings of anxiety, tension, guilt, and insecurity.
Because of low self-esteem, the political man focuses on the acquisition of power. Values held by revolutionary leaders result from guilt feelings acquired during childhood when the child is confronted with parental authority in terms of standards and conscience.	Focus on identity crisis, a pivotal event. Overall, a focus on the intersection of historical realities and personal conflicts.	Need for a role model for the follower. Deference and security as personality needs for the leader. Leader viewed as a moral agent.

In conclusion, Downton identifies the two types of charismatic leadership as revolutionary and institutionalized. In other words, charisma can be an agent of change, as well as a conservative force.

Power and Revolutionary Leadership

Studies of revolutionary leadership, in particular, emphasize the dynamics of conflict and power as a central phenomenon. Power struggles and violent conflicts vis-à-vis the status quo emerge as the revolutionary leadership struggles to realize the collective purpose, which is the realization of actual social change manifested in the satisfaction of human needs and expectation. Revolutionary leadership in this sense will fall into the category that James MacGregor Burns calls transforming leadership.[30] A transforming leader has a good understanding of potential followers and therefore recognizes and exploits their needs and demands. He not only identifies and exploits the needs and demands of potential followers, but also seeks to involve the follower fully in whatever social cause is in existence. As leader-follower interactions continue, the followers become more immersed in efforts to achieve the collective goal, while leaders may be converted to moral agents—that is they exhibit the kind of leadership that can bring about social change that will satisfy the existing needs of the followers. For MacGregor Burns:

> Leadership over human beings is exercised when persons with certain motives and purposes mobilize, in competition or conflict with others, institutional, political, psychological, and other resources so as to arouse, engage, and satisfy the motives of followers.[31]

The two actors involved are leaders and followers, with the leader playing the role of spokesman. Examples are Lenin's calls for peace, bread, and land; or Gandhi's calls for Indian independence from the British. A major factor is that both leaders and followers hold identical goals. What the leaders do is create a strong correspondence between their desires or motives and those of the followers in order to realize their common purposes.

In revolutionary leadership, relationships, collective effort, and purposeful behavior are important. Dynamic relationships with cadre and rank and file are necessary ingredients along with effective collective effort sustained toward the definite goal: success of the revolution. In a revolutionary situation where many aspects of society have become burdensome to the masses, as well as to the cadres and leaders, leadership is tantamount to leaders motivating or inducing followers to engage in action that would help produce the overthrow of the illegitimate system and usher in a system that is more in line with the expectations, aspirations, or desires of both leaders and followers. That leader may be more motivated and more skilled than the followers is reason for the former to initiate contact and induce, or provide incentives to, the latter to become more activist. The leader does the motivating and the inducing, and thus revolutionary leadership could be described overall as mobilizing, inspiring, or exhorting.

Conclusion and Critique

Many theories of leadership stress the varied biological, psychological, and social forces that affect the child and adolescent as the sources of political leadership. These early influences, which produce and shape the impulse for revolutionary leadership in an individual, are especially sharpened by parental attitudes and behavior, peer pressure and relations, type of schooling, and youthful attitudes toward leaders and leadership positions. The

Table 7.2: Mao Tse-tung

Mao Tse-tung (1893–1976), founder of the People's Republic of China in 1949, is
regarded as a prominent theorist of Marxian communism. Like many great persons,
Mao as a child was frequently in conflict with his strict father. But with the moral
support of his devoutly Buddhist mother, he successfully learned how to coexist with
his father. As a child, he also studied the traditional Confucian classics, and he never
entirely identified with the middle-class intellectuals who dominated Chinese
university life. Beginning in 1911, Mao was exposed to the radical tides of political
change and the new culture sweeping the country. Between 1913 and 1918, he
immersed himself in radical writings, and even organized a group of students with a
radical bent. The Chinese Radicals, as they became known, were heavily influenced
and motivated by the success of the Russian Revolution, which had established a
government of fairness to its citizens.

Upon the establishment of the Chinese Communist Party (CCP) in Shanghai in 1921,
Mao was a founding member and leader of the Hunan branch. As early as 1927, in
his "Report on the Peasant Movement in Hunan," Mao realized that the revolution
would be led by peasants and that the leader of the peasants would become leader of
China after the revolution. In 1928 when he fled from Chiang Kai Shek, he
established with Chu Teh a rural-based guerrilla army in the mountains of South
China. This was a significant development in his revolutionary career because he
now had a guerrilla force operating in a rural environment with peasant support.

During the early 1950s, Mao became chairman of the CCP, chief of state, and chairman
of the military commission. In the late 1950s, Mao embarked on two goals: (1) the
rapid transformation of rural ownership through elimination of the last vestiges of
rural private property; and (2) the initiation of the Great Leap Forward, a program
whose goal was to initiate rapid industrial growth through the use of people's
communes. The consequences of these policies were popular resistance and
administrative confusion, the effects of which were exacerbated by disastrous
shortfalls and severe food shortages. After a brief loss of influence and position as
chief of state, Mao regained leadership by launching the Great Proletarian Cultural
Revolution, which reached its peak between 1966 and 1969. Its objective was to teach
the Chinese masses that it was "right to revolt," and for them to get directly involved
in decision making.

In sum, Mao's greatest achievements were the unification of China through the
destruction of nationalist power led by Chiang Kai Shek, the creation of a Unified
People's Republic, and the leadership of the most populous and greatest socialist
revolution in the history of the world.

For further details, see Ross Terrill, *Mao: A Biography* (New York: Harper & Row, 1980);
and Philip Short, *Mao: A Life* (New York: Henry Holt and Co., 1999).

Table 7.3: Fidel Castro

Fidel Castro (1926–) was born into a family of comfortable means. In 1953 Castro launched an armed struggle against Cuban dictator Fulgencio Batista. The attack was a failure with most rebels either killed, or like Castro, jailed. In 1955, following an amnesty from Batista, Castro left for Mexico to plot an invasion of Cuba. At the end of 1956, Castro and eighty two fellow rebels landed in eastern Cuba and took refuge in the Sierra Maestra mountains, which they used as a base to launch their guerrilla warfare against Batista. After decisive attacks on some major Cuban cities, on January 1, 1959, Batista fled to the Dominican Republic. On January 8, 1959, Castro entered Havana after a triumphant ride through Cuba. In April 1961, Castro declared Cuba a socialist state and three days later on April 19, 1961, Castro's troops defeated the CIA-backed Cuban exile invasion force at Bay of Pigs.

Chronology of Key Events of Fidel Castro's Revolution

August 13, 1926—Fidel Castro Ruz was born in Biran, eastern Cuba, in a stable middle-class home.

July 26, 1953—Castro launches what was initially a failed armed struggle against Cuban dictator Fulgencio Batista.

May 1995—Castro, who had been jailed for his failed insurgency, was granted amnesty by Batista.

December 1956—Castro, who had left for Mexico soon after his release from jail, landed in eastern Cuba with eighty two fellow rebels. After the initial clash with Cuban forces, those who survived, including Castro, took refuge in the Sierra Maestra mountains where they launch a guerrilla war.

December 28, 1958—Ernesto "Che" Guevara, the Argentine-born guerrilla commander in Castro's army, lauched a decisive attack on the key city of Santa Clara and captured it.

January 1, 1959—Batista fled to the Dominican Republic. Castro's revolution is successful.

January 8, 1959—Castro rode in triumph through eastern Cuba to Havana.

April 16, 1961—Castro declared Cuba a socialist state.

For more details, see Lionel Martin, *The Early Fidel: Roots of Castro's Communism* (Secaucas, NJ: L. Stuart, 1978); and Peter G. Bourne, *Fidel: A Biography of Fidel Castro* (New York: Dodd, Mead, 1986).

child as an adult becomes preoccupied with the acquisition of power in order to compensate for, or triumph over, childhood experiences with and feelings of inferiority, guilt, impotence, or failures vis-à-vis parental expectations. The overall objective of the impulse for power is to achieve a sense of self-esteem.

Some of the major leaders analyzed by psychobiographers either had an intense positive attachment to one parent and intense negative attachment to the other, or an intensely traumatic, or negative youthful experience. Hitler was in constant conflict with his Austrian father, who wanted his son to become a civil servant like himself. Instead of his father's preference for education at a technical high school, Hitler preferred the more prestigious *gymnasium*. He wanted to become a painter or artist, to the great surprise of his father. At the height of the conflict between Hitler and his father over the issues of education and career, the father collapsed and died in the street. Among other experiences and societal developments, the economic dislocation and political turbulence of the early 1930s was the context Hitler needed for the consolidation of coercive and raw power. Lenin also lost his father suddenly at the early age of sixteen. Lenin, along with his older brother Alexander, had feelings of guilt over his father's death. Alexander was later executed after an abortive attempt to assassinate Czar Alexander III. Perhaps it was the combination of guilt over his father's death and intense, undying anger over his brother's execution that cemented Lenin's revolutionary impulse during this period. These two factors plus his early indoctrination in Marxism and the socioeconomic and political climate produced by World War I helped him in his drive toward revolution.

In their attempt to overcome their own psychological conflicts and attain self-esteem, leaders directly strike a cord with the longings of potential followers. As leader and followers interact, a sociopolitical movement develops based on a symbiotic relationship involving leader, cadres, and rank and file. All actors, in other words, through mutual support, collectively address their aspirations, demands, or expectations, thereby diminishing their individual fears, guilt, anxieties, or political-economic concerns.

The most common criticisms against psychoanalytical theories are that, in spite of their intriguing character, they are least amenable to scientific testing because they are based largely on speculation or intuition. In other words they cannot be replicated or verified. They are also limited to very few individuals, and ignore historical and socioeconomic variables. In particular, they tend to engage in an overstretch of their logic and explanations within arguments that are very unidimensional. For example, Why do some individuals with serious Oedipal conflicts become revolutionaries while others do not? Why would Lenin's older brother's execution constitute a catalyst that set him on a revolutionary course?[32]

The psychohistorical approach seems more like an improvement on the psychoanalytical because it introduces historical factors into the analysis. However, it is weakened by most of the intuitive and nonscientific aspects that are still a part of it. Because these works are confined to very few individuals, the problem of the extent of explanation still remains. For example, although seemingly compelling and intriguing, the events Erikson used are largely suspect in terms of the turning point that he believes they represent.

The psychohistorical explanations in general are entertaining because they have the qualities of a novel.[33]

Charisma, on which many of the sociological theories are based, is considered an ambiguous and elusive concept. What is sometimes referred to as charismatic leadership is simply media hype and sensationalism. In other words, the mass media manufacture or fabricate charisma. Media sensationalism creates false exaggerations about an individual's leadership qualities. Mere success, for example, is easily equated with charisma. While it has some intuitive value, the concept's empirical utility is seriously limited. Besides, it is not easy to determine whether all revolutionary leaders are charismatic. It is more likely that not all revolutionary leaders are charismatic, and nor are all charismatic leaders revolutionary. Finally, the problem with charismatic leadership is that it is an ephemeral, or short-lived phenomenon. This is because charisma is largely personal in nature, and its continued validity rests on continued performance and proof. In the end, Weber contends, charisma is unstable, and either becomes traditionalized or rationalized, or a combination of both.

Notes

1. For a more comprehensive and detailed analysis of the role of revolutionary leaders, see Mostafa Rejai and Kay Phillips, *Leaders and Leadership: An Appraisal of Theory and Research* (Westport, CT: Praeger, 1997); and James MacGregor Burns, *Leadership* (New York: Harper and Row, 1979).
2. Far a more detailed analysis, see Barbara Kellerman, ed., *Political Leadership: A Source Book* (Pittsburgh, PA: University of Pittsburgh Press, 1986).
3. See, for example, Sigmund Freud, *Group Psychology and the Analysis of the Ego*, ed. James Strachey (New York: W. W. Norton, 1989).
4. See Harold D. Lasswell, *Psychopathology and Politics* (New York: Viking, 1960); and *Power and Personality* (New York: Viking, 1962).
5. Harold D. Lasswell, *Power and Personality*, pp. 175, 263–64.
6. E. Victor Wolfenstein, *The Revolutionary Personality: Lenin, Trotsky, Gandhi* (Princeton, NJ: Princeton University Press, 1967).
7. See Erik H. Erikson, *Identity, Youth and Crisis* (New York: W. W. Norton, 1968).
8. E. Victor Wolfenstein, *The Revolutionary Personality: Lenin, Trotsky, Gandhi*, p. 308.
9. Jean Piaget, *The Origins of Intelligence in Children* (New York: International University Press, 1952).
10. For more on Gandhi's life, see Malcolm Yapp, *Gandhi* (St. Paul, MN: Greenhaven Press, 1980).
11. Erik H. Erikson, *Gandhi's Truth* (New York: Norton, 1969).
12. E. Victor Wolfenstein, *The Revolutionary Personality: Lenin, Trotsky, Gandhi* (Princeton, NJ: Princeton University Press, 1967), 82–3.
13. See N. Valentinov, *The Early Years of Lenin* (Ann Arbor: University of Michigan Press, 1969).
14. E. Victor Wolfenstein, *The Revolutionary Personality: Lenin, Trotsky, Gandhi*, p. 39.
15. Adolf Hitler, *Mein Kampf* (Boston: Houghton Mifflin, 1943), 5, 10.
16. For details, see Walter C. Langer, *The Mind of Adolf Hitler* (New York: Basic Books, 1972).
17. Mostafa Rejai and Kay Phillips, *Leaders of Revolution* (Beverly Hills, CA: Sage Publications, 1979).
18. For more details, see Mostafa Rejai and Kay Phillips, *Leaders and Leadership: An Appraisal of Theory and Research* (Westport, CT: Praeger, 1997).

19.   See Erik H. Erikson, *Childhood and Society* (New York: Norton, 1963); and E. Victor Wolfenstein, *The Revolutionary Personality: Lenin, Trotsky, Gandhi.*

20.   See Erik H. Erikson, *Young Man Luther: A Study in Psychoanalysis and History* (New York: Norton, 1962); and *Gandhi's Truth: On the Origins of Militant Nonviolence.*

21.   Erik H. Erikson, *Young Man Luther: A Study in Psychoanalysis and History.*

22.   Erik H. Erikson, *Gandhi's Truth: On the Origins of Militant Nonviolence.*

23.   See A. Schweitzer, "Theory of Political Charisma," *Comparative Studies in Society and History,* 16 (1974): 150–81.

24.   Max Weber, *The Theory of Social and Economic Organization,* ed. and trans. A. M. Henderson, and Talcott Parsons (New York: Free Press,1975) 328.

25.   Max Weber, *Essays in Sociology,* ed. with an introduction H. H. Gerth and C. Wright Mills (New York: Oxford University Press, 1958).

26.   Max Weber, *The Theory of Social and Economic Organization,* ed. with an introduction Talcott Parsons (New York: Free Press, 1984), 361–63.

27.   A. R. Wilner, *Charismatic Political Leadership: A Theory,* Research Monograph no. 32 (Princeton: Center of International Studies, 1968).

28.   Robert Tucker, "The Theory of Charismatic Leadership," *Daedalus* 97 (1968): 731–56, 737–38.

29.   J. V. Downton Jr., *Rebel Leadership: Commitment and Charisma in the Revolutionary Process* (New York: Free Press, 1973).

30.   James MacGregor Burns, *Leadership* (New York: Harper & Row, 1978).

31.   James MacGregor Burns, *Leadership,* p. 18.

32.   For detailed critiques of the revolutionary leader approach, see W. T. Daly, *The Revolutionary: A Review and Synthesis,* Sage Professional Papers in Comparative Politics. (Beverly Hills, CA: Sage, 1972); and K. J. Ratnam, "Charisma and Political Leadership," *Political Studies* 12 (1964): 341–54.

33.   For details, see P. Razen, *Eric H. Erikson: The Power and Limits of a Vision* (New York: Free Press, 1976); and Mostafa Rejai, "Theory and Research in the Study of Revolutionary Personnel," in *Handbook of Political Conflict: Theory and Research,* ed. T. R. Gurr (New York: Free Press, 1980).

Key Terms

authority	Oedipal conflict
charisma	passive resistance
charismatic authority	psychobiographical analysis
ego	rational-legal authority
id	revolutionary elite
identity	superego
legitimacy	traditional authority
nonviolence	

Discussion Questions

1. Outline the differences between the psychoanalytic and psychohistoric approaches to revolutionary leadership.
2. Discuss the three types of authority inherent in the sociological explanations of revolutionary leadership.
3. What is charisma? Discuss and critique its usefulness to leadership.
4. Analyze any one of the approaches to revolutionary leadership and apply it to the revolutionary history of a specific leader.

CHAPTER **8**

Revolutions
Causes and Types

Introduction and Definitions

Revolution as a topic of study has engaged the minds of classical philosophers such as Plato and Aristotle, renaissance thinkers like Machiavelli, and more modern figures such as Karl Marx, Alexis de Tocqueville, Émile Durkheim, and Max Weber. It, no doubt, constitutes one of the most dynamic subfields in the study of violent conflicts. While riots, violent demonstrations, or civil wars challenge state integrity, a revolution is more profound, dramatic, and intense with regards to its impact on the status quo.

The term revolution itself is used in reference to any radical change in society or the international system. One of the more popular twentieth-century developments that deserved the label of revolution has been the phenomenal changes in global telecommunications characterized by technologies ranging from the radio to the fax to the World Wide Web. During the eighteenth century, the transition from agricultural to industrial production brought about the industrial revolution, a development that generated many other worldwide activities with profound political and socioeconomic effects in Asia, Africa, and Latin America. A revolution thus implies a radical and profound alteration of political, economic, and social activities within a society.[1]

Revolution as a concept is often used loosely. For example, many soldiers have described their overthrow of an incumbent government (coup d'état) as a revolution. Often, the changes that resulted are not profound enough to justify describing their takeover as a revolution. In 1992, for example, young army officers whose average age was only twenty-seven years overthrew the twenty-three-year-old civilian regime in the West African state of Sierra Leone, and described their five year rule as a revolution.[2] They did not effect any dramatic, profound, or long-lasting change in political or economic activity that would qualify their rule as a revolution.

Many theorists of revolution consider revolutions to be only those upheavals that effect a radical alteration of values, a total revamping of the state and society with enormous consequences for the people and institutions. Examples of revolutions with such profound effects are the French, Russian, Chinese, Cuban, Iranian, and American, among others. According to Stanislav Andreski, the French and Russian revolutions approximate the type of perfect revolution because they had the following four characteristics: (1) an overthrow of the government by its own subjects, carried out from within the state; (2) the old ruling power elite replaced by a new one from within the state; (3) mass insurrection, involving violence or the threat thereof; and (4) a transformation of the old social system.[3] Many transformations labelled revolution do not satisfy all of these requirements. Besides, a transformation of the social system is often impossible to attain because there are always lingering remnants of the old order.

Along the lines of what constitutes the near perfect revolution, a distinction is often made between the "Great Revolutions," such as the French, Russian, American, or English, whose effects are very profound to the point of reconstituting the state, and less profound illegal and/or violent transfer of power. In the former case, known as the Exclusivist School, only some transformations qualify as revolutions because of the dramatic changes they generate.[4] In other words, in a revolution the end result of the change should be quite different from the prerevolution state. In the latter case, known as the Inclusivist School, the focus is on illegal and/or violent transfers of power even if they produce no profound effect on the state, citizens, and society at large. Under this focus, coups d'état qualify as revolution, whereas a legal accession to power, such as the Nazi ascendancy in Weimar Germany that resulted in a profound transformation of society would not qualify as a revolution. For the Inclusivist School, the emphasis is not on the end result of the change but on the turbulence or illegal and/or violen nature of change. The focus is how the change was accomplished, instead of what the end state is.

Since revolutions such as the great revolutions (the French, Russian, Chinese, and so on) involve change, analysts have often focused on the dimensions of revolutionary change. In other words, a revolution involves changes or alterations of the following: (1) values or the myths of the society, (2) the social structure, (3) institutions, and (4) elite leadership or class composition. These alterations are always accompanied by nonlegal or illegal transfer of power, as well as violent behavior especially at the time of the regime's collapse.[5] Changes in values involve operating on a new paradigm (conception of reality) or a new Weltanschauung (worldview). This could be a change from capitalist values to socialist ones. Whether the new values are voluntarily embraced by most people is open to question, because revolutions are generally characterized by coercion and crowd behavior as opposed to behavior and decisions based largely on individual choice. But an entirely new society and people enter the scene, and an entirely new worldview is embraced.

An alteration in the social structure of the society is an integral part of the revolution. One of the best illustrations of social-structural alteration is the change in class relations generated by alterations in the economic system. Marxism appropriately depicts such alterations through the transition from one economic system (mode of production) to another: for example, the transition theoretically from capitalism to socialism and then to communism, if feasible, entails a total alteration of class relations of dominance and stratification in politics and economics.

Institutional alteration refers to changes in the political institutions. In past great revolutions such as the French, or Russian, the monarchy was abolished and replaced by a legislature. There is, of course, a great deal of overlap between institutional, structural, and value alterations. As emphasized by A. S. Cohan, institutional alteration may simply be a reflection of the alterations in other dimensions such as in values or social structure.

Alteration of the elite is often inevitable with revolutions. The new rulers may come from different classes and groups. In other words, it involves the replacement of one hegemonic group by another. Many coups and other violent transitions in developing countries short of profound transitions include this displacement of one ruling group by another. The emergence of new rulers may not have any significance in terms of other alterations.

Finally, there is often disagreement over whether or not violence is integral to revolutions. In other words, are revolutions by definition violent acts? For many theorists, any discussion of revolutions that excludes violence is absurd. It is, however, useful to make a distinction between violent revolutionary acts such as the storming of the monarch's palace, and nonrevolutionary violent acts, such as looting, and outright vandalism, which may not be in support of a revolution. In terms of violence and revolutions, many theorists subscribe to the Sorelian (Georges Sorel, 1847–1922) notion of power transition.[6] It was Sorel who argued that power had to be wrestled from the middle class to the working class, and that such a process could be achieved only through a general strike that, in order to accomplish its goal, must be violent. He became a leader and theoretician of revolutionary syndicalism, or the revolutionary trade unionist movement advocating control of government and industry by trade unions, and to be achieved through such direct action as general strikes and sabotage. On the other hand, there is the notion of the nonviolent revolution reflected in Gandhi's philosophy of nonviolent resistance to overthrow British colonial hegemony over India, or Martin Luther King Jr.'s use of civil disobedience in the civil rights struggles in the United States in the 1960s. However, where the great revolutions are concerned, the notion of nonviolence is simply absurd, or a contradiction in terms.

The idea of a revolution as a fundamental societal change has transformed many countries in the world. In 1920, a group of scholars began to study the most famous revolutions of the West. Using the nomothetic method, the group identified the most common patterns or similarities among the great revolutions. Based on this study, which lasted ten years, they developed ten principles in are an attempt to explain past and predict future revolutions. This attempt at identifying sets of stages through which revolutions are supposed to pass has become known as the "Natural History School" of revolutions.[7] These ten stages are:

1. A period of initial political alienation during which a significant cross-section of society that includes poets, teachers, playwrights, bureaucrats, and even members of the aristocratic class, among others, cease to support the regime. They generally become estranged from the regime and all it stands for, as manifested in the criticism, sarcasm, and cynicism directed at it.
2. The regime, in response to criticism, will embark on major reforms through new policies and co-optation of some critics. This is usually the regime's first sign of weakness, and it opens itself up to increased pressures from the revolutionaries.
3. The revolution or fall of the regime begins with an actual political crisis that the incumbent government is unable to adequately handle. This catalyst, accelerator, or precipitating factor could be a natural disaster, a power struggle within the ruling elite, or defeat in war.
4. After the revolution, there is a short period of euphoria and unity among the revolutionaries, after which disunity develops with three factions (conservatives, moderates, and radicals) struggling for power. Their disagreements largely revolve around how much political or economic change the revolution should accomplish.
5. The moderate faction is usually the first to hold on to power.
6. The moderates are opposed by the radicals, who become more effective as extremist centers of mass mobilization are organized with the intent of seizing power.
7. The radicals eventually accede to power and effect extreme measures. Only in instances where the target of the revolution

is an external or alien power (for example, colonial rule) are the moderates likely to retain power and survive, such as in the American Revolution or the Algerian Revolution.

8. The vigilance coupled with the disorder produced by revolutionary fervor and struggle for power usher in a reign of terror under the extremists. During the French Revolution, the guillotine represented that coercive reign of terror.

9. The continuous struggle between defenders of the old regime, as well as external enemies of the revolution, eventually produces new effective leadership in the form of an absolute ruler. In France it was Napoleon, in England, Cromwell, and in Turkey, Ataturk.

10. Finally, the revolution accomplishes most of its pressing goals, power is consolidated, and moderation takes over. During this stage excesses committed during the revolution are condemned because power has shifted back to the moderates either because radicals are defeated or have died.

A significant addition to the literature of the Natural History school is David Schwartz's outline of a similar revolutionary process with an emphasis on the other stages such as the origin of revolutionary organizations following initial political alienation by the populace.[8] This is followed by revolutionary appeals, revolutionary coalition- and movement-building processes, nonviolent revolutionary politics, and outbreak of revolutionary violence. In similar fashion, the eruption of revolutionary violence is followed by rule of the moderates, accession of the extremists, a reign of terror, and a final period of moderation and pragmatism when the situation settles down into a status quo.

Determinants and the Types of Revolutions

A revolution is often a politicoeconomic revolt caused by injustice, abuse of power, and intense misery brought on by state economic failure such as a recession. The onset of state bankruptcy, or an extensive natural disaster such as a flood, famine, or drought act as catalysts for the outburst of violence. Between 1846 and 1849, for example, Europe was wracked by revolutions that were sparked by rising food prices after a poor harvest and the recession that followed the industrial expansion in the early 1840s.[9] There were revolts in Germany, Hungary, Austria, Czechoslovakia, Italy, and France. The revolts were fueled by a "contagion effect": groups initiated revolts as they learned of revolts in other countries, and the state's weakness to put them down.

Industrialization coupled with a rapid growth in population contributed to the emergence of an impoverished, immiserated (very miserable) urban working class. The consequences were increased hunger riots, which were often dealt with by military force. The hardships of the 1840s depression, the resulting popular unrest, and the growing paralysis of the Hapsburg government created a crisis in Prague by the end of 1847. Prague's urban population had rapidly increased at this time due to the rural exodus to cities and the beginnings of mechanized industry. In 1844 textile workers protested low wages, broke machines, and attacked Jewish factory owners and small businessmen. Again in 1847, workers protested against unemployment, food shortages, and high food prices; and such protests recurred in 1848.

Increasingly in much of continental Europe, intellectuals felt the lack of individual rights, as compared with those realized in the Glorious Revolution of 1688 in England, or in the United States with the Declaration of Independence in 1776 and the 1787 Constitution, and in France with the 1789 Revolution.[10] Thus, they began to express their discontent by spreading liberal ideas through their literary works.

Apart from mass frustration due to economic dislocation or a paralyzing political crisis, other factors that are critical in determining revolutions are the marginalization of capable and astute individuals whose exclusion from power creates in them a feeling of relative deprivation. Vilfredo Pareto (1848–1923) argued that the overthrow of the elite is at times due to the lack of co-optation of such competent people in society.[11] Similarly, divisions among the elite can pit some elite members against the incumbent government. The consequence is the formation of dissident elite groups that end up pursuing a revolutionary solution to the points at issue. Revolution could also be facilitated by widespread and powerful motivations that end up galvanizing the majority of a state's population behind the goal of revolution. Such critical factors for revolutionary movements are enhanced by adherence to a principle of noninterference in the affairs of another nation. The consequence is that other governments do very little to prevent a revolution from erupting in a particular nation.

In both classical and more modern theorizing about revolution, the eruption of violence generally follows a process that comprises either interests, beliefs, solidarity, or organization, or a combination of all factors. For example, for John Stuart Mill, individual interests that lead to individual action ultimately result in collective action. Such a process originates from decision rules. In other words, the distribution of wealth "is a matter of human institution solely." It "depends on the laws and customs of society."[12] The rules by which the distribution of wealth is determined affect individual interest, individual action, and in the end collective action. Similarly, in Max Weber's theorizing, collective action results from an interaction between interest, belief, and organization. Weber, however, makes a distinction between routine (outside the realm of instability) and nonroutine (instability) situations.[13] In the former context beliefs determine organization and interests determine collective action, whereas in the latter situation, interests lead to beliefs, which shape organizations and ultimately lead to collective action. The Marxian model discussed in the next chapter follows a process of organization of production, out of which develops conflicting interests based on class, then solidarity, and collective action. Collective action or revolution brings about the fundamental societal changes related to values, institutions, and other social-structural dimensions.

A more modern theorist, Charles Tilly formulated his theory along a similar process-like approach. His model of collective action, also known as resource mobilization or political process, consists of five elements: (1) interests of actors, (2) organization as the first step a group takes to act in its own interest, (3) mobilization (the process of collectively marshaling resources necessary to pursue the collective interest), (4) opportunity includes situations either conducive or nonconducive to the realization of the collective interest, and (5) collective action. The last element is dependent on, and results from, the changing combinations of the preceding four.[14]

Most of the post 1960s works on revolution have been inspired by the seminal works of two authors: Barrington Moore Jr.'s *Social Origins of Dictatorship and Democracy* (1966), and Eric Wolf's *Peasant Wars of the Twentieth Century* (1969).[15] Both works focus on agrarian classes or the reaction of peasants to the intrusions of modernization. According to Moore, the factors that determine the nature of revolutions are the impact that the processes of commercialization of agriculture and state expansion have on agrarian classes such as peasants and landlords. For example, he argues that fascism is a result of bureaucrats and landlords joining in a political coalition. Moore focuses largely on England, France, the United States, China, Japan, and India in his analysis.

Wolf analyzes revolutions in Mexico, Russia, China, Vietnam, Algeria, and Cuba. According to him, peasant rebellions are generally defensive in character. Such rebellions occur because peasants wish to protect their traditional lifestyles from the strains generated by the encroachment of modernity. The sources of such strains are population growth, commercialization and growth of markets, and the instability caused by changes in political elites brought on by power struggles. In other words, these factors correspond respectively to crises of demography, ecology, and power and authority.[16]

In the first factor, the mere increase in population size placed a serious strain on inherited and existing cultural arrangements related to agricultural and land issues. As population increased, so also did the commercialization of land and agriculture increase. Land and other resources were increasingly viewed as commodity items to be traded. Such commercialization did not take into account the needs of the rural populations. As a result, in places such as Mexico, Algeria, or Cuba, forced purchases and outright seizure were common. In China and Vietnam, inflated rents deprived many of land and

Table 8.1: Some Major Revolutions

REVOLUTION	DATE
English Revolution	1640–60
American Revolution	1765–75
French Revolution	1789–95
Mexican Revolution	1810–1920
Japan (Meiji) Revolution	1865–80
Boxer Rebellion	1899–1900
Turkish Revolution	1908–22
Russian Revolution	1917–21
Nazi Revolution	1923–35
Chinese Revolution	1937–49
Mau Mau Rebellion	1950–56
Algerian Revolution	1954–62
Cuban Revolution	1956–60
Iranian Revolution	1978–82

resources. Generally, the peasant economy suffered under the weight of taxation, demands for redemption payments, and by increased pressure on peasants to produce more industrially produced commodities. The combined effects of all these burdens and pressures disrupted the ecological balance of peasant society. Increasingly peasants were deprived of pasture, forest, and farm land. To a large extent, commercialization or commodification posed a serious threat to peasant communal existence. Commercialization in turn generated a rapid turnover in the elite class. Merchants, labor, and industrial leaders, who comprised the new elite, challenged the traditional elite (tribal chiefs, the mandarin, the landed nobleman) who controlled land and other fixed social resources.

Peasants, according to Wolf, are not easily galvanized into revolt. There are only two segments of the peasantry that have the influence and capacity to engage in sustained rebellion. These are: (1) a landowning "middle peasantry"—that is a peasant population that is well entrenched in a land of its own and cultivates it with the help of family labor, and (2) a peasantry that is outside the direct control of landlords.

Types of Revolutions

Contributions to the study of revolutions have also come from Chalmers Johnson. In his 1964 book, *Revolution and the Social System,* he used four criteria—targets, perpetrators, goals, and initiation—to develop six kinds of revolutions.[17] Although the term revolution is used overall, three are rebellions, which imply unsuccessful attempts to overthrow the system. The six are:

1. Jacquerie: a mass rebellion of peasants with limited goals. Many peasant rebellions would fall into this category, including the French peasant rebellion of 1358 and the Russian peasant rebellion between 1773 and 1775.
2. Millenarian rebellion: usually prophet-led, or with religious leaders as instigators, with the goal of creating an ideal society. Examples are the Taipong rebellion in China (1851–64), Zapata in Mexico (1910–19), and the Boxer Rebellion in China (1899–1900).
3. Anarchistic rebellion: described as antinationalistic and utopian. Examples are the Vendée counterrevolution (1793–96) during the French Revolution, the Tibetan rebellion in 1959; and the American Civil War (1861–65).
4. Jacobin communist revolution: described as the classic revolution because it involves fundamental societal change. Examples are the French Revolution (1789–99), the Turkish Revolution (1908–22), the Mexican Revolution (1910–34), and the Russian Revolution, Kerensky (March 1917–21).
5. Conspiratorial coup d'état: an elite-based revolution with elitist goals. Examples are the Russian Revolution, Lenin (October 1917), Irish Rebellion (1916), and Cuban Revolution (1959).
6. Militarized mass insurrection: an example of the elite leading the masses with nationalistic goals. Examples are the Chinese Revolution (1937–49), Algerian Revolution (1954–62), Ireland (1916–23), the Philippines (1946–54); and Malaya (1948–58).

Often in studies of revolutions, a distinction is made between revolutions against traditional monarchies or imperial or premodern states, and revolutions against modern dictatorships. Examples of the first type, revolution against traditional monarchies, are the classic revolutions of France in 1789, Russia in 1917, and China in 1911 to 1949. These revolutions occurred in societies dominated by traditional elites and by substantial peasant participation in revolts. Examples of the second type of revolution against dictatorship are Mexico in 1911, Cuba in 1959, Nicaragua and Iran in 1979, and the Philippines in 1986. These are societies characterized by semimodernity in both state and institutions. In these revolutions, a greater role was played by urban groups compared to peasants or rural groups. Such partially modernized societies are characterized by neopatrimonial rule comprised of a modern bureaucratic and party-based government centralized under the authoritarian rule of a single individual.[18] Such a leader's rule is based on an extensive system of patronage, rather than adherence to impersonal laws. Many of the actions and policies of the incumbents are directed into successful efforts to maintain or retain power. Clientelism, nepotism, and corruption are all subsumed under neopatrimonialism. Clientelism is a relationship of reciprocity between unequals. It is in existence in the form of patron-client relationships and political patronage. Political patronage, the distribution of public jobs or specific favors by party stalwarts, or by the single leader, in exchange for electoral support, is more appropriate as an analytical tool for understanding politics in such societies characterized by semimodernity.

The French Revolution   The French Revolution (1789–99), is an example of a revolution against a traditional monarchy or a premodern state. Its origins can be traced back to a financial crisis caused by France's involvement in foreign wars between 1740 and 1783. In particular, France's involvement in the American War of Independence (1778–83) further contributed to the national debt. This large public debt persisted because of a lack of tax reform that shielded the privileged classes (the clergy and nobility) from taxation. The population was divided into three estates: the third estate was made of the bourgeoisie (comprised of city workers, and the middle class) and peasants. They were the majority of the population. The second estate was made up of the nobility. They numbered roughly 400,000, with most of them being of minor rank. The first estate was comprised of all members of the clergy. Although the first and second estates enjoyed privileges over the third estate, and were richer, they were exempt from taxes.[19] The inequality among the three groups caused great discontent within society, and especially within the third estate. Thus, the French Revolution was, to a very large extent, a struggle for equal rights.

Other longstanding causes leading to the French Revolution were, first, the continuing grievances of the peasants who were constantly burdened with huge amounts of taxation. Second was the emergence of new critical ideas, especially among the bourgeoisie influenced by the new Age of Enlightenment. Moreover, the French troops who had served in the American Revolution were heavily influenced and even motivated by ideas such as the right to take up arms against tyranny, no taxation without representation, and a republic is superior to a monarchy, among others.[20] These revolutionary ideas quickly found fertile soil in France because of the incompetence of King Louis XVI (1774–92), who was weak and indecisive, and preferred to put his personal interest above the interest of the state.

Even with the greatly increased debt by the mid-1780s, the privileged orders still resisted attempts to tax them and demanded the calling of a representative assembly, the estates-general. The summoning of the estates-general only created more disputes over representation, elections, and voting. The bourgeois leaders of the third estate united in their struggle against the aristocracy. Their goal was to achieve equality by destroying the privileges of the clergy and the nobility, and put in place a system in which promotions would be based on merit, not birth, and in which all were subject to taxation and the requirements of the law.[21] By July 1789, the struggle pitted the king and the privileged orders on the one hand, and the bourgeois on the other. When the king prepared to use force against the national assembly (estates-general), the sans-culottes—the artisans and workers of Paris—prevented him from doing so. They attacked the Bastille on July 14, 1789, thereby saving the assembly and ensuring the success of the Revolution because the king lost control of Paris and the towns.

The precipitating factor that sparked the Revolution was the conflict in May 1789 between the crown and the privileged estates on the one hand, and the third estate on the other. In particular, the latter declared itself the national assembly and chose to disregard the king's authority by claiming the right to manage the affairs of the state. Some of the troops that the king intended to use to crush the revolt deserted to join the Parisians besieging the Bastille.

The fall of the Bastille marked the loss of authority by the crown, as real power passed to the elected representatives of the people. The king also lost authority in the countryside as a result of a peasant revolt that spread over most of France between July and August of 1789.

Finally, a principal reason for the eruption of the French Revolution was that France experienced unmanageable difficulties, in particular, bankruptcy after expending a great deal of resources in the success of the American Revolution against the English crown. King Louis XVI was incapable of generating new funds through taxation because the upper classes (nobility and clergy) would not relinquish their privilege of exemption from taxation. It was the third estate, made up of mostly the rising middle class (bourgeoisie) and professional people, who bore the brunt of taxation. The depressing economic system acted as a catalyst for the revolutionary outbursts because the harvest was poor, and food prices so exorbitant as to cause riots. The king was blamed for all the woes of the winter of 1789. In the final analysis, the French Revolution accomplished many significant things. A previously despotic and absolutist society saw the adoption of the rights of man and citizen, proclamation of equal rights, the end of privileges that caused a great deal of burden for the emerging and lower classes, the establishment of the constitution and a republic, as well as the institution of codified laws, among many other accomplishments.

Table 8.2: A Select Chronology of the French Revolution

1778:	France declares war on Great Britain and sends an army to North America.
February 6, 1779:	The United States and France sign a treaty in support of American independence from Britain.
1783:	Treaty of Versailles signed, recognizing the independence of the United States.
May 5, 1788:	The French estates-general meets at Versailles. It was the first such meeting since 1614.
June 17, 1788:	The third estate (also known as the commoners) of the estates-general meets separately and declares itself to be a national assembly. King Louis XVI closed their meeting place, so they repair to the tennis court at the Louvre (Jeu de Paume).
June 6, 1789:	Members of the national assembly swear an oath not to disband until a constitution is in place.
June 27, 1789:	Louis XVI legalizes the national assembly, permitting all three estates to meet together and vote on the basis of one person one vote.
July 14, 1789:	Parisian mob storms Bastille Castle, captures it, hoping to find arms. It was used as a royal prison. The mob kills its governor, the Marquis de Launey, and releases its seven inmates who were common prisoners and not political prisoners.
August 4, 1789:	Equality of rights is proclaimed throughout France during the night.
August 14, 1789:	Out of fear, nobles and clergy in the national assembly renounce their privileges, thereby ending feudalism in France.
August 1789:	Adoption of the Declaration of the Rights of Man and of Citizens.
October 5, 1789:	Parisian mob marches on Versailles. Louis XVI and Marie Antoinette are transferred to the Tuileries Palace in Paris, where they are held in confinement.
June 20–21, 1791:	Louis XVI and Marie Antoinette, in disguise, attempt to escape from France, but are apprehended at Varennes, and are brought back to Paris.
1791:	Louis XVI accepts a constitution.
October 1, 1791:	Legislative assembly convenes.
June 20, 1792:	An insurrection in Paris fails.
August 10, 1792:	A Paris mob, inflamed partly by the writings of Jean-Paul Marat, storms the Tuileries Palace and sets up a new city government. Robespierre is elected to the Commune of Paris.
September 2, 1792:	Mobs across France storm jails and kill hundreds of royalist sympathizers who had recently been confined in them.

Table 8.2: Continued

September 21, 1792:	National Convention meets for the first time, abolishes the monarchy, establishes a republic, and tries King Louis XVI for treason. The king is convicted by a majority of one vote.
January 21, 1792:	King Louis and Queen Marie Antoinette are guillotined in Paris. The executions enraged European monarchies, causing them to band together in the Brunswick Manifesto.
July 27, 1794:	Robespierre is arrested and guillotined the next morning.
October 5, 1795:	Napoleon, charged with protecting the Directory, rings the Tuileries with cannon. As the mob charges, Napoleon fires the cannon into the crowd, killing many and forcing the crowd to disband.
November 9, 1799:	Napoleon becomes First Consul.

Revolutions from Top to Bottom

Another distinction among theorists of revolution is that between revolutions from below (such as the Chinese, Russian, or Cuban) and revolutions from above (such as that of Turkey in 1923 and the Meiji Restoration in Japan in 1868). In instances of the latter, traditional rulers were ousted from power and extensive programs of modernization were put in place.

The underlying cause of the Turkish Revolution of the early 1920s was the effects of World War I on Turkey. The immediate cause was the attempt by the victorious Allies to control the Anatolian territory.[22] In order to prevent this from happening Kemal Atatürk (1881–1938) organized an army of national resistance. In opposition to the Sultan's (Mehmet V) weakness and ineffective government, a national assembly (First Turkish Grand National Assembly) met in Ankara, April 23, 1920. It elected Mustafa Kemal president and overturned the harsh terms embodied in the Treaty of Sévres (August 1920), which would have deprived Turkey of some of her richest provinces. In 1923, the Turkish Nationalists abolished the Ottoman Sultanate, and established the Republic of Turkey with Atatürk as its first president.

Atatürk then embarked on a process of Westernization that he believed was the only way to make Turkey strong. Westernization meant, to a large extent, destroying Islamic institutions. Accordingly, he abolished the Sultanate and Caliphate, and established a republic; implemented secularism nationwide; the *waaf* (religious endowments) and the *ulama* (religious leaders) were put under government control; religious courts were abolished; the Gregorian calendar replaced the Muslim calendar; religious brotherhoods were suppressed; sacred tombs were closed as places of worship; Western clothing styles replaced traditional clothing, in particular the wearing of the fez was forbidden and replaced by the hat; and a new civil code based on that of Switzerland replaced the *Sharia* (Muslim Law).[23] Atatürk embarked on many other reforms that totally revolutionized and modernized Turkish society.

Japan's Meiji Restoration (enlightened rule) constitutes another example of revolution from above. The immediate causes of the Meiji Restoration was the arrival of Westerners (British, Russian, French, Dutch, and Americans) into Japanese territory. The Japanese saw this as a direct attack on traditional Japanese values. The Shi-Shi segment of the Samurai class from southwestern Japan were especially opposed to the intrusion of foreigners in their political, economic, and cultural life. However, after a series of conflicts in which the Westerners bombarded their cities with cannons, they came to the realization that in order to expel the barbarians (Westerners), they had to learn to use their guns and their technology in general. Thus, the new slogan became: Japanese spirit, Western technology.

In time, the people of southwestern Japan (in particular, the Satsuma-Chosu regions) armed themselves with Western weapons. They then joined forces to topple the Shogun's army near Kyoto. The army then marched from the old capitol, Kyoto, to Yedo, which they renamed Tokyo for eastern capitol. They crowned the sixteen-year-old Prince Mutsuhito emperor in 1868. Meiji (1852–1912) reigned as emperor of Japan from 1867–1912.[24] The goal was to launch a series of Western reforms and establish a unified administration headed by the emperor as the sovereign.

With the collapse of the feudal order under the Tokugawa Shogunate, the Meiji government adopted a rationalistic system with a strong government vis-à-vis the West, as opposed to the spiritualistic mindset of the old Samurai class based on Chinese Confucianism. The emphasis was on removing the threat posed by the Western powers through industrialization. Japan was thus transformed in less than half a century into an industrialized world power. In addition, a centralized bureaucracy replaced the balance of power politics during the Tokuguwa era. A conscript army replaced the military authority of the Samurais. Freedom of movement and employment were instituted, thereby doing away with the rigid class structures of the old order. In order to enhance education and industry, the government imported foreign advisors and technology. In 1872, a centralized school system was established. In 1873, the old feudal system of taxation was abolished for a new system of taxes. In 1889, Japan became a constitutional monarchy with a bicameral legislature known as the Diet.[25] These changes and more continued throughout the Meiji period and have led some historians to refer to the Meiji Revolution, rather than the Restoration, which implies a return to the past. A noteworthy aspect of the Meiji Restoration was the willingness of the feudal lords to surrender their privileges in order to create a strong

Japan. In the end, Japan became strong enough to resist Western domination and to get rid of the unequal treaties that gave Westerners a privileged position in Japan. Through the restoration of absolute power in the person of the emperor, Japan achieved equality of opportunity, and modernization.

Just as many distinctions can be made with regard to revolutions, so also are there many causes of revolutions. For instance, there are revolutions caused by defeat in war. For example, the defeat of Napoleon Bonaparte ushered in a period (1815–30) of revolution in France, Belgium, Poland, Spain, Italy, and Portugal. Similarly, the Prussian victory over France in the Franco-Prussian War of 1870 to 1871, was followed by insurrection in France. Defeat also preceded revolutions in Russia, Hungary, Germany, and Turkey from 1917 to 1919. Defeat weakens the rulers materially and psychologically and tips the balance. There are also instances of revolutions caused by political reform. In other words, revolutions often occur after conditions have substantially improved or are in the process of improving. According to Alexis de Tocqueville's observations of the French Revolution, conditions were in fact improving when the revolution erupted.[26] Enlightened reforms in the past that touched on serfdom produced peasant insurrections. One such insurrection was the 1789 peasant insurrection caused by the 1780 reforms of Joseph II of Austria. Moreover, what is sometimes referred to as the black revolution in the United States broke out only after the Supreme Court decision in Brown versus Board of Education, outlawing racially segregated schools. Reforms generally raise the political capabilities of revolutionaries, thereby instigating them to further action. Reforms could also be interpreted as a sign of weakness on the part of the incumbent regime, thereby raising the bravery of the revolutionaries to press for more changes.

Revolutions can also be caused by a lack of unity among the power elite, leading to attacks, deprivations, or removal of protection from powerful individuals. In such a situation, senior military officers, large landowners, religious leaders, and important business tycoons, among others, could be the target of actual attacks of repression. The response of such people is often called a "palace revolution," a "coup d'état," "insurrection," "putsch," or "fascist revolution."[27] There are many instances in which, for example, senior military officers have staged a coup d'état against a president who retires them earlier than usual, or marginalizes them. Two examples are the coups d'état in Pakistan and the Ivory Coast in 1999. In October 1999, chief of the army staff General Pervez Musharraf overthrew Prime Minister Nawaz Sharif, and in December 1999, former army chief Robert Guei led a coup that toppled Ivorian president Henry Konan Bedie.

In conclusion, a revolution defined as a fundamental societal alteration of political-economic and social institutions is not just a phenomenon of the eighteenth, nineteenth, or early twentieth centuries, but is endemic to human existence. Revolutions have targeted traditional monarchies, as well as semimodern dictatorships. They have emanated from below with extensive participation by all classes, and from above, initiated by a power elite with aims at modernizing society. Revolutions have also been described as either left-wing or right-wing in orientation. The latter's goal is to restore traditional institutions along with maintaining social order and traditional authority, whereas in the former the aim is to change major political, economic, and social relations in order to achieve greater equality through institutional change. The Russian, Chinese, Cuban, and Nicaraguan revolutions are widely considered leftist, whereas the Iranian revolution falls squarely in the realm of right-wing revolutions.

Notes

1. For a detailed analysis of the linguistic and conceptual dimensions of the term revolution, see Ilan Rachum, *Revolution: The Entrance of a New Word Into Western Political Discourse* (Lanham: University Press of America, 1999).
2. For details, see Earl Conteh-Morgan and Mac Dixon-Fyle, *Sierra Leone at the End of the Twentieth Century: History, Politics, and Society* (New York: Peter Lang, 1999).
3. Stanislav Andreski, *Wars, Revolutions, Dictatorships: Studies of Historical and Contemporary Problems from a Comparative Viewpoint* (London: Frank Cass, 1992).
4. For details, see A. S. Cohan, *Theories of Revolution: An Introduction* (New York: John Wiley and Sons, 1975).
5. For more details on the dimensions of revolutionary change, see A. S. Cohan, *Theories of Revolution: An Introduction.*
6. Georges Sorel was a French social philosopher and journalist who was a leader and principal theoretician of the revolutionary syndicalist movement. His most important work is *Reflections on Violence* (1908; trans. 1912).
7. See, for example, David C. Schwartz, "Political Alienation: The Psychology of Revolution's First Stage," in *Anger, Violence, and Politics: Theories and Research,* eds. I. K. Feierabend, R. L. Feierabend, and T. R. Gurr (Englewood Cliffs, NJ: Prentice-Hall, 1972); L. P. Edwards, *The Natural History of Revolution* (Chicago: University of Chicago Press, 1927); and Crane Brinton, *The Anatomy of Revolution* (New York: Vintage Books, 1938).
8. David C. Schwartz, "Political Alienation: The Psychology of Revolution's First Stage."
9. See, for example, Priscilla S. Robertson, *Revolutions of 1848: A Social History* (Princeton: Princeton University Press, 1952); and Charles Tilly, *European Revolutions, 1492–1992* (Cambridge, MA: Blackwell, 1993).
10. For an analysis of varied types of revolutions, see Andrew Wheatcroft, *The World Atlas of Revolutions* (New York: Simon and Schuster, 1983).
11. Vilfredo Pareto, *The Rise and Fall of the Elites* (New York: Arno Press, 1979); and Harry Eckstein, "Theoretical Approaches to Explaining Collective Political Violence," in *Handbook of Political Conflict,* R. T. Gurr (New York: Free Press, 1980), 135–66.
12. For details, see Stephen J. Andriole and Gerald W. Hopple, *Revolution and Political Instability* (New York: St. Martin's, 1984); and George Soule, *Ideas of the Great Economists* (New York: The New American Library, 1952).
13. See, for example, Charles Tilly, *From Mobilization to Revolution* (Reading, MA: Addison-Wesley, 1978).
14. Charles Tilly, "Speaking Your Mind with Elections, Surveys, or Social Movements," *Public Opinion Quarterly* 47 (Winter): 461–78.
15. Barrington Moore Jr., *Social Origins of Dictatorship and Democracy* (Boston: Beacon Press, 1966); and Eric Wolf, *Peasant Wars of the Twentieth Century* (New York: Harper, 1969).
16. For details, see Jack A. Goldstone, ed., *Revolutions: Theoretical, Comparative, and Historical Studies* (New York: Harcourt Brace College Publishers, 1986), chapter 3.

17. Chalmers Johnson, *Revolution and the Social System* (Stanford: Hoover Institution, 1964).

18. For details on neopatrimonialism, see Christopher Clapham, ed., *Private Patronage and Public Power* (London: Frances Pinter, 1982).

19. There are numerous works on the French Revolution. See, for example, Patrice Higonnet, *Class, Ideology, and the Rights of Nobles During the French Revolution* (Oxford: Clarendon Press, 1981).

20. For details, see Norman Hampson, *The French Revolution: A Concise History* (New York: Scribner 1975).

21. See, for example, John Markoff, *The Abolition of Feudalism: Peasants, Lords, and Legislators in the French Revolution* (University Park, PA: Pennsylvania State University Press, 1996).

22. For details, see Gunsel Renda and C. Max Kortepeter, eds., *The Transformation of Turkish Culture: The Ataturk Legacy* (Princeton, NJ: Kingston Press, 1986).

23. See Henry E. Allen, *The Turkish Transformation: A Study in Social and Religious Development* (New York: Greenwood Press, 1968).

24. See, for example, George M. Beckmann, *The Making of the Meiji Constitution: The Oligarchs and the Constitutional Development of Japan, 1868–1891* (Lawrence: University of Kansas Press, 1957).

25. For details, see Thomas M. Huber, *The Revolutionary Origins of Modern Japan* (Stanford, CA: Stanford University Press, 1981).

26. Alexis de Tocqueville, *The Old Regime and the Revolution* (Chicago: University of Chicago Press, 1998).

27. The literature on coups d'état is immense; for a good survey see Maxwell A. Cameron, *Presidential Coups d'État and Regime Change in Latin American and Soviet Successor States: Lessons for Democratic Theory* (Notre Dame: The Helen Kellogg Institute for International Studies, 1998); and Eric Carlton, *The State Against the State: The Theory and Practice of the Coup d'État* (Aldershot: Scholar Press, 1997).

Key Terms

contagion effect	nonviolent revolution
coup d'état	palace revolution
fascism	political patronage
modernization	resource mobilization theory
"Natural History School"	revolution
of revolutions	revolution from above
neopatrimonial rule	revolution from below
nomothetic method	revolutionary syndicalism

Discussion Questions

1. What is a revolution? Discuss the various dimensions, distinctions, and alterations involved in revolutionary change.
2. Analyze the difference between revolutions from above and revolutions from below. Give examples whenever appropriate.
3. What is the "Natural History School" of revolutions?
4. Analyze the causes of, and outcome of, any major revolution.

CHAPTER **9**

The Marxist Explanation of Revolutionary Change

Karl Marx (1818–83) is considered the most famous conflict theorist. His explanation of conflict and social warfare inspired many other theorists and revolutionaries. Society for Marx is inevitably conflictual because of inherent contradictions manifested especially in the division of society into classes that reflect the mode of production, or economic system. In other words, Marxism relies on structural (societal) assumptions, or the effects of social structures to explain individual behavior as a determinant of social change.

In order to construct his theory of revolution, Marx utilizes the ideas of the renowned philosopher G. W. F. Hegel (1770–1831). Hegel theorized that one opinion (a thesis) countered another functioning as another opinion (an antithesis).[1] In a dialogue entailing both a thesis and antithesis it is assumed that both were partly correct and therefore produced a synthesis of the two. Thus a dialectical progression is often viewed as starting with a thesis, then its antithesis, and finally a synthesis. Of the numerous interpretations of Marxism, the Hegelian aspects of Marx's thought, which places emphasis on dialectics and the basic role of human praxis, are viewed as determining the nature of social change. The collective input of the thesis and antithesis into the synthesis made it superior to both. For Marx, freedom, or the most free society is to be realized through a process of historical evolution characterized by class warfare. Thus, Marx's teleology sketches how and why people create progressively nonexploitative (freer) societies by way of a unilinear path of social evolution to the freest society that would eliminate all economic distress in political systems.

According to Marx, all social organization results from a society's mode of production (or political economy). The aspect of the political economy that underscores economic factors is identifiable with another major interpretation of Marxism—that which emphasizes the positivist or scientific character of Marx's thought. The focus of this interpretation is social and economic conditions as determinants of the nature of revolutionary change.[2] It views the economic or material conditions of a person's existence as closely related to human consciousness. The mode of production is made up of the division of labor and technology that organizes society into different property relationships or income groups. Each income group then becomes the basis of a class that determines the social consciousness or social awareness of this group throughout its history. In addition, Marx argues, the mode of production produces three broad classes: capitalists (the bourgeoisie) the landlords, and laborers (the proletariat), with each characterized by its own social beliefs shaped by work experience or praxis. Specific social attitudes are a reflection of relative status in society underlined by praxis. Class conflict occurs because each class soon realizes that its material success depends on the economic failure of the other two classes. Society becomes a persistent conflict of economic interests generated by relative status. The conflict in turn defines each class's political attitudes.

According to Marxism, there are numerous contradictions inherent in capitalism as a mode of production. These contradictions are located in what Marx refers to as productive forces and relations of production (or productive relations). The former, according to many scholars, may refer to the skills and status of workers and the way in which labor is organized generally. These factors are in turn dependent on the state of technology. The latter has been defined as the social and personal relations among those involved in the production process of a given system of production.[3] Thus factors such as inequality, patterns of stratification and dominance, or property relations are involved in relations of production. Since historical materialism is the dialectical process of moving from one economic system to another, some relations of production are higher than others, leading to the final nonstratified, nonexploitative, or nonconflictual stage of communism.

Contradictions are especially inherent in a given system of relations of production. Some of the numerous contradictions inherent in the structure of capitalism are: (1) profit maximization that underlies production at the expense of the satisfaction of human needs and the development of human beings; (2) the contradiction inherent in the private ownership and control of productive processes and the social aspects of production itself; and (3) the anarchic nature of production itself because of the lack of planning among factories producing similar goods.[4] Marx predicts that as capitalism develops, these contradictions become more evident resulting in economic crises. For example, if bourgeois capitalists fail to maximize profits they are likely to postpone reinvestment thereby leading to rupture in the smooth working of the economic process and subsequently economic crisis. Similarly, since workers are paid a meager wage and the capitalists appropriate the surplus value accruing from production, underconsumption increases because of the worker's inability to consume goods in society, which in turn affects the growth of the means of production, as well as the generation of profits. Besides, the anarchic nature of production itself could lead to overestimating of demand for products. An imbalance between supply and demand, leading to more production than is necessary, may lead to a loss of profits and a decision to curtail production. A severe combination of these crises could lead to chronic depression and even a collapse of capitalism thereby generating the preconditions for a higher form of society.

Other effects of capitalism's internal contradictions are those that increasingly produce dissatisfaction with capitalism and also intensify the immiseration (increasing misery) of the working class. The increasing misery of the workers eventually generates the preconditions of socialism in the form of cooperative or socialist work relations with bourgeois capitalism. Immiseration intensifies because of increasing inequality between workers and capitalists to the point of impoverishment, and because of capitalism's ability to create needs it cannot satisfy due to insatiable wants and the lack of resources on the part of poorly paid workers.

Also there is a contradiction between the inclination of capital to become concentrated (centralization of economic power) and the necessity of competition for efficient functioning of capitalism (decentralization of economic power). This contradiction is obvious in this age of globalization as mergers take place between giant companies to create conglomerates, while at the same time the Western world emphasizes the spread of markets and democracy. Privatization in particular is pervading many sectors of society ranging from the industrialized nations to the less developed ones.

Marx and his collaborator Friedrich Engels attribute the founding of "scientific" socialism to themselves because of their systematic analysis and exposure of the inequities and stratification inherent in the economic structure of societies and social classes.[5] But many critics believe that the writings of Marx reveal a heavy dose of moralism. In other words, Marx was an extreme moralist whose philosophy is tantamount to an outright disapproval of the capitalist economic system and Western society as immoral, inhuman, and dehumanizing. For Marx, there is a fundamental discrepancy between the essence of humanity, which is characterized by voluntary productive activity, and human existence, which has been reduced to forced and alienated labor.

History as Class Conflict

Class warfare as a political conflict eventually ensues as each class develops its own ideology, organizes around a political party, and advances its interests at the expense of the other two classes. History, according to Marx, is therefore a constant conflict among classes as shaped and determined by the evolution of the mode of production and changes over times. As Marx and Engels wrote: the history of all hitherto existing societies is the history of class struggles.[6] This representation of society as one of class conflict is dynamic as humanity moves from one mode of production to a higher mode of production. Marx identifies five stages of social development, with each stage better than the previous one in the total wealth available to society. Yet, where private property is integral to any stage class conflict is the consequence, pitting the owners of the means of production against the nonowners or proletariats.

Underlying this class conflict is productive labor, which exists in an impoverished state because the owners of the means of production appropriate the surplus value that accrues from the process of production. In other words, the existence of private property is consistently inimical to labor, which constitutes the only source of all wealth. For Marx, the constant class conflict and the poverty suffered by labor due to exploitation constitute a fundamental social evil whose source he calls alienation. Marx borrowed the concept of alienation from Hegel. Hegel had argued that alienation (*Entfremdung*) results when individuals felt coerced to obey an unjust state—that is a state that dominates everyone's will without their consent.[7] Alienation ensues because the alienated feel exploited, manipulated, resentful, and confused. According to Hegel, social harmony occurrs only when a state is ruled with the consent of its people. According to Marx, a mode of production based on private property would result in both personal alienation (humans lose the value of their labor) and social alienation—constant class conflict that pits one class against the rest in a perennial and mutually destructive struggle for supremacy. Thus, private property becomes the source of personal and social injury and injustice.

Class consciousness is thus an integral aspect of Marxism. It stems from the emphasis on social and economic conditions as determinants of the nature of social change, or from the view of human consciousness being in large part a reflection of the material conditions of the person's existence. In order to establish the interactive (or dialectical) relationship between activity and consciousness, Marx outlines three criteria to establish categories of work, or objective classes: (1) ownership versus nonownership of the means of production, (2) control versus lack of control over what is produced, and (3) productive versus nonproductive work. The theory of class consciousness is shaped by these dichotomies.

Alienation is also a central aspect of Marxism and constitutes the most important characteristic of work in society and in the capitalist economic system. Alienation and its impact on the workers is severe as the worker becomes alienated from work in general, from the product of his labor, from other fellow workers, and from humanity as a whole. Work that is supposed to develop human beings instead becomes a heavy burden, especially for the proletariat under a capitalist system. Marx would say industrial production, for example, ruins the worker's mind and body. Because the production activity does not contribute to the full potential of the worker, the worker is rendered unhappy by the activity. Thus, the interests of the workers increasingly become opposed to the interests of the dominant classes who appropriate the products and surplus value. It is especially because of their exploited, unhappy, and alienated situation in capitalist society that the proletariat would become revolutionary, eventually transforming their temporary bourgeois consciousness into socialist consciousness.

Marx argued that the laborer receives only a meager wage from the owners of the means of production. The rest of the value of production is appropriated by the latter constantly driven by the profit motive. The landlords and capitalists could not exist unless they constantly generate profit, and since personal alienation deprives the workers of most of the wealth generated, the owners of the means of production (landlords and capitalists) find it in their interest to keep the laboring classes (the proletariat) poor—or even very poor. At the same time, this private property imperative in the form of rents, profits, and wages widens and intensifies class conflict.[8] The consequence is intrasocietal division based on class, causing the general body of humanity to make war on itself. When society's inbuilt contradictions reach their highest point, or when the time is right, one class challenges the power of another to cause a revolution. Thus, any mode of production based on private property simply generates one revolution after another to the eventual free society.

For Marx, man is characterized by change and flexibility in response to changes in historical epochs and societies. Since man is a "productive being," he is therefore a reflection of the economic system that envelopes him. Thus, in order to change man, the economic foundation of society must be changed. Although Marx puts the emphasis on economic forces, he at the same time argues that human society comprises two main dimensions: an economic base or substructure and a superstructure. The economic base consists of institutionalized material and economic forces and the overt division of society into social classes. Using the state as an instrument of domination, the ruling class seeks to preserve and perpetuate its control. According to Marx, the economic base and its material economic forces are predominant and therefore determine the shape and direction of the superstructure. The superstructure comprises all other sectors or aspects of society such as culture, religion, art, politics, ideas, and ideology. In other words, the superstructure is merely a reflection of the foundation of society, the economic base.

Wages, Labor, and Alienation

Marx argues that wages are determined by the social struggle between the capitalist bourgeoisie class and workers. The relationship between the two is asymmetrical in the sense that the capitalist can survive much longer without the worker than can the proletariat (worker) without the capitalist. Besides, while mergers and close collaboration among capitalists tend to be effective and socially accepted, for workers, such cooperation and collaboration is at times prohibited and tends to produce negative consequences. In fact, collaboration among workers is actually prohibited if capitalists succeed in gaining control of authoritative (state) institutions—for example, the banning of labor unions in South America in the 1970s. The proletariat is always at a disadvantage vis-à-vis the capitalist. For example, while the capitalist and the landowner can rely on rent and interest on capital as alternative sources of income, the worker has neither of the two to supplement his industrial income. This situation causes a great deal of competition among the workers.

In Marxism, the condition of the worker is a precarious one not just because of his lack of income on rent and interest on capital, but because the worker's likelihood of gaining employment is dependent on the demands for workers in general.[9] Where the supply of workers far exceeds the demand, a segment of the labor force experiences deprivation and even starvation. Stated differently, the worker is reduced to a mere commodity whose survival is dependent on whether he can find a buyer to buy his labor. At times, it becomes very difficult for the worker to redirect his skills into other segments of production because of the considerable division of labor in the capitalist system. In times of economic downturn, the worker is the first to be adversely affected because of his subordinate position in the capitalist hierarchy. Under capitalism, the worker struggles for both his physical means of subsistence and to get work. The condition of the worker in society can be summarized in terms of a situation where: (1) if the wealth of society declines the worker is most adversely affected; and (2) if the wealth of society increases, the demand for workers usually exceeds the supply. At the same time, the increase in wages for workers gives rise to overwork among the workers because the more they are determined to earn, the more they should be prepared to expend their time and energy in the service of greed. Marx then goes on to argue that because of overwork and slave labor, the workers shorten their life span, which benefits the working class as a whole because an ever-fresh supply of labor becomes necessary.

The development and progression of capitalism produces an accumulation of capital that in turn increases the division of labor, and the division of labor increases the number of workers. The consequence is that the worker becomes dependent and confined to a narrow area of specialization with its routine type of labor. The increase in the class of people solely dependent on work intensifies competition among workers, thereby lowering their value as there is a surplus of labor and wages.

As capitalism develops, and as the worker becomes increasingly impoverished, so does the scope and magnitude of this production.[10] At the same time, the competition among capitalists results in the accumulation of capital in a few hands and thus the existence of the most terrible monopoly. In the end, the distinction between tiller of the soil and the factory worker disappears. The consequence is that society becomes characterized by two classes: the propertied and the propertyless workers. A system of two broad classes also implies that workers are increasingly devalued and their devaluation is in direct proportion to the increasing value of the things they produce. In other words, labor produces two things: commodities and itself the worker as a commodity. The product of labor is material as it has produced a concrete object or as Marx classified it as the objectification of labor. But at the end of the production process, the worker becomes nothing but a servant of what he has produced because he does not own it, and second, because he receives merely a means of subsistence, a meager wage. He is therefore no better than a slave worker. In Marx's own analysis:

> According to the economic laws the estrangement of the worker in his object is expressed thus: the more the worker produces, the less he has to consume; the more values he creates, the more valueless, the more unworthy he becomes; the better formed his product, the more deformed becomes the worker; the more civilized his object, the more barbarous becomes the worker; the more powerful labor becomes, the more powerless becomes the worker; the more ingenious labor becomes, the less ingenious becomes the worker and the more he becomes nature's servant.[11]

In other words, labor produces deprivation for the worker, whereas for the rich it produces benefits, profits, and a wonderful life.

Labor, according to Marx, is not an integral part of the worker because he naturally hates work, which makes him unhappy. The consequence is that work is considered coercion and not a voluntary act. Again, according to Marx:

> First, the fact that labor is enternal to the worker, i.e., it does not belong to his intrinsic nature; that in his work, therefore, he does not affirm himself but denies himself, does not feel content but unhappy, does not develop freely his physical and mental energy but mortifies his body and ruins his mind. The worker therefore only feels himself outside his work, and in his work feels outside

himself. He feels at home when he is not working, and when he is working he does not feel at home. His labor is therefore not voluntary, but coerced; it is forced labour. It is therefore not the satisfaction of a need; it is merely a means to satisfy needs external to it. Its alien character emerges clearly in the fact that as soon as no physical or other compulsion exists, labour is shunned like the plague.[12]

In other words, the worker becomes alienated to work as well to the product of his labor. Work activity is alien to him; it is independent of him. Thus, he becomes increasingly dissatisfied, or even frustrated to the point where workers as a collectivity begin to develop revolutionary feelings as they become more conscious of their pitiful condition.

Historical Developments

According to Marx, the history of human development and the revolutions that are integral to it follow a unilinear path of teleological development characterized by five stages or modes of production. The first stage, called primitive communism, occurred before agriculture and represented the beginning point of all human history. It is characterized by an economy of hunting and gathering where private property did not exist. As population increased during this stage, game became more scarce, and hunting increasingly difficult. Eventually, gathering became more important than hunting as overpopulation increased. At that point, agriculture began, eventually placing an enormous value on land and thereby creating private property. Thus agriculture represented the second stage of human production. Priests and kings as organizers of society took possession of the land to create the first social revolution. Their ascendance to power produced inequality, spawned wars between cultures, and in turn generated labor in the form of slavery. According to Marx, this second stage was one of oriental slavery because it had its origins in the orient—the ancient near East and Egypt. The great agricultural empires of Mesopotamia, Egypt, Persia, and later Rome were created by oriental slavery. Adequate or excess food supply, as well as succeeding empires were the result of continued population growth and expanding agricultural production. Warfare was the primary means by which these empires replenished their supply of slaves. Eventually, this mode of production reached its highest point in the vast and powerful Roman Empire.

When the Roman Empire could no longer expand because it had reached its geographical limits, it could no longer acquire fresh slaves by warfare. The slave population of Rome also declined because slaves could not reproduce their own numbers because they were so miserable. Thus, a social transformation began in the second half of Roman history as the empire tried to replace their slaves with serfs. Rome was not successful in this effort, and soon after the empire collapsed under the onslaught of barbarian invasions. Feudalism, the third stage of historical development, was instituted by the German tribes that took over after Rome's collapse. Building on what the Romans had already started, they consolidated their rule by replacing slavery with serfdom, and by dividing the Roman Empire into greater political estates and locked laborers (serfs) into land tilling through an inherited socioeconomic status from which they could not escape. Although conditions for serfs were good enough for them to reproduce their numbers, their income still bordered on subsistence at a level of misery approaching famine. Because feudalism defined private property by real estate alone, it therefore equated social status and political status with land. It meant that real estate deliberately excluded the value of capital from legal definitions of wealth. Since cities were associated with capital, those whose work revolved around trade developed severe hostility toward those who controlled land and denied the legitimacy of money as a form of wealth.[13] Owners of capital thus demanded social recognition and organized corporations with the aid of kings. Thus, the focus on capital (capitalism) developed naturally out of this mutual antagonism between capital and real estate and spawned the seeds of the fourth estate. Because of the fundamental hostility between the two, capital facilitated the occurrence of the next revolution.

The inherent contradictions within feudalism saw capitalism destroy feudalism. This destruction (revolution) was manifested in the industrial revolutions that occurred in France and Great Britain in the nineteenth century. Capitalism replaced serfs with wage-earning and industrial laborers. The proletariat, as the wage earners are called, were virtually wage slaves and were just as miserable as serfs and lived at the margins of subsistence. Like serfs, however, the proletariat (industrial working class) increased its population and became the overwhelming majority of the population. As they acquired literacy, skills in the use of new technology, and modern values because of their location in cities, they would become conscious of their long history of misery and mobilize into a massive revolutionary party. The new historical awareness would set the stage for the teleos of human history: communism. Communism is the fifth and final stage of social-economic development. When this final revolution occurs, private property will cease to exist and, with its demise, social warfare (class conflict) will come to an end.

The proletarian revolution becomes quite significant because in contrast to all previous revolutionary transitions, it results in the abolition of private ownership of the means of production, and consequently of all class divisions, class struggles, and the state. Humankind eventually reaches a society of peace and harmony following a brief period of the "dictatorship of the proletariat," during which the last attempts of the bourgeoisie to overturn the revolution and restore the previous order are defeated. With that, the transition to a "classless society" is realized. Thus, in Marxism the communist revolution finally eliminates alienation from man's economic condition and ushers in a period of voluntary and spontaneous productivity.

In sum, each stage in this historical materialism, or this vision of world history, is based on a unilinear path of development dictated by the mode of production and private property. Each stage involves an inverse relationship between total productivity and general misery of the laboring population. Each step also lays the foundation for the next stage of socioeconomic development. For Marx, all these steps lead to a final stage, the teleos, or the ultimate end of the historical process. Communism for Marx, is that teleos.

In the communist manifesto written in 1848, Marx and Engels emphasized that proletariats could only succeed in their struggle against capitalists if they overthrew the bourgeoisie by conquering political power, thereby eliminating class exploitation. Thus their most important message is that proletarian internationalism is a necessary condition for success in the constant struggle of labor against capital, in the effort to eliminate the remnants of the bourgeoisie and bourgeois power. With the elimination of coercive bourgeois power, the state would wither away and usher in free association, or true communism. The manifesto is thus a severe denunciation of bourgeois civilization, and a call for the proletariat to mobilize and bring about the free society: "The proletariat have nothing to lose but their chains. They have a world to win. Workingmen of all countries, unite!"[14] Marx basically regarded bourgeois capitalism as inherently unstable and contradictory, and as early as 1848 had predicted its collapse.

Marxism contends that the workers would increase their strength as they organize and mobilize in trade unions and political parties, and would eventually seize power by violent revolution in countries (such as Germany) with authoritarian traditions; whereas in countries with democratic traditions (for example Britain and the United States), the transition could be peaceful. Proletarian revolution would begin in the most industrially advanced capitalist countries and would then spread worldwide. Following revolution there would be the dictatorship of the proletariat, a transitional socialist stage to the consolidation of a communist society. The state, "the executive committee of the bourgeoisie," an instrument of class oppression, would continue to exist, but would now be ruled by the majority, the proletariats, and goods would be distributed according to each individual's contribution. When stratification by classes disappears, there would be no need for a state, which would wither away, and a new principle for the distribution of resources would be: "from each according to his ability and to each according to his needs."

The Scope of Marx's Influence

Considered the most important social and political theorist of the nineteenth and twentieth centuries, Marx's influence was immense starting in the 1880s in France and continuing to the post–World War II era and its Cold War conflicts. Marxism became the motivation for the Russian Revolution of 1917, Chinese communism under Mao Zedong, and communist parties everywhere. It became the foundation of development ideologies like Afro-Marxism in some African countries during the Cold War. Marxism also underlined many proxy wars like the Angolan Civil War between 1975 and 1990s. It motivated U.S. intervention in, and eventual war with, Vietnam in the 1960s and 1970s. In sum, it became the basis of all the tensions, suspicions, and rivalries between the United States and U.S.S.R. from 1947 until the disintegration of the latter in the early 1990s.

The writings of Karl Marx influenced many other revolutionaries, in particular Vladimir Lenin. The aspect of Marxism that asserts that capitalism uses war to further its own ends is Marxism-Leninism. In *Imperialism: The Highest Stage of Capitalism*, Lenin argues that imperialism (overseas capitalist expansion through colonialism in particular) is an inevitable outgrowth of capitalism.[15] When capitalism has reached the stage where it is characterized by monopolies, the state comes to depend more and more on capital exports. But because of a lack of opportunities for expansion within the capitalist countries themselves, the export of capital to ensure an uninterrupted increase in profits becomes essential. The perpetuation of increasing profits causes capitalist countries to struggle for political and military control of overseas territories as markets. In other words, the scramble for colonies by European states in the nineteenth century was done to secure raw materials and markets for manufactured surplus goods, as well as a source of cheap labor.

In the struggle for colonies, capitalist or imperialist nations at times went to war with one another. In particular, World War I was seen as proof of this struggle to obtain overseas territories, especially as Germany competed fiercely with Britain and France, because Germany also wanted to have the power, wealth, and prestige that came with an expanded market and source of raw materials. Thus, in Lenin's view, the only way to eliminate international conflict and ensure peace is to eliminate, through revolution, capitalist states themselves. Revolution involves transforming the domestic economic systems of the capitalist states and establishing in their place a "world proletarian" system based on socialism. Stated differently, before the final communist system, socialist states would ensure peace since they are in agreement over basic issues of resource allocation and are not disposed to the militarism that characterized the advanced capitalist states. In practice, however, during the Cold War, the socialist states of China and Russia were just as prone to go to war with each other as the capitalist states. For example, the Sino-Soviet conflicts of the 1950s and 1960s also qualify as military conflicts.

The notion of capitalist expansionism became a central issue of the Cold War in relations between the Soviet Union and the capitalist West. Stalin, for example, was concerned about the goal of capitalist encirclement, a strategy whereby communist states are totally encircled and contained by the West.[16] However, Stalin's successor, the next Soviet president, Kruschev, made reference to socialist encirclement, a development whereby as capitalist states weakened, they are encircled by socialist states. As the Cold War progressed, the notion of peaceful coexistence was also seen as a possibility between capitalist and socialist states. It would be a policy of accommodating capitalist states. This idea of peaceful coexistence did not end the military competition between the East and West, as well as the many wars of national liberation sponsored by the Soviet Union in the Third World.

Lenin's theory has been criticized by many critics for only focusing on economic motivations while ignoring political, psychocultural, ideological, religious, or idiosyncratic causes of war. The theory seems to be more valued for the period from 1870 to 1914 but is weak in relation to the current stage of advanced capitalism and what seems to be almost a lawlike generalization in the social sciences that advanced capitalist democracies never go to war with each other. On the other hand, those more favorably inclined to Lenin's theory argue that the current inequality between advanced capitalist states and Third World states is a result of the actions of imperial capitalist states during the past centuries. Dependency and world system approaches to explaining the international political economy are such examples.[17]

Dependency emphasizes a power structure of economic asymmetry between advanced capitalist states and developing countries. In particular, Latin American scholars like Raul Prebisch and Fernando Cardoso, among others, used the dependency approach to explain why Latin American states are poor in relations to advanced capitalist states. They argue that asymmetry in power capabilities between the North and South is a result of deliberate economic exploitation whereby the advanced capitalist states like the United States keep the developing countries poor by keeping them as suppliers of raw materials, markets for their surplus goods, and investment outlets for multinational corporations. This exploitation of the poor countries is possible because of the Bretton Woods institutions (the World Bank, the International Monetary Fund, and the World Trade Organization, formerly known as the General Agreement on Tariffs and Trade). These institutions were established after World War II by U.S. leadership during the July 1944 meeting of 44 countries hosted by the U.S. in Bretton Woods, New Hempshire to discuss the postwar economy. Their functions

Table 9.1: Karl Marx

Karl Marx was born May 5, 1818. He descended from a long line of rabbis, and from a comfortable middle-class home in Germany. At the age of seventeen he began his advanced studies in the faculty of law at the University of Bonn. Later he enrolled at the University of Berlin where he embraced the Hegelian movement, and as a result abandoned his earlier interest in romanticism. In October 1842, Marx became editor, in Cologne, of the influential liberal newspaper *Rheinische Zeitung*, supported by industrialists. Marx emigrated to France in 1843 when the Prussian government was forced to close the newspaper because of Marx's critical articles on economic questions. In Paris, Marx associated with French socialists; he became a communist and described his views in the *Economic and Philosophical Manuscripts (1844)*. It was also in Paris that he became a lifelong friend of Friedrich Engels (1820–95). In 1844 both Marx and Engels were expelled from Paris. Marx moved to Brussels where he spent the next three years, and developed his materialist conception of history in the German ideology. In 1847 Marx and Engels wrote the *Communist Manifesto*, and its completion coincided with the wave of revolutions in Europe. After moving back to Paris in 1848, Marx finally sought refuge in London in 1849. In London, Marx lived in poverty and his main source of income came from Engels. In the 1850s and 1860s he produced detailed works on capital, wage labor, and other economic issues. Marx died on March 14, 1883, after a serious deterioration in health, and was buried at Highgate Cemetery in North London.

are to stabilize exchange rates, give international assistance to war-damaged economies, and ensure low tariffs. Their collective structures and policies known as the Bretton Woods system focus on public management of the international political economy. The developing countries, according to dependency explanations, are kept poor by institutions like the World Bank and the International Monetary Fund, which are controlled by advanced capitalist states. Moreover, the global economy dominated by the Bretton Woods institutions has been divided by states into an international division of labor in which the capitalist states produce manufactured goods and the developing countries supply raw materials. The consequence is that the developing countries are always dependent on the rich capitalist states because of adverse terms of trade from the value of raw materials. Dependent states find themselves always short of foreign exchange, unable to import high technology, and always requesting more foreign aid from donors. The domestic consequences for the dependent country are chronic unemployment, structural imbalances among economic sectors of society, misery, and frustration that at times lead to ethnic tensions and violence.

Similar to the dependency approach is world systems analysis, which argues that developing countries are plagued by poverty because they were incorporated into capitalism as peripheral states to supply raw materials,

Table 9.2: Friedrich Engels

Friedrich Engels was born in Barmen in 1820, the son of a wealthy German industrialist. As a young man, his father sent him to Manchester, England, to work at his cotton factory. While there he was shocked by the impoverished condition of the working classes. In 1844 Engels began contributing articles to a radical journal called *Franco-German Annals*. Later that year Engels and Marx met and the two realized that their views on capitalism and society were, to a large extent, in complete agreement. They therefore decided to collaborate in their writings, with Marx tackling more difficult abstract concepts, and Engels capable of communicating their ideas through writing to a wider mass audience. In 1845 because of pressure on the French government by the Prussian authorities Karl Marx was expelled from France. Marx and Engels decided to move to Belgium, a country that observed more freedom than other European countries. Since Marx lacked any independent financial means, Engels helped to support him and his family. He gave Marx the royalties to *Conditions of the Working Class in England,* which he completed in 1845, while he was working at his father's cotton factory in Manchester. He also found alternate sources of support for Marx among sympathizers. In July 1845 Engels took Marx to England to meet with several of the Chartist leaders who had become friends to Engels. In January 1846, they returned to Brussels to set up a system that would link together socialist leaders living in different parts of Europe. That very year socialists held a conference in London, at the end of which they formed a new organization called the Communist League. In 1847, following a conference to develop a strategy of action, the Communist League committee decided that its goal was to launch a successful revolution against the bourgeoisie. Meanwhile, Marx and Engels were working on a pamphlet that would become the *Communist Manifesto* published in February 1848. That same year, Engels helped form an organization called the Rhineland Democrats whose leaders were arrested, but Engels managed to escape from the country. Engels and Marx next moved to London where the Marx family experienced such poverty that Engels returned to work for his father in Germany in order to help support them. From Germany he kept in constant touch with Marx. His support enabled the Marx family to survive. When Marx died in London in March 1883, Engels devoted the rest of his life to editing and translating his works. In particular he edited the second and third volumes of *Das Kapital* from Marx's drafts and notes.

serve as markets, and provide a source of investment for the core of capitalism: the advanced capitalist states. In other words, for world systems analysts, the international capitalist economy is divided into core capitalist states, the semiperiphery of capitalism (middle capitalist states), and the periphery: the Third World. This process of global capitalist incorporation is said to have started as far back as the fifteenth century. The consequence is a structure of power, wealth, and prestige that is responsible for the global inequality among states and even within states. Details on world systems analysis are found in chapter 6.

Critique and Conclusion

Marxist theory has often been critiqued for its heavy dosage of economic determinism, because at the core of its analysis is historical materialism that regards economic forces as the major determinants in the formation of society. Class struggle centers on the ownership of the means of production. The ruling class (the holders of economic power) control and shape all political institutions and cultural beliefs, which they use to perpetuate themselves in power. Engels, for instance, claims that economic factors (the economic base) determine political factors (the political and ideological superstructure). However, he later (1890) denied that he and Marx ever claimed that all historical developments are determined by economic factors, though he thought they are, in the final analysis, decisive.[18]

To many critics of Marxism, nearly all of Marx's predictions have been proved wrong. For example, capitalism has not only become more humane, but the worker has not experienced any progressive immiseration. Instead, workers are better off in advanced capitalist societies, and even own shares in many of the big companies that dominate the economic landscape. However, neo-Marxists argue that the breakdown of capitalism has not materialized because of: the exploitative aspects of foreign trade, which benefit the advanced capitalist countries; intervention by governments to rescue major firms and states that are on the verge of collapse; and state expenditure and regulation of the economy. Marxists, in addition, point to certain developments in capitalism as a mode of production that tend to support Marxist predictions about the demise of capitalism. These are developments such as the concentration of capital and the growth of monopolies in advanced capitalism. Most of these monopolies stave off the contradictions of capitalism through their imperialist activities. Workers in advanced capitalism are enabled to maintain their standard of living through the foreign exploitation involved in expansive capitalism. Moreover, another factor in advanced capitalist societies that seems to have delayed revolutionary consciousness among workers are cleavages. These are cleavages that undermine working-class unity such as ethnic, racial, or gender discrimination.

Finally, Marxian theory, it might be said, aims instead at interpreting the social and political world. In the process Marxism presents a theory of liberation because the transitions from one economic system to another are rarely peaceful. As Marx himself asserts in his *Contribution to the Critique of Political Economy:*

> At a certain stage of their development, the material productive forces in society come in conflict with the existing relations of production, or—what is but a legal expression of the same thing—with the property relations within which they

have been at work before. From forms of development of the productive forces these relations turn into their fetters. Then begins an epoch of social revolution. With the change of the economic foundation the entire immense superstructure is more or less rapidly transformed.[19]

Thus civil violence is integral to the transition process from one mode of production to the other. A complete change would also involve transformation of both formal institutions in the economic and political realms and their related patterns of dominance and principles of authority. Finally, critics of Marxism are skeptical about whether the contradictions in capitalism will be intense enough to lead to violent challenges against the status quo, especially in late capitalism.

Upon closer examination, Marxism raises numerous questions that challenge the plausibility of its logic. Marx puts too much faith in human nature and its potential for realizing the ideal society. Can any society exist without some level of organization and stratification? Can human life ever be free of all drudgery in this world of imperfection? Moreover, Marx's overemphasis on material forces ignores the fact that political, spiritual, and even intellectual forces could be just as decisive, if not more decisive in shaping the economic system. The idea of class also could be conceptualized more broadly to include aspects other than ownership versus nonownership. Finally, since conflict is endemic to any society at any period of history, the idea that class conflict and violence will ultimately lead to a nonviolent, nondivisive, and freest society is unrealistic.

In conclusion, for Marx, revolution or collective political violence is a class-based movement that grows out of objective structural contradictions within capitalist society. The principal focus in analyzing any society is its mode of production and the way in which labor is organized and its impact on class relations. The contradictions inherent in productive forces and relations of production are expressed in class conflict. Thus, a successful revolution involves a transition from one form of stratification and dominance inherent in a mode of production to a completely new mode of production with its own disjuncture in productive forces and relations of production.

Notes

1. Hegel was an idealist who emphasized the significance of spiritual and cultural forces and ideas in human history. He also glorified the idea of the state as the manifestation of the highest spiritual force, which he called *Geist*, or universal spirit. Although an idealist, he generally defended and justified the status quo whether it related to religion, politics, or culture. For details, see Mostafa Rejai, *Comparative Political Ideologies* (New York: St. Martin's Press, 1984).
2. For details on Marxism, see D. McLellan, *Karl Marx: His Life and Thought* (London: Macmillan, 1973).
3. See Robert C. Tucker, *The Marxian Revolutionary Idea* (New York: Norton, 1969).

4. For further details, see B. Salert, *Revolutions and Revolutionaries* (New York: Elsevier, 1976).
5. Friedrich Engels (1820–95) was a wealthy German industrialist who worked and lived in England. He became Marx's lifelong friend, collaborator, and benefactor. Marx collaborated with Engels starting in 1845.
6. Karl Marx and Friedrich Engels, *Manifesto of the Communist Party* (New York: International Publishers, 1964).
7. For further details on the influences of other theorists on Karl Marx's thought, see Steven Wallach, *Synopsis of World History: A Study in Culture* (New York: American Heritage Custom Publishing, 1996).
8. See Karl Marx, *Early Writings*, trans. and ed. T. B. Bottomore (New York: McGraw-Hill, 1964).
9. For details, see Karl Marx, *Economic and Philosophic Manuscripts of 1844* (Moscow: Progress Publishers, 1974).
10. See, for example, Karl Marx, *Early Writings*, trans. and ed. T. B. Bottomore (New York: McGraw-Hill, 1964).
11. Karl Marx, *Economic and Philosophical Manuscripts of 1844*, p. 65.
12. Karl Marx, *Economic and Philosophical Manuscripts of 1844*, p. 66.
13. For more details, see Richard N. Hunt, *The Political Ideas of Marx and Engels*, 2 volumes.
14. Karl Marx and Friedrich Engels, *Manifesto of the Communist Party*.
15. V. Lenin, *Imperialism: The Highest Stage of Capitalism* (New York: International Publishers, 1933).
16. See, for example, William Taubman, *Stalin's American Policy: From Entente to Detente to Cold War* (New York: Norton, 1982).
17. On dependency and world systems approach see, respectively, Raúl Prebisch, *Latin America: A Problem in Developments* (Austin: University of Texas at Austin, 1971); Samir Amin, *Accumation on a World Scale: A Critique of the Theory of Underdevelopment* (New York: Monthly Review Press, 1974); and Immanuel Wallerstein, *The Capitalist World-Economy: Essays* (New York: Cambridge University Press, 1979).
18. See, for example, Joel Krieger, ed. *The Oxford Companion to Politics of the World* (New York: Oxford University Press, 1993), 569–75.
19. Karl Marx, *A Contribution to the Critique of Political Economy* (New York: The International Library Publishing Company, 1904 [1983]), 159–61.

Key Terms

alienation
bourgeoisie
capitalist encirclement
class conflict
class consciousness
dependency approach
division of labor
economic base
imperialism

international division of labor
militarism
peaceful coexistence
political superstructure
praxis
proletariat
socialist encirclement
world systems analysis

Discussion Questions

1. What is class conflict? Discuss it in relation to capitalism and other economic systems in Marxism.
2. Analyze alienation as an integral aspect of Marx's critique of capitalism.
3. Discuss historical materialism in relation to the economic systems contained in Marxism.
4. How convincing is the dependency approach in explaining North-South relations?
5. Outline and critique some of the major inbuilt contradictions in capitalism as an economic system. Are they relevant today?

CHAPTER **10**

Interethnic or Identity Sources
of Violent Conflicts

Many of the 23 to 25 million war-related deaths in developing nations in the last half century could be attributed to violent conflicts underlined by significant overtones of identity or ethnonationalism. In terms of scope, intensity, and duration, these internal wars claim a growing number of lives, accelerate economic destructiveness, and undermine efforts to promote human rights, democracy, and socioeconomic progress. This increase in the number of ethnonationalist conflicts means that ethnicity and identity are becoming focal points of mobilization as a combination of disputes that have followed the process of decolonization, and those which have reemerged and intensified following the end of the Cold War.

While ethnicity has a positive dimension—defining identity and fostering self-determination—it is at the same time very destructive to human life and can cause untold suffering. It is therefore becoming quite apparent that even as the dangers of a nuclear holocaust become remote, this post–Cold War era is fraught with the disruption of economic activity and societal security in many states of the world because of intense and protracted ethnopolitical conflicts. Thus, the end of the Cold War and the beginning of a new millennium has challenged North-South relations and institutions to redefine their goals in line with changing environmental demands and new types of conflict. The objective of this chapter is to: (1) conceptually situate the nature of ethnopolitical conflicts in general; and (2) analyze the scope, intensity, and underlying causes of ethnonationalist conflicts in the international system along with their implications for humanitarian intervention.

The addition of post–Cold War conflicts to the existing nation-building conflicts continues to strengthen the perception of an international system increasingly gripped by anarchy. The real challenge to peacemaking arises from the seemingly unresolvable and protracted nature of many decolonization, nation-building, and now post–Cold War/new millennium conflicts. All three types of conflicts could be interactive, thereby making them more complex in relation to world stability.

Factors that enhance ethnic feelings may include perceptions of shared culture, nationality, language, religion, and race. An ethnic group is therefore a group of people who consider themselves to be distinct from others because of a shared belief of common ancestry, ties with a specific territory, a perception of a shared culture, and belief in common destiny. This conceptualization of an ethnic group is in essence summarized in terms of mental and/or physical attachment to a historic homeland, and the perception or practice of a shared culture that is often manifested as a common language, religion, race, or customs.

Ethnonationalist Conflicts: An Overview

Violent ethnic conflicts are becoming so widespread that they are now the direct cause of the external displacement of more than twenty million persons.[1] In these ethnonationalist conflicts, as in all conflicts, the source of dispute arises from at least one object of contention among two or more groups. The object of contention may involve incompatibilities over at least one issue, although in many ethnonationalist conflicts there are more. Conflict may revolve, for example, around exclusivist behavior manifested in interethnic discrimination, and situations of strong competition over limited resources. Besides, the consciousness of being one in relation to other ethnic groups translates into both subjective and objective elements that encompass multiple levels. Broader social-structural processes interact with personal and interpersonal psychocultural dynamics and are affected by the wider global systemic developments.

However, since ethnonationalist violence erupts over differences such as defining the proper boundaries of a political community, determining the goals and policies of a political community, the equitable distribution of resources within the state, or the struggle over scarce resources, one could argue that ethnonationalist conflict as such does not exist. What does exist is political, socioeconomic, and other sources of conflict between groups that manifest themselves along ethnic or identity lines. On the other hand, in a situation in which the exclusivist character of ethnicity is used as a powerful mobilizing symbol, ethnic discrimination becomes a significant factor in the scope, intensity, and even duration of the conflict.

Ethnonationalism and Protracted Conflicts

Not unlike the concept of nationalism, the behavioral manifestations of ethnonationalism are susceptible to variation in terms of revival or dormancy. In other words, the salience of personal and social ethnic identity may vary with the zeitgeist (spirit of the times). Generally, situations of imagined or real threat, intense discriminations, and heightened competition over dwindling resources awaken the consciousness of being one in relation to other ethnic groups. The ethnic identity factor (other than other social cleavages) becomes central to the self-identity of some group of individuals. In such a situation, ethnicity as a group phenomenon becomes the process of enhancing the security of an individuals's social identity. The ebb and flow of strong ethnonationalist sentiments continue to underscore Max Weber's original idea that "an ethnic group is a human collectivity based on assumption of common origin, real or imaginary."[2] The ethnic collectivity is solidified in times of danger or potential harm to the group.

Ethnocommunal groups, moreover, are identified not by the perception of a particular trait or combination of traits, but by the shared perception that the defining traits, whatever they are, make the group exclusive (that is, set the group apart). In addition, the ethnocommunal group is politically salient if it satisfies one or both of two primary criteria: it experiences economic or political discrimination, and it has organized and mobilized its resources in support of collective interests. Ethnopolitical violence is heightened by the fact that the group is a beneficiary of, or suffers from, systematic discriminatory treatment vis-à-vis other groups within the polity. Such interethnic discrimination may be a consequence of widespread social practice or deliberate government policy or both. In the most extreme situation, the ethnic group's most fundamental right (the right to physical survival) is threatened by systematic discrimination.

The concept of ethnonationalist conflict underscores the outcome of structural and perceptual incompatibilities that generate mutually opposed and overt behaviors that may be violent, protracted, and intractable. The dynamism inherent in social reality produces complex, interconnected, and embedded conflicts over time and space. Brecher and Wilkenfeld describe a protracted conflict as a situation that exhibits an extended duration of hostile exchange, very high stakes, spillover to many other areas, and conflict processes over time rather than specific events.[3] Although protracted, they share many characteristics with other conflicts in that they arise from an attempt to correct the injustices of deprivation, repressed identity for the parties involved, an absence of group security, and an attempt to guarantee effective political participation as a means to ensure: (1) retention of predominant control over its territory and use of resources; (2) security—safety and preservation of the group; (3) maximum feasible freedom in relation to civil/political, economic/social/cultural rights relative to other groups; (4) continued acceptance of the group by others, and in particular by the state; and (5) guaranteeing its long-term political and socioeconomic opportunity base. When these concerns are threatened or seem unrealizable to the group, the consequence is usually ethnonationalist violence.

Intractable conflicts, because they acquire features not related to the original conflict issues, become especially resistant to resolution. They tend to therefore widen in scope, increase in destructive intensity, and even lengthen in duration. The main instruments of communication between the disputing parties become violence. The parties are likely to maintain rigid and uncompromising positions, express intense hostility, and view the conflict in zero-sum terms, making their positions resistant to resolution. Based on the mutually exclusive goals of the parties, the conflict is conceptualized as inevitable, integrated into the life of the group, and elevated to the level of religion. The conflict in this sense becomes a vested interest of the groups's identiy. Ethnonationalist conflicts that have many characteristics of protraction and intractability fall into four broad categories: (1) separatist movements (Armenians in Azerbaijan, or Kurds in Iraq)—the effort by an ethnic group to become politically independent, or part of an effort by a nation to prevent the group from doing so; (2) rivalry for autonomy or political power or territorial control (Chechen/Ingush in Russia, Islamists in Algeria and Egypt, Hutu and Tutsi in Rwanda or Burundi)—conflict between ethnic groups in one nation, or between an ethnic group and the government over access to and control of economic, political, and territorial opportunities within the nation; (3) conquest (Bosnian Muslims and Serbs, Croats and Serbs)—ethnonationalist violence involving a war between two or more nations where ethnic differences between the groups is a major factor; and (4) survival (Turks and other nonethnic Germans in Germany, or Gypsies in Romania)—conflict occurs as part of an attempt by a national government or majority group to forcibly assimilate, harm, remove, or drive out an ethnic minority.[4]

It is quite common for ethnonationalist conflicts to originate from socioeconomic crises of the state and patterns of ethnopolitical domination. Asymmetrical or competitive relations between ethnic groups largely determine a society's state and ethnic structures and in turn affect the domestic context from which ethnonationalist wars erupt. The centrality of state politicoeconomic crisis indicates that the issue of distributional equity in resource allocation is a more important source of violent conflict. The probability of the conflict becoming protracted is high because the parties to the conflict occupy the same territory. In other words, at the core of many ethnonationalist conflicts is a struggle over values and claims to finite resources, power and status, where the objective of one group is to eliminate, dominate, or injure the other.[5] Such interethnic rivalry is predicated mainly on the fact that one ethnic group had what the other wanted—the motivating factor could be land, more economic opportunities, and the like. The sociocultural distance between ethnic groups often produce situations in which dominant groups systematically deny other groups a fair share of the country's resources. The structure of inequality is aggravated during periods of economic crisis and austerity, as dominant groups strive to ensure their advantageous economic, political, or social position. Widening inequality is sometimes accompanied by state oppression, resulting from a challenge against the dominant group, or the persecution could lead to a rebellion by the oppressed group. Thus, the level of violence in ethnonationalist conflict situations becomes a function of intensity of motivation. Violence is directed toward the outgroup because important economic, power, or security goals are involved.

While these post–Cold War ethnonationalist conflicts do not have the potential of involving the vital interests of nations with more lethal weapons, they nonetheless underscore the fact that the awkward incompatibilities between nation (peoples) and state (territory) are manifested in conflictual ethnocommunal coexistence with serious implications for regional and world stability. The state as the primary source of political authority is coming under pressure from the violent clash of its ethnic communities. These grass roots resurgences of violent interethnic conflicts are challenging the nation-state's viability. If the divisive nature of these deeper sociohistorical and cultural forces continue to widen in scope and increase in intensity, the outcome could be more zones of turmoil that are essentially impossible to recognize. The post–Cold War trend of inward-looking ethnic assertion is, in many instances, bound to lead to separatism and hypernationalism. The consequence could be a clash of hypernationalisms as ethnocommunal groups look to separate themselves from their current locus of control.

Contending Views on Ethnonationalism

Perspectives on ethnonationalist conflicts and violence are generally divided into two approaches: primordialism, and instrumentalism or constructivism. Primordialism is based largely on emotive theories of ethnic violence and on the psychological sources of ethnic identity. As an explanation of ethnonationalism, it revolves around group identity and the emotive power that underlies it. The basic group identity consists of factors and endowments held in common by the group, which keep resurfacing to reassert the common emotional bond of the group vis-à-vis other groups. These endowments constitute basic personal characteristics that shape how group members perceive the world and the world perceives them. Facial marks, racial characteristics, tattoos, or other visible markers help reinforce group solidarity. Family names, relative language, and regional location reinforce the group's common identity. Anthony Smith, a moderate primordialist, defines an ethnic group as one characterized by these five traits: a group name, a believed common descent, common historical memories, elements of shared culture such as language or religion, and either actual, historical, or sentimental attachment to a specific territory.[7] In other words, ethnonationalist conflict in a primordial sense would be motivated by inherent biological drives, such as defense of kin and territoriality, or the desire to reverence one's ancestors. Thus, for primordialists, ethnic identities are given and flow directly from cultural identities. Critics of this primordialist view point out that the shared history and felt kinship ties are usually fictitious.[8] This means that most modern ethnic or national identities are quite recently defined or redefined. However, the primordialist perspective helps identify the powerful psychological motivations of ethnic identity, which eventually motivate ethnic solidarity and ethnopolitical violence.

Instrumentalists are typically rational choice analysts applying their approach to the origin of group identity rather than the determinants of group behavior. Robert Bates, who strongly adheres to the instrumentalist view, argues that ethnic groups are a product of the changes generated by modernization, which forces coalitions to form in a rational attempt to compete for scarce goods.[9] Instrumentalists emphasize conflicts between clientelist networks underlined by ethnicity or politicized ethnicity based on clientelism. This view may be too narrow because ethnic violence occurs in many parts of the world that have little bearing on clientelism and economic benefits. It is probably the force of primordial sentiments that makes the masses respond to the ethnic manipulation of ethnic elites. Nonetheless, instrumentalists maintain that ethnic identities are not immutable but have been formed and re-formed on a regular basis. It is, in other words, ethnic elites who play the critical role in influencing the nature of ethnic identities. The instrumentalist view, despite its shortcomings, helps explain several aspects of ethnopolitical conflicts even when economic goods are not the major point at issue. It emphasizes the fact that elites may be using ethnopolitics as an instrument in pursuit of their own personal goals. The elites, in the process of ethnicizing politics, may redefine even nonethnic issues in ethnic terms. In the final analysis, the divide between instrumentalists and primordialists is not as rigid as the above analysis may appear to suggest. For example, whereas the primordialists argue that the ethnic identities can be materially affected by the process of modernization, the instrumentalists on the other hand underscore the ethnic constraints on elite autonomy.

Instrumentalism as a model of ethnic conflict attempts to explain how ethnic identities can be formed and re-formed. In other words, primordialists explain why people are so strongly attached to their ethnic groups,

Table 10.1: Major Themes: Primordialism vs. Instrumentalism/Constructivism

PRIMORDIALISM	INSTRUMENTALISM/CONSTRUCTIVISM
Focus on psychological sources of ethnic identity.	Focus on rational choice explanations of ethnicity.
Emphasis on determinants or characteristics (racial, visible markers, other endowments) held in common by the group.	Emphasis on origins of group identity such as the result of ethnic manipulation by elites, socialization, etc.
Based on inherent biological drives (e.g., defense of kin), ascriptive characteristics, ethnocentrism, etc.	Based on social construction of ethnicity in order to gain political or economic objectives.
In-group/out-group orientation where in-group relationships are less conflictual and out-group interactions conflictual.	Cultural differences are manipulated by elites underlined by clientelist networks.
Natural division of people into ethnic groups thereby making ethnic differences a permanent feature of society.	Ethnic groups are not fixed and permanent because they are formed and re-formed only as instruments to achieve a specific goal.
Ethnic similarities foster in-group cooperation, but lead to conflict with out-groups.	"Creations" of ethnicity could permanently divide societies and foster ongoing enmity and violence.

whereas instrumentalists explain why people may be galvanized into action in support of their group, and how elites can help form and re-form identity. Accordingly, ethnic identity, and its meaning (individuals and values included), is an ideology. The ideology is generally either newly invented or newly interpreted by ethnic or nationalist intellectuals.[10] Their function is to "construct" ethnic identity made possible because of history "discovered." It requires only a belief in shared ancestry, not the fact of common descent. Another important point is that the intellectuals "discover" the common history and identity of their ethnic group and work to "regenerate" their group. The process could divide once united people into two hostile groups. Once ethnic groups come to be defined or "discovered" it could lead to suspicious, negative comparisons. In this case, ethnic groups are not permanent and fixed, but are easily malleable either because of primordial attachments or manipulation by the ethnic elite.

Finally, Stuart Kaufman provides a "mobilization-spiral model" of ethnic war as an alternative to explaining ethnonationalist conflicts.[11] Building on the dynamic aspects of Charles Tilly's mobilization model, interaction becomes crucial in his explanation because an ethnic conflict is a process that involves the active interaction of ethnic mobilization and countermobilization. At the core of the mobilization-spiral model is the security dilemma that confronts an ethnic group within the context of state breakdown, where each group's efforts at self-preservation constitutes a threat to the other group, thereby pitting both groups in a classic sequence of conflict escalation. According to the mobilization-spiral model, ethnic war can erupt when groups concerned about ethnic extinction become hostile and are mobilized by elites engaged in outbidding. The outbreak of war is dependent, however, on the existence of a security dilemma and the conditions that create the opportunity for the group to engage in violent conflict. Thus, the critical cause of ethnonationalist conflict is the interaction of three factors: interethnic hostility, elite outbidding within groups, and a security dilemma confronting them. "Opportunity" defines some of the circumstances necessary to facilitate outbidding and a security dilemma. According to Kaufman, the necessary conditions for a mobilization-spiral process of ethnic war are: mass hostility due to dissatisfaction and emotional heat; ethnic elite outbidding—a competition by elites to formulate extremist ethnic policies; and a security dilemma in which groups are forced (due to anarchy) to resort to self-help to ensure their survival. All three necessary conditions are dependent on the existence of economic deprivation, opportunity, and a situation of de facto anarchy.

Sources of Interethnic Conflicts

Ethnopolitical conflicts are an increasingly obvious feature of the modern world. From Burundi or Rwanda to Ireland and the former soviet Union; from Canada to South Africa; or from Sudan to Sri Lanka and Spain, ethnic groups and conflict have become an integral part of national political life. The various analyses of ethnic conflicts identify three broad factors that seem to be especially important in the increase in scope and intensity of violence underlined by ethnic differences. The first factor focuses on the degree of differentiation along geographic and economic lines within a country and its relationship to ethnic cleavages. In Senegal, for example, it is the Casamance region, the source of most agricultural produce, that is in rebellion against the Senegalese government. Similarly, in Spain, it is the Basque and Catalan regions, the most prosperous, that are the most rebellion prone. In various other countries in the world, the relatively well-off openly express their opposition to "subsidizing" the other less well-off groups that may be occupying other regions of the country. Geographic and economic boundaries within states are universal, and groups take the resulting boundaries seriously.

The extensive bureaucratization of the state and the growth of the welfare state in some countries constitutes a second factor of ethnic conflicts. The state, in this case, is viewed as intrusive by certain groups, and therefore threatening or destructive of particularity. In Europe, for example, political mobilization is increasingly along regional and cultural lines, rather than along socioeconomic lines.

The increasing globalization (internationalization) of economic and political activity is the third source of ethnic conflicts.[12] Local groups engage in countermobilization as, for example, economic power, processes, and control shift to global networks. The growth of the North American Free Trade Agreement (NAFTA) and the continued integration of the European Union is bound to produce dissatisfied groups who see economic and political control slipping away from them. Similarly, the increase in the international flow of migrants is introducing, and in many cases has already created, new ethnic groups, such as Turks and other nonethnic Germans in Germany, Indians in Britain, or Algerians and Moroccans in France, which increase the level of insecurity among indigenous groups and intensify the in-group out-group divide.

Ethnic conflicts intensify and become intractable because of competing identifying markers such as certain patterns of behavior or systems of symbols, cultural characteristics that celebrate difference rather than similarities with other groups; for example, ceremonies, rituals, events, and various cultural traits. Intractable conflicts are conflicts that make it extremely difficult or even impossible to get the major parties to coexist peacefully, or to agree to a mutually acceptable peace formula.[13] They are conflicts that are therefore not easily controlled or managed because of the competing obstinacy and uncompromising positions of the actors involved. Prominent among intractable conflicts are the Catholic-Protestant conflict in Northern Ireland, the Sinhalese-Tamil conflict in Sri Lanka, the Muslim-Christian conflict in Sudan, and the Israeli-Palestinian conflict in the Middle East. Such conflicts are intractable because of factors such as geography, history, and longevity.

John Agnew has identified two major sources of intractable conflicts: spatial and temporal.[14] Spatiality in ethnic conflicts comprises issues such as competing territorial claims, ritualization of symbolic places, and competition for control over spatial economic policy or location of development projects. Conflicts over such issues are often seen in zero-sum terms to take the form of mutually exclusive positions. Temporal factors are a manifestation of the cumulative temporal nature of ethnic conflict. Thus, over time, material stakes accumulate, new symbolic issues emerge, and competing interests may convert to competing principles. In the latter situation, the point is reached where even interests that are always negotiable are viewed as principles that are never negotiable. The intractability of ethnic conflicts is often directly proportional to their longevity.

In spatiality, territorial claim becomes the source of mutually incompatible goals. The ensuing awareness of group membership the claims produce tends to exclude ethnic cooperation along alternative social identities such as class or region. For example, in the 1950s, Sinhalese ethnonationalism expressed in language and religion (Buddhism) not only lay claim to the entire island of Sri Lanka, but it excluded Tamils and undermined the possibility of negotiating language rights and questions of political devolution for Tamils. The consequence has been organized rebellion by Tamil Tigers for an independent Tamil state in the north and east of Sri Lanka.

Similarly in Northern Ireland, conflict revolves around competitive territorial claims. Since 1969, the scope and intensity of contending territorial claims and intergroup violence have strengthened between the Protestant Unionist majority and Catholic Nationalist minority. Groups on both sides of the conflict either lay claim to the whole of Ireland and/or regard the existing boundaries of Northern Ireland to be sacrosanct and outside the bounds of negotiation. The conflict has over time intensified into zero-sum attitudes.

Moreover, provocative acts that produce violent conflicts and help prolong or even deepen ethnic hatred are competitively expressed. Public rituals or folk histories annually expressed by both sides reinforce group identity and conflict. For example, both Protestants and Catholics engage in commemorative ceremonies, processions, or demonstrations that celebrate symbolic places, battles, or rebellions. They often escalate into violence because marches, for example, are often directed near or through a neighborhood occupied by the other ethnic group.

In addition, the distribution of resources, location/allocation of development projects, and access to societal opportunities in general are done along ethnic lines with obvious discriminatory outcomes. Thus, both primordial and instrumental overtones underlie the allocation of resources. Processes, networks, or organizing principles become dependent on the dynamics of interethnic conflict. New projects related to housing, health, or transportation can be located in areas occupied by the dominant group. In Northern Ireland, for example, between 1945 to 1972, the dominant Protestant elite directed new industrial investment to the predominantly Protestant eastern region of Northern Ireland.[15] Such policies of controlling and directing spatial policy to benefit the dominant group is common in many ethnic-plagued societies in the world.

Temporal sources of intractable conflicts emphasize the dynamism in such conflicts because new "causes" are generated over time that add to the impossibility of resolution. Some sources of temporal intractability are: (1) the existence of new material stakes linked to the internationalization of the conflicts; (2) criminal organizations benefiting from operations of paramilitary groups within the rival ethnic groups; and (3) creation of new employment opportunities for rival interested parties related to linkages with the rest of the economy. Even in situations of violent conflict, some individuals and groups both within the country and outside acquire power, wealth, and prestige from the daily routine of the ethnic conflict. Examples are the benefits gained by arms dealers in the various wars raging in many countries, or quasi-criminal operations related to a wide range of business and other activities such as protection rackets or direct control of the taxi business, and domination of security (prisons, courts) jobs by the Protestant majority in Northern Ireland.

With time, ethnic conflicts generate new symbolic issues whose objective is to produce action from the other side. Examples are the deaths of hunger strikers and sectarian killings in the Irish conflict, or suicide bombings in the Israeli-Palestinian conflict. In intractable conflicts attempts at resolving the conflict through power sharing are often viewed by the dominant group as a prospective sellout or betrayal and therefore a reason for continued intransigence.

Finally, intractable conflicts enhance rival stereotyping, ethnocentrism, and bellicose attitudes. The loss of life, earnings, or overall freedom caused by ethnic conflicts tend to transform the interests that underlie the conflict into struggles over principles such as human rights. Such a situation enhances extremism because interests can be negotiated, principles cannot.

In his monumental study of ethnic groups, *Minorities at Risk,* Ted Gurr uses the concept of communal groups to refer to "psychological communities: groups whose core members share a distinct and enduring collective identity based on cultural traits and lifeways that matter to them and to others with whom they interact."[16] While these traits or common experiences (religion, beliefs, language, region, and so on) may be important, it is actually the shared perception about them that is helpful in identifying the group. Differential treatment of a group, either through deprivation or favoritism, raises the self-consciousness of that group relative to others. Where differences are minimal, communal identity becomes less salient as a unifying force. As differences in treatment become more equitable, groups tend to be indistinguishable from one another over time. Examples are the insignificance in terms of social relations between Anglo-Saxons and Normans in England; or that between Protestants and Catholics in western societies, except in Northern Ireland. But distinctiveness stands out where discrimination persists. In particular, the political saliency of communal groups is determined by one or both of these two important conditions: benefits, or suffering from institutionalized discriminatory practice relative

Table 10.2: A Select Number of Ethnic Conflicts by Region

Europe

Britain: Northern Ireland, where the Protestant majority in Northern Ireland favors continued union with Britain while the Catholic minority wants to join with the rest of Ireland.

Romania: Romania's ethnic Hungarians, mostly in Transylvania, want greater autonomy and the right to educate their children in their language. There have been sporadic attacks on Gypsies as well.

Russia: Chechen rebels want greater autonomy and even separation from Russia. So far there have been two Russian-Chechen wars over the territory of Chechenya.

Africa

Uganda: The army of President Yoweri Museveni composed mainly of Baganda and Banyarwanda ethnic groups continues to wage sporadic warfare with northern rebels, mainly from other ethnic groups.

Burundi: Ethnic clashes between the majority Hutu and minority Tutsi groups have led to thousands of deaths since the early 1990s.

Angola: The Angolan Civil War, which started in 1975, still continues with supporters of the government mainly from the urban dwellers, while rebel support is mainly from Ovimbundu-speaking people and peasants.

Middle East

Azerbaijan: Azerbaijan is fighting to end a rebellion by Nagorno-Karabakh, an enclave within Azerbaijan populated largely by Christian Armenians who favor independence or affiliation with Armenia.

Iraq: In the north, two major Kurdish parties rule in an enclave protected militarily by the United States and its allies.

Egypt: Many deaths have occurred as a result of clashes between Islamic militants and government security forces and in attacks by militants on foreigners and Coptic Christians.

Asia

Tajikistan: Tens of thousands of Tajik Muslims have been driven from their land by resurgent communist armies seeking to suppress Islamic political power.

Papua New Guinea: Rebels on the island of Bouganinville declared independence in 1990. The Papua New Guinea government subdued the rebellion in 1991 after fighting that claimed about 3,000 lives.

Indonesia: Sporadic but intense clashes between militant Muslim groups and Christians have erupted in the past few years in a number of islands in Indonesia. A separatist movement also exists in northern Sumatra, where Indonesians are said to have killed several hundred people.

Latin America

Colombia: Colombia has experienced many decades of violent conflicts involving the government and narcoterrorist groups, as well as mutual attacks between right-wing and left-wing rebel groups.

Mexico: Sporadic violent conflicts between Mexican government forces and Zapatista rebels fighting for the rights of neglected Indian groups.

Brazil: Indian groups in the Amazon region are pressing the government to recognize their rights. The Indian groups experience violence from the national government and other key actors that attempt to forcibly remove them from their traditional lands.

to other groups; and the group has mobilized in the past in favor of interests. For instance, blacks in the United States experienced systematic discrimination for a long time due to the widespread practice of differential treatment, deliberate government policy, or historical legacy.

In Gurr's analysis, the four historical processes of conquest, state building, migrations, and economic development are responsible for the inequalities that divide dominant groups and subordinate groups. One or more of the four processes predominate from region to region. The more sharply distinct a communal group is from a dominant group, the more it tends to suffer from political and economic inequalities. Political differences are found in access to positions of political power, access to civil service positions, recruitment to military and police service, voting rights, equal legal protection, and so on. Similarly, economic inequalities include: inequalities in income, inequalities in land and other property, access to higher or technical education, presence in commercial activities, and so on.

Grievances that are often articulated by ethnic minorities were cogently expressed by the Conference on Security and Cooperation in Europe (CSCE)[17] as follows:

> Persons belonging to national minorities have the right to exercise fully and effectively their human rights and fundamental freedoms without any discrimination and in full equality before the law.
>
> To belong to a national minority is a matter of a person's individual choice and no disadvantage may arise from the exercise of such choice.
>
> Persons belonging to national minorities have the right freely to express, preserve and develop their ethnic, cultural, linguistic or religious identity and to maintain and develop their culture in all its aspects, free of any attempts at assimilation against their will. In particular, they have the right
>
> —to use freely their mother tongue in private as well as in public;
> —to establish and maintain their own educational, cultural and religious institutions, organizations or associations; . . .
> —to profess and practice their religion; . . .
> —to establish and maintain unimpeded contacts among themselves within their country as well as contacts across frontiers with citizens of other states; . . .
> —to disseminate, have access to and exchange information in their mother tongue;
> —to establish and maintain organizations or associations within their country and to participate in international non-governmental organizations.
>
> Persons belonging to national minorities can exercise and enjoy their rights individually as well as in community with other members of their group.
>
> *Conference on the Human Dimension of the Conference*
> *on Security and Cooperation in Europe (CSCE), June 1990*

In general, communal groups or ethnic minorities pursue their interests either through nonviolent protests, violent protests, or rebellion. These strategies of political action are in order of increasing intensity. The stronger their feeling of deprivation, the more intense the political strategy employed.

Where conflict between minority group and the larger society is not ongoing, it could mean that the conflict has been resolved through the granting of independence to the group such as the Ukrainians in the USSR between 1944 and the mid-1950s. In some cases the minority group is granted regional autonomy such as were the Basques in Spain in 1980. In the case of the Kurds in Turkey, political recognition has been the outcome since 1961. Defeat of the minority group could also be an outcome.[18] Generally, state policies toward minorities fall under one of the following: (1) containment, which involves segregation, restricted access to societal opportunities, and even restricted political activities; (2) assimilation, or involving the minority group in dominant language and culture, job training, residential and social integration, and the like; (3) pluralism, which involves protection of cultural and religious diversity, education in multiple languages, and group representation in legislative assemblies, and the like; and (4) power sharing, or separate schools, media, economic activity organized communally, and guaranteed participation in decision-making bodies.

Ethnonationalist Violence in Africa

Actual and potential ethnocommunal violence exists in most regions of the world, with Africa increasingly perceived as a zone of violent ethnopolitical conflict. Senegal, Rwanda, Somalia, and Burundi represent only some of the states experiencing violent conflicts with overtones of ethnicity. The protracted nature and intractability of struggles in Africa have also promoted a chaotic, destabilized atmosphere both within and across borders. The consequence is often the stifling of economic progress, the weakening of state political infrastructure, and the further deterioration of human health and welfare. Some analysts argue that many of Africa's ethnic wars are merely a consequence of ethnic groups forming coalitions in a rational attempt to compete for scarce goods (instrumentalist view) as a result of social changes produced by the process of modernization. In particular, Robert Bates and Donald Rothchild point out that ethnic conflicts in Africa are, in large part, conflicts between clientelist networks, defined ethnically, over the distribution of economic goods by the state.[19] John Saul underscored this view when he wrote that "there is a clear sense—in which politicized ethnicity is merely clientelism writ large."[20]

Some of the factors underlying many of Africa's violent ethnic conflicts revolve around consolidation of power within a state by a dominant group, and discrimination resulting from competition for scarce resources. Many of Africa's wars are still largely nation-building conflicts and thus often internecine and genocidal in nature. Many African nations have either experienced or are currently plagued by several distinct types of conflict underlined by ethnocommunal divisions: wars of independence (Algeria or Mozambique), wars of secession (Biafra, or Eritrea), transnational wars (Somalia versus Ethiopia in 1977), war over ideology (Angola during the Cold War in the 1970), war over religious differences (Sudan), and several coups and countercoups. Conflicts over democratization are also part of the instability. Accordingly, Africa's conflicts are conflicts of national integration, suggesting that such conflicts are endemic to pluralistic or multiethnic states in their nation-building efforts, where the allocation of resources is perceived to be unfair, and where competitive relations and suspicions characterize intercommunal interactions.

Africa's many conflictual situations have been aggravated by a combination of artificial states and a transfer of power to a hand-picked ethnic group by departing colonial powers. The consequence is that ruling groups are perceived to be ethnic-based, and to deprive others of political and societal opportunities. Ethnic conflicts in African states are often manifested along the lines of political party identity. They are more often the justification for the centralization of power within a single party or the establishment of military oligarchies. During the Cold War, in particular, dictators have often consolidated their power and legitimized their activities through a single party system, or through a symbiotic relationship between the ruling party, the military, and the incumbent regime. The outcome is often exclusion of other ethnic groups. Ethnic-based power consolidation practices have been part of the political process in many African states. This outcome in African politics is due in large part to the creation of ethnic identity among many peoples of Africa as a result of modernization. In some parts of Africa, for example, ethnic labels and literary languages were first created (instrumentalist view) by European missionaries and anthropologists. The new demarcations united some people and marked them off from others. The resulting "tribal" divisions were often used as a basis for administrative and political practices. As the social and political usefulness of the new identities increased, they became increasingly accepted by the "tribal" group itself. For example, the identification of the Hutu-Tutsi distinction in Rwanda as an ethnic difference was the creation of German and Belgian colonial administrators, as was the enmity between the two groups.[21] However, knowledge of this has not mitigated the violent intensity of their group conflict.

Other factors such as population pressure, scarcity of resources, the impact of the global political economy, and drought help to aggravate longstanding ethnic tensions and can thus accentuate the effects of economic discrimination along ethnic lines. Ethnonationalist violence motivated by the interconnection between environmental degradation and scarcity is becoming a regular phenomenon in Africa. For example, the violent conflicts between Senegalese and Mauritanians in the spring of 1989 were underlined by the effects of scarcity related to environmental degradation. For details, see chapter 12.

Some ethnonationalist conflicts in Africa are based on violence as a consequence of active rivalry between multiple groups, such as the Oromo-Somali-Eritrea-Tigrean opposition to Amhara dominance in Ethiopia. The Mbundu-Ovimbundu-Bakongo conflict in Angola also represents an example of violence emanating from multiple ethnic groups with disagreements over such key issues as the definition of the proper boundaries of the political community. This phenomenon of actual and potential ethnonationalist violence in African states underscores Manfred Halpern's concept of emanation to explain the sacredness of relationships like the tribe, ethnic group, nation, or religion in Africa.[22] All over the world, individuals live out their lives submerged as emanations of another—a political movement, a leader, a dogma, or an ethnic group. In other words, the traditional Africans, based on this notion of emanation, view themselves as an extension not only of a kinship group but of their entire ethnic community (primordialist view). This is also the relationship that motivates mutual massacres among ethnic groups in some countries. In such conflicts, many willingly fight and die for the preservation of their group, such that the emotionally based motivation surpasses any rational cost-benefit analysis.

Finally, certain forms of ethnonationalist violence are produced by a perception of vertical political and economic dualism where one group monopolizes privilege in a country. This perception is accentuated by the fact that the various indigenous cultures making up all but a handful of African states speak different languages, and are, or may be, products of different sociocultural histories. This sharpens the sense of distinctiveness from other groups, even when a people are nation minded. Interethnic animosities and primordial distinctiveness are resuscitated by the stress and tension created by the struggle for educational, employment, and other opportunities. There are those rare moments when ethnic groups see themselves as alien to one another, such that ethnic atrocities or genocide are committed with ease, resulting in a certain degree of dehumanization caused by a sense of cultural distance. The outbreak of interethnic bloodletting has to do with power and control, and the focus on, and consciousness of, these fuel ethnic violence and mutual bloodletting.

Yugoslavia: A Post–Cold War Ethnic Conflict

The Yugoslavian conflict of the 1990s can be categorized as a conflict generated by the centrifugal ethnonationalisms of the end of the Cold War. The region (the Balkans) where Yugoslavia was situated is one with a complex ethnic and religious history, aggravated by the suppression of pluralistic and democratic rule during the era of communism, as well as by the ambitions and power struggles between Yugoslavian leaders.

After a group of Slavic peoples migrated into the Balkans (a region in the southern corner of Europe) around the sixth or seventh century, they were soon converted either to Eastern Orthodox Christianity or to Roman Catholicism.

Further complicating the religious composition of the area was the conquest in the fifteenth century by Ottoman Turks of most of the Balkans. Over the centuries a large portion of the population was converted to Islam. By the eighteenth century, Bosnia-Herzegovina had a majority Muslim population.[23] This overlap in ethnicity and religion gave Yugoslavia its mosaic character: the Slovenes and Croats in the north, the Bosnian Muslims in the center, and the Serbs and Macedonians in the south. Ethnically they were all South Slavs. Apart from small minorities of Albanians and Hungarians that were not Slavic ethnic groups, most of the population spoke a common language—Serbo-Croation—except for slight differences in accent and vocabulary. The dialects of the Slovenes and the Macedonians are different enough to count as separate languages. In terms of religious identity, the Slovenes and Croats are Catholics, the Serbs and Macedonians are Eastern Orthodox, and the Albanians and the majority of Bosnians are Muslims.

The violent conflicts of the 1990s that rocked the region were exacerbated not so much by differing religious affiliations, as by a legacy of centuries of interethnic violence and bloodletting that had solidified a perception of mutual rivalry and ethnoreligious separateness among peoples who were largely identical. The fact of a shared language and ethnicity, for example, between a Serb and a Croat, does not help dilute the awareness of difference that is more based on the subtleties of ethnonational identity than on religious identity.

World War II was one source of the legacies of interethnic hatred, when the Serbs suffered under a particularly harsh German occupation during which some Yugoslavians cooperated with the Germans.[24] In particular, the Ustase, a party of the Croats led by Ante Pavelic, established a fascist puppet Croat state that assisted the Nazis in rounding up and murdering hundreds of thousands of Serbs, Jews, and Gypsies. According to estimates, as many as 700,000 may have been exterminated. The consequence is a legacy of bitterness and vendetta that is being played out today. Other Yugoslavian groups, including some Croats, fought valiantly against the Germans. Under Josip Broz Tito, a communist, they were able to transform Yugoslavia into a communist dictatorship until the death of Tito in 1980.

Under Tito, ethnonationalism was suppressed. Yugoslavians were forced to identify themselves as citizens and communists. In order to realize his objective of a Yugoslavia where no ethnic group was preeminent, Tito set up a federal system based on power sharing with Yugoslavia divided into six republics: Slovenia, Croatia, Bosnia-Herzegovina, Serbia, Macedonia, Montenegro, and two Serbian-supervised autonomous provinces—Kosovo and Vojvodina.[25] The eight representatives of the republics and provinces were to act as a collective head of state, with the actual presidency of the state rotating annually among them. Tito was actually the absolute ruler of Yugoslavia until his death in 1980. The constitution he had designed was never really applied, and when it was put to the test in 1980, it failed.

The Rise of Violent Ethnonationalism

By the mid-1980s, Yugoslavia had begun to experience severe strains. The first were economic problems that caused deprivation, tensions, and jealousy. One reason was that Croatia and Slovenia—both closer to the West ideologically and physically—were doing far better than the southern republics, including the Serbs. Thus Serbian jealousy toward the richer north was aroused. On the other hand, Serbian-supported communist rules and regulations on greater economic liberalization were resented by the Croats and Slovenes.

In 1986 Serbia argued that because the two autonomous provinces contained Serbs, the provinces should be run by Serbia itself, and should no longer be autonomous. In October 1988, the Serbian leader Slobodan Milosevic was able to coerce the leadership of Vojvodina into turning over power to him. In November 1988, Milosevic had some of the Kosovo leadership dismissed or arrested. He declared Kosovo to be an integral part of Serbia, and many Serbs considered Kosovo their spiritual home. It was at Kosovo in 1389 that the Turks utterly defeated a Serbian army and launched their conquest of Serbian lands. Although Kosovo is now 90 percent ethnic Albanians, it has occupied a key place in Serbia's national mythology.

It was the extension of Serbian sovereignty over Vojvodina and Kosovo that motivated other leaders to leave the federation before Milosevic annexed their territory. Slovenia, followed by Croatia, were the first to leave the federation.[26] Yugoslavia under Milosevic supported the idea of a united Yugoslavia, but only if the Serbs were the dominant force, and this was exactly what the Croats and the Slovenes were trying to avoid.

In June 1991, the Croatian and Slovenian parliaments declared the independence of their respective countries. Bosnia waited until October 1991 to declare its independence; it was followed in November by Macedonia. Then followed four years of war in the states of the former Yugoslavia. There was war between Slovenia and Yugoslavia (now dominated by Serbia). The war between Croatia and Serbian irregulars allied with the Yugoslavian army would last until 1995. The war in Bosnia became the most vicious and bloody.

Montenegro, whose population is culturally almost identical to Serbia's, was not at war because it had already been taken over by a group of leaders with close ties to Milosovic.

The Kosovo Conflict

During the wars in Croatia and Bosnia between 1991 and 1996, Kosovo was relatively quiet. By this time, however, Milosevic had forcibly introduced direct rule in Vojvodina and Kosovo. Ethnic Albanians in Kosovo expressed their displeasure at Belgrade and elected a "government" run by a moderate, Ibrahim Rugova. Meanwhile, the Serbs introduced extreme segregation and discrimination enforced by their police forces.

The 1995 Dayton peace accords that ended the war in neighboring Bosnia did not include Kosovo. Kosovo Albanians had expected that the accords would also address their plight, but this did not happen. Instead a separatist group using violent methods, the Kosovo Liberation Army (KLA), began sporadic attacks on Serb police and officials in 1996.[27] A sharp escalation of the conflict was temporarily dampened with a U.S.-brokered truce that saw the introduction of hundreds of international cease-fire monitors into Kosovo. But eventually, the Serbs refused to accept a Western-sponsored peace accord that the ethnic Albanian side had signed.

In February 1998, Milosevic sent Serbian troops to Kosovo to take back KLA-controlled areas. After several unsuccessful attempts at restoring peace to Kosovo, NATO took military action against Serbia in the spring of 1999. On March 24 it launched an air campaign that lasted for eleven weeks. On June 9, 1999, Serbia finally agreed to sign a UN-approved peace agreement with NATO. Serbian troops were forced to withdraw from Kosovo, and a peacekeeping mission composed of U.S. and European troops became responsible for restoring trust between Serbs and Kosovo Albanians.

The problems of ethnicity can be summarized in terms of psychological, economic, and political models of ethnic conflict. Psychologists in large part emphasize frustration-aggression-displacement explanations focusing on the role of inherent human inclination to aggression and group narcissism, which produces or intensifies hostility of one ethnic group against another. Displacement models explain interethnic violence in terms of the occasional release of the accumulated aggression of one group on to another group in societies where intergroup violence is legally prohibited. Rationalizations such as projection, transfer, reinforcement, and pseudospeciation often serve as justifications for displacement. Relative deprivation models, on the other hand, underscore the perception by groups of the gap between what their actual status is and their desired status in relation to other groups. The focus is therefore on intergroup differences manifested in the extent of economic inequality and the gap in political opportunities in a society. Models of ethnic divisions of labor focus on factors that generate ethnic identity and ethnic mobilization. The scope and intensity of interethnic conflict tends to be greater in situations where differences in economic status and occupations are reserved for the dominant ethnic group, while other ethnic groups are confined to lower-status occupations. Thus, economic discrimination is equated with ethnic discrimination.

Interethnic conflicts will continue to persist and pervade the international system because what may be the most essential criterion for ethnicity—for example, language—does not necessarily guarantee ethnic commonality. Often, where language is shared, religion divides, and vice versa. The reality of multiple identities (ethnicity, religion, race, and so on) has not precluded the salience of a single identity among individuals. Individuals choose to embrace one over the other for reasons of prestige, expediency, or in response to societal or peer pressure.

Notes

1. This data is based on early 1990s figures; see *Refugees* no. 93 (August 1993), a special focus on ethnic conflict (Geneva: UNHCR).
2. As quoted in Karl P. Magyar, ed., *Challenge and Response: Anticipating U.S. Military Security Concerns* (Maxwell AFB: Air University Press, 1996), 15.
3. Michael Brecher and Jonathan Wilkenfeld, *Crisis, Conflict and Instability* (New York: Pergamon Press, 1989), 127.
4. Further details of these four categorizations are found in David Levinson, "Ethnic Conflict and Refugees," *Refugees* no. 93 (August 1993): 4–9.
5. For examples on the Liberian conflict, see Earl Conteh-Morgan and Shireen Kadivar, "Ethnopolitical Violence in the Liberian Civil War." *The Journal of Conflict Studies* 15, no. 1 (spring 1995): 30–44.
6. For details on these models, see John McGarry and Brendan O'Leary, eds., *The Politics of Ethnic Conflict Regulation* (London: Routledge, 1993); and Rajat Ganguly and Raymond C. Taras, *Understanding Ethnic Conflict: The International Dimension* (New York: Longman, 1998).
7. Anthony D. Smith, *The Ethnic Revival* (Cambridge: Cambridge University Press, 1981).
8. See, for example, Walker Connor, *Ethnonationalism: The Quest for Understanding* (Princeton: Princeton University Press, 1994), 220–21; and Stephen Van Evera, "Hypotheses on Nationalism and War," *International Security* 18, no. 4 (spring 1994).
9. See Robert Bates, "Modernization, Ethnic Competition, and the Rationality of Politics in Contemporary Africa," in *State vs. Ethnic Claims: African Policy Dilemmas*, ed. Donald Rothchild and Victor A. Olorunsola (Boulder, CO: Westview, 1983).
10. For details, see Leroy Vail, *The Creation of Tribalism in Southern Africa* (Berkeley: University of California Press, 1980); and Crawford Young, ed. *The Rising Tide of Cultural Pluralism: The Nation-State at Bay?* (Madison: University of Wisconsin Press, 1993).
11. Stuart J. Kaufman, "Causes of Ethnic War: A Theoretical Synthesis," paper presented at the International Studies Association Meeting, San Diego, California, April 1996.
12. For more negative effects of globalization, see Andrew Hurrell and Ngaire Woods, eds., *Inequality, Globalization, and World Politics* (Oxford: Oxford University Press, 1999).
13. For details on intractable conflicts, see Louis Kriesberg, Terrell A. Northrup, and Stuart J. Thorson, eds., *Intractable Conflicts and Their Transformation* (Syracuse, NY: Syracuse University Press, 1989).
14. John Agnew, "Beyond Reason: Spatial and Temporal Sources of Ethnic Conflicts," in *Intractable Conflicts and Their Transformation*, ed. Louis Kriesberg, Terrell A. Northrup, and Stuart J. Thorson.

15. See John Agnew, "Beyond Reason: Spatial and Temporal Sources of Ethnic Conflicts."
16. Ted R. Gurr, *Minorities at Risk: A Global View of Ethnopolitical Conflicts* (Washington, DC: United States Institute of Peace Press, 1993), 3.
17. U.S. Commission on Security and Cooperation in Europe, Document of the Copenhagen Meeting of the Conference on the Human Dimension of the CSCE (Washington, DC: U.S. Government Printing Office, 1990), 16–17.
18. For details, see Ted R. Gurr, *Minorities at Risk: A Global View of Ethnopolitical Conflicts.*
19. See, for example, Donald Rothchild, "Collective Demands for Improved Distribution," in *State vs. Ethnic Claims: African Policy Dilemmas,* ed. Donald Rothchild and Victor A. Olorunsola (Boulder, CO: Westview, 1983); and Robert H. Bates, *Prosperity and Violence: The Political Economy of Violence* (New York: W. W. Norton, 2001).
20. Quoted in Rothchild, p. 189.
21. For details on this see, for example, Rene Lemarchand, "Burundi in Comparative Perspective: Dimensions of Ethnic Strife," in *The Politics of Ethnic Conflict Regulation,* ed. John McGarry and Brendan O'Leary (London: Routledge, 1993), 151–71.
22. Manfred Halpern, "Changing Connections to Multiple Worlds: The African as Individual, Tribesman, Nationalist, Muslim, Christian, Traditionalist, Transformer, and as a World Neighbor, Especially with Israel and the Arabs," in *Africa: From Mystery to Maze,* ed. Helen Kitchen (Lexington, MA: D.C. Heath, 1976), 9–44.
23. See John B. Allcock, *Explaining Yugoslavia* (New York: Columbia University Press, 2000).
24. See, for details, Karin S. Bjornson and Kurt Jonassohn, *The Former Yugoslavia: Some Historical Roots of Present Conflicts* (Montreal: Concordia University, 1994).
25. See, for example, Duncan Wilson, *Tito's Yugoslavia* (Cambridge: Cambridge University Press, 1979).
26. For further details, see Misha Glenny, *The Fall of Yugoslavia: The Third Balkan War* (New York: Penguin, 1996).
27. For details, see Sabrina P. Ramet, *Balkan Babel: The Disintegration of Yugoslavia from the Death of Tito to the War for Kosovo* (Boulder, CO: Westview Press, 1999).

Key Terms

artificial states
constructivism
ethnic group
ethnic mobilization
ethnonationalism

ethnonationalist conflict
identity
instrumentalism
intractable conflicts

primordialism
protracted conflict
pseudospeciation
zeitgeist

Discussion Questions

1. What is an ethnic group? How serious are ethnic conflicts in terms of deaths and refugees?
2. What are the contending views of ethnonationalist conflicts? Identify one and briefly discuss its main characteristics.
3. Outline and discuss as many sources (reasons) of interethnic conflicts as possible.
4. Analyze in some detail one example of ethnic conflict in any region or country of the world.

CHAPTER 11

Genocide
Types, Causes, and Activators

Introduction

Numerous instances of genocide abound in the history of the human race, with some more well known in terms of scope, intensity, and publicity than others. Some of the more famous ones are the Nazi genocide (now known as the Holocaust) of the Jewish people of Europe between 1933 and 1945, the deliberate and rather systematic murder of over one million Armenians in 1921 by the Turkish state, the genocidal policies and actions of the Khmer Rouge in Cambodia in the late 1970s and 1980s, and the relatively more recent genocidal massacre of close to one million Tutsi and some moderate Hutus in Rwanda in 1994. Some of the less well known instances of genocide include the 1637 extermination of Pequot Indians by the colonists in Mystic, Connecticut, the extermination of the aboriginal inhabitants of Tasmania, and the German massacres of the Herero in southwest Africa in 1904.[1]

According to Article II of the UN convention on genocide as adopted December 9, 1948, genocide means any of the following acts committed with intent to destroy, in whole or in part, a national, ethnic, racial, or religious group as such:

1. Killing members of the group;
2. Causing serious bodily or mental harm to members of the group;
3. Deliberately inflicting on the group conditions of life calculated to bring about its physical destruction in whole or in part;

4. Imposing measures intended to prevent births within the group;
5. Forcibly transferring children of the group to another group.[2]

The UN definition is restrictive because it intentionally excluded the purposeful and deliberate annihilation of political groups and social classes. Thus, every assault on a group may be rationalized as a defense against a political movement.

The term genocide was coined by Raphael Lemkin in his book *Axis Rule in Occupied Europe,* published in 1944.[3] His definition included both lethal and nonlethal acts: "killing members of the group," and "deliberately inflicting conditions of life calculated to bring about its physical destruction in whole or in part," and "forcibly transferring children of the group to another group." In 1946, largely because of Lemkin's prodding, the UN for the first time considered the issue of preventing and punishing genocide. The General Assembly adopted the term and defined it in 1946 as "a denial of the right of existence of entire human groups."

Types of Genocide

Genocide as the systematic slaughter of whole categories (religious, ethnic, racial, and even political, etc.) of human beings in order to eliminate, in its entirely, the group to which they belong. As a phenomenon, it could be located in the past, in the present, and most definitely in the future, as both necessary and sufficient conditions for genocidal massacres interact to produce such inclination. Until the end of the Cold War, and the increase in hypernationalisms (and genocides in Bosnia and Rwanda in particular) genocide was thought by many to be a thing of the past best documented by the Nazi Holocaust, with the belief that our current knowledge of what happened would keep such atrocities from being repeated. In terms of scope, Stalin's slaughter of the kulaks (independent peasants of the USSR) was even more devastating than Hitler's genocide.[4] But Stalin and his lieutenants effectively concealed the scope of the killings and branded the victims as enemies of revolution or at least opponents of economic development programs. Even after true knowledge of the extent of both Stalin's and Hitler's genocides became known, it still did not reinforce the belief that genocides would be a part of the future, especially the late twentieth century. The genocides between Hutu and Tutsi ethnic groups in Burundi and Rwanda over the years, while in proportion were equal to that of the Nazi Holocaust, were not considered as important because of the geostrategic insignificance of those two countries in the overall equation of world politics. The Stalin and Hitler genocides occurred a long time ago. However, the attitude that genocides are rare, a thing of the past, and likely to occur only in less developed countries such as Burundi or Rwanda is being increasingly challenged by recent developments involving forced removal of whole groups, and extensive mass killings in the Balkans and elsewhere.

Currently, because of the pervasive effect of media reporting related to the global telecommunications revolution and what is often referred to as the "CNN effect," the world is made more aware of genocidal threats or tendencies in many remote regions. While the international law tenets of noninterference are still intact, the globalizing trends of human rights, and democratization in particular, have sensitized more to the realities of mass murders and thereby pressure their governments to put a stop to moral atrocities committed by foreign governments against their own subjects.

Genocide is in reality mass murder because of its malicious and intentional killing of a large number, or an entire group, of persons. While war is governed by rules, in genocide there is the deliberate and calculated intention to kill a whole category of persons. Again, unlike war, in genocide the intention is the elimination of an entire group. While the killing is always deliberate or intentional, the reasons for killing have differed from case to case. Many studies have categorized genocides in terms of ideological, colonial, pragmatic, and retributive justifications, among many others.[5]

Appropriate examples of genocides of ideology are Stalin and kulaks, and the Khmer Rouge in Kampuchea. Based on these two examples alone, ideological genocides could be described as genocides that attempt to enforce a worldview or conception of reality on others. Ideology is the rationale that "legitimized" the genocidal intent by placing it in the context of, say, Marxism-Lenisism, national socialism, or militant socialism. One weltanschauung (worldview) or theory or faith is imposed on everyone, and those who oppose it or are considered unfit to accept it are eliminated. During the Cold War, the world witnessed ideological genocide in Kampuchea by the Khmer Rouge, and in China during Mao's Cultural Revolution. Genocide was rationalized in the name of the need to ensure the implementation of progressive ideals.

Ideological genocide is also referred to as political because of the deliberate and planned killing of members of political associations, movements, and parties rather than of ethnic groups or nationalities who resist the imposition of the ideology. For example, Barbara Harff and Ted Gurr describe revolutionary genocide as the "mass murder of class or political enemies in the service of new revolutionary ideologies."[6] In particular, the Nazi genocide of more than five million Jews and other groups constitutes a genocide predicated on ideological fervor, but is shocking in terms of its scope, intensity, and irrationality. Genocide extended to the extermination of those Jews who had contributed to German greatness and who would have continued to contribute to the competitiveness, modernization, and greatness of

Germany. This included eminent scientists, inventors, skilled workers, and millions of innocent, loyal, and apolitical citizens. The fervor of the attempt to make Europe free of Jews was pursued to the point where enormous resources were devoted to the task of killing Jews and other groups such as the 200,000 Roma. The reason was that the mere existence of Jews was a threat to the racial purity and soul of the Aryan race. Jews were considered nonhumans, or worse still, antihumans. Some scholars describe the Jewish Holocaust as a genocide of ethnic purification. The case of the Turks against the Armenians also falls into this category of ethnic purification. Another description of such genocide is ideological xenophobia because the objective was to cleanse the nation by eliminating all alien groups.

Genocides and Indigenous Peoples

Many instances abound of genocides of colonization. The more well known cases are those of the Germans in 1904 against the Herero people of southwest Africa, and more recently that of Indonesia against the people of East Timor. In the case of the Herero 64,000 people were killed. East Timor saw several thousand killed between 1975 and 1999 when the East Timorese finally won their independence as a result of political pressure on Indonesia from the international community. In the case of Germany in southwest Africa, it was quite normal to occupy the land of weaker peoples during that period (the nineteenth and first part of the twentieth centuries). Within the tradition of that time was the acceptability of colonization, "right of democracy," and subduing natives in favor of modern Europeans. In terms of the systemic value of the time, colonies were the coveted goals of great powers, and thus Germany also wanted to have a place in the sun, especially since it had lagged far behind Britain and France in terms of the national prestige that came with possessing colonies. Accordingly, when German colonists encountered the Hereros in southwest Africa in 1892, they decided to deprive them of their land as part of the colonization process. It was decided that they should be moved into reservations, but when the Hereros, realized they were being stripped of their land, they rebelled. It was then that the Germans embarked upon a systematic, deliberate elimination of the Hereros, reducing their numbers from about 80,000 in 1904 to 14,000 by 1911.[7] The goal of the Germans under General Lothan von Trotha was to remove the Herero from the country altogether, mostly through extermination.

Genocide of colonization, at times, is addressed by different names. For example, developmental genocides or genocide against indigenous people like the Herero, is referred to by Harff and Gurr as hegemonial genocides.[8] Genocide in such cases is justified and rationalized by the need to enhance development and progress. Any obstruction of these goals by indigenous, inferior peoples elicits a response of genocide. In other words, the colonizers are often conscious and self-assured of their cultural, economic, and military superiority vis-à-vis the indigenous people. Thus, any resistance to dispossessing native or indigenous populations of their land unleashes a genocidal response. What may be labeled genocide of colonization before the second half of the twentieth century, is today referred to as developmental genocide. North America has many examples of developmental genocide, mostly in the nineteenth century, when the Native Americans (Indians) of the great plains were displaced from their lands by herders and farmers.[9] Currently, displacement of indigenous peoples is ongoing in the South American countries of Brazil, Peru, Colombia, and Venezuela, among others, because of the encroachment of modernity in the form of extractive industries, plantations, and development projects such as new cities and roads. In all of these examples, genocide is the intentional or unintentional destruction of peoples who are an obstacle to the exploitation of resources for development purposes.

Genocide and Power Politics

Another categorization of genocide is what some analysts have referred to as pragmatic genocide. This is the kind of genocide underlined by power struggles between two groups. Examples are the recurring genocidal massacres between the Hutu and Tutsi in Burundi and Rwanda. In 1963, for example, between 10,000 and 12,000 Tutsis were killed. In 1994, between 500,000 and 800,000 Tutsi and some moderate Hutu were also exterminated by Hutus in Rwanda.[10] In cases of pragmatic genocide, the major motivation is power struggle, to try to decide once and for all who is the most powerful; and this could be decided by eliminating members of the other group. Fear, a desire for revenge, and a perceived need to effectively deter challenges from the target group are the causes of pragmatic genocides. Such genocides have been recurrent and have especially predominated the post–Cold War era. In Burundi and Rwanda for instance, the level of hatred, the competition for scarce resources, and the desire to dominate have generated genocidal massacres between the Hutus and Tutsis since the 1950s. In the former Yugoslavia, the level of hatred resulting from the experiences of World War II, coupled with the struggle for dominance, were played out in ethnic cleansing or mass exterminations between Serbs, Croats, and Bosnian Muslims in the early 1990s. The lack of restraint for genocide stems from the rationale that the other group is dangerous, it is the enemy, and therefore it should be eliminated so that there will be no survivors left to initiate revenge. It is often a question of settling old scores, or a case of past grievances being played out in the present.

Retributive genocide shares certain traits with pragmatic genocide. Retributive genocide often occurs during decolonization, or at the end of a war because a specific group was allied with the colonizers or the enemies against the rest of the population. Examples of such genocides are many in the history of colonialism and decolonization. Colonialism by its very nature depends on divide and rule in order to subdue the colonized, and often one group is used by the conquerors, or favored by the colonizers at the expense of all the other groups. Two prominent and popular examples again are the Hutu in Burundi and the Tamil in Sri Lanka, who were deliberately favored for advancement by their colonial masters and thus their subsequent massacre by the radical movements.[11] Often these retributive genocides are also hegemonic struggles whose objective is to expand or maintain the state after a colonial power has withdrawn its hegemony, leaving the rival groups to struggle to fill in the power vacuum left by the sudden withdrawal. Previously submissive or oppressed groups either contend for power or claim the right to secede. Hegemonic wars often lead to state disintegration such as the fragmentation of the former Yugoslavia.

Another example of hegemonic war resulting in a genocide of decolonization was the Biafran War (1966–67), which was waged to prevent the secession of Biafra (mostly Ibo-speaking people) from the Nigerian Federation six years after decolonization. According to estimates, between 600,000 and one million Biafrans died in the struggle between the Nigerian government and secessionist Biafra.[12] Generally, the end of colonial or communist hegemony unleashes ethnic tensions, some of which escalate into attempts to secede from the state or federation, resulting in war between the state and a specific ethnic group. Since opposition to the state very often coalesces around ethnic or regional groups, targeting such a group or region often results in hegemonic genocide or repressive politicide. Other examples include government massacre of Chinese in Malaya (1948–56), Baluchi tribesmen in Pakistan (1958–74), and Kurdish nationalists in Iraq (1959–75).

The sequence of escalation toward genocide often starts with the withdrawal of the hegemon or collapse of legitimate authority. This, coupled with the existence of historic rivalry, a history of grievances, heightened competition for land, employment, and other scarce resources, leads to a breakdown in restraint between rivals. Genocide may result, especially if one or more of the group leaders adopt an uncompromising stance toward resolution of a potential crisis. The cases of the former Yugoslavia and the Hutus and Tutsis fit squarely the category of retributive genocide because in each, the perpetrator's objective was to destroy a real enemy. It is often used to settle old scores underlined by religious, racial, or ethnic differences.

In the broadest terms, therefore, genocide may occur as part of an effort by an ethnolinguistic, racial, religious, or regional group to become politically independent, or as part of an effort by a nation to prevent the group form doing so. An example is the Timorese (Antoni) in Indonesia before 1999. This is genocide as a result of separatist efforts by a group opposed by the state. In addition, genocide may occur as a result of rivalry for autonomy, political power, or territorial control. This is usually part of a conflict between a group in one nation, or between an ethnic group and the government over access to and control of economic resources, political power, territory, or political autonomy within the nation. Examples are Albanians in Serbia (1999), Igbo in Nigeria (1966–67), and the Hutu and Tutsi in Rwanda and Burundi over the years. During the Cold War, genocides for purely political (ideological) reasons, now commonly referred to as politicides, were part of the political landscape in some countries. For instance, the right-wing death squads and disappearances that characterized Chile, Argentina, and El Salvador fit the definition of repressive politicide. They were directed almost exclusively at leftists in Argentina (1976–80), Chile (mid-1970s to mid-1980s), and El Salvador (1980–90). Furthermore, genocide may occur as part of a war between two or more nations where ethnic differences between the groups is a major factor. The objective of the war might be the conquest or elimination of the other ethnic group, or its removal from all or some of its territory through mass killing. Examples are Bosnian Muslims and Serbs and Croats and Serbs. Finally, genocide may occur as part of an attempt by a national government or majority groups to forcibly assimilate, harm, remove, or drive out an ethnic minority. Examples are Shiite Muslims in Iraq and Amazonian Indian groups in Brazil.

In conclusion, what has often baffled many observers is what may be referred to as the "abnormal normality" inherent in genocides.[13] Participants in genocide seem to "sear their conscience with a hot iron" in order to perpetuate the most heinous of crimes (the total extermination of another group) on behalf of their own group, political cause, or religion. The deliberate, coolly calculated, systematic slaughter of many innocent victims takes on a normality that is often difficult to comprehend from the outside. The hunting down of the victims, the voluntary participation by most who take part in the killings, the rationalization of the massacres, and the excitement by some participants at the annihilation of the enemy are all factors that indicate the abnormal normality of genocide. In other words, individuals who engage in perpetrating genocide become so much captives of the conventional standards of their times that even the brightest minds fall prey to such collective psychosis directed against the most disadvantaged and often very innocent in society. Perhaps the only things explainable about genocide that may make it a reality is that: (1) most people will obey even the most outrageous instructions in order to conform to the dominant spirit of the times; (2) people often think that the evil that befalls others will never

Table 11.1: Motivations for Genocides

TYPE OF GENOCIDE	EXAMPLES	CAUSES
Genocides of ideology/political genocides/ revolutionary genocides	Stalin's slaughter of the kulaks; Nazi Holocaust; China during the Cultural Revolution; Khmer Rouge against Cambodians	Genocide in order to enforce an ideology or particular worldview
Genocide of ethnic purification	Nazi Holocaust; Armenian massacre by Turkey	Ideological xenophobia caused by the desire to cleanse the nation of all alien groups
Genocides of colonization/ developmental genocides/ hegemonial genocides	Germans against the Herero people of southwest Africa during the nineteenth and early twentieth centuries; Indonesia against E. Timor; displacement of Native American (Indians) by herders and farmers	Attempts to deprive natives of their land as part of the colonization processes
Pragmatic genocide	Hutu and Tutsi in Burundi and Rwanda; former Yugoslavia between Serbs, Croats, and Bosnian Muslims	Fear, a desire for revenge, competition for scarce resources moves one group to try to eliminate the other
Retributive genocide/ decolonization/ postwar/post–Cold War genocides	Hutu in Burundi; Tamil in Sri Lanka; Tutsi in Rwanda massacred following decolonization	Due to hegemonic struggles following the withdrawal of the colonizing power; desire for revenge

happen to them, and so they prefer to remain silent and uninvolved in any efforts to combat evil; (3) people often defer serious decisions and seemingly controversial or sensitive issues to their elected officials for resolution; and (4) people tend to be more followers than leaders, and thus tend to be easily influenced by the predominant mode of behavior. In the final analysis, entire populations tend to surrender their own individual decision making or thinking to the leader of the group or to some authority figure such as Stalin, Hitler, Idi Amin, or Pol Pot.

Table 11.2: A Selected Chronology of the Nazi Genocide (The Holocaust, 1933–45)

1933

February 28: Sterilization (of inferiors) laws enacted; implemented three weeks later. Constitutional rights "temporarily" suspended until 1945.

March 19: Dachau concentration camp established

April 1: General boycott of all Jewish businesses for one day.

April 7: All Jews removed from civil service.

Jews denied admission to the bar

May 10: Burning of books written by Jews and political opponents.

July 14: Law mandating sterilization of those with hereditary diseases such as epilepsy, schizophrenia, etc. Some 300,000 to 400,000 people are sterilized under this law.

August: Euthanasia is preferred over sterilization for "inferiors."

November 24: Law passed against habitual and dangerous criminals, which allows beggars, the homeless, alcoholics, and the unemployed to be sent to concentration camps.

1934

August 2: Hitler becomes head of state and commander-in-chief.

Beginning 1934: Mental hospitals encouraged to neglect patients.

1935

May 21: Jews removed from the military.

Summer 1935: No Jews (*Juden Verboten*) signs increase in business and elsewhere.

July 26: Marriage between Aryans and non-Aryans outlawed.

September 15: First of Nuremburg Laws (Anti-Semitic passed).

October 18: Law forbids marriages between "hereditary ill" and "healthy" people. Forces the abortion of children of the "hereditary ill" up to the sixth month of pregnancy.

1936

Sachsenhausen concentration camp established.

May 10: Burning of books written by Jews.

July 12: German Roma and Sinti (Gypsies) are arrested and deported to Dachau.

1937

Spring: Sterilization of the "Rhineland Bastards" begins.

July 16: Buchenwald concentration camp opens.

1938

Neuengamme and Mauthausen concentration camps established

June 15: Arrest of all previously convicted Jews.

July 23: Announcement that Jews will need identity cards beginning in 1939.

July 25: Jewish doctors will only be allowed to treat Jewish patients.

August 17: Jews required to insert "Sara" or "Israel" as middle name.

September 30: Jewish physicians lose their licenses.

October 6: Passports of Jews marked with a J.

October 26: Approximately 17,000 Polish Jews expelled from Germany.

Table 11.2: Continued

November 9: *Kristallnacht* (Night of the Broken Glass).
November 12: 26,000 Jews arrested and sent to concentration camps.
November 15: Expulsion of Jewish children from German schools.
December 13: Compulsory expropriation of all Jewish businesses and industries.

1939
Ravensbruck concentration camp established.
January 30: Hitler predicts that Jews will be "exterminated" in the event of
   another war.
October 1939: Medical killing became official policy. An estimated 275,000 people
   became victims of "euthanasia."
November 23: All Jews in Poland mandated to wear *Judenstern* (Jewish Star of David).

1940
Early 1940: Gas first used as killing method.

1941
June 22: Mobile killing units (*Einsatzgruppen*) follow the German army and commit
   mass slaughter throughout Eastern Europe. By the spring of 1943, these special
   killing units had killed more than one million Jews and tens of thousands of others.
July 8: Jews in Baltic States forced to wear the Star of David.
July 31: Heydrich appointed by Goering to carry out the "Final Solution."
September 23: First gassing experiments at Auschwitz.
October 23: Massacre in Odessa, 34,000 Jews dead.

1942
January 20: Waunsee conference on Nazi "Final Solution."
June 23: Auschwitz opens as death camp and work center.
December 16: Himmler orders the "final solution of the gypsy question."

1943
November 3: *Erntefest* (Harvest Festival) operation launched to kill all remaining Jews
   in the central and southern region of Poland. About 40,000 Jews are shot to death
   on this one day.

1944
May 15–June 8: 476,000 Jews deported to Auschwitz from Hungary to be murdered
   by gassing.

The April 1994 Rwandan Genocide

Historical Background

The Rwandan genocide of April to June 1994 was the culmination of events
from the past interacting with factors, actors, and situations in the present.
   While social and ethnic categories and differentiation between Hutu and
Tutsi were already present before the advent of European colonialism, it was
the German and Belgian colonial policies of indirect rule that aggravated

and formalized the polarization and politicization of ethnicity. Interactions between Hutu and Tutsi generally fall into two different phases. The first phase involved peaceful Tutsi immigration into Hutu areas. The basis of socioeconomic interaction between the two comprised of cattle products exchanged for agricultural products. This period of peaceful coexistence was generally followed by the establishment of direct Tutsi administrative and military rule.[14] Eventually, the Tutsi extended their control over the factors of production, which involved gradual restriction over access to land, cattle, and labor.

German and Belgian policies, in addition, favored the entrenchment of Tutsi dominance. Influenced largely by the so-called Hamitic hypothesis, this European policy was manifested in 1933 in the compulsory introduction of identity cards, thereby reinforcing and speeding up the process of ethnic division of Tutsi, Hutu, and Twa. The Hamitic hypothesis argued that the Hamites, supposedly a branch of the Caucasian race, had introduced everything of value in Africa. The thesis also linked physical characteristics with mental capacity. In the case of Rwanda the Tutsi were "Hamites," and "resembled the negro only in the colour of their skin."[15] The Tutsi, based on the Hamitic thesis, resembles more closely a white person. He is, in terms of physical characteristics, "a European who happens to have a black skin...." In sum, Tutsi were considered to be related to Europeans and, therefore, the Europeans could easily work with them. This served as a justification for the colonial policy of divide and rule. Thus, the policy of identity cards meant that all citizens had to closely identify with their respective ethnic group, which in turn translated into differential access to societal and political opportunities.

In other words, under European colonialism, a policy of "ethnogenesis" was instituted based on rigid divisions and separation of Hutu and Tutsi. The consequence is that Rwandese society became divided into haves and have-nots corresponding respectively to Tutsi and Hutu.

However, twenty-five years later, the Belgians abruptly changed their policy of enhancing Tutsi hegemony. The reasons for the policy shift were the general decolonization process unfolding in the rest of Africa, including independence in the Congo (Zaire).[16] These two factors impelled the Belgian administration and the Catholic church to attempt to redress the injustices of the past. This meant a shift in support from the minority Tutsi to the majority Hutu. The shift in policy contributed to the Hutu revolution of 1959 to 1961, through which Rwanda experienced a dramatic transition from a Tutsi-dominated monarchy to a Hutu-led independent republic in less than three years. However, this policy change introduced a new dimension of interethnic instability and a potential future of violence based on ethnic rivalry.

The previous creation of ethnicity in the 1930s also produced a social construct of Tutsi superiority and Hutu inferiority. These feelings of superiority, inferiority, contempt, and mistrust soon permeated the entire Rwandese society and developed into a culture of fear and suspicion. This social atmosphere was largely responsible for the outburst of violence at the time of independence when the fortunes were reversed. Since then, ethnicity has been repeatedly exploited for purposes of political gain and hegemony. The events of 1959 to 1961 also generated tens of thousands of Tutsi refugees into neighboring countries. Their armed incursions into Rwanda aggravated the perennial ethnic divisions and contributed to the immediate factors of the 1994 genocide.

Independence and Policy Reversal

The Belgian policy reversal favoring the majority Hutu constituted a major change in Rwandan society because it led to the abolition of the monarchy as well to the dismantling of all political and administrative Tutsi structures the Belgians had in the past relied on to implement their policy of indirect rule. The catalyst for the Hutu revolt of 1959 to 1961 was the rigid and inflexible attitude of a conservative Tutsi political and administrative elite that refused all attempts at democratization. The transition to Hutu hegemony marked the beginning of a cycle of violent clashes as part of the struggle over control of the Rwandese state, viewed as a zero-sum game in which the winner controlled all resources. The accession to power by the Hutu meant the virtual exclusion from public life for all Tutsi. Tutsi citizens also had to endure all sorts of abuses. In reality, the 1959 Hutu revolt was followed by a succession of crises in which the victims were largely Tutsi chiefs and subchiefs.[17] For example, of the 43 Tutsi chiefs and 549 subchiefs in office in early November 1959, 21 and 314 respectively were eliminated through murder, expulsion, or exile.

At the same time, between 1962 and 1990, during the first and second republics, increasing intra-Hutu tensions—mainly between groups from the northern regions and the rest of the country—developed and came to form an important factor underlying the cleavage between Hutu in the 1990s. The northern Hutu constitute a distinctive and independent subculture based in part on their strong awareness of a pre-Tutsi past. They tended to be strongly suspicious of any compromise or conciliatory gestures toward the exiled Tutsi community in places such as Uganda, Tanzania, or Zaire. President Juvenal Habyarimana's informal council (Akazu), composed of his immediate family members, belonged to this northern Hutu group. The northern Hutu were also largely hostile to the Hutu groups favoring negotiation or dialogue with the Tutsi-led Rwandese Patriotic Front (RPF).[18] The Akazu played a leading role in the genocide of April 1994 in terms of organization, mobilization of Hutu, and transmission of instructions to the Interahamwe party militias.

The war between the Tutsi-dominated Rwandan Patriotic Army (RPA) and the Hutu-dominated government had a devastating effect on Rwanda's economy. First, it adversely affected both coffee and food production because of its displacement of hundreds of thousands of peasant farmers in the northern part of the country. In particular, it brought to a halt road transportation between Rwanda and the Kenyan part of Mombassa, which is Rwanda's primary overland route to the outside world. Furthermore, it destroyed the country's third largest earner of foreign exchange, its fledgling tourist industry. Finally, the war effort diverted funds away from other sectors of the economy. These effects combined with continued demographic pressure on available resources to aggravate stress and instability in the Rwandian sociopolitical environment. To a very large extent, international financial donors overlooked these potentially explosive political consequences when requiring and imposing their structural adjustment programs for Rwanda's economic recovery.

Immediate Causes of Genocide

The considerable popularity enjoyed by President Habyarimana in the Hutu as well as in the Tutsi community began to erode from 1985 onward due to the general political and economic crisis. Economically, the scarcity of land was a formidable problem. Population increase in the already densely populated country had resulted in a situation in which the average peasant family did not possess more than 0.7 hectare of land. Militarily, between January and February 1993, a major attack by the RPA in the most fertile part of the country resulted in a massive displacement of 13 percent of the country's overall population and a drop by 15 percent of agriculturally marketed production in one year.[19] These factors provided the Hutu extremists the justification to engage in violence. Politically, these economic and military developments led to the buildup of party militias (Interahamwe) and the setting up of a pro-Hutu party Coalition pour la Défense de la République (CDR). In particular, both were opposed to demands for political liberalization.

The CDR was composed of extremists from the Mouvement Révolutionnaire National pour le Développement (MRND). It was set up officially in March 1992 with the explicit agenda of Hutu extremism, and expressions of ethnicity in general. Its opposition to the reform process meant that it did not hesitate to criticize the president over the concessions he was forced to make in the course of the Arusha peace talks.

Among the immediate causes of the genocide are: (1) the dislocations and economic hardships of structural adjustment requirements, and (2) the murder in neighboring Burundi of its first democratically elected Hutu president. The structural adjustment package may have contributed to increased impoverishment of the rural Hutu population, thereby making large numbers of people susceptible to the hate propaganda to join the militias and to participate in genocidal massacres.[20] Some of the provisions of the adjustment package may have also generated in varying degrees resentment among civil servants and nonagricultural wage and salary earners, leading to increased susceptibility to hate propaganda and either active or tacit participation in the genocide.

The murder of Burundi's Hutu president Melchior Ndadaye by Tutsi soldiers of the Burundian army on the night of October 20–21, 1993, contributed to the already worsened political climate. Most observers of the Rwanda/Burundi political environment underscored this event as the critical factor for the ensuing genocide in Rwanda. According to Linden:

> Perhaps the single most important trigger enabling those who were determined to abort the process to win the day was ironically an assassination in Burundi on 21 October 1993, that of the new "Hutu" president, Melchior Ndadeye, one of the first fruits of a process of democratization of its "Tutsi" regime. Tens of thousands died in the wake of the coup and some 70,000 Burundian "Hutu" fled into southern Rwanda. The message of these events to many around Habyarimana was doubtless that the Tutsi would never genuinely accept (Hutu) majority rule within the context of a government of national unity. In other words, the extremists were right: Arusha was too much, too far, too fast.[21]

Rene Lemarchand likewise expressed a similar view of the significance of the event in neighboring Burundi:

> (Ndadaye's) death at the hands of an all-Tutsi army carried an immediate and powerful demonstration effect to the Hutu of Rwanda. The message came through clear and loud: "Never trust the Tutsi!" Thus, with Ndadaye's death varnished what few glimmers of hope remained that Arusha might provide a viable forum for a political compromise with the RPF.[22]

Thus, the violent overthrow and murder of President Ndadaye, along with other internal factors, subverted the implementation of an enlarged transitional government and political liberalization in general.

During the early 1990s, there were serious attempts by some in the Hutu-dominated regime in Rwanda to effect a policy of outright political and military marginalization of the RPF, and of the Tutsi population as a whole. From 1990, specific incidents of political and ethnic harassment occurred. For example, in mid-October 1990, a group of Hutu incited by local authorities took revenge on a group of Tutsi in the region of Kibilira, killing 300 people and generating numerous refugees in the process. Mainly Tutsi citizens accused of sympathizing with the RPF were sentenced to death. More than 8,000 citizens were arrested without clear motives.[23] As a result of a temporary territorial success for the RPF in the Ruhengeri area, military and civilian authorities took revenge on the Bagogwe, a Tutsi subgroup, causing at least 500 deaths. The Bagogwe would become further victims of terror as the conflict unfolded.

By the end of 1991, the south of the country became involved in the conflict for the first time. According to African Rights:

> The 1992 Bugesera massacre marked an important turning point in the development of the methods of killings, because of the central role played by extremist propaganda. For four months before the killing started, extremist politicians and ideologues had been active in the area, inciting Hutu populace.[24]

In particular, the mayor of the area, who belonged to the central committee of the MRND, was the driving force behind the terror.

These initial killings and violence were directed at Tutsi and reform-minded Hutu in different places. They reveal a particular strategy and plan adopted by local authorities, with strong support from the highest levels of the regime. Thus, there was increasing involvement of party militias, multiplication of the number of individual killers, and a deliberately created climate of insecurity and unsafety. The members of the party militia were recruited widely across Rwanda. Many were unemployed youth armed after the February 1993 offensive of the RPF. Both the political and ethnic polarization and the increased arming of Hutu extremists received tacit support from President Habyarimana who did not objected to the role of regime supporters in the gradually widening conflict after the latter half of 1990.

In spite of the talks and agreements between the RPF, the government, and other parties in 1993, Rwandese society tended to polarize more and more into anti- and pro-RPF (and Tutsi) parties and groups. Habyarimana's supporters tended to equate opponents of the MRND regime with enemies of the Hutu people. Moreover, events in neighboring Burundi added to the polarization. Violence was deliberately fueled by the media, which agitated the Hutu population against their presumed enemies. For example, in July 1993, Radio-Télévision Libre des Mille Collinès (RTLMC) started to broadcast, officially to counterbalance Radio Muhabura (RPF) and the official Radio Rwanda.[25] The RTLMC's role was pivotal in inciting violence against Tutsi and moderate Hutu.

The Rwandan genocide of 1994 began first with the creation of a poisoned political climate and of ethnic polarization. Second, from 1992, direct means in the form of militias, spreading of weapons, creation of extremist movements, political assassinations, and planned massacres were used along with the deliberate inciting of hatred and a climate of terror and fear. Moreover, the planning originated from the leadership in the army, the presidential guard, and the administration, among others, who had a vested interest in maintaining the status quo.

The April 1994 Genocide

The catalyst that intensified and made extensive the violent episodes of 1993 was the April 6, 1994, incident in which the plane carrying Juvénal Habyarimana as well as the president of Burundi (Yprien Ntarymira) was hit by a rocket and exploded as it was approaching the airport. All passengers and crew were killed. According to some commentators, the plane crash became an excuse for and part of the plan to instigate the genocidal violence. It was, in other words, "an eminently rational act from the standpoint of the immediate goals of Hutu extremists."[26]

The violence that followed amounted to one of the most atrocious in the history of humankind. Within a period of less than three months, at least 500,000 people were killed, in addition to thousands and thousands maimed, raped, and psychologically scarred for life. Two million became external refugees in neighboring countries, and one million became internally displaced. The massacres took the form of a well-organized, systematic, and meticulous plan. Most observers agree that the massacres were organized in advance and directed from the top in terms of local and national government officials, the army, the presidential guard and the MRND party. According to African Rights:

> The killers include the professional Interahamwe, soldiers, gendarmes, Presidential Guardsmen and local government officials who actually supervised and carried out the killings. Some of these people have been witnessed, with their clothes literally drenched in blood, at the scene of the massacres or at roadblocks. And above them, there are the architects of genocide—the men who held the highest offices in the land, who controlled the government, army and radio stations, and who planned and implemented the killings from on high. Few of these people actually wielded machetes or even guns, but it was their policies and words that put guns and machetes in the hands of so many people in Rwanda. Some traveled the country inciting hatred, or spoke on the radio, others were active behind the scenes encouraging the extremists and lending them logistical, financial, political and diplomatic support.[27]

According to Lemarchand, by 1992, the plan, mechanism, and entire apparatus of genocide was already in place. He identifies the actors and the structures, or institutional apparatus, as follows:

> It involved four distinctive levels of activity, or sets of actors; (a) the akazu ("little house"), that is the core group, consisting of Habyarimana's immediate entourage, i.e., his wife (Agathe), his three brothers-in-law . . . and a sprinkling of trusted advisers . . . ; (b) the rural organizers, numbering anywhere from two to three hundred, drawn from the communal and prefectural cadres (préfets,

sous-préfets, conseillers, commanaux, etc.); (c) the militias (Interhamwe), estimated at 30,000 forming the ground-level operatives in charge of doing the actual killing; and (d) the Presidential Guard, recruited almost exclusively among northerners and trained with a view to providing auxiliary slaughterhouse support to civilian death squads.[28]

The killings did not take the form of spontaneous outbursts, but were systematic and based on instructions from the highest level.

There was a sequence to the massacres. Almost immediately after the aircraft was shot down at 8:30 P.M., a selective assassination of opposition politicians (mostly Hutu) began. The leadership of every opposition party was targeted in a similar way. The second target group for assassination, after leading opposition politicians had been killed, were dissenting civilians, both Hutu and Tutsi. These inlcuded journalists, human rights activists, representatives of various civil society groups, and civil servants. According to African Rights, twenty-seven journalists were reported killed immediately after April 6. Next, after the killing of the opposition, the widespread massacre of Tutsi started. Most people, either willingly or by force, seem to have participated in the killings.[29] The first targets were Tutsi men and boys, including even the smallest boys. Killings, rapes, maimings, and torture were used extensively and across all age groups. People were also burnt alive, thrown dead or alive into pit latrines, and often forced to kill their friends and relatives. Some of the worst massacres were directed against people seeking refuge in churches.

One of the strategies used by the planners of the genocide was the sowing of confusion during and immediately following the plane crash. The objective was the deliberate creation of fear and ignorance so that neither Rwandese nor foreigners knew what was happening. The strategy included the setting up of roadblocks, a nationwide curfew, and the disruption of telephone links. These were instituted immediately. At the same time an effective campaign of disinformation by RTLMC and Radio Rwanda were taking place. The Rwanda crisis was blamed on the RPF and its alleged violation of the cease-fire agreements. It took the international press almost three weeks to really grasp the magnitude of the genocide taking place in Rwanda, particularly, in the rural areas. By July 1994, the RPF took over the governance of Rwanda. To show its preparedness for peace, the RPF included in the new government Hutu moderates who had survived the massacres.

In conclusion, many genocides have been caused by a long history of conflict between perpetrators and victims. The preceding violent conflicts before the actual mass killings are often intensified by general economic dislocation resulting in severe economic times.[30] The interaction between a legacy of conflict and economic hard times is manifested in the most vicious propaganda against the target group.[31] The group is described in subhuman terms, accused of betraying the nation, and especially accused of causing the catastrophic economic hard times experienced by the rest of the people. In preparation for the actual genocide, extremism generally prevails, and paramilitary armies and other groups are formed and incited to carry out the actual killing.

Notes

1. See, among other works, David Svaldi, *Sand Creek and the Rhetoric of Extermination: A Case Study in Indian-White Relations* (Lanham, MD: University Press of America, 1989); and W. P. DuPreez, *Genocide: The Psychology of Mass Murder* (London: Boyars/Bowerdean, 1994).

2. *U.N. Genocide Convention* (Washington, DC: Bureau of Public Affairs, Department of State, 1986).

3. Raphael Lemkin, *Axis Rule in Occupied Europe* (New York: H. Fertig, 1973); or see James Joseph Martin, *The Man Who Invented "Genocide": The Public Career and Consequences of Raphael Lemkin* (Torrance, CA: Institute for Historical Review, 1984).

4. See, for example, W. P. DuPreez, *Genocide: The Psychology of Mass Murder* (London: Boyers/Bowerdean, 1994); and R. J. Rummel, *Lethal Politics: Soviet Genocide and Mass Murder since 1917* (New Brunswick: Transaction Publishers, 1990).

5. For more details, see Frank R. Chalk, *The History and Sociology of Genocide: Analyses and Case Studies* (New Haven: Yale University Press, 1990); and George J. Andreopoulous, ed., *Genocide: Conceptual and Historical Dimensions* (Philadelphia: University of Pennsylvania Press, 1994).

6. Barbara Harff and T. R. Gurr, "Toward Empirical Theory of Genocides and Politicides: Identification and Measurement of Cases since 1945," *International Studies Quarterly* 32 (1988) 63.

7. For more details, see W. P. DuPreez, *Genocide: The Psychology of Mass Murder* (London: Boyers/Bowerdean, 1994); and Jon Bridgman, *The Revolt of the Hereros* (Berkeley: University of California Press, 1981).

8. Barbara Harff and T. R. Gurr, "Toward Empirical Theory of Genocides and Politicides: Identification and Measurement of Cases since 1945."

9. See, for example, David Svaldi, *Sand Creek and the Rhetoric of Extermination: A Case Study in Indian-White Relations* (Lanham, MD: University Press of America, 1989).

10. For details, see Filip Reyntjen, *Burundi: Breaking the Cycle of Violence* (London: Minority Rights Group, 1995); and Arthur J. Klinghoffer, *The International Dimension of Genocide in Rwanda* (London: Macmillan Press, 1998).

11. See David Little, *Sri Lanka: The Invention of Enmity* (Washington, DC: United States Institute of Peace, 1994).

12. See, for example, Ken Saro-Wiwa, *On a Darkling Plain: An Account of the Nigerian Civil War* (London: Saros, 1989).

13. In terms of varied conceptualizations and case studies on genocide, see Frank R. Chalk, *The History and Sociology of Genocide: Analyses and Case Studies* (New Haven: Yale University Press, 1990); and George J. Andreopoulous, ed., *Genocide: Conceptual and Historical Dimensions* (Philadelphia: University of Pennsylvania Press, 1994).

14. For details, see *The International Response to Conflict and Genocide: Lessons from the Rwanda Experience,* published by the Steering Committee of the Joint Evaluation of Emergency Assistance to Rwanda, March 1996.

15. *The International Response to Conflict and Genocide,* chapter 3, p 1.

16. See, for example, Catharine Newbury, *The Cohesion of Oppression: Clientship and Ethnicity in Rwanda, 1860–1960,* (New York: Columbia University Press, 1988); and A. Lema, *Africa Divided: The Creation of "Ethnic Groups"* (Lund: Lund University Press, 1993).

17. See, *The International Response to Conflict and Genocide*, chapter 3.
18. The RPF is a creation of the Tutsi refugees who fled Rwanda, mainly between 1959 and 1966. For details, see C. Watson, *Exile from Rwanda: Background to an Invasion* (Washington, DC: U.S. Committee for Refugees, 1991).
19. See, *The International Response of Conflict and Genocide*, chapter 4.
20. The SAPs contributed to increased inflation associated with devaluation and deficit financing in the early 1990s. For details, see *World Bank, Implementation Completion Report: Rwandese Republic Structural Adjustment Credit* (Washington, DC, 1995).
21. I. Linden, "The Churches and Genocide: Lessons from Rwanda," *Svensk Missionstidskrift* 83 (March 1995): 5–15.
22. Rene Lemarchand, *Rwanda: The Rationality of Genocide* (1995).
23. Africa Watch, *Rwanda. Talking Peace and Waging War. Human Rights since the October 1990 Invasion* (1992).
24. African Rights, *Rwanda: Death, Despair and Defiance* (London, 1994).
25. See *The International Response to Conflict and Genocide: Lessons from the Rwanda Experience*, chapter 4.
26. Rene Lemarchand, *The Rationality of Genocide*, 1995.
27. African Rights, *Rwanda: Death, Despair and Defiance* (London, 1994).
28. Rene Lemarchand, *Rwanda: The Rationality of Genocide* (1995). See also G. Prunier, *The Rwandese Crisis (1959–1994)* (London: Hurst, 1995).
29. See again, African Rights, *Rwanda: Death, Despair and Defiance* (London, 1994).
30. For details on the activators of genocidal movements, see R. Melson, "Revolutionary Genocide: On the Causes of the Armenian Genocide of 1915 and the Holocaust," *Holocaust and Genocide Studies* 4 (1989): 161–74.
31. On early warning indicators of genocide, see F. H. Littell, "Essay: Early Warning," *Holocaust and Genocide Studies* 3 (1988): 483–90.

Key Terms

civil society groups
CNN effect
decolonization process
developmental genocide
genocide
genocides of colonization
Hamitic hypothesis
hegemonial genocides
hegemonic wars

ideological genocide
ideological xenophobia
policy of ethogenesis
pragmatic genocide
retribution genocide
revolutionary genocide
structural adjustment package
zero-sum game

Discussion Questions

1. Discuss some of the problems related to the definition of genocide.
2. What is the difference between ideological genocide and retributive genocide? Give specific examples where appropriate.
3. Analyze some of the reasons for genocides. Where appropriate apply these reasons to specific genocidal events.
4. Identify a specific genocide and give an account of it.
5. What are some of the causes of the genocides that occurred at the end of the Cold War?

CHAPTER **12**

Environmental
Degradation–Violent
Conflict Nexus

The literature linking environmental deficiencies or degradation and violent conflict is on the increase. Researchers exploring the linkage have posited a number of possible connections: (1) unnatural or extreme weather conditions stifle economic activity, uprooting populations and creating discontent and misery; (2) deforestation is a cause of ethnic tensions in some regions of the world; (3) depletion of fish stocks produces forced migration or expanded operations by farmers, resulting in tensions with neighbors; (4) decreases in crop yield as a result of inefficient agricultural practices generate strife in some societies; and (5) intraregional and interstate conflict can ensue from upstream pollution or appropriation of freshwater supplies.

Population projections, when linked to environmental degradation and the availability of natural resources, present an alarming future scenario. Local renewable resources—cropland, forests, freshwater, and the like—are being depleted and degraded by logging, overgrazing, overcultivation, or pollution, among other causes. Stated differently, there is growing evidence between increasing scarcity of renewable resources (environmental scarcity) and the incidence of a link violent conflict, especially within states at the end of the twentieth century.

The aim of this chapter is to survey the current literature associating environmental degradation and existence of, or potential for, violent conflicts. Environmental conflicts are violent conflicts, of short or long duration, among groups within different states, generated by environmental degradation. Such conflicts are ultimately caused by an overuse, overstrain, or impoverishment of either resources or living space.

Thomas Homer-Dixon is one of the foremost to assert a direct connection between the degradation of the environment and the eruption of, or potential for, eruption of violent conflicts among groups.[1] He identifies six types of environmental change that have implications for violent conflict. These are: water and land degradation, deforestation, decline in fisheries, and, to a minor extent, global warming and stratospheric ozone depletion. Peter Gleick, on the other hand, considers global climatic changes as constituting the ultimate source of all environmental conflict.[2] He identifies four principal consequences of global climate change caused by human activities: availability of freshwater resources, quality of freshwater resources, changes in agricultural productivity and trade, and rise in sea level. Both Homer-Dixon and Gleick underscore the vulnerability of developing countries to this effect of environmental deficiencies and violent conflicts.

Norman Myers also emphasizes the vulnerabilities of the developing world, by arguing that environmental weaknesses serve as determinants of the sources of conflict, exacerbate other primary causes of conflict, and largely help to shape the nature of the conflict.[3] In particular, Myers outlines as the major causes of conflict, five types of environmental problems: (1) access and availability of water, (2) deforestation, (3) desertification, (4) species extinction and gene depletion, and (5) greenhouse gases. In an already socially fragile world, Myers believes that these environmental issues could help to destabilize societies. They may be triggers to violent conflict when coupled with dislocated economics, unjust social systems, coercive political systems, and population explosion, among other factors. Jill W. Goodrich and Peter Brecke, in their framework linking environmental change and violent conflict, emphasize environmental pressures defined as environmental consequences of extensive anthropogenic (human-caused) activities.[4] The pressures in turn produce negative effects, or physical and social consequences. Either because of direct or indirect social consequences, physical consequences result in negative social effects. Eventually, environmental conflict is the outcome of these negative social effects.

According to Stephan Libiszewski, the type of scarcity produced by environmental degradation determines the role of the environment in a conflict. He outlines four types of scarcity: (1) physical scarcity, (2) geopolitical scarcity, (3) socioeconomic scarcity, and (4) environmental scarcity. In the first type, physical scarcity, a resource is available in a finite amount. Geopolitical scarcity refers to the unequal distribution of a resource. A socioeconomic scarcity has to do with inequality between and within societies in the distribution of purchasing power and of property rights related to the provision or access to natural resources. These three types of scarcity, according to Libiszewski, are traditional conflicts of resource distribution, and therefore different from environmental scarcity, which is "resources that have traditionally been regarded as plentiful and naturally renewable but are becoming scarce because of the failure of human beings to adopt sustainable methods of their management."[5] In other words, environmental conflict results from environmental degradation that produces environmental scarcity of a resource. Other factors, no doubt, also contribute to the outbreak of violence, such as the socioeconomic consequences of environmental deficiency.

Environmental Degradation and the Declining Capacity of the State

Many studies on the state of the environment view economic deprivation, migratory behavior, or ethnolinguistic clashes to be connected in varying degrees with environmental degradation. The combined effect of the socioeconomic variables of overpopulation, land scarcity, overgrazing, or civil strife, among others, tend to effectively undermine the capacity of the developing state to mobilize the resources of the country toward sustained national development.

Homer-Dixon emphasizes group identity, simple scarcity, and relative deprivation as three types of environmentally induced conflict; intergroup conflict occurs because environmental scarcity has forced substantial population movements, which in turn generate conflicts. The migration of one group to the territory of another in search of greener pastures because of deprivation resulting from environmental stress results in clashes between the two groups, who are usually of different ethnolinguistic or ethnocultural makeups. In other words, differences in group identity could become the trigger for such conflict. In the second type of conflict, simple scarcity conflict, conflict occurs because of competition for a single renewable resource. The most desired renewables are resources necessary for human survival such as water, fish, and productive farm land. According to Homer-Dixon, river water generates the most contention.[6] These renewables easily produce conflicts because they are collective property that can be seized or controlled. In the third type of conflict, Homer-Dixon makes reference to the concept of relative deprivation and its relationship to environmental conflicts. Relative deprivation conflicts are manifested in civil strife and insurgency caused by unequal distribution. Such conflicts occur because a society's level of resource and wealth production decreases due to environmental deficiencies, as an individual's level of discontent increases because of a "widening gap between their actual level of economic achievement and the level they feel they deserve."[7] This results in class animosity within the lower classes toward the power elite, who are perceived as the cause of the former's plight.

Environmental scarcity in general tends to undermine the capacity of the state to adequately provide for its citizens, thereby resulting in the state's gradual loss of legitimacy vis-à-vis citizens. This state incapacity and loss of legitimacy is particularly common in developing countries. Scarcity leads to a barrage of economic and political demands on government to alleviate the problems caused by the loss of renewable resources. Solutions such as constructing dams or irrigation systems, providing fertilizer plants, or implementing reforestation programs entail expenditure of enormous resources that the state, in its diminished capacity, cannot provide.

Environmental Changes and Conflict in Developing Countries

A significant change in one sector (for example, population growth) of society generally interacts with, is affected by, or impacts other aspects of society, often with unanticipated consequences for the entire ecosystem. Homer-Dixon and Jessica Blitt underscore environmental change, population growth, and unequal social distribution of resources as the sources of environmental scarcity and as the principal causes of many ongoing conflicts in developing countries. It is the human cause of decline in quantity and quality of a renewable resource that leads to environmental change, especially when such decline occurs faster than it is renewed by natural processes. A per capita reduction of the resource occurs as population growth occurs, leading to the division of the resource among increasing numbers of people. Unequal resource distribution translates into the resource being concentrated in the hands of a few people within the population. As quantity and quality diminish, the resource pie becomes smaller. When coupled with population growth, the quantity available to groups and individuals becomes equally smaller. As often happens, some groups end up with a disproportionate share of the scarce resource even in the midst of scarcity.

The three sources of environmental scarcity—environmental change, population growth, and equal distribution—interact to produce resource capture and ecological marginalization.[8] Resource capture occurs when groups within a society shift resource access and availability in their favor because of the scarcity that resulted from a decrease in the quality and quantity of renewable resources coupled with population growth. This creates animosity between the disadvantaged groups in society and the power elite. Economic marginalization results from unequal resource access coupled with population growth, which forces segments of the population to migrate to regions that are ecologically fragile. Lack of knowledge and capital to protect local resources plus the large number of people combine to decrease both the quantity and quality of renewable resources.

In explanations of environmentally induced conflicts in developing countries, experts in this field particularly emphasize the relationship between human activity, environmental change, and social disruption, all of which interact to generate conflicts. For Homer-Dixon in particular, the combined effect of human activity on the environment is largely a function of two factors: the product of total population in the area and physical activity per capita, and the vulnerability of the ecosystem in that area to those particular activities. Using this environmental change and acute conflict framework, Homer-Dixon then formulates a number of environmental scarcity models.[9] The models of environmental scarcity, he argues, contain four primary social effects that may, either singly or in combination, substantially increase the probability of acute conflict in developing countries. These primary social effects result from a change in the environment, and are: decreased agricultural production, economic decline, population displacement, and disruption of institutions and of legitimized and authoritative social relations. He then identifies six types of environmental changes as plausible causes of violent intergroup conflict: greenhouse warming, stratospheric ozone depletion, deforestation, degraded agricultural land, overuse and pollution of water supplies, and depletion of fish stocks. According to Homer-Dixon, the latter four environmental changes require special attention because they will be the primary causes of social turmoil in the decades ahead, more so than greenhouse warming or ozone depletion, which fall into the category of climate change.

From his analysis of environmental scarcity and violent conflicts, Homer-Dixon hypothesized three relationships: (1) that decreasing supplies of physically controllable environmental resources, especially river water, trigger "simple scarcity" conflicts; (2) that large population movements caused by environmental stress spawn "group identity" conflicts, with the level and intensity of such conflicts varying from context to context; and (3) that environmental scarcity simultaneously increases economic deprivation, which disrupts key social institutions, which in turn causes "deprivation" conflicts such as civil strife and insurgency.

In particular, environmental scarcity is a function of three types of scarcity: supply-induced scarcity, demand-induced scarcity, and structural scarcities.[10] The first type of scarcity is also known as environmental change and results in ecosystem degradation, sensitivity caused by human activity like logging, fishing, or extraction of water. In some cases, resource degradation can be irreversible, especially where the topsoil is shallow. Demand-induced scarcity occurs as a result of an increase in the overall demand for a resource caused by either population growth or an increase in per capita consumption of the resource. Scarcity is aggravated even more if the supply of the resource remains constant. Structural scarcity occurs from the unequal distribution of resources achieved through legislation or other means. The consequence is that the resource becomes accessible and concentrated in the hands of a privileged few, the power elite, at the expense of the bulk of the population. Supply-induced scarcity describes a diminution in the quantity or quality of the resource, while demand-induced scarcity results from an increase in the number of people competing for the resource, leading to a smaller portion or none available for more people. Structural scarcity results when, because of the insecurity arising from scarcity of the resource, the power elite ensures for itself a larger share of the resource, thereby reducing the amount available for the rest of the population. These three often mutually interact and occur simultaneously.

The existence of environmental scarcity does not necessarily produce social dislocation and violent conflict. Violent conflict is exacerbated by factors such as: (1) the inability of the market or the state to provide alternative sources of the scarce resource, or to develop substitutes for the resources, or (2) the actions of the power elite through either legislation or by force to skew the distribution of the scarce resource in their favor instead of ensuring distribution to benefit the greatest number. The consequence is that even in the midst of scarcity, the power elite end up controlling a disproportionate amount of the resource relative to their small size. In the process, they also stubbornly maintain institutional rigidity, oppose reform to alleviate scarcity problems, and undermine any capacity the economy may have to launch innovations that would effectively deal with the problem. Developing countries are not just woefully lacking in adequate institutions to deal with new problems, they also often lack the financial capital to embark on any new ventures to alleviate the scarcity problem. Resources may include financial or human capital.

The existence of the above conditions will definitely aggravate the scarcity problem resulting in five kinds of social consequences: constrained agricultural productivity, limited economic productivity, migration, social segmentation, and disruption of legitimate institutions.[11] In other words, along with other societal factors (for example, the nature of interethnic relations) these five effects are produced. Food and cash-crop production are definitely affected by various kinds of environmental scarcity, especially water scarcities, topsoil erosion, or deforestation. Often the least-advantaged groups suffer the very adverse effects of environmental scarcity, since they lack access to financial capital, the technology to alleviate the problem, or decision-making power to steer legislation in their favor. As the prospects for productive agriculture diminishe's some individuals become poorer and thereby may decide to migrate to other regions of the country, only to find that the local people may not be that welcoming. The result may be social friction.

The migration of peoples, either as individuals or in groups, raises the awareness of cultural, ethnic, regional, religious, or other preexisting differences. The outcome is increased polarization of society and rivalry for the scarce resource, which then result in ethnocommunal tensions and the potential for disrupted village systems, districts, provinces, and even the entire state system itself. Environmental scarcity is thus characterized by these mutually reinforcing effects because as agricultural production falls, the state is confronted with new problems related to mass migrations, falling tax revenues, and challenge from small coalitions of elites (rent seekers) whose goal is to exploit the situation for profit by monopolizing scarce resources. These rent seekers in practice constitute a state within the state because of the inordinate power they wield, and because of their capacity to evade paying taxes and consistently influence policy in their favor.

As the effects of environmental scarcity increase, they generate new negative effects that eventually increase the grievance of the adversely affected populations, and given the opportunity, they are likely to use violence to address those grievances. The affected groups are more likely to act if they perceive themselves to be relatively deprived. But even a perception of relative deprivation is not sufficient to cause rebellion. The affected groups have to be aware of their common interests, organize, mobilize their resources, and engage in rebellion against the state. It becomes easier to engage in rebellion when individuals belonging to a group are already organized around distinct social cleavages based on ethnicity, religion, class, and so on.

Civil violence should be viewed as a last resort for the affected groups. Violence is likely to occur because of structural inflexibilities associated with the political system that offer little opportunity for aggrieved groups to express their frustration peacefully and gain redress. Aggrieved groups soon realize that the violent route is the only feasible alternative available to them. If they are convinced that they are likely to succeed if they challenge the state, then violence becomes the rational option to take.

Finally, since environmental scarcity is located within states, the state may itself be confronted by challenger groups using guerrilla tactics to fight their battle. Such conflicts are often difficult to control because the challengers may soon learn that, at least in the short run, the barrel of a gun provides them with an abundance of loot or resources they have never before acquired. Violence resulting from the mutual interaction of environmental scarcity, grievances, and changing structure of opportunities can take the form of guerrilla warfare, coups d'état, interethnic clashes, or even revolution, which could lead to a revamping of the entire society.

Conflict, the Environment, and Refugeeism

In Brazil, the Horn of Africa, Haiti, India, and many other countries millions have been displaced as a result of environmental degradation. Many areas of the world are becoming increasingly uninhabitable because of deterioration of agricultural lands, desertification, salinization, water pollution, and natural and man-made disasters. Some of these factors result in massive, rapid, and unplanned movement of persons, especially when they are underlined by violent conflicts. The close interaction between natural disasters, civil conflict, persecution, and overpopulation, among other factors, have caused people to migrate from their homes either temporarily or permanently because their land can no longer sustain them.

The most important causes and dynamics of environmental migration are: elemental disruptions (cyclones, volcanoes, earthquakes, and other natural disasters); slow-onset disruptions (global warming, deforestation, land degradation, erosion, salinity, siltation, water logging, or desertification); accidental disruptions (accidents in the manufacturing, transportation, and application of chemicals); disruptions caused by development (dams and irrigation projects may bring benefits to some while causing the displacement of others); and environmental warfare.[12] Each category ranges in effect from mild to moderate to catastrophic.

In environmental warfare, the environment becomes the major victim of violent conflict. In countries such as Sudan, Somalia, Chad, Afghanistan, or Angola, environmental degradation is both a cause and a result of armed conflict and persecution. These countries experience both ecological disasters and armed conflict, often followed by drought and famine and increased possibility for further intergroup conflict. Bombs, tanks, and other weapons can destroy local infrastructure such as dams, which in turn destroys the habitat of an entire area. The consequence is either temporary movements to escape the fighting or permanent movements because of the permanent destruction of habitat.

The mass movements caused by warfare in turn result in ecological degradation. The United Nations High Commissioner for Refugees, Sadako Ogato, told a United Nations Conference on Environment and Development (UNCED) preparatory meeting in September 1991 that "environmental degradation has increasingly become both a cause and a symptom of population."[13] There is thus a strong correlation between the arid and semi-arid areas of the poorest countries of the world and the majority of refugees. Refugees need fuel wood to cook and thus are forced to gather and use up more fuel wood from their surroundings. While the refugee effect on environmental degradation is globally very small, it is nonetheless very visible in areas highly populated by the sudden mass movements of people. In the end, both the refugees and the local population suffer the ensuing degradation. For example, in the early 1990s, Mozambican refugees in parts of Zimbabwe rapidly depleted the resources of deadwood around their camps, and were soon obliged to cut down living trees.[14] In such situations the relationship between the refugees and their hosts becomes strained by the competition for increasingly limited resources.

The Link between Environmental Degradation and Population Growth

Ecology and resource consumption are becoming increasingly interwoven. What seems to be a perennial doubling of economic activity draws raw material from land and water. Pollution and the tendency to waste are elements associated with some technologies. In regions of the world where there is overpopulation relative to renewable resources, scarcity can lead to competition. Scarcity, coupled with ethnic competition, and grievances arising from long-standing socioeconomic and political factors, constitute power incentives for individuals and groups to take control of rational politics, by force if necessary.[15] Frequently, it is only the winners in general elections who have access to resources ranging from land and water to jobs in state-owned enterprises. Such a winner-take-all situation is a powerful incentive to join conflict groups and reduces an individual's inclination to engage in political apathy.

Population pressure, scarcity of resources, the impact of the global political economy, and drought, among other factors, aggravate long-standing ethnic tensions and can thus accentuate the efforts of economic discrimination along ethnic lines. In times of drought and famine ethnic conflicts are further aggravated when the affected tribal groups attempt to move into new regions in search of pasture for their starving animals. For instance, in the spring of 1989, the killing of Senegalese farmers by Mauritanians in the Senegalese River basin triggered explosions of ethnic violence in the two countries. In Senegal almost all of the 17,000 shops owned by Moors were destroyed, and their owners were deported to Mauritania. In both countries several hundred people were killed, and the two nations nearly engaged in war.[16] In drought-stricken areas, famine relief is used by the dominant group as a political weapon, resulting in unequal distribution and monopoly over the distribution. The dominant groups ensure that their groups receive assistance first. In the mid-1980s, the Amhara-dominated regime of Ethiopia was widely accused of using food aid as a political weapon, preventing the distribution of food to areas suspected of collaborating with Eritrean rebels.

In may parts of the developing world, negative human influences on the environment abound. These influences are often directly associated with drought, famine, and rapid vegetation modification. The twin processes of forest degradation and desertification are considered to be critical to the long-term ecological viability of many developing regions. In Africa, for example, they affect socioeconomic security related to food production. The many post–Cold War conflicts raging in developing countries cause significant damage to the forest. In Liberia and Sierra Leone, for example, many military engagements between fighting factions occurred in forest zones. In such conflicts, resources such as timber are exploited by rebels to finance war-related activities. This situation in war-ravaged countries, coupled with cash crops that take away land for food crops, leads to increased stress and violence. Land degradation, desertification, and the use of the forest as a battle ground all have significant negative effects on natural variables such as species diversity and soil maintenance. The direct socioeconomic impacts relate to the general human security of these war-ravaged countries in terms of reduced food production, limited income-earning opportunities, affected settlement patterns, and human mobility.

Forest degradation largely affects rural inhabitants in developing countries. The vast majority of the six billion inhabitants of the world subsist as the rural poor. Land degradation coupled with unequal patterns of land ownership intensify poverty by depriving numerous peasants of productive land. Their only option is to continue farming fragile lands, cutting down rain forest and plowing in semi-arid areas. The annual increase in the numbers of these land-deprived peasants puts further strain on their security. The catalyst for the 1995 Chiapas rebellion in Mexico was the government's response to the requests for more land reforms and more assistance in farming by indigenous groups. In the 1970s, a major factor in the mass opposition against the Shah of Iran was demographic pressure on the agricultural sector of the economy. Between 1950 and 1976, the Iranian population was reported to have nearly doubled from approximately 17 million to 32 million. The lack of land for the millions of peasants led to a rural exodus, which in turn contributed to unemployment and a strong feeling of relative deprivation as transitionals in the cities became aware of growing disparities.[17]

In Africa and other developing areas, according to reports by the Food and Agricultural Organization (FAO) and the World Food Programme (WFP), civil strife has become a greater threat to food security. As national and international efforts continue to reduce poverty, more and more people are sliding into abject poverty, and live on less than one dollar a day. In 1972, the Club of Rome's study entitled "Limits to Growth" emphasized that infinite growth was impossible in a world characterized by finite resources.[18] The most essential resource in terms of population growth is land, and that is in finite supply. Even technological progress cannot, according to the limits to growth thesis, expand all physical resources indefinitely.

As populations increase, especially in developing countries, so does the potential for violent conflict over resources. One resource that is already an issue of serious dispute and of potential interstate violence is water. About one-fifth of the world's population already struggles to obtain enough clean drinking water to survive, and their numbers are increasing. In both the Middle East and the Indian subcontinent, there have been increased conflicts between states about the quantity and quality of water use. Water use generally falls under the management of global commons. Disputes and conflicts over such commons tend to revolve around the threats to security caused by others' use of the same resource.

The Nile River happens to be the common property of many nations, including Egypt, Sudan, Tanzania, Uganda, and Ethiopia. Egypt is perennially dependent on adequate Nile flows and thus is continually concerned that Tanzania might develop irrigation from lake Victoria, which is a part of the Nile system. Egypt has even threatened force against Tanzania regarding such a move. Similarly, Egypt is concerned that Ethiopia or Uganda might one day take action to block rights to the Nile waters. In the Middle East, Syria and Iraq complain of water shortages because of Turkey's construction of the Atatürk Dam, which contains the Euphrates River. In China, the Three Gorges Dam is expected to displace one million people, and consume more than 115,000 acres of the country's richest farm land.[19] Similarly, many large-scale dam projects have displaced hundreds of thousands of rural inhabitants all over the world, with severe consequences related to poverty.

Decline in agricultural production is associated with soil and water loss among the growing rural poor communities of developing regions. This linkage in turn feeds directly into the challenge of poverty, food shortages, and unemployment worldwide. In other words, fragile ecosystems are increasing in number just as nationals are experiencing socioeconomic stress related to abject poverty, inadequate resources, and natural disasters. Fragile ecosystems generally transcend national borders and include deserts, semi-arid lands, wetlands, and coastal areas, among others. For instance, desertification affects about one sixth of the world's population, 70 percent of all dry lands, amounting to 3.6 billion hactares, and one quarter of the total land area of the world. This process of desertification is in direct contrast to the population momentum that continues to put additional pressure on the limited land, intensify competition among groups, and raise tensions, which in some countries contribute to state failure.

Environmental Security as High Politics

The problem of environmental degradation has generated discussions of environmental security. As a concept, environmental security describes the governmental, intergovernmental, and nongovernmental attempts to grapple with growing international environmental problems in general. It has in fact become part of the larger literature on human security broadly defined. As environmental changes and degradation have become more manifest in depletion of the ozone layer, erosion of fertile soils, water pollution,

Table 12.1: Environment-Related Conventions

1. Basel Convention on Transboundary Movement of Hazardous Waste, 1989
2. Convention on Biological Diversity, 1992
3. Convention on Climate Change, 1997
4. Convention to Combat Desertification, 1994
5. Convention on International Trade in Endangered Species (CITES), 1973
6. The Convention on the Conservation of Migratory Species of Wild Animals (CMS), or the Bonn Convention
7. The Montreal Protocol designed to protect the stratospheric ozone layer, or Montreal Protocol on Ozone Depleting Substances, 1987
8. Inter-American Convention for the Protection and Conservation of Sea Turtles, 1998
9. Convention of Fishing and Conservation of the Living Resources in the Baltic Sea and Belts, 1958
10. Agreement on the Conservation of Seals in the Wadden Sea, 1990

global warming, and the like, they have assumed the salience of "high politics," or national and international security threats.[20] Environmental insecurity therefore implies any developments that destroy positive human-environment relationships. Where negative human-environment relationships appear threatening, concepts such as ecological security, sustainable development, and ecocide, among others, are used to describe the need to pay careful attention to the environment. However, just like the concept of national security in the international relations or foreign policy literature, environmental security is viewed by some scholars as a catch-all concept that includes, among others, the following principles: equality of rights over natural resources, prohibition of ecological aggression, monitoring of ecological security, prevention of environmental aggression, sustainable development, and international responsibility for the environment.

The reality in terms of developments in national and regional conflicts seem to equally reveal that instead of just warfare resulting from environmental degradation, it may indeed be a fact that an increasing number of new conflicts are over natural resources. For instance, some observers claim that a principal cause of the Arab-Israeli war of 1967 was water scarcity. Similarily, a major reason for group violence in the Horn of Africa is food scarcity. However, while environmental scarcity may not necessarily lead to interstate wars, or intergroup competition over resources, it can nonetheless contribute to tensions based on group identity, which could eventually escalate into civil strife. In other words, environmental scarcity could destabilize social institutions thereby making it harder for the state to maintain law and order, especially in cases where ethnic elites may choose to incite civil strife by exploiting the differences based on ethnic identity.

In other words, a major factor in environmental scarcity that is at times overlooked is the resource maldistribution that tends to aggravate violent ethnic conflict in regions of ethnocultural diversity. For instance, land, water, and food resource scarcity in states of the former Soviet Union, coupled with maldistribution, are said to have produced several hundred conflicts between 1988 and 1996, with approximately 300 of those conflicts falling under the category of border and territorial disputes.[21] Interethnic tensions, rivalries and violence, and refugees were the result of fierce competition over land and water, in-migration, population increases, and natural resource depletion. While conflicts over resources may not apply to all of the conflicts in the former Soviet Union, there are nonetheless six large areas affected by ethnoterritorial conflicts: Caucasus and Transcaucasus, Central Asia, Baltic States, Moldova and the Ukraine, the Volga-Urals region, and southern Siberia.[22]

While the Russian-Chechen War was fueled by political, religious, and ethnic causes, there is also a significant level of resource (especially oil) factor involved. Despite the dissolution of the U.S.S.R. in 1991, the Russian Federation still contains more than 7 million ethnolinguistically diverse Muslim peoples. Two of these groups—the Tartars and the Chechens—are important to the Russian Federation for two main reasons. The first has to do with a critical resource—oil. Both Chechenya and Tartastan possess substantial oil reserves. The second reason is political: both republics refused to ratify the 1992 Russian Federation Treaty that established the present Russian Federation.[23]

Russia did not hesitate to go to war, first in 1996, and then again in 1999, because the several thousand Muslim fighters, mostly Chechens, who invaded the neighboring republic of Daghestan in August 1999 declared that their goal was to detach Daghestan from Russia and to establish a Muslim Northern Caucasus federal state from the Black Sea to the Caspian.[24] If they had succeeded in their objectives, it would have endangered the security of oil transportation from the region. Chechen rebel success would have affected the objective of building pipelines to export oil from the Caucasus. Prior to 1999, the Chechens were able to steal oil and generate cash flow over which Russia had no control because it lacked control over the pipeline that runs from Baku, the capital of Azerbaijan, to Novorssrysk in Russia. Russian plans to build a pipeline bypass via Daghestan were jeopardized by the summer incursions of the Chechens.

One of the serious developments in international affairs is the fact that environmental degradation and scarcity have a transboundary impact capable of affecting interstate relations. For example, population and environmental degradation by their very nature and effects transcend interstate borders. This means that the idea of complex interdependence is in reality now also manifested not just in production networks, trade, investment, and global communications, but also in the reality of cross-boundary environmental degradation. The state has become not only permeable and penetrable as a result of transboundary environmental effects, but is now also liable to conflict with other states as a result of environmental degradation and scarcity. The 1987 Brundtland Report, entitled *Our Common Future*, underscored this development very well:

> Environmental stress is both a cause and an effect of political tension and military conflict. Nations have often fought to assert or resist control over raw materials, energy supplies, land, river basins, sea passages and other key environmental resources. Such conflicts are likely to increase as these resources become scarcer and competition for them will increase.[25]

However, despite the scope of interdependence in the world, states and societies compete for power and economic prosperity with little thought for their impact on either the earth itself or on others.

The perennial struggle for power and resources has thus produced many disputes between and among nations, several of which are unresolved. In the area of water as a resource issue, for example, there are the outstanding disputes between Egypt, Ethiopia, and Sudan over the Nile; the Iraq-Syria-Turkey dispute over the Euphrates; and the Cambodia-Laos-Thailand and Vietnam disputes over the Mekong River, among many others.[26] The disputes often revolve around issues of flooding, water flow/diversion, irrigation, dams, agrochemical pollution, industrial pollution, and salinization, among others.

Ecological damage is increasingly becoming a feature of the international system as states compete for power and prosperity, or as multinational corporations strive to enhance their scope of market operations. Instances of ecological damage are seen in the Iran-Iraq conflict, the United States-led war against Iraq in 1990 to 1991, the release of hazardous chemicals into the Rhine at Basel, Switzerland, in 1986, the nuclear explosion at Chernobyl in 1986, or the 1989 Exxon Valdez oil spill off Alaska. While these wars and accidents may be infrequent, the most damage to the environment is done by the sum total of industrial and agroindustrial systems, as well as utilities and transportation systems.

In sum, environmental degradation caused by the combined and interacting effects of human activity and population growth is producing environmental scarcity in the areas of renewable resources, aggravating long-standing ethnic animosities, and contributing to the eruption of violent resource wars in some parts of the world. The environment as an issue has increasingly become the focus of both state and nonstate actors because of its security implications related to resource scarcity, conflicts, refugees, pollution, and ozone depletion, among other factors.

Notes

1. Thomas Homer-Dixon, "Environmental Scarcities and Violent Conflict: Evidence From Cases," *International Security* 19:1 (summer 1994): 146–71.
2. Peter Gleick, "Climate change and International Politics: Problems Facing Developing Countries," *Ambio* 18:6 (1989): 333–39.
3. Norman Myers, *Ultimate Security: The Environmental Basis of Political Stability* (New York: W.W. Norton & Co., 1993).
4. Jill W. Goodrich and Peter Brecke, "The Pathways From Environmental Change to Violent Conflict: Connecting the Physical and Social Sciences," paper presented at the 40th Annual International Studies Association Meeting, Washington DC, Feb. 16–20, 1999.
5. Stephan Libiszewski, "What Is an Environmental Conflict?" *Occasional Paper*, no. 1 (Zurich: Center for Security Studies and Conflict Research, July 1992).
6. Thomas Homer-Dixon, "Environmental Scarcities and Violent Conflict: Evidence From Cases."
7. Thomas Homer-Dixon, "On the Threshold: Environmental Changes as Causes of Acute Conflict," *International Security* 16:2 (fall 1991): 109.
8. See Thomas Homer-Dixon and Jessica Blitt, "Introduction: A Theoretical Overview," in *Ecoviolence*, ed. Thomas Homer-Dixon and Jessica Blitt (Lanham: Rowman & Littlefield Publishers, Inc., 1998).
9. Thomas Homer-Dixon, "On the Threshold: Environmental Changes as Causes of Acute Conflict."
10. See Thomas Homer-Dixon and Jessica Blitt, "Introduction: A Theoretical Overview," in *Ecoviolence*.
11. For details, see Thomas Homer-Dixon and Jessica Blitt, "Introduction: A Theoretical Overview," in *Ecoviolence*.
12. See, for example, Susan F. Martin, "The Inhospitable Earth," *Refugees* no. 89 (May 1992): A UNHCR publication.
13. See "Refugees and the Environment," *Refugees* no. 89 (May 1992): A UNHCR publication, p. 5.
14. For details, see Gus Le Breton, "Carrying a Heavy Load," *Refugees* no. 89 (May 1992): A UNHCR publication.
15. For a detailed analysis of the linkage between scarcity, ethnic competition, and violence, see "The International Response to Conflict and Genocide: Lessons from the Rwanda Experience," published by Steering Committee of the Joint Evaluation of Emergency Assistance to Rwanda, March 1996 (http//:131.111.106.147/policy/pb020.htm).
16. For details, see Earl Conteh-Morgan and Shireen Kadivar, "Ethnopolitical Violence in the Liberian Civil War," *The Journal of Conflict Studies* xv, no. 1 (spring 1995).
17. See, for example, Roger Burbach, *Chiapas and the Crisis of Mexican Agriculture* (Oakland, CA: Institute for Food and Development Policy, 1994); and *Encyclopaedia Iranica*, ed. Eshan Yarshater (London: Routledge and Kegan Paul, 1982).
18. See, for example, H. S. D. Cole et al. eds., *Models of Doom: A Critique of the Limits to Growth* (New York: Universe Books, 1973).
19. For details on water disputes, see Michael Renner, Mario Pianta, and Cinzer Franch, "International Conflict and Environmental Degradation," in *New Directions in Conflict Theory: Conflict Resolution and Conflict Transformation*, ed. Raimo Vayrynen (London: Sage, 1991).
20. See, among others, Norman Myers, "Environmental Security," *Foreign Policy* 74: 29–41; and Arthur Westing, "The Environmental Component of Comprehensive Security," *Bulletin of Peace Proposals* 20, no. 2 (1989): 129–34.

21. See Michael Renner et al., "International Conflict and Environmental Degradation," in *New Directions in Conflict Theory*, ed. Raimo Vayrynen.

22. For details, see V. V. Stepanov, "Hotbeds of Interethnic Tension," *Herald of the Russian Academy of Sciences* 64, no. 2: 98–105.

23. See David Damrel, "The Religious Roots of Conflict: Russia and Chechnya," *Religious Studies News* 10, no. 3 (Sept. 1995).

24. For details, see Ariel Cohen, "Chechen War Fueled by Politics," *The Austin Review*, Friday, December 17, 1999, front page.

25. *Our Common Future*, the report by the World Commission on Environment and Degradation (1987): 290.

26. On water disputes, see Michael Renner et al., "International Conflict and Environmental Degradation," in *New Directions in Conflict Theory*, ed. Raimo Vayrynen.

Key Terms

demand-induced scarcity
demographic pressure
desertification
ecocide
environmental degradation
environmental migration

environmental scarcity
environmental security
high politics
human security
resource capture
supply-induced scarcity

Discussion Questions

1. What are some of the major causes of environmental-related conflicts?
2. Discuss the relationship between environmental degradation, conflict, and refugees.
3. How is human activity related to environmental scarcity and violent conflicts?
4. Define and discuss the concept of environmental security.
5. Are environmental degradation and scarcity always related to violence?

CHAPTER 13

Terrorism
Internal and External Dimensions

Introduction

Terrorism is often considered an old form of violence with more modern characteristics. It involves the purposeful or deliberate inducement of fear, through the use of threats or violence as methods of effecting change by dissatisfied entities. Although terrorism is often regarded as a method limited to small groups such as the Italian Red Brigades, the Japanese Red Army, Hamas, or Islamic Jihad, it has nonetheless been the preferred method of many despotic regimes, especially during the Cold War era in Argentina, Chile, or El Salvador. It entails inducing strong fear, uncertainty, outrage, and ultimately inflicting violence on the target population. In other words, terrorism is used by both state and nonstate actors to pursue political and social-economic goals.

Conceptual and Definitional Problems

Just as there are many competing explanations of what causes other forms of collective political violence such as revolutions, genocides, or ethnopolitical violence, so also are there many definitions of, and disagreements over, what constitutes terrorism. The result is that the term *terrorism* has been used to refer to a variety of similar and contradictory phenomena such as guerrilla warfare or wars of national self-determination.[1] At the heart of the definitional and conceptual disagreements are two factors: (1) the lack of agreement over what constitutes terrorist activities and related phenomena such as guerrilla movements or violent protest movements; and (2) the

254 · Collective Political Violence

difficulty of making a distinction between activities related to "legitimate" acts of national self-determination struggles and "illegal" acts of violence against governments. In other words, where terrorism is concerned, what may constitute genuine struggles for national self-determination may be labeled terrorism by those that may not approve of the activities of the group. It is therefore commonly said that "One man's terrorist is another man's freedom fighter." Terrorism thus becomes a purely subjective matter: a cruel act of terrorism to some may be a legitimate act of self-determination to others.[2] What is often labeled terrorism is manifested in various activities: bombings, assassinations, kidnappings, extortions, hijacking, arson, and the like. Complicating the problem is the fact that most or all of these methods are also used by guerrillas, freedom fighters, or insurgents.

Terrorism as a concept serves no useful analytic purpose because it has become a catch-all label for virtually all types of civil strife: insurgency, urban and rural guerrilla warfare, coups de'état, or riots. Second, terrorism serves no use as a tool for analyzing violence because it is underlined by contending political objectives. What to some is viewed as terrorism is merely a struggle for national self-determination to others. Terrorism, as a result, becomes a vehicle for verbal attacks against enemies, for judging rivals, or to score propaganda points against the opposing side.

The fact that terrorism defies precise definition is due to its value-laden (subjective) nature: it is often used to condemn, judge, or show support for one group vis-à-vis another. It defies precise definition because of the multiple actors, past and present, on the world's stage whose activities may be labeled terroristic: the Revolutionary Armed Forces of Colombia (FARC), the Ku Klux Klan in the United States, the Red Brigade, the Basques, skinhead groups in Germany and other parts of Europe, and so on; or in the area of state terrorism, Mao's Cultural Revolution, Pol Pot's regime in Kampuchea, Idi Amin's reign of terror in Uganda, Stalin's purges in the Soviet Union, and the Pinochet regime in Chile, among many others.

Select Definitions of Terrorism

Despite the conceptual difficulties inherent in the concept and phenomenon of terrorism, many scholars have nonetheless attempted a definition. Some differences that have emanated from terrorism as a concept are: whether terrorism can be attributed to both the opposition and those who govern (the state); whether state terrorism should be viewed as unavoidable or not; whether terror from revolutionaries is different from state or regime terror; whether state support is a component of international terrorism; whether violence is a necessary element of terrorism; and whether it is possible to make a distinction between war and terrorism.[3] In other words, the difficulty of defining the concept is related to the lack of consensus about what constitutes terrorism. For example, is all political violence terrorism? What ordinary crimes qualify as terrorism? How is terrorism different from guerrilla warfare? Do we focus on objectives to determine differences? Can the repressive or coercive behavior of governments be labeled terroristic? Below are selected definitions of terrorism:

> Terrorism is violence or the threat of violence calculated to create an atmosphere of fear and alarm—in a word, to terrorize—and thereby bring about some social or political change.
>
> —Brian M. Jenkins

> Terrorism—is—any type of political violence that lacks an adequate moral and legal justification, regardless of whether the actor is a revolutionary group or a government.
>
> —Richard A. Falk

> Political terrorism may be defined as the threat and/or use of extranormal forms of political violence, in varying degrees, with the objective of achieving certain political objectives/goals. Such goals constitute the long range and short-term objectives that the group or movement seeks to obtain.
>
> —Richard Shultz

> Terrorism is the deliberate and systematic use or threat of violence to coerce changes in political behavior. It involves symbolic acts of violence, intended to communicate a political message to watching audiences.
>
> —Martha Crenshaw

> The purposeful act or the threat of the act of violence to create fear and/or compliant behavior in a victim and/or audience of the act or threat.
>
> —Michael Stohl

> —acts of violence and other repressive acts by colonial, racist and alien regimes against peoples struggling for their liberation—; tolerating or assisting by a state the organizations of the remnants of fascists or mercenary groups whose terrorist activity is directed against other sovereign countries; acts of violence committed by individuals or groups of individuals which endanger or take innocent human lives or jeopardize fundamental freedoms, [provided this definition does] not affect the inalienable rights to self-determination and independence of all peoples under colonial and racist regimes and other forms of alien domination.
>
> —Non-Aligned Movement, 1973

> —terrorism is [coercive, life-threatening] action intended to induce sharp fear and through that agency to effect a desired outcome in a conflict situation.
>
> —Raymond Duvall, Michael Stohl, and Ted R. Gurr

From the above definitions, one can conclude that the term *terrorism* has no widely accepted definition. It lacks conceptual precision, and as a result confusion tends to surround the concept. However, based on the various definitions of the concept, certain indisputable elements predominate: (1) it is characterized by violence, actual or threatened; (2) its goal or objective is political in nature; (3) its perpetration can cause injury and death not only to the source of the political injustice, but to innocent persons as well; and (4) its strategy is the use of violence and terror to mobilize public opinion and thereby secure its political goal.

Causes of Terrorism

Virtually all definitions of terrorism emphasize the deliberate choice involved in acts of violence. But, although environmental circumstances may exist that are conducive to the formation of terrorist groups and the perpetration of terrorist acts, only a few people affected by negative political and socioeconomic circumstances practice terrorism. In analyzing the causes of a phenomena, social scientists often make a distinction between long-term causes and immediate causes, or preconditions and precipitating factors. The former are conditions that lay the foundation for, while the latter are specific events that speed up or immediately precede, the occurrence of the phenomenon. With regard to terrorism, some analysts identify modernization manifested in sophisticated network of transport and communication that give the terrorists ease of mobility and publicity as a precondition of terrorism. Another precondition of terrorism is urbanization due to the complex and crowded nature of cities, which provide a variety of targets, ease of mobility, enhanced communication, and a source of new recruits among transients and transitionals who have migrated from rural areas to the cities, or those who are simply unemployed and generally dissatisfied with the status quo.[4] Cities provide the attentive public, as well, for effective communication of the terrorists' goals. The overpopulation and impersonality of city life also enhance secrecy and anonymity.

A society with a historical legacy of violence may become a breeding ground for terrorism. The society may already be one in which violence has been used for centuries to the point where it becomes ingrained in the national consciousness, or is a part of the sociopolitical and historical habits and traditions. In Ireland, for example, incidents of political violence extend as far back as the eighteenth century. There have been so many terrorists incidents in Ireland that any new occurrence does not seem to surprise many people. The political culture of Ireland, in other words, includes a subculture of terrorist activities.

Terrorism in one society may have a "contagion effect" on another society because of imitation and interdependence factors. Acts of terrorism are communicated to the world in a matter of minutes. Ideologies are transnationalized from one region to another.[5] Maoism, for example, was adopted by the

Shining Path of Peru, and by the National Union for the Total Independence of Angola (UNITA) in the 1970s. Various other liberation movements in developing countries, especially during the Cold War, were influenced in varying degrees by Soviet or Chinese communism, or by the Cuban Revolution.

Terrorist activities can also widen and intensify because of a government's lack of political will or inability to vigorously fight terrorism. Combating terrorism may entail a curtailment of civil rights because of the need for roadblocks, identity cards, searching luggage, or homes. Modern democratic regimes are not likely to opt for the widespread implementation of such security measures because they undermine civil liberties. Besides, the clandestine nature and small size of terrorist organizations may make it very difficult to prevent their activities.

As with many of the causes of collective political violence, terrorism is a result of the accumulation of grievances. In other words, most terrorists are not mad people who just decide to perpetuate terrorist acts. They are usually a subentity (ethnic, religious, regional, and so on) constituting a minority discriminated against by the majority.[6] Terrorism is often the work of an extremist faction of a discriminated minority whose objective is to redress grievances, to ensure equality, civil liberties, or equal opportunity with the rest of society. However, terrorism is not always a case of discrimination, deprivation, or oppression of a minority. Stated differently, factors of discrimination or oppression do not constitute necessary and sufficient conditions of terrorism. For example, not all deprived people resort to terrorism. On the other hand, some of the affluent groups or individuals who do not experience any deprivation or oppression can resort to terrorism. An example is the terrorism from advanced industrial societies like Germany, Japan, and Italy. Terrorist groups in these countries are not affected by discrimination and can even be described as privileged. These groups resort to terrorism because they believe the incumbents have not implemented their own vision of society. The terrorism they inflict on society could be described as a form of ideological terrorism aimed at forcing both members of the right and left to subdue to their own worldview.

Lack of political rights and civil liberties, which translate into a lack of opportunity for political participation, constitutes another condition for terrorism. A group is not necessarily experiencing economic deprivation, but the focus of the group is primarily political because of blockages to the legal expression of opposition. It is a situation of rigid structural inflexibilities in the political realm that deprive an entire group of human rights. In such a society, terrorism is likely to be effective if the government lacks the ability or even the political will to effectively contain terrorism.

Finally, terrorism is always a case of dissatisfaction by a small group either with a larger movement, or acting on their own. A small group acts on behalf

258 · Collective Political Violence

of a wider popular constituency, often without their consent. It is a case of militancy by a small group within a sea of widespread passivity.

Internal and External Factors

The varied definitions of terrorism emphasize an element of rational political choice, a behavior that is coolly calculated and based on the notion of using extreme measures to effect a certain outcome. To paraphrase Carl von Clausewitz, terrorism is nothing but the continuation of politics by other means. The frequency and scope of terrorist activities tend to make terrorism a "normal" response to issues of gross inequalities and injustice in the international system. An understanding of the widespread nature of terrorism may require a conceptualization of terrorism in terms of levels of analysis: internal and external causes. The internal causes focus on the domestic factors: individual, governmental, societal, or wider cultural variables within states that may motivate terrorist activities. On the other hand, a focus on external factors underscores the nature and attributes of the international system that encourage the resort to terrorism as a method of influence. Issues such as the foreign policies of other states, the availability and diffusion of military capabilities, the global telecommunications revolution, and the increasing trend of global inequality and its corresponding socioeconomic deprivation. However, in a world of rapid globalization, it is hardly possible to come up with a clear-cut categorization of internal and external causes. Terrorism is thus an issue that could concomitantly be caused in varying degrees by both internal and external factors.

Based on our familiarity with other explanations of collective political violence, terrorism could likewise be explained by psychological, psychosocial, rationalistic, or social-structural factors, among others. For example, if terrorism is coolly calculated or deliberate, then it becomes tempting to argue that it is motivated by what has been referred to as "root" causes or societal conditions such as political-economic deprivation, oppression, despair, hopelessness, or persecution of members of the terrorist group. These conditions, among others, are obstacles that prevent members of the terrorist group from satisfying their basic needs, thereby forcing them to turn to terrorism as a last resort.[7] Terrorism, according to the "root causes" theory is a revolt against desperate conditions or circumstances whose objective is to bring about a change in their circumstances.

Countering the root causes school of thought are those who view terrorism as a pathological behavior by individuals who decide to wage a struggle against traditionally accepted rules and norms of society. Terrorism is therefore not connected to issues of deprivation, oppression, or gross inequalities. Terrorism is rather unprincipled behavior based on heinous crimes that are not justified, or motivated by deprivations, because after all many individuals and groups all over the world suffer intolerable injustice, but do not use the insanity of terrorism to vent their dissatisfaction. For example, according to Moshe Decter, what makes terrorism unprincipled and pathological is that: "Its victims are virtually and invariably unarmed, undefended, unwary civilians. The terrorist murders, maims, kidnaps, hijacks, tortures, bombs and menaces the innocent without the justification of military necessity."[8]

At times, the goals and objectives of terrorists may appear pathological because they may not be clearly articulated or even realistic, although they may resort to terrorism in order to communicate such objectives and in the process acquire political leverage. For example, it is difficult to imagine how the actions of groups like the Japanese Red Army or the Italian Red Brigades could lead to the overthrow of their governments and put them in power. However, for many their goals are not to overthrow the system, but mainly to direct attention to their cause, or gain recognition in society. Terrorism by its very nature is often violent and contains scenes of bloodletting, bombings, and other attention-grabbing activities. In an age of global telecommunications and what is now popularly known as the "CNN effect," media exposure may be a priority of some of the groups. The pervasiveness of the media could be a motivating factor for use of intense violence in order to grab the headlines.

A primary objective of terrorism is to psychologically weaken the incumbent regime by undermining its effectiveness through widespread fear and insecurity. As the regime is rendered more incapable of providing law and order, as well as physical security, it gradually loses legitimacy in the eyes of the people because of widespread insecurity and demoralization. The fear and insecurity is a result of violent incidents, guerrilla warfare, or deliberate activities aimed at undermining the regime's efficiency and effectiveness. The bombings by Tamil Tigers in Sri Lanka or the attacks of Islamic militants in Algeria are examples of attempts to psychologically demoralize the incumbent regimes.

Often intermixed with the aim to create fear and insecurity is the goal of generating sympathy for the terrorists' cause, and thereby creating hostility and loathing toward the regime, which is then perceived as responsible for the plight of the disgruntled group.

In addition, terrorism is used as a provocative strategy. The counterresponse of the regime tends to underscore the repressive behavior of the state because a counterreaction often involves greater repression and persecution, which increase media exposure for the terrorists and elicit sympathy for them, and thereby generate condemnation of government tactics and increased support for the terrorists' cause. An example would be the Intifada uprisings in the West Bank in the 1980s and 1990s, against Israeli occupation.

Moreover, terrorist activities are a function of intraorganizational control, discipline, and morale building. The effectiveness and organizational performance of the organization should be manifested in frequent or occasional acts of terrorism.[9] This goal of ensuring effectiveness is often aggravated by factional rivalry as factions compete for influence within the organization. The consequence is more intense and frequent incidents of terrorism against innocent individuals. Instances of factionalism are common in the Palestinian resistance movement.

Terrorism also may be used as a last resort. Often the minority that is relatively very weak vis-à-vis the regime resorts to terrorism as its only weapon. Terrorism is a weapon that can be very effective, even against the most powerful regime. It is a relatively inexpensive and uncomplicated way of addressing the military balance between regime and terrorists.

Furthermore, an additional reason for terrorism is the need to strike at the opportune moment on the part of the terrorists. The terrorists may calculate that it is quite expedient not to postpone the vigorous pursuit of the organization's objectives. They may consider it politically and militarily expedient to strike when the regime is at its weakest. For example, a national liberation movement seeking independence exploits a situation in which the colonial power has been rendered materially and psychologically weak by involvement in a long foreign war; examples include the IRA against Britain after World War I and the National Liberation Front (FLN) against France after the Indochina War.

Finally, as in coups d'état, the contagion effect also applies to terrorism as a political strategy. The success of one terrorist group in its overall objective motivates other terrorist groups to press on and intensity their efforts. For example, the success of one independent movement encourages another similar movement to press on with its demands for independence, as when the liberation movements in the Portuguese colonies of Mozambique, Angola, and Guinea-Bissau in Africa were pressured to keep up with nationalists in neighboring African countries and other parts of the world in the 1960s and 1970s.

State Violence and Terror

Terrorists come in all ideological persuasions. Examples include the Maoist Shining Path (Sondero Luminoso) of Peru, the Irish Republican Army, the anarchists of the nineteenth century, the Japanese Red Army, or the Italian Red Brigades, to ultraconservative status quo-oriented ones such as the Ulster Defense Leagues of Northern Ireland or the right wing death squads in Central and South America in the 1970s and 1980s, which were responsible for the abduction and murder of thousands.

The rather illegitimate violent activities of past and current terrorist organizations convey the idea that terrorism is carried out solely by nonstate actors, small groups, or subnational entities. This is one of the myths of terrorism, among many others.[10] Terrorism is in reality the domain of both state and nonstate actors. The concept itself originated with the French revolutionary period between 1793 and 1798. Terrorism (French *Terrorisme*) was practiced by the Jacobin and Thermidorian regimes in France, right down to the era of fascist or communist states and right-wing, or dictorial regimes in the developing countries of Africa, Asia, Latin America, or the Middle East. Such states employed terror in the form of deliberately instilling of fear in the population, unlawfully confiscating of property, torturing, maiming, illegal arrests, and ultimately assassinating or disappearing opposition members. However, for some reason, the myth persists that terrorism is the activity of nonstate, subnational entities.

The insecurity that characterizes many regimes is directed at nonelites or challengers whose activities are considered threatening. Actual or anticipated opposition impels the power elite to choose terror as a policy or strategy. According to Raymond Duvall and Michael Stohl, terror has two goals: (1) to produce disorientation and/or compliance through immobilization of the target of terror; and (2) to mobilize public opinion in order to create attitudes favorable to the interests of the user.[11] Internally, the state can choose one of two methods to accomplish its goals: either direct the terrorism (state-directed terrorism) itself, or tolerate it (state-tolerated terrorism). An example of the former is the Reign of Terror in France during the French Revolution between 1792 and 1794; or in Iran during the Shah's reign. Examples of the latter are El Salvador and Guatemala during the 1970s, which were characterized by right-wing private death squads. In cases where the state's enemies are outside the country, the state can export terrorism (state-exported terrorism) through selective assassination of opponents. Examples are the selective assassination of Libyan leader Qadafi's opponents abroad, or Trotsky's murder in Mexico in 1940.

States can institutionalize terrorism (institutionalized state terrorism) in order to combat actual or anticipated threats. Some examples are Stalin's purges of opponents in the 1930s, the French counterinsurgency against Muslim Revolutionaries in Algeria in the 1960s, or state terror in Chile and Argentina during the 1970s and 1980s, among many others. In such instances, regimes rely on ongoing terror as an instrument of rule. On the other hand, state terrorism can be situationally specific, where it becomes a strategy in response to a specific kind of open challenge or threat, but ceases after the threat subsides.[12] In the final analysis, state terrorism and violence is a consequence of: (1) open challenge or threat by an opposition; (2) serious ideological differences between the incumbent regime and the opposition; (3) social-structural imbalance expressed in the form of a sharp cleavage between the state and specific groups in society; and (4) the role of international actors in sponsoring challenges against an incumbent regime.

Table 13.1: A Random Selection of Terrorist Activities

January 3, 2000: Four rocket-propelled grenades were fired at the Russian Embassy in Beirut, killing two policemen and wounding six.

August 7, 1998: Deadly bombings of U.S. embassies in Kenya and Tanzania. More than 700 people died and almost 6,000 were wounded.

January 5, 1997: A bomb exploded at a mosque in Rustenburg, injuring two people. The Boere Aanvals Troupe claimed responsibility for the attack.

March 2, 1997: A Hamas satchel bomb exploded at the Apropo Café in Tel Aviv, killing three persons and injuring 48, including a six-month-old child.

October 15, 1997: The Tamil Tigers carried out a bomb attack on Sri Lanka's new World Trade Center in the financial district of Colombo.

June 1996: Nineteen U.S. airmen killed in the bombing of the Khubar Towers housing facility in Saudi Arabia.

December 21, 1988: Pan Am flight 747 was bombed in flight over Lockerbie, Scotland. The bomb killed 259 people on board and 11 on the ground.

October 7, 1985: The Italian cruise ship Achille Lauro was hijacked by four Palestinian gunmen off the coast of Egypt. An American passenger in a wheelchair was the only casualty of the hijacking.

September 23, 1983: A bomb exploded on board an Omani Gulf jet en route from Karachi to Abu Dhabi, killing 111 people.

October 6, 1981: Egyptian president Anwar al-Sadat was assassinated in Cairo by Islamic extremists within his own army.

April 1978: Former Italian prime minister Aldo Moro was kidnapped and murdered by the Red Brigades who thought that by eliminating him they would cause the collapse of the capitalist establishment and pave the way for a Marxist-Leninist revolution.

September 5, 1972: Eight Arab commandos broke into the Olympic compound in Munich, West Germany. At the end of their terror, 11 of the 18-member Israeli Olympic team had been killed.

It is generally the case that regimes facing external threat are likely to use more violence against domestic opponents.

The belief persists in the minds of many that terrorists are pathological cases, they constitute the mentally unbalanced, and their activities are devoid of any coherent and well-defined political objectives. If such a myth gains widespread acceptance, it leaves very little room for addressing the socioeconomic and political grievances articulated by terrorists. However, the terrorist acts of West Bank Palestinians or the IRA, for example, are actually not committed within a political vacuum.

The view that all terrorists are criminals underscores the above myth that they are psychopaths. Both myths are intended to deny terrorists any possible "legitimacy" in the international arena. The political acts committed by terrorists are thus put in the same category as criminal activities with purely individual motives. Such classifications could also include states that collude with organized criminal organizations in perpetrating political acts that are in every respect criminal. Examples abound of collusion between the CIA and the Mafia, or governments that cooperate with right-wing death squads. The excuse of governments is usually that such activities are carried out in the name of national security.

All terrorist acts are in the final analysis terroristic, even if they are carried out by "freedom fighters." The cliche, one man's terrorist is another's freedom fighter constitutes an obstacle to making any progress in eradicating terrorism.

Not all insurgent violence is political terrorism because some insurgents refuse to terrorize the population for fear of alienating it. If political terrorism is used, it may be used only for propaganda purposes because many groups realize that legitimacy and popular support do not arise from fear, terror, and force. On the other hand, groups that decide to terrorize do not do so in order to produce chaos. Their objective is to impel the regime to prevent chaos by resorting to state terror, which may eventually discredit it. While in the short run chaos may ensue from terrorist activities, the ultimate objective is to demonstrate the inability of the regime to effectively govern the society.

In some cases, governments may acquiesce or give tacit support to the terror perpetrated by vigilantes, especially if their activities support the maintenance of law and order. Examples abound of Latin America in the 1970s and 1980s, the KKK in the American South during and following Reconstruction, South Africa during Apartheid, and in Northern Ireland, among others.

Terror is often exported and therefore is not just an internal problem. Both governments and groups are guilty of exporting terrorism.[13] The regime of Khadaffi of Libya is notorious for its support of many terrorists groups and liberation movements. Israel and the United States—the CIA, in particular—support terrorist activities to further their national security objectives. In terms of individuals and groups, the Saudi-born Osama bin Laden in 1998 exported his terrorism to Kenya and Tanzania by bombing the U.S. embassies in those countries. The consequence was hundreds of deaths of mostly Kenyans and Tanzanians. In the past there have been many incidents of terrorism in European soil related to the Palestinian cause.

The myth is often widespread that terrorism is coordinated and funded by one or two major state actors in the international system. During the Cold War, the United States accused the Soviet Union of playing that role, along with Syria and Libya. The scope of such funding is usually not as widespread as alleged. The United States has often been concerned about the role of what it calls "rogue states" in the perpetration of terrorist activities. Thus, Iraq, Libya, and North Korea would tend to figure at the top of such a list. But more recently, attention has focused on an individual multimillionaire, Osama bin Laden.

Finally, terrorism has been quite effective both in the past and in recent history. The Palestinians and their goal of autonomy and push toward statehood could in large part be attributed to terrorist activities linked to causes in the 1970s and 1980s. These activities forced the Western powers to more seriously attend to the Palestinian problem. The same argument could be made for the IRA cause in Northern Ireland.

The United States and Domestic Terrorism

Between 1985 and 1986, a great many terrorist acts were directed at Americans overseas, especially in Europe. Terrorism directed at American citizens also widened in scope to include ordinary Americans. Before 1986, terrorism was directed mostly at government officials and other largely visible targets. For instance, the seizure of the U.S. embassy in Tehran in 1979 involved mostly diplomats, not ordinary Americans. Similarly, the truck bombing of the Marine barracks in Beirut in 1983 was directed at members of the U.S. military. However, with the hijacking of TWA 847 in the summer of 1985, ordinary Americans suddenly became targets of terrorism. For seventeen days, American passengers became hostages, at the end of which TWA closed down its Cairo-Athens and Cairo-Rome connections. In 1986, American tennis players were conspicuously absent from the Italian Open tennis tournament in Rome. The U.S. Tennis Association had decided it was too dangerous to send its players there. During the summer of 1986 many Americans either postponed or canceled travel to Europe. According to the U.S. State Department, terrorism before the end of the Cold War was essentially a problem for the Western nations. For example, in 1985 there were conservatively 695 terrorist incidents worldwide. Only one occurred in Eastern Europe. Four took place in North America, but 25 per cent of all the terrorism overseas was directed at American targets.[14]

The United States is also currently concerned not just with international terrorism against U.S. citizens, but also with domestic terrorism manifested in antigovernment sentiment and the rapid increase in self-styled militia and paramilitary groups characterized to a large extent by extremist views on race, religion, federal governmental authority, gun control, or taxation. According to Lynn Fischer of the U. S. Department of Defense Security Institute, the reasons for the increase in antigovernment terrorism since 1990 are related to the ready availability of materials and easy access to instructions and explosives information on the internet, the copy-cat effect of the Oklahoma City bombing in 1995, anger or revenge against specific persons or agencies, or simply a manifestation of cultural and sociological trends in the United States.[15] In other words, terrorism is not just a concern of Americans who travel or live overseas, but of Americans anywhere within the borders of the United States. For example, in the destruction of the

Alfred P. Murrah Federal Building in Oklahoma, more than 100 federal employees and members of their families were killed.

Since the tragic event of the Oklahoma City bombing, other domestic terrorist acts have been attempted. In March 1995 in central Minnesota, two members of an antitax Minnesota militia, the Patriots Council, were convicted of making an illegal batch of ricin, a toxic derivative of the castor bean, that they planned to use against law-enforcement officers who had served legal papers on members of the group. The two members were convicted under the Biological Weapons and Anti-Terrorism Act of 1989. Members of the group had planned to poison U.S. agents by placing ricin on doorknobs and also to blow up a federal building.

On November 13, 1995, in Muskogee, Oklahoma, Ray Willie Lampley, a self-proclaimed "anti-government prophet," and three others were charged for plotting a series of bombings against abortion clinics, homosexual gathering places, welfare offices, and offices of the Anti-Defamation League and the Southern Poverty Law Center. The four members of the Oklahoma Constitutional Militia were arrested before any of their plans were carried out.

On May 20, 1996, in Laredo, Texas, an explosion blew out the windows of a five-story office building that housed an FBI field office staff of twelve agents. There were no injuries or structural damage. It is not known whether the FBI was the intended target; the building housed a bank and several other offices. An anonymous caller claiming responsibility for the blast said he belonged to "Organization 544."

There are several other instances of either successful, abortive, or threatened terrorist violence against U.S. federal officials or buildings. Among many others, are the plot to bomb the office of the U.S. Internal Revenue Service in Austin, Texas, in August of 1996; the plot to blow up the Criminal Justice Information Services Division complex near Clarksburg, West Virginia, in October 1996; and earlier the World Trade Center bombing in New York City in February 1993.

Related to incidents of domestic terrorism are extreme militant activities associated with animal rights, environmentalism, and abortion. G. Davidson Smith refers to these acts of violence as "single issue terrorism." It is violent radicalism on the part of groups or individuals "protesting a perceived grievance or wrong usually attributed to governmental action or inaction."[16] While there are legitimate and generally moderate animal welfare societies, there has also emerged over the past decades radical or extremist elements prepared to use threats, violence, and destruction of property in order to achieve their objectives. In the case of a single issue like abortion, it has included murder.

These activists, whether related to animal rights, environmental protection, or abortion, come from varied walks of life and socioeconomic levels.

However, many tend to be on the left, politically. The pro-life angle of the abortion struggle is drawn largely from the right. Many animal rights supporters and environmental extremists are comprised of the young, largely idealistic, and impatient university students who attempt to speed up the achievement of their goals through direct action. For example, the Militant Vegan and Arkangel, are examples of animal rights organizations, both of these are international in scope, publicize their goals and operations through the Internet and newsletters, and maintain addresses of targets: doctors, scientists, or research labs. The extremist segment of each movement publishes instructions on how to perpetuate terrorist activities such as vandalism or sabotage, and bomb-making details. In abortion extremism, the first fatality caused by bombing at an abortion clinic occurred in the United States on January 29, 1998, in Alabama. By June 2000, the United States had already experienced five murders related to the abortion issue.

In the area of animal rights, perhaps the best-known extremist group in Europe and North America is the Animal Liberation Front (ALF) founded in 1976.[17] It has engaged in a series of break-ins at universities and medical laboratories, vandalized, engaged in arson, and released animals, mostly in Canada. The AFL made the FBI's domestic terrorism list in 1987 because of a multimillion dollar arson at a veterinary lab in California. Other extremist animal rights groups include: the Hunt Retribution Squad (HRS) in Britain and the Animal Rights Militia (ARM) in both the United States and Britain, an offshoot of the ALF. A tacit and alleged supporter of these groups in the United States is the People for the Ethical Treatment of Animals (PETA), a powerful Virginia-based lobby group.

In the area of environmental activism, the most frequent targets are resource exploitation and hydroelectric developments, followed by the nuclear power industry, chemical manufacturers, and industrial polluters, among others. Earth First and its followers, for example, have shown a willingness and capacity to use violence, especially sabotage, as a tactic to defend the environment. The movement's sabotage (or ecotage in enviro-speak) technique involves tree spiking, a dangerous practice because for loggers using chain saws and mills, spikes can cause saw blades literally to explode, causing serious injury. The extremist environmentalists also advocate homicide, and violence against farms, animal research facilities, logging companies, and hunters in order to discourage animal and environmental abuses.

In the United States abortion will continue to be a hot and emotional issue. The extreme right-wing groups involved commit criminal acts in support of their cause. The extreme antiabortionists also have their own handbook, *The Army of God,* which provides details on techniques of sabotage of clinics, silencers for guns, and C4 explosives, among other things.[18] Since 1993, in the United States five people have been killed, and eleven more persons wounded. Critics have been the targets of graffiti, noxious gases, and numerous threats.

In conclusion, as groups in society continue to develop strong feelings over issues related to either the environment, animal rights, or abortion, more militant activity is bound to occur. In other words, many of these single issues are not amenable to simple, clear-cut solutions. The danger is that certain individuals in groups who feel their preferences are not being satisfied may decide to resort to one or any number of acts of terrorism: bombings, arsons, vandalism, assassinations, and the like.

More Modern Types of Terrorism

Just as terrorism is perpetrated by both state and nonstate actors, so also are there different types of terrorism.

Bioterrorism is a terrorist attack that uses germs to kill instead of bombs. It is believed that biological weapons are potentially as deadly as nuclear weapons.[19] The likely agents of a bioterrorist attack would be smallpox and anthrax. Unlike explosives, biological weapons are harder to detect and are therefore silent killers. For example, the Aum Shinrikyo cult in Japan used a nerve gas, Sarin, to kill twelve people in an attack on the Tokyo Subway in 1995.

Terrorists could exploit the ease of production for many of the biological pathogens or toxins. The ease of use therefore becomes the key factor for the increased popularity of biological weapons. According to the CIA, a biological agent is the biological material that is delivered either via a weapon, or administered to a person. Biological agents for bioterrorism fall into two categories: pathogens and toxins. Pathogens in turn are divided into three kinds: bacteria, viruses and fungi. Pathogens are organisms that produce a disease in a human.[20] In particular, bioterrorism is widely associated with the bacterium forms of the pathogens. Bacteria are the smallest organisms that are made from one cell and have the ability to reproduce freely. Some of the most deadly disease from bacteria include anthrax, brucellosis, cholera, pneumonic plague, and typhoid. The second pathogens are viruses, which are the simplest of the three forms. These microorganisms are capable of invading surrounding cells and reprogram them to make more viruses. This is because the viruses cannot reproduce by themselves. Some of the mostdeadly viruses are smallpox, hepatitis, AIDS, and encephalitis. The third pathogen form is fungi. These organisms are larger and more complex than bacteria and can reproduce by forming spores. Fungi have a more difficult developmental and delivery process, and are therefore not closely associated with bioterrorism or biological warfare.

It is toxins that are very closely associated with both bioterrorism and biological warfare. Toxins are poisonous compounds produced by living

Table 13.2: International Terrorism Conventions*

1. Convention of Offenses and Certain Other Acts Committed on Board Aircraft (Tokyo Convention, agreed 9/63—safety of aviation).
2. Convention for the Suppression of Unlawful Seizure of Aircraft (Hague Convention, agreed 12/70—aircraft hijacking).
3. Convention for the Suppression of Unlawful Acts Against the Safety of Civil Aviation (Montreal convention, agreed 9/71—applies to acts of aviation sabotage such as bombings aboard aircraft in flight).
4. Convention of the Prevention and Punishment of Crimes Against Internationally Protected Persons (agreed 12/73—protects senior government officials and diplomats).
5. Convention on the Physical Protection of Nuclear material (Nuclear Materials Convention, agreed 10/79—combats unlawful taking and use of nuclear materials).
6. International Convention Against the Taking of Hostages (Hostages Convention, agreed 12/79).
7. Protocol for the Suppression of Unlawful Acts of Violence at Airports Serving International Civil Aviation (agreed 2/88—extends and supplements Montreal Convention).
8. Convention for the Suppression of Unlawful Acts Against the Safety of Marine Navigation (agreed 3/88—applies to terrorist activities on ships).
9. Protocol for the Suppression of Unlawful Acts Against the Safety of Fixed Platforms Located on the Continental Shelf (agreed 3/88—applies to terrorist activities on fixed offshore platforms).
10. Convention of the Marking of Plastic Explosives for the Purpose of Identification (agreed 3/91—detection of plastic explosives, e.g., to combat aircraft sabotage).
11. International convention for the Suppression of Terrorist Bombing (agreed 12/97—expands the legal framework for international cooperation in the investigation, prosecution, and extradition of persons who engage in terrorist bombings).

Source: U.S. State Department, Office of Counterterrorism.

*The overwhelming number of these eleven major multilateral agreements apply to flight safety, or the prevention of hijackings. They stress the need for all states that are party to them to cooperate in making hijacking incidents subject to severe penalties. They especially call on parties to extradite offenders and assist with criminal proceedings. The fifth convention addresses the nonproliferation of nuclear material and especially prohibits the possession, use, transfer, theft, and threat of use of such material with the intent to cause death, injury, or property damage. It is not surprising that the United States is a party to all these agreements because it is so often a target of hijacking, and is vulnerable to many other types of terrorism.

organisms, usually proteins that act on particular cell receptors. Toxins are known for their widespread utilization in chemical agents. Toxins used for bioterriorism purposes are gained through the process of removing the toxin from the host organism and introducing it to a suitable environment that can be delivered as an agent.

Biological agents can be delivered in countless ways, all with varying degrees of severity. The most common way used by bioterrorism is the spreading of the agent through aerosol, food and water contamination, or being injected. Aerosols are simply agents (usually toxins) that are delivered airborne.[21] Since aerosols are best suited for affecting large populations, agents released through air ducts and from sprayers are two common, low-cost modes of operation. The method of food and water contamination is by far easier. It is more effective for small targets and not for large populations. Those affected immediately suffer the consequences, which are often fatal. Injection is most personal, and is usually made through person-to-person contact. In 1978, for example, the injection method was made famous through the use of an "umbrella gun," during which the Bulgarian secret police used the toxin ricin stored in a hypodermic needle attached to an umbrella tip to kill two Bulgarian defectors.

Bioterrorists are more prone to resort to biological warfare because of ease of manufacture. No specialized facilities are required for production of biological agents. The CIA has developed three general classification of production. For biological products, there is pilot scale, industrial scale, and laboratory scale. Laboratory scale is the lowest level of production that is less than fifty liters, while pilot scale is fifty to five hundred liters, and industrial is over five hundred liters. The scale of production depends upon the effect desired and the final end product. Laboratory and pilot scale can be utilized by bioterrorists for strategic, covert operations. Industrial scale is mainly used for production of a wider scope, usually at the governmental or state level.

Cyberterrorism is at times referred to as cyberwarfare or infowarfare.[22] It is a relatively new type of terrorism that has both a military dimension and a general internet "war" aspect. An attack on a nation's military computer system could adversely affect a military's Command, Control, Communication, and Intelligence (C^3I) network. Similarly, cybercrime, cyberfraud, or electronic threats and stalking are very common. Generally, a cyberterrorist attack could target and cripple a nation's power plants, telecommunications, banking, transportation, and emergency services, as well as other infrastructure. On a few occasions, for example, computer hackers have successfully broken into Pentagon computers in the United States.

Narcoterrorism describes the linkage of the trade in drugs and terrorism. It is an alliance of two very pernicious transnational threats: terror and drugs.[23] Narcoterrorists, in other words, deal in weapons, launder enormous profits from the traffic in drugs, and acquire capabilities that make them effective enough to even challenge incumbent governments. An example is the FARC in Colombia vis-à-vis the Colombian government.

In sum, terrorism has been quite difficult to define because the aims and motives of terrorists are broad-ranging and touch on issues either supported or vehemently opposed by a variety of individuals. For example, in the struggle for national self-determination, a group may use terrorism, but are still considered a freedom fighters in the eyes of its supporters. Or it may be a case of ideological terrorism spawned by a struggle between right-wing government and an opposition group. Religious terrorism tends to be quite common, such as that sponsored by some Islamic groups, or fundamentalists of a particular religion. The abortion debate in the United States has produced terrorism related to that single issue. Individuals or groups involved in such issues as abortion or animal rights tend to be fanatical to the point of at times using extreme violence.

The types of attack inherent in terrorism are as varied as the number of terrorist organizations. They range from bombings (including letter bombs, hand bombs, car bombs, suicide bombings, and bomb threats), hostage taking, kidnapping, mortar attack, shooting, to chemical attacks. The favorite targets of terrorists are embassies, airports, aircrafts, buildings, buses, and places of worship, among others. The terrorist groups or freedom fighters in the international system have used one or more of these methods of attack.

The Impact of 9/11 on the United States

Terrorism that is endemic to the history of the world has gradually transformed itself from a local/national problem to a global one characterized by intimidation, threats, violence, and coercion of entire societies and governments in order to secure ideological, political, economic, or social objectives. The terrorizing of a population or target group takes many forms, such as the expropriation of property; banishment and execution used by the Roman Emperors between the first and fourth centuries AD; the methods of torture and arbitrary arrest used during the Spanish Inquisition; the intimidation and killings by the Ku Klux Klan directed at blacks during and after Reconstruction; and the violent tactics of anarchists in Russia, Western Europe, and the United States in the nineteenth century that led to the assassination of monarchs and heads of state, among other examples. In the twentieth century terrorism as a strategy became not only more ideological, it widened its scope as a result of improved transportation and communication networks, as well as the growing sophistication of instruments of violence, especially explosives. During the 1970s and 1980s, terrorism continued to be global, expanding from a few hundred to several thousand a year into the mid- and late 1990s. The Arab-Israeli conflict, the Irish conflict, and other West European terrorist groups were mostly responsible for the widened scope of terrorism.

Terrorism · **271**

A major aspect of the growing sophistication and widened scope of terrorism was manifested in the attack on America's homeland on September 11, 2001, by the Al Quaeda terrorist network spearheaded by Saudi-born Osama bin Laden. He is also believed to have ordered the bombings of the U.S. embassies in Dar es Salaam in Tanzania, and Nairobi, Kenya, in August 1998. Those attacks killed more than two hundred people. All this is part of his call for a Muslim Jihad, or holy war, against the United States.

In 1979, a twenty-two-year-old bin Laden entered the war against the Soviets in Afghanistan, fighting alongside the Afghan resistance fighters known as the Mujihadin. Eventually, the Soviets withdrew from Afghanistan, and the Mujihadin claimed victory.[24] Bin Laden is also opposed to the reigning Saudi Monarchy, the Fahd family because it allowed the United States to use the country as a staging ground for attacks on Iraqi forces in Kuwait and Iraq during the 1991 Gulf War. Bin Laden and the fundamentalists also detest the U.S. presence in Saudi Arabia because the country is considered holy and the home to Mecca, the birthplace of Mohammed and the location of the Great Mosque of Mecca, considered by Muslims to be the most sacred spot on Earth.

In 1998, bin Laden issued a "fatwa," a religious ruling, calling for Muslims to kill Americans and their allies. Three other groups, including the Islamic Jihad in Egypt, endorsed the ruling. The September 11, 2001, attacks on the United States were preceded by warnings that strikes would be directed at the United States, Israel, and U.S. forces in Saudi Arabia, among others.

Two years after the attacks on the World Trade Center and the Pentagon many argue that the government is infringing on the constitutional rights of U.S. citizens in its efforts to prevent future catastrophes.[25] The Bush administration's sweeping U.S.A. Patriot Act rushed through Congress in October 2001 is considered the source of the current threats to the freedom of Americans. Under the measure, detentions are kept secret, wiretaps are easier to do, and visa applications, especially by Muslims and Arabs, take much longer to be approved. Secret searches and deportation of noncitizens suspected of belonging to terrorist organizations are common. The Patriot Act even allows major probes of law-abiding citizens for intelligence purposes. The once permissive and friendly attitude toward immigrants has dramatically changed into a national vigilance largely directed at immigrants. For example, after September 11, 2001, the government detained between 1,100 and 1,500 individuals with suspected terrorist ties nationwide. But only a few have gone through due process. The fate and identity of the rest are still top secret.

In May 2002, the FBI's twenty-seven-year prohibition against spying on religious and political organizations was lifted as the bureau shifted its emphasis to counterterrorism. Supporters of the Patriot Act and national vigilance argue that during periods of crisis, the public will support

Table 13.3: Key Participants in U.S. Homeland Security

Federal Bureau of Investigation (FBI)
Collects intelligence on domestic threats, including foreign-influenced terrorist groups. Has set new priorities on counterterrorism, cybercrimes, and communication with state and local police. More agents now deployed overseas.

U.S. Coast Guard
Has stepped up defenses for high-risk vessels and coastal facilities (power plants, refineries). Developing high-tech tracking for all vessels in U.S. waters.

Defense Department
Tracks the war-making capabilities and intentions of other nations through the Defense Intelligence Agency. The National Security Agency focuses on cryptology and electronic surveillance.

Epidemiological Intelligence Service
Serves as an early-warning and response unit against bioterrorist attacks.

Department of Homeland Security
Its goal is to implement a broad national plan to secure the United States from terrorist attacks. Federal agencies, state and local governments, the private sector, and citizens are all involved.

Transportation Security Administration
Designed to make air travel safe; this new agency uses federal security agents and sophisticated bomb-detection machines.

Treasury Department
Has new powers to expose suspicious money transactions, enabling the United States to freeze assets of terrorists groups.

Federal Emergency Management Agency
Provides resources, manpower, and training to state and local firefighters, police, and emergency medical technicians.

Immigration and Naturalization Service
Protects U.S. borders with increased manpower plus new technology to track noncitizens. Databank of all foreign students.

substantial limits on their civil liberties, including limits on free speech, the press, privacy, and rights to a fair trial. They, however, oppose such restrictions once the threats subside.

The terrorist activities of Al Qaeda directed against the United States have become very transnational. Terrorists in the twenty-first century are no longer recognizable and consequently they are difficult to target. It is also unlikely that terrorism will ever subside to the degree where U.S. interests would be considered secure in all parts of the world. The motives that produce terrorism are pervasive and have even been institutionalized: abject poverty, religious radicalism, political grievances, and the readily available instruments of violence and terror ranging from small arms to biological and chemical agents. So far peacekeeping and/or peacemaking has been unable to deal with a conflict where one of the parties is elusive, a nonstate actor, or a seemingly unidentifiable entity bent on destroying the United States. The final chapter of this book will focus on how the various aspects of peacekeeping are dealing with the changing nature of political violence in the international system.

Notes

1. For a vast array of definitions of terrorism, see Alex P. Schmid, *Political Terrorism* (Amsterdam: North Holland Publishing Co., 1983); for a distinction between terrorism and other types of collective political violence, see David Fromkin, "The Strategy of Terror," *Foreign Affairs* 53 (July 1975).
2. See, for example, "Liberty and Terrorism," *International Security* 2 (fall 1977): 56–7.
3. For details, see Brian M. Jenkins, "International Terrorism: The Other World War," in *International Terrorism: Characteristics, Causes, Controls,* ed. Charles W. Kegley Jr. (New York: St. Martin's Press, 1990), 27–38.
4. For a wide-ranging explanation of terrorism, see Peter C. Sederberg, "Terrorism: Contending Themes in Contemporary Research" in *Annual Review of Conflict of Knowledge* (New York: Garland Publishing, 1991); Martha Crenshaw, "The Causes of Terrorism," in *International Terrorism: Characteristics, Causes, Controls,* pp. 113–26.
5. See, for example, Charles W. Kegley Jr., T. Vance Spurgeon, and Eugene R. Wittkopf, "Structural Terrorism," in *Terrible Beyond Endurance? The Foreign Policy of State Terrorism,* ed. Michael Stohl and George Lopez (Westport, C.: Greenwood Press, 1988), 13–31.
6. For details, see Peter Lupsha, "Explanation of Political Violence: Some Psychological Theories versus Indignation," *Politics and Society* 2 (1971: 89–104.
7. See Moorhead Kennedy, "The Root Causes of Terrorism, *The Humanist* 46 (Sept.–Oct. 1986): 5–9.
8. Moshe Decter, "Terrorism: The Fallacy of Root Causes," *Midstream* 33 (March 1989):8.
9. See, for example, J. Bowyer Bell, *The Secret Army* (New York: John Day Co.: 1970).
10. For a detailed analysis of myths of terrorism, see Michael Stohl, "Demystifying the Mystery of International Terrorism," in *International Terrorism: Characteristics, Causes, Controls,* pp. 81–96.
11. For details, see Raymond D. Duvall, and Michael Stohl, "Governance by Terror," in Michael Stohl, ed. *The Politics of Terrorism* (New York: M. Dekker 1998).
12. For details, see Ted R. Gurr, "The Political Origins of State Violence and Terror: A Theoretical Analysis," in *Government Violence and Repression: An Agenda for Research,* ed. Michael Stohl and George A. Lopez (New York: Greenwood Press, 1986).
13. On the internationalization of terrorism, see James Adams, *The Financing of Terror* (New York: Simon & Schuster, 1986); and Stephen Sengaller, *Invisible Armies: Terrorism in the 1990s* (New York: Harcourt, Brace, Jovanovich, 1987).
14. For further details, see U.S. Department of State, Patterns of Global Terrorism, 1995.
15. Lynn Fischer, "The Threat of Domestic Terrorism," DOD Security Institute, The Terrorism Research Center, 1996–1999.
16. G. Davidson Smith, "Single Issue Terrorism," *Commentary* no. 74: 1.
17. For details, see Susan E. Paris, "Animal Rights Terrorism Must be Stopped," *Mass High Tech,* August 1995.
18. See *Washington Post,* January 17, 1995.
19. See, for example, Yonah Alexander, "Will Terrorists Use Chemical Weapons?" *JINSA Security Affairs* (June-July 1990).
20. For more details, see Ron Purver, *Chemical and Biological Terrorism: The Threat According to the Open Literature* (Ottawa, Canada: Canadian Security Intelligence Service, June 1995).
21. For further details, see *Chemical/Biological/Radiological Incident Handbook* (Central

Intelligence Agency, 1998); and *Weapons of Mass Destruction Terms Handbook,* Defense Special Weapons Agency, DSWA-AR-40H, June 1, 1998.

22. See *Cybercrime, Cyberterrorism, Cyberwarfare: Averting an Electronic Waterloo, A Global Organized Crime Project* (Washington, DC: Center for Strategic and International Studies, 1998); and Infowar website.

23. For examples, see Stephen G. Trujillo, "Peru's Maoist Drug Dealers," *The New York Times,* April 8, 1992; "Colombia's Bloodstained Peace," *The Economist,* June 6, 1992; and Judith Miller, "South Asia Identified as Terror Hub," *The New York Times,* April 30, 2000.

24. See, for example, Yonah Alexander, and Michael S. Swetnam, *Usama bin Laden's al-Qaida: Profile of a Terrorist Network* (Ardsley, NY: Transnational Publishers, 2001).

25. For details, see Brad Smith, "Critics Alarmed Over Post-9/11 Crackdown," *Tampa Tribune,* September 2, 2002, p. 12.

Key Terms

biological agent
bioterrorism
C^{3}I
contagion effect
cyberterrorism
domestic terrorism

factionalism
guerrilla warfare
ideological terrorism
narcoterrorism
oppression
paramilitary groups

precipitating factors
preconditions
single-issue terrorism
state terrorism
terror

Discussion Questions

1. Discuss the difficulties inherent in conceptualizing and defining terrorism.
2. What are the causes of terrorism?
3. Analyze state violence and terror by emphasizing what it is, discussing examples, and stressing its significance.
4. Discuss the problem of domestic terrorism in the United States.
5. Are biological and chemical terrorism real dangers for the international system? Discuss your answer by emphasizing specific concepts and examples.

CHAPTER **14**

New Scenarios in Violent Conflicts and Peacekeeping

The many dimensions of collective political violence (civil wars, revolutions, genocides, and the like) explored in this text indicate that violent conflicts are endemic to all societies and take many forms. Moreover, with the transition from the twentieth to the twenty-first century, the potential for new security threats related to information warfare, cyberterrorism, and bioterrorism looms large. Many of the ongoing conflicts are simply a recycling and intensification of traditional conflicts based on ethnicity and related to social structural imbalances that produce individual and/or group frustration. In particular, it could be argued that many of the irregular conflicts taking place in many developing countries are a consequence of the intensification of economic inequality or sociopolitical exclusion. While many are benefiting from increased trade and investment, millions still are experiencing abject poverty. The consequence is a widening gap between the rich and poor, and among groups in society. According to World Bank figures, in the late 1990s, the average percentage of income received by the lowest 20 percent in relation to the highest 20 percent in selected Latin American countries was 3.6 percent to 51 percent; and Asia it was 7.2 percent to 45.1 percent; in Africa in was 6.8 percent to 44.1 percent; and for developed countries it was 8.1 percent to 38.7 percent.[1]

Extreme inequality is an instigator of ethnoreligious and other tensions that could be politicized and transformed into rebellion. This situation of gross inequalities coupled with rapid population growth is often a recipe for more future insurgencies and attacks against the rich and powerful. In many of the developing regions, thousands and even millions are born into a permanent environment of poverty characterized by lack of educational, health, and employment opportunities. Those born in the next twenty to twenty-five years will constitute a majority in the megacities and sprawling urban areas of the developing world. With few or no opportunities to enjoy the fruits of capitalism, they will most likely constitute a powder keg ready to explode at any time. Extremist political and religious movements, bandit organizations, xenophobia, narcoterrorists, or Mafia-like extortionists could be the consequence.[2] Already, in some developed countries, all sorts of xenophobic or subnationalist groups are emerging with an emphasis on exclusivity, ultranationalism, or racial supremacy. Some even condone the expulsion and/or annihilation of those they consider part of the out-group, such as immigrants or ethnoracial minorities.

The intensification of inequality has probably fueled the struggle for lucrative but easily smuggled commodities such as diamonds, and with it has emerged a new kind of warfare that some would label "irregular warfare." In irregular warfare there are open attacks on unarmed civilians, the use of rape, abductions, and looting by boys often as young as ten years. They are, to a large extent, internal wars being fought over resources, or booty. For example, between 1989 and 1996, out of 101 wars, 95 were internal.[3] At the same time most of the victims are civilians. According to Michael Klare, during World War I, 90 percent of the casualties in battle were soldiers, and only 10 percent were civilians; in the wars of the late twentieth century, the ratio was totally reversed with 80 percent of the casualties in recent wars civilians, and only 20 percent combatants.[4]

The targeting of civilians is producing not only a massive flow of refugees, but also is adding to the number of people with missing limbs, orphaned children, or those that have lost their entire childhood years. Often, the violence perpetrated in civil wars is done by neighbors against neighbors. Individuals and groups kill without remorse, and violate peace agreements, or even turn their guns against peacekeeping troops. A great deal of the violence in civil wars has been made possible by the proliferation of small arms, especially the AK-47, grenades, and mines. However, the United Nations and the great powers tend to focus instead on the control of larger and more sophisticated weapons while ignoring these light weapons. The great powers ignore the trafficking of light weapons because they, as the arms-producing nations, make huge profits selling such weapons to zones of conflict.[5] Rebels often fight very hard to control regions endowed with lucrative resources like diamonds, gold, oil, or timber, in order to exploit these resources as a source of income to procure more weapons and continue the war effort. The determination of rebel groups, coupled with the lack of professionalism by government troops, has made peacekeeping in zones of conflict very risky, and has even shaped the character of peacekeeping since the end of the Cold War.

Peacekeeping and the End of the Cold War

The United Nations in its original conception of peacekeeping focused on interstate wars and not on internal wars. However, with the end of the Cold War, the increase in civil wars created a dilemma for UN peacekeeping. The charter of the UN has no provisions addressing internal conflict. This means that the international community and regional organizations have had to improvise, or invoke defense protocols to deal with each new eruption of domestic conflict. In varying degrees, Rwanda, Somalia, or Angola, among others, have been failures for UN peacekeeping.

The increased scope and intensity of violent conflicts (genocides and civil wars in particular) have combined to give peacekeeping increased stature, respectability, and potential. Its new and evolving role has been demonstrated in election monitoring in various countries (Haiti, Nicaragua, Angola, and Cambodia, among others), in interposition between warring factions, and in purely humanitarian functions. Increasingly, the UN in particular has been called upon to supervise and monitor elections.[6] Before the 1990s, UN participation in electoral processes was considered unprecedented, and it would have turned down a request to do so. However, more recent examples of UN election supervision have been complemented by a UN peacekeeping component to ensure security. Examples are Namibia in 1989 to 1990; Western Sahara in 1991, and Cambodia in 1992 to 1994. Elections in this case are seen as a conflict settlement arrangement. Similarly, since the end of the Cold War and the eruption of more violent conflicts in Africa, and the former Yugoslavia in particular, the UN has been called upon to speed up peaceful settlement of such conflicts and to ensure the delivery of humanitarian assistance to starving and homeless populations. UN intervention within countries in situations of extreme anarchy and suffering may have led to a modified principle of nonintervention, incorporated in Article 2, paragraph 7 of the UN charter. For example, in 1991, UN Security Council Resolution 688 called upon Iraq to "allow immediate access by international humanitarian organizations to all those in need of assistance in all parts of Iraq." In the past the Security Council had been reluctant to approve humanitarian assistance as the major or primary function of a peacekeeping operation. The increased scope of human suffering caused by post–Cold War conflicts has forced the council to abandon that position. Humanitarian protection has now become a part of the major mandate of UN peacekeeping in many zones of conflict. In other words, though never envisioned in the UN charter, peacekeeping in its various forms has become an integral part of cooperative efforts to end regional and national conflicts that erupted following the end of the Cold War.

By the early 1990s, it had become evident that UN Security Council authorizations for peace operations were undergoing substantive change, mostly from traditional methods of preventive diplomacy, interpositions, to an authorization on the use of force. The reasons underlying such a transition are no doubt shaped by developments in the international system, as well as the imperatives of interstate, and interethnic violence. The reasons could be placed under four categories. First, the momentum and euphoria generated by one of the most broad-based collective security efforts in the post–World War II era—the coalition of some twenty-eight states led by the United States and authorized by the Security Council. The 1991 Gulf War was thus a watershed event in the latter part of the twentieth century. It served to generate increased dependence on Security Council authorization of force, and even encouraged regional organizations to invoke their defense protocols and seek regional-backed use of force to contain intraregional conflict. Second, former UN secretary-general Boutros Boutros-Ghali personally decided to seize upon and exploit to the fullest the changing aspects of global cooperation. Taking office in June 1992, he expounded his vision of peacekeeping in *Agenda for Peace,* where among other things, he recommended authorization of the use of force.[7] The new cooperative spirit among nations regarding violence and humanitarian intervention particularly encouraged the secretary-general to emphasize increased peacekeeping and the use of force. A third factor is the realization by states that Security Council authorization elicits less criticism when it comes to intervention within a sovereign state. It has therefore become more expedient and even safer to fly the UN flag (the "fig leaf") in some multilateral operations than to unilaterally follow the prescriptions of Article 51 and suffer the slings of critical world opinion. Such multilateral operations also have the advantage of attracting both the financial and military support of other countries. Finally, Security Council authorizations of direct military intervention and use of force is related to the effects of what is now labeled the "CNN effect," or the graphic media focus on carnage and suffering produced by internecine conflicts such as in the former Yugoslavia in the early 1990s, in Somalia, or Sierra Leone, among others.

It was the Yugoslavian crisis of the early 1990s that ignited the long-standing issue of the right of the UN to intervene in internal disputes. For example, India and other nonpermanent members of the Security Council opposed the U.S. proposal that authorized the use of force in Yugoslavia under Chapter VII of the UN charter as a way to allow deployment of troops without the consent of Serbian militia leaders and to preclude demands for its removal. If allowed, according to the nonpermanent members, it would constitute a fundamental change in the traditional peacekeeping operations because it would eliminate the requirement for consent.[8] However, the decision for UN intervention in Yugoslavia's domestic conflict was not totally at odds with past UN practice and principle of nonintervention. In reality, the UN has often authorized action when it has realized that civil wars have threatened other states. Through the authorization to intervene, it has operated within the terms of the UN charter. In particular, Paragraph 7, Article 2 of the charter makes a distinction between conflicts that fall within domestic jurisdictions and conflicts that threaten "the maintenance of international peace and security (Article 24)." In the latter conflicts the UN not only has the authority, but it is permitted to "take effective collective measures for the prevention and removal of [such] threats to peace" (Article 1) and to ensure the restoration of peace and security.

Since conflicts erupt that pose a threat to regional peace and security, the end of the twentieth century has seen more peacekeeping without the consent of key domestic actors. For instance, since Iraq is viewed as posing a threat to peace and security in the Middle East region, the UN Iraq-Kuwait Observer Mission (UNIKOM), was deployed along the border between Iraq and Kuwait after the removal of Iraqi forces from Kuwait without consent. In previous decades and under different circumstances, the need for unanimous consent of the parties to the conflict would have been required.

The increasingly blurred distinction between intervention and nonintervention is related to the changed nature of civil wars and their spillover effects, and the refugees they generate.[9] In terms of actual and potential conflict situations, three possibilities seem especially worthy of note: (1) the unity, authority, and legitimacy of many nation states may be forced to disintegrate under the mounting weight of centrifugal forces of ethnicity and nationalism, thereby further casting doubt on the effectiveness of traditional methods of peacekeeping; (2) the distinction between civil and international conflict-related issues may become increasingly obscure; and (3) the intersection of domestic problems of social heterogeneity and globalization issues may have become inextricably woven into a worldwide international security problem manifested largely in civil strife, refugeeism, starvation, and the outbreak of deadly diseases. It is therefore no surprise that because of the increased intensity of conflicts, the early 1990s saw a corresponding marked increase in peacekeeping operations. Between mid-1988 and December 1996, a total of twenty-eight peacekeeping operations were set up, compared to only five at the beginning of 1988.[10] The increase in the number of operations also corresponded to an increase in peacekeeping activities such as supervision of the truce between warring parties, observation or presence, interposition or a buffer force between forces, maintenance and patrol of a border, or the disarming of warring factions.

Along with this expansion of peacekeeping activities, the concept and practice of peacekeeping seems to have undergone a paradigm shift from *peacekeeping* (the deployment of military forces to forestall the escalation of a dispute) to *preventive diplomacy* (efforts made to abort disputes before they widen and intensify) to *peacemaking* (proactive intervention to encourage warring parties settle their dispute) to *peace enforcement* (the mandate to "impose" a ceasefire, or do battle with violators if need be) to *peace-building* (assist in reconstruction efforts after conflict resolution in order to prevent a fresh eruption of the conflict). Instances have occurred in which the blood-letting, carnage, and starvation were such that peace enforcement has been encouraged. Somalia, Liberia, Bosnia, Kosovo, are some cases in point.

As a result of the increased importance of peacekeeping as a response to conflict situations, in 1992 Secretary-General Boutros Boutrous-Ghali proposed steps the UN might take to strengthen the its peace and security capabilities. Among others are: (1) to activate the UN military force anticipated in Article 42 of the charter to respond to acts of actual or imminent aggression through the provision of military forces, facilities, and equipment; (2) to use peace enforcement in cases where cease-fires have become difficult to maintain; this involves the use of heavily armed troops who have volunteered for such duty; and (3) to strengthen peacekeeping capabilities related to logistics, equipment, personnel (military, civilian, or police), training, and finance.[11] However, member states of the UN are often unwilling to finance requests for new peacekeeping initiatives. For example, at the end of 1995 UN members were in arrears $3.7 billion even when emergencies like that of the former Yugoslavia required the separation of combatants. On April 30, 1996, the UN officially went broke. Only 55 of the 185 member states had paid their dues in full.[12] Thus, the one big obstacle standing in the way of the UN Security Council fully developing its capacity to maintain international peace and security as envisaged in the UN charter is the unwillingness of members to shoulder the financial costs of peacekeeping. In the recent past, regional organizations have been more active in trying to maintain peace within their regions.

Regionalized Peacekeeping

With the end of the Cold War, peacekeeping widened in scope as new conflicts erupted to the point where some regional organizations and alliances were impelled to contain them. Even a few regional economic organizations were forced to focus greater attention on their defense protocols. Regional peacekeeping, whether by NATO or the Economic Community of West African States (ECOWAS), underscores the power of community expectations, and the practices of cooperation through which a number of states from the same region form or sustain collectivity that possesses an effective authority with respect to the goals and survival of the community.[13] Interdependence and the spillover of violent conflicts has compelled some regions to enlarge their power in order to maintain political order, mobilize consent, control anarchy, and otherwise attempt to shape the social and political lives of its members. Moreover, regional organizations could engage in elastic interpretation of defense protocols when the need for military humanitarian intervention arises.

The direct deployment of regional forces in civil wars for the purposes of peacekeeping constitutes a fundamental change in the system of practice relating to conflict resolution among members of regional organizations. The shift from a largely noninterventionist tradition of regional politics to a new practice of active peacemaking is a manifestation of an end of millennium environment with its new conception of security, politics, and economics. For independent states to organize a multinational force to directly intervene in the affairs of another state is a rare phenomenon, and would have been almost unthinkable during the Cold War.

However, demands and challenges exist that challenge regional peacekeeping missions. These demands and challenges originate both internally and externally. Among the domestic sources eroding peacekeeping's competence, two are especially important. One is the already discussed increase in ethnonationalism, which has emboldened new groups to contest state authority and thereby lessen the legitimacy of state and regional-level actors. The other is the accessibility to military technological gadgets on the part of disgruntled and/or power-hungry groups. The process of light arms militarization links the Third World disgruntled and the arms dealers of both advanced industrial countries and the developing world.[14] These two factors in combination have fragmented weak states and thereby made peacekeeping a more complicated exercise increasingly vulnerable to stalemate and paralysis in so far as its ability to address and resolve intractable conflicts are concerned.

In addition to the combined effect of light arms proliferation and increased ethnonationalism, other reasons for the weakness of regional peacekeeping are: (1) lack of resources; (2) the absence of a security-oriented body like the UN Security Council, and (3) a lack of cooperation from the UN. The question of funding peacekeeping operations as well as the lack of a body like the UN Security Council reduce the ability of regional organizations to respond quickly to crisis situations. The Arab League and the OAU, for example, both require that decisions be reached by consensus, a policy that has often frustrated attempts to act in a decisive and concerted fashion. For instance, the emergency meeting called by the Arab League after Iraq's invasion of Kuwait ended with some states committing themselves to cooperation with the West and others condemning such cooperation and arguing that this was an "Arab problem" that required an "Arab solution."[15] Similarly, within ECOWAS, decisive action related to troop contribution and peacekeeping initiatives are often hampered by a lack of consensus between anglophone and francophone states.[16] Nigeria, which often plays the role of leader, is often hampered not just by a lack of resources but also by the reluctance of francophone West African states.

Similarly, the Conference on Security and Cooperation in Europe (CSCE), because of the conditions under which it was created by the Charter of Paris in 1990, is beset by many procedures that do not make for quick decisive action.[17] For example, it may be difficult to decisively and quickly convene a meeting because the mechanism for the convening of a meeting of the Council of Ministers requires the approval of only one-third of its members, but that mechanism may be hard to invoke. Moreover, any decisions taken by the council must be reached by consensus, a requirement that effectively prevents the CSCE from rapidly responding to conflicts. If the CSCE is to play a more dynamic and useful role, it must provide the means to authorize peacekeeping under special circumstances. Often lack of support or cooperation from the U.N. hampers regional peacekeeping efforts. For example, the OAU's peacekeeping effort in Chad failed to achieve its objective because its request to the UN for certain types of assistance went unheeded. The Western members of the Security Council did not support the OAU's request for UN financing, largely because France opposed it, and equally opposed the African solution based on compromise among the Chadian leaders and a consensus of support from African leaders.[18] France did not want Libya to be part of such an African compromise because of Libya's anti-Western and pro-Communist backing of African states with similar ideologies.

Finally, regional organizations are also constrained by the Security Council because although Article 52 of Chapter 7 states: "Nothing in the present Charter precludes the existence of regional arrangements or agencies for dealing with such matters relating to the maintenance of international peace and security as appropriate for regional action." And the first part of Article 53 states that "the Security Council, where appropriate shall utilize such arrangements or agencies for enforcement actions under its authority." However, the remaining part of Article 53 has caused much controversy between regional organizations and the UN. It states that "no enforcement action shall be taken under regional arrangements or by regional agencies without the authorization of the Security Council with the exception of measures against the enemy state, as defined." Article 54 of Chapter 7 also constrains regional organizations: "The Security Council shall at times be kept fully informed of activities undertaken or in contemplation under regional arrangements or by regional agencies for the maintenance of international peace and security." This provision in large part places the Council above the regional organizations, a situation that understandably frustrates governments in regions beset by violent conflict.

Privatized Peacekeeping?

An additional effect of the intensity of post–Cold War violent conflicts is the privatization of peacekeeping. The phenomenon of private military security armies is not new. But rather, their reemergence with the end of the Cold War is a response to the scope and intensity of violent political change, the complexities involved in new security challenges, insurgencies, and humanitarian crises. The demise of East-West bipolarity and the attendant weakening of the military-strategic hold on spheres of influence produced cracks in international security structures and political-military coalitions. Besides, these private military companies have become a part of the ongoing privitization of functions sweeping across both the developed and developing nations.[19] The increasingly interlinked and regionalized civil wars of the developing world impel state governments to call on these armies in order to contain often well-armed and well-trained rebel armies. These privatized armies legitimize their behavior and operations by supporting only recognized incumbent regimes, and utilizing only widely accepted legal and financial instruments to negotiate agreements. On the whole, their behavior is characterized as professional, useful, and distinctly corporate in character, and therefore in line with the growing emphasis on economic expansion and efficiency. Just as any transnational corporation they are motivated largely by economic gain, at times participating directly in combat.

Private military companies can both facilitate and obstruct the quick resolution of a conflict. To well-armed rebels they are viewed as an obstacle, whereas for weak incumbent governments they are the means of forcing rebel armies to the negotiating table. In the Sierra Leone civil war, they were largely responsible in forcing the stubborn Revolutionary United Front (RUF) to the bargaining table in 1996. The existence of rich mineral deposits, along with weak governments whose national armies have divided loyalties creates a viable market for private military assistance.[20] Thus, the access to natural resources, or the lure of contracts that amount to millions of dollars, become the rationale for privatized military security operations. For instance, Vinnell Corporation based in the United States negotiated contracts worth more than $170 million for training Saudi Arabia's national guard and air force. In Angola, Executive Outcomes was hired to protect that nation's oil wells and also ended up involved in the award of a diamond concession. Even nonprofit organizations such as the Red Cross are beginning to hire armed guards to protect their installations in zones of severe conflict.[21]

With the post–Cold War retrenchment of great powers from weakly cohesive states and the rise of competing ethnic nationalisms and challenges against the state, private military companies are now filling up the void created by the withdrawal. These privatized security companies now shoulder some of the costs the Western powers would have been accused of not being willing to undertake in countries of less strategic importance. For the Western powers such as the United States, the first and obvious principal considerations are the financial and human costs, followed by probable political costs if an intervention mission proves to be too costly and a failure.[22] For example, in Somalia, the human costs on both sides, the generally combative character of the intervention, and the desecration of dead Americans in October 1993 led to an immediate withdrawal of U.S. troops from the mission. In other words, while the motivations for great-power intervention in nonstrategic areas of the world have declined, for private security companies like Executive Outcomes, Vinnell Corporation, Military Professional Resources, Inc., and Sandline International, among others, the lure of diamonds, oil revenues, and substantial contracts have made them willing participants in the irregular warfare of far away places.

Moreover, in contrast to the traditional militaries of the great powers, private military companies are more professionally equipped and better trained to engage in the irregular wars and low-intensity conflicts of many developing areas where the boundaries between civilians and rebels is often blurred, and where the leader-follower hierarchy may not be well defined. Many fighters, for instance, within Executive Outcomes participated in low-intensity civil wars in Angola, Mozambique, and South Africa. In addition to experience with low-intensity conflict, some private military companies boast of sniper and special-forces training, rapid deployment, and tank warfare.

Unlike the great powers, private armies do not have to be concerned about being caught in a quagmire. Their decision to contain rebel armies is solely motivated by financial gain. The United States, for example, in its decision to intervene in any conflict is concerned about coming up with a well-defined political-military objective, a quick decisive strike force, and assurance of domestic political support. Critics of current Western response to crisis in areas of nonstrategic importance to the West point to the inclination to view the travails of non-Western cultures with less urgency, as evidenced by the Western passivity to the genocidal massacres of Rwandan Tutsi by Hutus in 1994.[23] In the United States, for example, the Rwandan crisis was viewed by many legislators as a remote incident, a tribal slaughter in one of the most "uncivilized" parts of the world.

The current Western attitude toward conflict in nonstrategic areas of the world coupled with the shift within great-power societies to combat increasing domestic problems—medical costs, education priorities, crime, urban youth unemployment, among others—have spawned the private armies that currently operate in many ongoing civil wars. Their common objectives are to improve client's military-security capability and thereby enable that client (often an incumbent regime) to contain more effectively rebel army challengers. Their activities range from guarding embassies, protecting assets of corporations working in war zones, and training national armies to function better in war, to active participation in war against rebel armies.

Finally, a symbiotic relationship is steadily developing between private armies, besieged governments, and mining companies. First, a threatened government is impelled to shore up its security and thereby guarantee its survival. It invites a private security army, which is lured in by the rich resources and contract. While the military company provides overall security, it especially protects operations of mining companies because revenues from these sources ensure its payments. If this trend continues, only nonstrategic countries with rich mineral deposits will be able to guarantee a modicum of internal security against rebel armies. Those without such resources will be caught in endless anarchy without any humanitarian or military security intervention.

In response to the changed security and political environment in regions of the world, peacekeeping has therefore become an integral and high profile component of world politics. The United Nations defines peacekeeping as "the deployment of international military and civilian personnel to a conflict area with the consent of the parties to the conflict in order to: stop or contain hostilities or supervise the carrying out of a peace agreement."[24] While this definition serves a useful purpose, no single definition or conceptualization of peacekeeping exists. Peacekeeping continues to evolve as new conflicts arise and demands to contain them are increasingly placed on regional economic organizations or alliance systems, as well as the United Nations. In addition to "privatized peacekeeping," and regionalized peacekeeping, the United Nations has conducted a total of more than 42 peacekeeping operations, 15 in the 40-year period between 1948 and 1988, and the others since 1989. In 1995, some 60,000 personnel were serving in 17 missions at an annual cost of about $3,500 million; in 1996 the number dropped to 26,000 military and civilian personnel in 16 operations with a total annual cost of about $1,600 million.[25] Conflicts in the Democratic Republic of Congo and in Sierra Leone, among others, continue to put demands on the UN for more peacekeeping forces. However, peacekeeping in developing regions like Africa is likely to remain ineffective if the advanced industrial powers continue their policy of staying away from conflicts in those states. For example, since the failed Somali operation by the UN, which involved the loss of 18 U.S. soldiers, the United States and its allies are now reluctant to get involved in the irregular conflicts of developing nations. UN peacekeeping

Table 14.1: Current Peacekeeping Missions

MISSION NAME AND LOCATION	ACRONYM	STARTING DATE
UN Truce Supervision Organization—Middle East	UNTSO	June 1948
UN Military Observer Group in India-Pakistan-Kashmir	UNMOGIP	January 1949
UN Peacekeeping Force in Cyprus	UNFICYP	March 1964
UN Disengagement Observer Force-Golan Heights	UNDOF	June 1974
UN Interim Force in Lebanon	UNIFIL	March 1978
UN Mission for the Referendum in Western Sahara	MINURSO	April 1991
UN Iraq-Kuwait Observation Mission	UNIKOM	April 1991
UN Observer Mission in Georgia	UNOMIG	August 1993
UN Mission in Bosnia-Herzegovina	UNMIBH	December 1995
UN Mission of Observers in Previaka-Croatia	UNMOP	January 1996
UN Interim Administration in Kosovo	UNMIK	June 1999
UN Mission in Sierra Leone	UNAMSIL	October 1999
UN Transitional Administration in East Timor	UNTAET	October 1999
UN Organization Mission in the Democratic Republic of the Congo	MONUC	November 1999
UN Mission in Ethiopia and Eritrea	UNMEE	July 2000

Source: United Nations Department of Peacekeeping Operations.

missions comprising mostly troops from the developing world are often poorly equipped and lightly armed, rendering them very ineffective when they have to deal with well-armed and determined rebel groups bent on violating peace agreements.

Pacific Settlement and Humanitarian Interventions

Although peace enforcement is becoming more widespread, the traditional methods of peaceful settlements of disputes and conflicts are still an integral part of international relations, and the work of the United Nations. For example, disputes between warring parties could be settled through *collective security,* or *collective self-defense.* The idea of collective security is based on the assumption that it is in the interest, and it is the responsibility, of all nation-states to maintain peace in the international system. It is a principle usually summarized as "all for one, one for all." Certain conditions must be satisfied for collective security to work. First, peace must be considered as indivisible, or all members of the international system must be concerned about threats to peace anywhere. Second, all members must agree in advance to mobilize force, resources, and organize to counter any such threat, even if it does not directly affect them. The prospects of encountering preponderant opposition for disturbing the peace is what usually dissuades potential aggressors from disturbing the peace. The first attempt at a universal collective security system was the establishment of the League of Nations in 1919. After the failure of the league to maintain international peace, the end of World War II saw the establishment of the UN as another attempt to adapt the assumptions of collective security to a universal system for preventing war.[26] The existence of many civil wars, and the occasional eruption of interstate wars, are indications that collective security is often undermined by ideological differences among major states (for example, communism versus capitalism during the Cold War), clashing economic interests, geostrategic interests, or a lack of agreement on what constitutes threats to peace. There is no perfect example of collective security at work. The Korean War in the early 1950s in which the United States led a unified force under the UN flag that fought against North Korean aggression came close to a successful implementation of collective security. The international coalition spearheaded by the United States that fought against Iraqi aggression directed at Kuwait in 1990 to 1991 is another example of an imperfect application of collective security.

Apart from collective security and collective self-defense, which may occasionally involve doing battle with the enemy, there are other methods of ensuring peace—that is through pacific settlement of disputes. Methods of pacific settlement are a key aspect of international law and practice. They are also emphasized in the UN charter as steps to be followed by states involved in disputes. In Article 33 of the UN charter, it is stated that before parties submit a dispute to a UN organ, they should "seek a solution by negotiation, inquiry, mediation, conciliation, arbitration, judicial settlement, resort to regional agencies or arrangements, or other peaceful means of their own choice."

Negotiation as a method of dispute settlement involves face-to-face discussion between or among the parties to the dispute or conflict with the aim of reaching an agreement. Outside parties are excluded from the process. As the bedrock of diplomacy, negotiation is the most common method for settling international differences.

Inquiry is a process whereby a neutral team of investigators establish the facts underlying a dispute. This is necessary because often controversy surrounds the facts and clarifications by an impartial body may facilitate settlement. The role of the investigators is not to suggest terms of settlement, but merely to report, with the hope that the report may help lay the ground-work conducive to settlement.

Mediation is a process of conflict settlement that involves a third party suggesting terms of settlement to warring factions, or parties in conflict. The third party (the mediator) is involved in the negotiations with the sole purpose of seeking terms of compromise acceptable to the factions. An effective mediator plays a skillful balancing act, and is supposed to be neutral so that he or she gains the confidence of the disputants.

In *conciliation,* the mediator or third party is a commission or interna-tional body whose assistance has been requested to find a solution satisfac-tory to the disputing parties. The United Nations is known for establishing special commissions to attempt conciliation.[27] As in mediation, the objec-tive of the commission is not to impose a solution, or favor one party, but to present terms of compromise acceptable to all parties. In October 1968, a protocol instituting a Conciliation and Good Offices Commission to be responsible for seeking a settlement of any disputes that may arise between states parties to the Convention against Discrimination in Education entered into force. This was a protocol adopted by UNESCO.

Arbitration involves the application of legal principles to a dispute based on conditions previously agreed upon by the disputants. The legal prin-ciples are applied by a panel of judges or arbitrators put together either by special agreement of the disputing parties or by an appropriate treaty. The disputants do not only submit the dispute to arbitration, but they also agree in advance to be bound by the decision. An agreement resulting from arbitration is known as a *compromis* and specifies the method of selecting the panel of judges, the time and place of conducting the hearing, and any conditions that would result in an equitable decision. Arbitration was used extensively by the ancient Greeks, and during the nineteenth and early twen-tieth centuries. Since 1945, it has been applied mainly in disputes involving issues of trade and investment.

Adjudication, or settlement by adjudication involves the use of an estab-lished international court for decision. Since the court is created by statute and is designated to resolve disputes among members, there are no prelim-inary limitations upon its procedures, evidence to be considered, or legal principles to be applied, except those stated in the statute that authorized its establishment. Nations wary of infringement upon their sovereignty have been reluctant to submit to the jurisdiction of international courts. The International Court of Justice does not receive many requests for judicial settlement. The United States, for example, jealous of its sovereignty, has re-fused to submit to the newly created International Criminal Court. Similar to arbitration, once the parties have agreed to submit a case to adjudication, the court's decision is considered binding, although adequate enforcement is often lacking. The European Court of Justice for the European Union is based on the idea of adjudication. Its functions are varied acting as an international court, a constitutional court, an administrative court, a civil court, and a court of appeal.

Good Offices as a method of dispute settlement is not mentioned in Article 33 of the UN charter, but nonetheless is frequently used. It involves the aid of a third party or state not involved in the dispute. The role of the third party may not be to offer any suggestions for terms of settlement, but strictly to serve as a channel of communications, or provide facilities for the use of the parties. The third party aims at promoting settlement and may therefore provide a neutral ground for negotiation, or offer to relay messages between the disputants without taking sides in the dispute. During the late 1980s the use of UN Good Offices succeeded in encouraging Soviet forces to withdraw from Afghanistan.

While these peaceful settlement methods are essential peacemaking strategies, they nonetheless often fail to prevent the escalation of many disputes into violent confrontations. As the scope and intensity of conflicts endure, UN peacekeeping, as well as regional peacekeeping initiatives, will continue to control anarchy, and alleviate some of the suffering caused by collective political violence in regions of the world. Perhaps the Rome Statute of the International Criminal Court, which entered into force on July 1, 2002, will act as a deterrent against heinous crimes that are so often a major aspect of civil wars. These crimes are enumerated in Part 2, articles 5-8 (see appendix 3) of the Rome Statute and include among others, genocide, crimes against humanity, and war crimes.

Many individuals would argue that peace enforcement or humanitarian military intervention constitutes a new trend of prescribing for the world. Are the many activities of UN peacekeeping—election monitoring, demobilization, rehabilitation, and so on—informed and influenced by principles of international law, or simply realpolitik and raw power? In other words, how can the UN or NATO ensure respect for the many interventionist peacekeeping and peacebuilding activities? How can the UN make new precepts related to conflict resolution legitimate in an international society characterized by diversity? In the absence of a sovereign world government how does the UN ensure obedience to universal rules of conduct for states?

Is humanitarian intervention involving activities such as feeding the starving, encouraging respect for human rights, or promoting socioeconomic development, a legal right? Many examples of humanitarian intervention today would during the Cold War be tantamount to a violation of the principles of nonintervention. Is the principle of nonintervention that underscores respect for order and avoiding war now outdated? Should the principle of nonintervention apply when the situation in a country is so serious that the moral conscience of the world is affronted?

Humanitarian or peacekeeping intervention involves questions about authorization. For example, Who gets to decide what is legal and what is not, and who gets to use force as a legal sanction against illegal uses of force? What is the relationship between politics and law, between power and authority? Can military intervention in another country be really humanitarian in terms of motives, stated purposes, methods of operation and in actual results? When humanitarian or peacekeeping intervention involves the use of tough action (military enforcement), or taking sides, can it qualify as "humanitarian"? Isn't humanitarian military intervention ethnocentric—that is characterized by contempt for local forces, or arrogance on the part of intervening forces? Who is there to guarantee obedience for the rules of international humanitarian law such as respect for inhabitants of occupied territories, or the rights and duties of the peacekeeping force? Peacekeeping interventions may, in the final analysis, be a case of a question about using "good" violence to reduce the incidence of "bad" violence. Peacekeeping and peace building may be attempts to address the relationship between injustice and resort to violence, as well as the need to construct a system of international governance in which the underlying grievances pertaining to questions of justice and injustice are also addressed.

Notes

1. World Bank, *World Development Indicators* (Washington, DC: World Bank, 1998), 68–70.
2. For more details on the consequences of uneven development, see Andrew Hurrell, "Security and Inequality," in *Inequality, Globalization, and World Politics*, ed. Andrew Hurrell and Ngaire Woods (Oxford: Oxford University Press, 1999).
3. See World Bank, *World Development Indicators* (Washington, DC, 1999).
4. See Michael T. Klare, "The New Arms Race: Light Weapons and International Security," at www.currenthistory.com/archiveapr97/klare.html.
5. See, for example, Anthony Sampson, *The Arms Bazaar in the Nineties* (London: Coronet, 1991).
6. United Nations, *Peacekeeping Data Tables*, Suite 7G. New York.
7. Boutrous Boutros-Ghali, *An Agenda for Peace* (New York: United Nations, 1992).
8. For details, see Indar J. Rikhye, *Strengthening U.N. Peacekeeping* (Washington, DC: United States Institute of Peace, 1992).
9. For data on refugees, see *Population Data Unit* (Geneva: United Nations High Commissioner for Refugees, 2001).
10. See United Nations, Department of Public Information.
11. Boutros Boutros-Ghali, *An Agenda for Peace*, 1992.
12. See *Tampa Tribune*, "The U.N. in Financial Crisis?" April 27, 1996, p. A4.
13. For details on ECOWAS, see Karl P. Magyer, and Earl Conteh-Morgan, eds., *Peacekeeping in Africa: ECOMOG in Liberia* (London: Macmillan, 1998).
14. See, for example, Nicole Ball, *Security and Economy in the Third World* (London: Adamantine, 1988).
15. For details, see Indar J. Rikhye, *Strengthening U.N. Peacekeeping* (Washington, DC: United States Institute of Peace, 1992).

16. See, for example, Karl P. Magyar and Earl Conteh-Morgan, eds., *Peacekeeping in Africa: ECOMOG in Liberia* (London: Macmillan, 1998).
17. See, for example, The Charter of the Organization for Security and Cooperation in Europe.
18. See, for example, George K. Kieh, "International Organizations and Peacekeeping in Africa," in *Peacekeeping in Africa: ECOMOG in Liberia*, ed. Karl P. Magyar and Earl Conteh-Morgan (London: Macmillan, 1998).
19. See, for example, David Shearer, "Outsourcing War," *Foreign Policy* 112 (fall 1998): 68–80.
20. See Al J. Venter, "Market Forces: How Hired Guns Succeed Where the United Nations Failed," *Jane's International Defense Review*, March 1, 1998.
21. For further details, see Adam Zagorin, "Soldiers for Sale," at Pathfinder.com/Time Magazine, 1997.
22. See "The Clinton administration's Policy on Reforming Multilateral Peace Operations," *Dispatch* 5, no. 2 (May 16, 1994).
23. Facts on File, *World News Digest* (August 4, 1994): 542E2.
24. Fact Sheet, "The U.N. and Peacekeeping," p. 1.
25. Fact Sheet, United Nations Peacekeeping Operations, p. 1.
26. See, for details, Evan Luard, *A History of the United Nations* (New York: St Martin's Press, 1989).
27. See, for example, Lawrence Finkelstein, ed., *Politics in the United Nations System* (Durham: Duke University Press, 1988); and Evan Luard, *The United Nations: How It Works and What It Does* (New York: St. Martin's Press, 1994).

Key Terms

humanitarian assistance
irregular warfare
peace building
peace enforcement
peacekeeping

peacekeeping activities
peacemaking
preventive diplomacy
private military security armies
regionalized peacekeeping

Discussion Questions

1. What is peacekeeping? In what ways has peacekeeping expanded since the end of the Cold War?
2. Identify and explain the following: peacemaking, preventive diplomacy, and peace enforcement.
3. Discuss regionalized peacekeeping, and analyze the reasons for its weakness compared to UN peacekeeping.
4. What accounts for the seeming increase in private military armies? Do you think it is a positive trend?

Glossary of Terms and Concepts

Aggression   Action or behavior intended to inflict physical or psychological harm, or destroy property.

Alienation   A condition of self-estrangement or psychological separation (as opposed to mutual identification or solidarity) with one's immediate environment, including, in Marxism, one's work, product of work, fellow workers, and society as a whole.

Altruism   Actions that benefit or enhance the welfare of others even at a cost of one's own well-being.

Anarchy   The absence of government. The international system is characterized as one of anarchy because of the absence of a world government to prevent instances of civil and interstate wars, as well as other forms of collective violence.

Animal rights   The promotion of actions and activities aimed at enhancing the ethical treatment of animals, especially objection to vivisection, dissection, hunting, animal sacrifices, and all forms of cruelty to animals.

Anomie   A social condition characterized by an imbalance or gap between a society's stated goals and the instructionalized means to achieve those goals.

Arms race   A condition of competitive defense spending as rival states arm against each other. It takes the form of an action-reaction process with one state basing the level of its defense spending on the defense spending of its rival.

Balance of power   A system of distributing power among two or more competing coalitions of nation states intended to prevent a predominance of power by any one coalition. It is a theory derived from power politics or realism that asserts that states strive to counterbalance each other through competition for power in the international system.

Basic human needs   Necessary elements for development and growth such as food, clothing, shelter, and freedom, among others.

Biodiversity   (Biological diversity) The emphasis in the ecological arena intended to ensure the interactions of diverse species so that ecosystems maintain their vitality and remain stable.

Biological determination   The view that behavior is in large part caused by innate, genetic, or biological factors, as opposed to environmental factors.

Biological weapons   Weapons that include viruses, rickettsiae and bacteria capable of multiplying within the target organism thereby destroying or disabling life in man, animals, or plants.

Bipolarity   A structure of power that revolves around a two coalition (each headed by a major power) system of nation-states that constantly balance each other in order to prevent unilateral dominance on either side.

Capitalism   A particular class-based economic system based on wealth accumulation through profit maximization by the capitalist (dominant) class in which the working class is subordinated and virtually every transaction is commodified, or translates into something to be bought and sold.

Capitalist contradictions   Karl Marx's identification of inbuilt contradictions of capitalism as an economic system that would lead to its downfall. Examples of contradictions inherent in the structure of capitalism are socialized production versus private appropriation, the existence of enormous material wealth versus economic misery and inequality, and labor versus money.

Chemical weapons   Weapons comprised of phosgene, chlorine, and mustard gases, among others, which are deadly chemicals that disable or kill members of the target community, and contaminate territory.

Civil society   The domain of nonstate associations and groups (for example, church, women's groups, universities, labor unions, etc.) formed by private citizens, to the government or state sphere of society.

Civil war   A major, well-organized, widespread violent conflict between the armed forces of a state and rebel forces composed largely of residents of the state.

Class conflict   The conflict and struggle between classes such as in Marxism between the bourgeoisie (capitalist class) and the proletariat (working class), or between slave owners and slaves in a slave society.

Class exploitation   The process whereby in capitalism, the surplus value generated by the productive labor of the working class is appropriated by the capitalist class. This is done primarily through the wage relation that binds the working class to the dominant class.

Cold War   The global ideological (capitalism vs. communism) struggle between the United States and U.S.S.R. between 1947 and 1989 for political, economic, and military dominance. Although labeled *Cold War,* the period caused many hot wars between the clients of the two superpowers.

Collective security   A universal system summarized as "one for all, all for one," wherein aggression against one is considered aggression against all. This means that all nation-states in the international system are committed to join together to punish an aggressor state that disturbs the peace. The League of Nations in the past, and now the United Nations, are the only two examples of collective security.

Colonization   The territorial expansion by European powers during the eighteenth and nineteenth centuries that resulted in the creation of overseas empires in Africa, Asia, the Middle East, and other regions.

Combatant   An individual directly engaged in armed conflict either through actions and/or direct military support. This also includes persons engaged in nonformal collective violence such as riots, genocide, terrorism, or ethnic conflicts.

Competition   A situation in which parties strive to improve their relative position in terms of things such as influence, power, or available resources.

Conflict   A situation of incompatible interests or perceptions that produce antagonistic or hostile behavior between people or groups. The behavior may be verbal and/or physical, aimed at hurting, damaging, or frustrating the other.

Conflict management   Efforts put forth to prevent a conflict from escalating, or to reduce its intensity and destructive nature.

Conflict resolution   The deescalation or deduction of a conflict situation toward a more compatible or peaceful behavior.

Conflict transformation   A significant and enduring process of change away from a protracted, mutually destructive struggle between adversaries toward a relationship of constructive and more cooperative interaction.

Conscription   The forceful recruitment ("the draft") of citizens into the armed forces.

Culture of peace and nonviolence   The worldview characterized by personal, institutional, and structural values, mores, and practices that promote and sustain activities that foster peaceful living such as justice, human rights, intercultural harmony, and ecological sustainability.

Culture of war and violence   The worldview characterized by personal, institutional, and structural values, mores, and practices the promote and sustain activities that destroy or diminish life and the equality of life on earth such as wars, other forms of physical violence, and various nonphysical expressions of violence.

Decolonization   The granting of independence to European colonies following World War II, a development that saw the emergence of many more sovereign nation states into the international system.

Demobilization   The process whereby combatants or warring factions are disarmed and disbanded, usually as part of the implementation of a peace agreement following a war.

Deterrence   A policy based on the threat of military intervention in order to prevent a rival nation from resorting to the use of military force.

Diplomacy   A system of promoting understanding and peaceful relations among states through negotiations and dialogue, as well as through institutional practices and discourses that have evolved over centuries of international relations.

Egalitarian society   A society based on the absence of class distinctions, or on relative equality between groups.

Ego   The component of the human personality that tries to resolve the conflict or struggle between the impulses of the id instinctual forces and the constraints of the superego social/moral imperatives.

Ethnic cleansing   A term that originated in the early 1990s (end of the Cold War) to describe the deliberate expulsion of one ethnic group by another from a territory through the use of widespread killings, mass rape, and torture.

Ethnic group   A group of people who consider themselves distinct from others based on cultural traits such as language, religion, race, and perceptions of a common historical heritage, shared experiences, and often common destiny.

Ethnocentrism   The belief that uncritically assumes the superiority of one's own group and culture over all others. It is characterized by attitudes, beliefs, and practices that distinguish the in-group ("we") from the out-group ("they"), implying that "they" by definition, do not measure up to "our" standards.

Ethnonationalism   The clamor by a specific ethnic group to possess its own sovereign state endowed with full citizenship based on common ethnicity.

External war   Hostilities between states or between culturally different political communities based on armed force.

False consciousness   The notion that workers and other groups in society are oblivious to the injustices they suffer because of capitalism's awesome ability to deceive and exploit.

Frame of reference   A guide or set of related beliefs that serve as a standard for behavior or for the evaluation of behavior or conduct and information.

Free-rider problem   The problem that rises when everyone hopes someone else will do something (e.g., vote, give a subsidy, volunteer to fight, etc.), and then no one does.

Game theory   A methodological approach based on the assumption of individual rationality in which two or more players are expected to make choices under specified constraints. Their decisions are usually interdependent—that is the effectiveness of one actor's decision depends on the decision taken by other actors or players.

Global warming   The gradual increase in the earth's temperature (both on its surface and lower atmosphere) caused by the entrapment of heat resulting from the accumulation of certain gases, mainly carbon dioxide.

Good offices   A method of enhancing peaceful settlement of a dispute in which a neutral third party supplies data and other types of information to facilitate communication between disputing parties, without making any substantial recommendations or suggestions on the possible terms of settlement.

Guerrilla war   A term literally translated "little war." It generally refers to any nonstate, irregular armed force that is engaged in a prolonged conflict at the domestic level against an incumbent government. The term was first used in reference to the Peninsular War of 1808 to 1814, to describe the hit-and-run tactics of the local Spanish forces opposing Napoleon's effort to extend his rule over Spain.

Hegemony   Political, military, economic, and sociocultural domination of a system by a single person, group, or nation. The United States, for example, exercised hegemony (leadership, dominance) in the international system between 1945 to the end of the Cold War.

Homicide   The killing ("murder") of another human being, especially when there are no extenuating circumstances to the killing, such as "accidental" firing of a weapon.

Homogeneity   The opposite of heterogeneity, it is a characteristic of strong similarity to one another, of some group, collection of people, or nation.

Instrumentalism   A perspective of interethnic relations based on the idea that interethnic conflict is a consequence of the politicization or manipulation of ethnic differences by political elites for personal or class benefits. That is, since ethnicity is socially constructed, ethnic conflicts are due less to the inherent tendency for ethnic cleavages to cause conflict than to elite manipulation.

Insurgency   An internal armed uprising by opponents of the government (insurgents) who resort to organized violence against government forces to either overthrow the government or achieve their political aims.

Internal war   Highly organized warfare between political communities within the same polity, characterized by widespread participation.

Irredentism   The annexation of, or the intention to annex, a neighboring state because of cultural similarity or association with the people who inhabit it.

Jihad A term mostly associated with radical Islam and translated as "holy war." It is also used within a broader context to include all endeavors made by Muslims on behalf of the Islamic faith.

Just war A war based on the principle that if a nation is attacked it is morally justified to defend itself. This means that a just war is defensive and not imperialistic, rejects any undue use of force, and does not inflict harm on noncombatants, among other factors.

Lebensraum A German term literally translated "living space." It refers to the need to acquire foreign territories in order to provide resources (mineral and agricultural) to sustain a world power in its competition with other world powers.

Liberalism A perspective within international relations theory that underscores such factors as the spread of democratic institutions in order to guarantee peace and individual rights and liberties, national and international interests, interdependence, or harmony of interests among nations would eliminate the inclination toward aggression. International organizations and international regimes can regulate disputes and ensure a harmony of interests, and collective security as exemplified in the UN system would also help guarantee peace and security.

Marginalization Excluding an individual, group, practice, or thought from the mainstream of social relations, institutions, or participation. In the end, it involves discrimination and exclusion.

Mediation A form of conflict resolution that involves an outside third party acting as a facilitator by restoring communication between the rival parties, clarifying points at issue, and providing a proper definition of the conflict situation. It often involves face-to-face negotiations, intended to arrest escalation of the violence. The suggestions are not binding.

Militarism Total domination of government and society by the military manifested in subordination of civilian control, the pervasiveness of military values, and virtual control of the political system by military institutions.

Military industrial complex The situation during the Cold War that produced the conjunction of an immense military establishment and a large arms industry in American society.

Minority group A subgroup of people that makes up the smaller of two or more groups within a given population. The dominant (numerically larger) group often singles out the smaller group for unequal treatment.

Nationalism The emotion of loyalty to the state and its government by the populace as a result of socialization.

Negative peace The presence of conditions of exploitation, gaping inequality, or oppression, among others, that subvert universal human rights and dignity. Social and economic justice and well-being are not being ensured for all.

Negotiation The most common method of peaceful settlement characterized by interactions between conflicting parties in order to normalize relationships, finalize agreements, reconcile conflicting positions, or identify complementary interests, among other things.

Nomothetic (as opposed to ideographic) The belief that commonalities or regularities exist among events, issues, or phenomena (for example, revolutions) that are worth identifying and expressed as lawlike generalizations.

Nonviolence The ethic that rejects aggression and violence as a means of achieving goals or resolving conflicts, utilizing instead civil obedience based on actions of openness and love.

Norms Moral standards of what "should," "ought," or "must" be as opposed to what "is."

Out-group A group to which an individual feels he or she does not identify, or does not belong.

Ozone layer Depending on the season and other factors, the ozone layer is a protective concentration of ozone in the stratosphere between 9.3 and 31 miles above the earth.

Pacifism The principle opposing all wars, as well as all preparations for war.

Peace building The process of assisting in reconstruction efforts after conflict resolution in order to prevent a fresh eruption of the conflict.

Peace enforcement The mandate to "impose" a cease-fire, or do battle with violators if need be.

Peacekeeping   The deployment of military forces to forestall the escalation of a dispute.

Peaceful society   A society that frowns upon physical violence or combat and utilizes instead deception and trickery. Values of cooperation, sharing, and harmonious interpersonal relationships largely guarantee a very low level of physical aggression.

Personality   An individual's behavioral and emotional characteristics that differentiate him or her from others, and that also describes that individual's reactions to various situations or events.

Political community   A group of people characterized by membership of a common territory, and apolitical official in charge of announcing group decisions.

Positive peace   The absence of conditions of exploitation, intolerable inequality, or oppression, among others, that guarantee the promotion of universal human rights and dignity. The emphasis is on developing social conditions that emphasize peace building. Social and economic justice and well-being are being ensured for all.

Positivism   The belief that the best way to understand social and natural phenomena is through the scientific method, and that human behavior is the result of biological, psychological, and environmental influences.

Power   The ability to get others to do what they would otherwise not want to do.

Praxis   Social action whose goal is to change a system, society, or the world.

Primordialism   The view that interethnic differences based on racial, language, religious, regional characteristics, and other visible markers produce interethnic conflicts because members of the same group emotionally identify with their in-group, but feel no such identity with those outside their ethnic group.

Prisoners' dilemma   A situation is which two parties are confronted with choices that would seemingly be in their self-interest, but end up hurting each other.

Proletariat   Wage earners, or those who do not own the means of production and therefore have little control over its disposition.

Public good   A good such that if one individual consumes it, it cannot feasiblely be withheld from others in the group. In other words, nonpayers cannot be excluded from consuming it. This is in contrast to a private good that can be consumed only by those who pay for it.

Rational choice   A decision-making approach in which the decision makers compare the expected utility of compelling policy options and select the option they believe will produce the most favorable outcome.

Realism   Also referred to as power politics, or realpolitik, a worldview within international relations theory that characterizes international politics as a struggle for power between states.

Rebellion   An organized interlinked series of violent collective actions by one or more political groups with the specific aim of overthrowing a state.

Refugee   According to the United Nations High Commission for Refugees (UNHCR), a refugee is a person who "owing to a well-founded fear of being persecuted for reasons of race, religion, nationality, membership in a particular social group, or political opinion is outside the country of his nationality, and is unable to or, owing to such fear, is unwilling to avail himself of the protection of that country" (Convention Relating to the Status of Refugees, 1951).

Relative deprivation   The feeling or perception of a gap or discrepancy between what one considers one's rights, dues, or expectations, and what one has actually attained. The feeling of deprivation is theorized to produce frustration and anger, and is therefore linked to the onset of rebellion.

Repression   The coerced treatment or subjugation of individuals or groups by violent or nonviolent means.

Resource base   Refers to the totality of the earth's natural resources, including water and air, on which human life depends.

Resource mobilization theory   A theory of social movement that emphasizes the capacity of competing groups to organize and use the adequate resources (means) to achieve their goals.

Revolution   The overthrow, and fundamental transformation of the values, institutions, social structure, class composition, of a state—usually through violent means.

Secession   The attempt of a political entity (e.g., region, or ethnic group) within a state to separate from the larger political unit, usually with an intent to establish its own independent sovereign state.

Self help   The assumption that because of international anarchy or the lack of a wold government, states must provide for and ensure their own security.

Social class   A large grouping or social entity sharing similar occupational, income, and educational interests and also characterized by similar location and interests as well as some form of mutual self-consciousness and identity.

Social contract   An actual or hypothetical agreement between state and society to form a system that would avoid the anarchy and violence of the survival of the fittest.

Social distance   The degree of relational separateness felt by one individual or group toward another.

Social movement   A group of actors in society who organize and mobilize with the intent to defend or change society or the position of a group within society.

Sociobiology   The study of the biological behavior of social behavior.

Sovereignty   A concept of international relations that attributes to the government of a state the highest or ultimate authority.

State of nature   An imagined or hypothetical situation characterized by violent competition and the lack of any organized government.

State terror   Deliberate and/or indiscriminate violence against, or killings of, individuals or groups by the state.

Strategy   The overall plan actors in conflict use to manage their conflict or achieve their political and military objectives.

Structural factors   Those attributes external to the individual or group that characterize the physical or social environment.

Structural violence   Indirect and insidious, or nonmilitary, violence perpetuated by socioeconomic injustices manifested in limited or no access to basic human needs, and a humane quality of life. It operates at different (local, national, international, and global) systemic levels, built into the structure of social and cultural institutions, and based on varying degrees of repression.

Structure   The fundamental unit of social order that is considered the locus for explanation of stability and/or instablility.

Subculture   A subcultural group that has its own distinctive values and norms, but also shares some of the values and norms of the dominant culture.

Superego   Also known as the conscience, it is that aspect of the personality that internalizes society's values and norms.

Superpower   A term of the Cold War era applied to the United States and the Soviet Union to denote the unrivaled combination of political, military, and economic power possessed by each.

Sustainable development   Economic development that emphasizes deliberate efforts to make available key economic resources and a livable and healthy environment for future generations.

System   A combined set of mutually reinforcing structures and processes, or a set of interacting parts.

Systems theory   A mode of analysis that examines the dynamic relationship between a whole and its parts and focuses on how a system's inputs produce desired outputs and therefore a balanced state.

Tactics   The immediate and short term aspects of a broad conception (strategy) of a military effort.

Teleology   the fact or quality of being directed toward a definite end, or having an ultimate purpose. For example, in Marxism, economic forces are theorized as moving toward a final end, a communist economic system with no class differences and no state.

Terrorism   Acts of violence that are either national or international, committed by individuals or organizations to publicize their cause, punish their enemies, or achieve their goals.

Treaty   A written contract or document between two parties that must be ratified before it is considered legally binding.

Typology   The organization of types or observations into separate and distinct categories through the use of concepts, variables, and theories.

United Nations   The single universal intergovernmental organization based on collective security presently operating in the international system. It is characterized by universal membership and general purpose functions ranging from peace and security.

Values   Preferences or entities for which one is willing to sacrifice time, money, or effort, among others.

Violence   The use of physical aggression (force) by an individual, group, or organization resulting in injury or abuse to others.

War   Well-organized, open, and widespread armed conflict between nations, or between factions within a state.

Warfare   Armed combat between two or more political entities.

War system   A series of mutually interrelated and reinforcing structures and trends that promote war.

Working class   The capitalist system's subordinate class, whose member survive by selling their labor capacity to the capitalist class or owners of the means of production.

World systems theory   A theory that attempts to explain stratification, dependence, and inequality in the world system by focusing on the effects of capitalism in producing core (advanced), semiperipheral, and peripheral capitalist states.

Xenophobia   Fear or distrust of foreigners seen as the out-group, and of the policies and objectives of other states. It is related to the mass emotion of nationalism, which perceives and stereotypes others as something to be feared or hated.

Zero-sum   A situation or interaction based on a loss for one being automatically a gain for the other.

Glossary of Conflict-Related Theorists

This glossary provides a brief biographical sketch of some of the major conflict-related thinkers discussed in the text.

Bentham, Jeremy (1748–1832)   English philosopher who formulated the utilitarian philosophy of "the greatest good for the greatest number." He advocated rational behavior in all situations in order to effectively maintain a balance between pleasure and pain.

Bodin, Jean (1530–96)   French political philosopher who in 1576 formulated the doctrine of state sovereignty. The state is sovereign when it is endowed with supreme and absolute power subject only to the principles of divine and natural law.

Durkheim, Émile (1858–1917)   In 1893 he wrote *De la division du travail social* in which he expressed the hope that trade unions and other segments of civil society would one day create a new moral order because a common value system is essential to societal stability.

Engels, Friedrich (1820–95)   German socialist philosopher, collaborator, and lifelong friend of Karl Marx. He was also an economic determinist who believed that the capitalist system will be replaced, and that societies will eventually progress toward classlessness. He coauthored the *Communist Manifesto* with Marx in 1848.

Erikson, Erik (1902–94)   He claimed that humans develop in stages. His eight psychosocial stages have been used to analyze revolutionary leaders. Erikson, like Freud, made significant contributions to the psychosocial analysis of conflict.

Freud, Sigmund (1856–1939)   In *Beyond the Pleasure Principle*, Freud attempts to explain the causes and effects of our drives. He argues that instinctual drives in man produce aggressive and egotistical behaviors that are checked by society's demand (culture) for conformity.

Fromm, Erich (1900–80)   German-born social scientist and philosopher who wrote many books on psychoanalysis, crime and punishment, and

theory of aggression. His *Anatomy of Human Destructiveness* is a detailed work that critiques several theories of violence and aggression. In the conclusion he offered his own explanation of human aggression.

Gandhi, Mohandas (1869–1948) Indian spiritual and political leader, called Mahatma ("Great Soul"). Leader of Indian independence movement and exponent and founder of "passive resistance," or nonviolent noncooperation.

Hegel, Georg Wilhelm Friedrich (1770–1831) German philosopher who expressed dialectical progression: an idea develops a thesis that is opposed by an antithesis. Out of this clash of ideas emerges a synthesis, or a new thesis or solution, all as part of the process of society progressing toward perfection and freedom.

Hobbes, Thomas (1588–1679) English philosopher and political theorist, best known for his views on conflict and violence developed in *Leviathan* (1651), especially his statements that "life is a war of all against all," or life as "nasty, short, and brutish." For Hobbes wars are in large part due to man's evil nature and the impulse to self-preservation.

Kant, Immanuel (1724–1804) In his theories, Kant expressed his belief in a conflict between man's sociability and his selfish nature. In order to ensure peace, Kant recommended a state that would guarantee and uphold individual freedom, curbing it only when it threatened the general welfare and freedom of others in society.

Lenin, Vladimir Illyich (1870–1924) Russian Marxist theorist, leader of the Social Democratic Party, and instigator of the Bolshevik Revolution of 1917. Among his influential works was *Imperialism the Highest Stage of Capitalism* (1916).

Lorenz, Konrad (1903–89) a 1973 Nobel Laureate and scientist of animal behavior. His book *On Aggression* generated a great deal of criticism because of its methodological leap from animal behavior to human behavior.

Marx, Karl (1818–83) German philosopher, economist, and political thinker. An active revolutionary and founder of the First International. Like his lifelong friend Engels, Marx believed capitalism would fail because of its inherent contradictions. His works inspired much of nineteenth-century socialist thought and greatly influenced the communist agitations of the twentieth century.

Mosca, Gaetano (1857–1941)   Italian sociologist and political economist, considered the founder of elitism, whose focus was the study of power and the groups who dominated decision making. Elitists also examined the manner in which power was obtained and maintained, elite-mass interactions, and the role of force, myth, and symbols in the exercise of power. These ideas were mostly clearly developed in *The Ruling Class* (1896).

Pareto, Vilfredo (1848–1923)   Italian economist and political philosopher born in Paris. Along with Mosca, and Robert Michels, he argued that power was always in the hands of a minority (an elite), and that political struggles are the result of disputes between groups dominated by a small elite. Elitism is a more realistic description of political reality compared to ideas such as popular sovereignty, egalitarianism, or government by the people. His major work was *The Mind and Society* (1916).

Sorel, Georges (1847–1922)   French philosopher and theorist of syndicalism. He was opposed to state enterprise, political institutions, and political parties. In his major work *Reflections on Violence* (1908), he proposed that it is by the "myth of the general strike" that socialism could be realized. The fascists would subsequently seize upon this notion and put it into practice.

Weber, Max (1864–1920)   German sociologist of the twentieth century who rejected Marx's theory of economic determinism. In his works, he stressed the interrelationship between ideology, social structure, and material interests. In particular, he is known for emphasizing the importance of ethical and religious factors in the formation of capitalism, notably in his famous work *The Protestant Ethic and the Spirit of Capitalism* (1904).

Appendix 1: United Nations Convention on the Prevention and Punishment of the Crime of Genocide (1951)

The Contracting Parties,

Having considered the declaration made by the General Assembly of the United Nations in its resolution 96 (1) dated 11 December 1946 that genocide is a crime under international law, contrary to the spirit and aims of the United Nations and condemned by the civilized world,

Recognizing that at all periods of history genocide has inflicted great losses on humanity, and

Being convinced that, in order to liberate mankind from such an odious scourge, international co-operation is required, Hereby agree as hereinafter provided:

Article I   The Contracting Parties confirm that genocide, whether committed in time of peace or in time of war, is a crime under international law which they undertake to prevent and to punish.

Article II   In the present Convention, genocide means any of the following acts committed with intent to destroy, in whole or in part, a national, ethnical, racial or religious group, as such:

    a) Killing members of the group;
    b) Causing serious bodily or mental harm to members of the group;
    c) Deliberately inflicting on the group conditions of life calculated to bring about its physical destruction in whole or in part;
    d) Imposing measures intended to prevent births within the group;
    e) Forcibly transferring children of the group to another group.

Article III   The following acts shall be punishable:

    a) Genocide;
    b) Conspiracy to commit genocide;

c) Direct and public incitement to commit genocide;

d) Attempt to commit genocide;

e) Complicity in genocide.

Article IV Persons committing genocide or any of the other acts enumerated in Article III shall be punished, whether they are constitutionally responsible rulers, public officials or private individuals.

Article V The Contracting Parties undertake to enact, in accordance with their respective Constitutions, the necessary legislation to give effect to the provisions of the present Convention, and, in particular, to provide effective penalties for persons guilty of genocide or any of the other acts enumerated in Article III.

Article VI Persons charged with genocide or any of the other acts enumerated in Article III shall be tried by a competent tribunal of the State in the territory of which the act was committed, or by such international penal tribunal as may have jurisdiction with respect to those Contracting Parties which shall have accepted its jurisdiction.

Article VII Genocide and the other acts enumerated in Article III shall not be considered as political crimes for the purpose of extradition. The Contracting Parties pledge themselves in such cases to grant extradition in accordance with their laws and treaties in force.

Article VIII Any Contracting Party may call upon the competent organs of the United Nations to take such action under the Charter of the United Nations as they consider appropriate for the prevention and suppression of acts of genocide or any of the other acts enumerated in Article III.

Article IX Disputes between the Contracting Parties relating to the interpretation, application or fulfilment of the present Convention, including those relating to the responsibility of a State for genocide or for any of the other acts enumerated in Article III, shall be submitted to the International Court of Justice at the request of any of the parties to the dispute.

Article X The present Convention, of which the Chinese, English, French, Russian and Spanish texts are equally authentic, shall bear the date of 9 December 1948.

Article XI   The present Convention shall be open until 31 December 1949 for signature on behalf of any Member of the United Nations and of any nonmember State to which an invitation to sign has been addressed by the General Assembly. The present Convention shall be ratified, and the instruments of ratification shall be deposited with the Secretary-General of the United Nations.

After 1 January 1950, the present Convention may be acceded to on behalf of any Member of the United Nations and of any non-member State which has received an invitation as aforesaid. Instruments of accession shall be deposited with the Secretary-General of the United Nations.

Article XII   Any Contracting Parry may at any time, by notification addressed to the Secretary-General of the United Nations, extend the application of the present Convention to all or any of the territories for the conduct of whose foreign relations that Contracting Party is responsible.

Article XIII   On the day when the first twenty instruments of ratification or accession have been deposited, the Secretary-General shall draw up a proces-verbal and transmit a copy thereof to each Member of the United Nations and to each of the non-member States contemplated in Article XI. The present Convention shall come into force on the ninetieth day following the date of deposit of the twentieth instrument of ratification or accession. Any ratification or accession effected, subsequent to the latter date shall become effective on the ninetieth day following the deposit of the instrument of ratification or accession.

Article XIV   The present Convention shall remain in effect for a period of ten years as from the date of its coming into force. It shall thereafter remain in force for successive periods of five years for such Contracting Parties as have not denounced it at least six months before the expiration of the current period. Denunciation shall be effected by a written notification addressed to the Secretary-General of the United Nations.

Article XV   If, as a result of denunciations, the number of Parties to the present Convention should become less than sixteen, the Convention shall cease to be in force as from the date on which the last of these denunciations shall become effective.

Article XVI   A request for the revision of the present Convention may be made at any time by any Contracting Party by means of a notification in writing addressed to the Secretary-General. The General Assembly shall decide upon the steps, if any, to be taken in respect of such request.

Article XVII   The Secretary-General of the United Nations shall notify all Members of the United Nations and the non-member States contemplated in Article XI of the following:

a) Signatures, ratifications and accessions received in accordance with Article XI;
b) Notifications received in accordance with Article XII;
c) The date upon which the present Convention comes into force in accordance with Article XIII;
d) Denunciations received in accordance with Article XIV;
e) The abrogation of the Convention in accordance with Article XV;
f) Notifications received in accordance with Article XVI.

Article XVIII   The original of the present Convention shall be deposited in the archives of the United Nations. A certified copy of the Convention shall be transmitted to each Member of the United Nations and to each of the non-member States contemplated in Article XI.

Article XIX   The present Convention shall be registered by the Secretary-General of the United Nations on the date of its coming into force.

Appendix 2: Chapter VII: UN Charter Action with Respect to Threats to the Peace, Breaches of the Peace, and Acts of Aggression

Article 39   The Security Council shall determine the existence of any threat to the peace, breach of the peace, or act of aggression and shall make recommendations, or decide what measures shall be taken in accordance with Articles 41 and 42, to maintain or restore international peace and security.

Article 40   In order to prevent an aggravation of the situation, the Security Council may, before making the recommendations or deciding upon the measures provided for in Article 39, call upon the parties concerned to comply with such provisional measures as it deems necessary or desirable. Such provisional measures shall be without prejudice to the rights, claims, or position of the parties concerned. The Security Council shall duly take account of failure to comply with such provisional measures.

Article 41   The Security Council may decide what measures not involving the use of armed force are to be employed to give effect to its decisions, and it may call upon the Members of the United Nations to apply such measures. These may include complete or partial interruption of economic relations and of rail, sea, air, postal, telegraphic, radio, and other means of communication, and the severance of diplomatic relations.

Article 42   Should the Security Council consider that measures provided for in Article 41 would be inadequate or have proved to be inadequate, it may take such action by air, sea, or land forces as may be necessary to maintain or restore international peace and security. Such action may include demonstrations, blockade, and other operations by air, sea, or land forces of Members of the United Nations.

Article 43   1. All Members of the United Nations, in order to contribute to the maintenance of international peace and security, undertake to make available to the Security Council, on its call and in accordance with a special agreement or agreements, armed forces, assistance and facilities, including rights of passage, necessary for the purpose of maintaining international peace and security.

2. Such agreement or agreements shall govern the numbers and types of forces, their degree of readiness and general location, and the nature of the facilities and assistance to be provided.

3. The agreement or agreements shall be negotiated as soon as possible on the initiative of the Security Council. They shall be concluded between the Charter of the United Nations Security Council and Members or between the Security Council and groups of Members and shall be subject to ratification by the signatory states in accordance with their respective constitutional processes.

Article 44 When the Security Council has decided to use force it shall, before calling upon a Member not represented on it to provide armed forces in fulfillment of the obligations assumed under Article 43, invite that Member, if the Member so desires, to participate in the decisions of the Security Council concerning the employment of contingents of that Member's armed forces.

Article 45 In order to enable the United Nations to take urgent military measures, Members shall hold immediately available national air-force contingents for combined international enforcement action. The strength and degree of readiness of these contingents and plans for their combined action shall be determined, within the limits laid down in the special agreement or agreements referred to in Article 43, by the Security Council with the assistance of the Military Staff Committee.

Article 46 Plans for the application of armed force shall be made by the Security Council with the assistance of the Military Staff Committee.

Article 47 1. There shall be established a Military Staff Committee to advise and assist the Security Council on all questions relating to the Security Council's military requirements for the maintenance of international peace and security, the employment and command of forces placed at its disposal, the regulation of armaments, and possible disarmament.

2. The Military Staff Committee shall consist of the Chiefs of Staff of the permanent members of the Security Council or their representatives. Any Member of the United Nations not permanently represented on the Committee shall be invited by the Committee to be associated with it when the efficient discharge of the Committee's responsibilities requires the participation of that Member in its work.

3. The Military Staff Committee shall be responsible under the Security Council for the strategic direction of any armed forces placed at the disposal of the Security Council. Questions relating to the command of such forces shall be worked out subsequently.

4. The Military Staff Committee, with the authorization of the Security Council and after consultation with appropriate regional agencies, may establish regional sub-committees.

Article 48 1. The action required to carry out the decisions of the Security Council for the maintenance of international peace and security shall be taken by all the Members of the United Nations or by some of them, as the Security Council may determine.

2. Such decisions shall be carried out by the Members of the United Nations directly and through their action in the appropriate international agencies of which they are members.

Article 49 The Members of the United Nations shall join in affording mutual assistance in carrying out the measures decided upon by the Security Council.

Article 50 If preventive or enforcement measures against any state are taken by the Security Council, any other state, whether a Member of the United Nations or not, which finds itself confronted with special economic problems arising from the carrying out of those measures shall have the right to consult the Security Council with regard to a solution of those problems.

Article 51 Nothing in the present Charter shall impair the inherent right of individual or collective self-defense if an armed attack occurs against a Member of the United Nations, until the Security Council has taken measures necessary to maintain international peace and security. Measures taken by Members in the exercise of this right of self-defense shall be immediately reported to the Charter of the United Nations Security Council and shall not in any way affect the authority and responsibility of the Security Council under the present Charter to take at any time such action as it deems necessary in order to maintain or restore international peace and security.

Chapter VIII: Regional Arrangements

Article 52 1. Nothing in the present Charter precludes the existence of regional arrangements or agencies for dealing with such matters relating to the maintenance of international peace and security as are appropriate for regional action, provided that such arrangements or agencies and their activities are consistent with the Purposes and Principles of the United Nations.

2. The Members of the United Nations entering into such arrangements or constituting such agencies shall make every effort to achieve pacific settlement of local disputes through such regional arrangements or by such regional agencies before referring them to the Security Council.

3. The Security Council shall encourage the development of pacific settlement of local disputes through such regional arrangements or by such regional agencies either on the initiative of the states concerned or by reference from the Security Council.

4. This Article in no way impairs the application of Articles 34 and 35.

Article 53 1. The Security Council shall, where appropriate, utilize such regional arrangements or agencies for enforcement action under its authority. But no enforcement action shall be taken under regional arrangements or by regional agencies without the authorization of the Security Council, with the exception of measures against any enemy state, as defined in paragraph 2 of this Article, provided for pursuant to Article 107 or in regional arrangements directed against renewal of aggressive policy on the part of any such state, until such time as the Organization may, on request of the Governments concerned, be charged with the responsibility for preventing further aggression by such a state.

2. The term enemy state as used in paragraph 1 of this Article applies to any state which during the Second World War has been an enemy of any signatory of the present Charter.

Article 54 The Security Council shall at all times be kept fully informed of activities undertaken or in contemplation under regional arrangements or by regional agencies for the maintenance of international peace and security.

Appendix 3: Rome Statute of the International Criminal Court
Part 2. Jurisdiction, Admissibility and Applicable Law

Article 5

Crimes within the jurisdiction of the Court

1. The jurisdiction of the Court shall be limited to the most serious crimes of concern to the international community as a whole. The Court has jurisdiction in accordance with this Statute with respect to the following crimes:
   (a) The crime of genocide;
   (b) Crimes against humanity;
   (c) War crimes;
   (d) The crime of aggression.
2. The Court shall exercise jurisdiction over the crime of aggression once a provision is adopted in accordance with articles 121 and 123 defining the crime and setting out the conditions under which the Court shall exercise jurisdiction with respect to this crime. Such a provision shall be consistent with the relevant provisions of the Charter of the United Nations.

Article 6

Genocide

For the purpose of this Statute, "genocide" means any of the following acts committed with intent to destroy, in whole or in part, a national, ethnical, racial or religious group, as such:

   (a) Killing members of the group;
   (b) Causing serious bodily or mental harm to members of the group;
   (c) Deliberately inflicting on the group conditions of life calculated to bring about its physical destruction in whole or in part;
   (d) Imposing measures intended to prevent births within the group;
   (e) Forcibly transferring children of the group to another group.

Article 7
Crimes against humanity

1. For the purpose of this Statute, "crime against humanity" means any of the following acts when committed as part of a widespread or systematic attack directed against any civilian population, with knowledge of the attack:
   (a) Murder;
   (b) Extermination;
   (c) Enslavement;
   (d) Deportation or forcible transfer of population;
   (e) Imprisonment or other severe deprivation of physical liberty in violation of fundamental rules of international law;
   (f) Torture;
   (g) Rape, sexual slavery, enforced prostitution, forced pregnancy, enforced sterilization, or any other form of sexual violence of comparable gravity;
   (h) Persecution against any identifiable group or collectivity on political, racial, national, ethnic, cultural, religious, gender as defined in paragraph 3, or other grounds that are universally recognized as impermissible under international law, in connection with any act referred to in this paragraph or any crime within the jurisdiction of the Court;
   (i) Enforced disappearance of persons;
   (j) The crime of apartheid;
   (k) Other inhumane acts of a similar character intentionally causing great suffering, or serious injury to body or to mental or physical health.
2. For the purpose of paragraph 1:
   (a) "Attack directed against any civilian population" means a course of conduct involving the multiple commission of acts referred to in paragraph 1 against any civilian population, pursuant to or in furtherance of a State or organizational policy to commit such attack;
   (b) "Extermination" includes the intentional infliction of conditions of life, inter alia the deprivation of access to food and medicine, calculated to bring about the destruction of part of a population;
   (c) "Enslavement" means the exercise of any or all of the powers attaching to the right of ownership over a person and includes the exercise of such power in the course of trafficking in persons, in particular women and children;
   (d) "Deportation or forcible transfer of population" means forced displacement of the persons concerned by expulsion or other coercive acts from the area in which they are lawfully present, without grounds permitted under international law;

(e) "Torture" means the intentional infliction of severe pain or suffering, whether physical or mental, upon a person in the custody or under the control of the accused; except that torture shall not include pain or suffering arising only from, inherent in or incidental to, lawful sanctions;

(f) "Forced pregnancy" means the unlawful confinement of a woman forcibly made pregnant, with the intent of affecting the ethnic composition of any population or carrying out other grave violations of international law. This definition shall not in any way be interpreted as affecting national laws relating to pregnancy;

(g) "Persecution" means the intentional and severe deprivation of fundamental rights contrary to international law by reason of the identity of the group or collectivity;

(h) "The crime of apartheid" means inhumane acts of a character similar to those referred to in paragraph 1, committed in the context of an institutionalized regime of systematic oppression and domination by one racial group over any other racial group or groups and committed with the intention of maintaining that regime;

(i) "Enforced disappearance of persons" means the arrest, detention or abduction of persons by, or with the authorization, support or acquiescence of, a State or a political organization, followed by a refusal to acknowledge that deprivation of freedom or to give information on the fate or whereabouts of those persons, with the intention of removing them from the protection of the law for a prolonged period of time.

3. For the purpose of this Statute, it is understood that the term "gender" refers to the two sexes, male and female, within the context of society. The term "gender" does not indicate any meaning different from the above.

Article 8

War crimes

1. The Court shall have jurisdiction in respect of war crimes in particular when committed as part of a plan or policy or as part of a large-scale commission of such crimes.

2. For the purpose of this Statute, "war crimes" means:

(a) Grave breaches of the Geneva Conventions of 12 August 1949, namely, any of the following acts against persons or property protected under the provisions of the relevant Geneva Convention:

  (i) Wilful killing;

  (ii) Torture or inhuman treatment, including biological experiments;

    (iii) Wilfully causing great suffering, or serious injury to body or health;

    (iv) Extensive destruction and appropriation of property, not justified by military necessity and carried out unlawfully and wantonly;

    (v) Compelling a prisoner of war or other protected person to serve in the forces of a hostile Power;

    (vi) Wilfully depriving a prisoner of war or other protected person of the rights of fair and regular trial;

    (vii) Unlawful deportation or transfer or unlawful confinement;

    (viii) Taking of hostages.

(b) Other serious violations of the laws and customs applicable in international armed conflict, within the established framework of international law, namely, any of the following acts:

    (i) Intentionally directing attacks against the civilian population as such or against individual civilians not taking direct part in hostilities;

    (ii) Intentionally directing attacks against civilian objects, that is, objects which are not military objectives;

    (iii) Intentionally directing attacks against personnel, installations, material, units or vehicles involved in a humanitarian assistance or peacekeeping mission in accordance with the Charter of the United Nations, as long as they are entitled to the protection given to civilians or civilian objects under the international law of armed conflict;

    (iv) Intentionally launching an attack in the knowledge that such attack will cause incidental loss of life or injury to civilians or damage to civilian objects or widespread, long-term and severe damage to the natural environment which would be clearly excessive in relation to the concrete and direct overall military advantage anticipated;

    (v) Attacking or bombarding, by whatever means, towns, villages, dwellings or buildings which are undefended and which are not military objectives;

    (vi) Killing or wounding a combatant who, having laid down his arms or having no longer means of defense, has surrendered at discretion;

    (vii) Making improper use of a flag of truce, of the flag or of the military insignia and uniform of the enemy or of the United Nations, as well as of the distinctive emblems of the Geneva Conventions, resulting in death or serious personal injury;

(viii) The transfer, directly or indirectly, by the Occupying Power of parts of its own civilian population into the territory it occupies, or the deportation or transfer of all or parts of the population of the occupied territory within or outside this territory;

(ix) Intentionally directing attacks against buildings dedicated to religion, education, art, science or charitable purposes, historic monuments, hospitals and places where the sick and wounded are collected, provided they are not military objectives;

(x) Subjecting persons who are in the power of an adverse party to physical mutilation or to medical or scientific experiments of any kind which are neither justified by the medical, dental or hospital treatment of the person concerned nor carried out in his or her interest, and which cause death to or seriously endanger the health of such person or persons;

(xi) Killing or wounding treacherously individuals belonging to the hostile nation or army;

(xii) Declaring that no quarter will be given;

(xiii) Destroying or seizing the enemy's property unless such destruction or seizure be imperatively demanded by the necessities of war;

(xiv) Declaring abolished, suspended or inadmissible in a court of law the rights and actions of the nationals of the hostile party;

(xv) Compelling the nationals of the hostile party to take part in the operations of war directed against their own country, even if they were in the belligerent's service before the commencement of the war;

(xvi) Pillaging a town or place, even when taken by assault;

(xvii) Employing poison or poisoned weapons;

(xviii) Employing asphyxiating, poisonous or other gases, and all analogous liquids, materials or devices;

(xix) Employing bullets which expand or flatten easily in the human body, such as bullets with a hard envelope which does not entirely cover the core or is pierced with incisions;

(xx) Employing weapons, projectiles and material and methods of warfare which are of a nature to cause superfluous injury or unnecessary suffering or which are inherently indiscriminate in violation of the international law of armed conflict, provided that such weapons, projectiles and material and methods of warfare are the subject of a comprehensive prohibition and are included in an annex to this Statute, by an amendment in accordance with the relevant provisions set forth in articles 121 and 123;

(xxi) Committing outrages upon personal dignity, in particular humiliating and degrading treatment;

(xxii) Committing rape, sexual slavery, enforced prostitution, forced pregnancy, as defined in article 7, paragraph 2 (f), enforced sterilization, or any other form of sexual violence also constituting a grave breach of the Geneva Conventions;

(xxiii) Utilizing the presence of a civilian or other protected person to render certain points, areas or military forces immune from military operations;

(xxiv) Intentionally directing attacks against buildings, material, medical units and transport, and personnel using the distinctive emblems of the Geneva Conventions in conformity with international law;

(xxv) Intentionally using starvation of civilians as a method of warfare by depriving them of objects indispensable to their survival, including wilfully impeding relief supplies as provided for under the Geneva Conventions;

(xxvi) Conscripting or enlisting children under the age of fifteen years into the national armed forces or using them to participate actively in hostilities.

(c) In the case of an armed conflict not of an international character, serious violations of article 3 common to the four Geneva Conventions of 12 August 1949, namely, any of the following acts committed against persons taking no active part in the hostilities, including members of armed forces who have laid down their arms and those placed *hors de combat* by sickness, wounds, detention or any other cause:

(i) Violence to life and person, in particular murder of all kinds, mutilation, cruel treatment and torture;

(ii) Committing outrages upon personal dignity, in particular humiliating and degrading treatment;

(iii) Taking of hostages;

(iv) The passing of sentences and the carrying out of executions without previous judgement pronounced by a regularly constituted court, affording all judicial guarantees which are generally recognized as indispensable.

(d) Paragraph 2 (c) applies to armed conflicts not of an international character and thus does not apply to situations of internal disturbances and tensions, such as riots, isolated and sporadic acts of violence or other acts of a similar nature.

(e) Other serious violations of the laws and customs applicable in armed conflicts not of an international character, within the established framework of international law, namely, any of the following acts:

    (i) Intentionally directing attacks against the civilian population as such or against individual civilians not taking direct part in hostilities;

    (ii) Intentionally directing attacks against buildings, material, medical units and transport, and personnel using the distinctive emblems of the Geneva Conventions in conformity with international law;

    (iii) Intentionally directing attacks against personnel, installations, material, units or vehicles involved in a humanitarian assistance or peacekeeping mission in accordance with the Charter of the United Nations, as long as they are entitled to the protection given to civilians or civilian objects under the international law of armed conflict;

    (iv) Intentionally directing attacks against buildings dedicated to religion, education, art, science or charitable purposes, historic monuments, hospitals and places where the sick and wounded are collected, provided they are not military objectives;

    (v) Pillaging a town or place, even when taken by assault;

    (vi) Committing rape, sexual slavery, enforced prostitution, forced pregnancy, as defined in article 7, paragraph 2 (f), enforced sterilization, and any other form of sexual violence also constituting a serious violation of article 3 common to the four Geneva Conventions;

    (vii) Conscripting or enlisting children under the age of fifteen years into armed forces or groups or using them to participate actively in hostilities;

    (viii) Ordering the displacement of the civilian population for reasons related to the conflict, unless the security of the civilians involved or imperative military reasons so demand;

    (ix) Killing or wounding treacherously a combatant adversary;

    (x) Declaring that no quarter will be given;

    (xi) Subjecting persons who are in the power of another party to the conflict to physical mutilation or to medical or scientific experiments of any kind which are neither justified by the medical, dental or hospital treatment of the person concerned nor carried out in his or her interest, and which cause death to or seriously endanger the health of such person or persons;

    (xii) Destroying or seizing the property of an adversary unless such destruction or seizure be imperatively demanded by the necessities of the conflict;

  (f) Paragraph 2 (e) applies to armed conflicts not of an international character and thus does not apply to situations of internal disturbances and tensions, such as riots, isolated and sporadic acts of violence or other acts of a similar nature. It applies to armed conflicts that take place in the territory of a State when there is protracted armed conflict between governmental authorities and organized armed groups or between such groups.

3. Nothing in paragraph 2 (c) and (e) shall affect the responsibility of a Government to maintain or re-establish law and order in the State or to defend the unity and territorial integrity of the State, by all legitimate means.

Index